More Praise for *Chasing the Scream*

"Wonderful. I couldn't put it down." —**Noam Chomsky**

"This book is as intoxicatingly thrilling as crack, without destroying your teeth. It will change the drug debate forever." —**Russell Brand**

"An astounding book." —**Amy Goodman, host of *Democracy Now***

"Superb." —**Piers Morgan**

"One of the best books I read this year." —**Chris Boddener, *The Atlantic***

"Gripping." —*The Financial Times*

"Hari's empathy and keen eye for detail bring a disparate group of characters to life." —*The New York Times Book Review*

"Incredibly entertaining...Enormously emotionally affecting...It really is an extraordinary book." —**Vanessa Feltz, BBC Radio**

"Hari...assembl[es] stories from all corners of what he calls a 'global battlefield.' Their combined testimony forms a convincing brief that drug prohibition may have spawned as much crime, violence, and heartache as drug use ever did." —*The Boston Globe*

"Incredibly insightful and provocative." —**B.J. Novak, writer and executive producer, *The Office***

"This book is, forgive the obvious phrase, screamingly addictive. The story it tells, jaw-droppingly horrific, hilarious, and incredible, is one everyone should know: that it is all true boggles the mind, fascinates, and infuriates in equal measure. Johann Hari, in brilliant prose, exposes one of the greatest and most harmful scandals of the past hundred years." —**Stephen Fry**

"*Chasing the Scream* vividly paints the war on drugs as the century-long bad LSD trip that it is; in doing so it sticks a big nail in its coffin." —**Ioan Grillo, author of *El Narco* and *Gangster Warlords***

"Johann Hari has written a drug policy reform book like no other. Many have studied, or conducted, the science surrounding the manifold ills of drug prohibition. But Hari puts it all into riveting story form, and humanizes it. Part Gonzo journalism, part Louis CK standup, part Mark Twain storytelling, *Chasing the Scream: The First and Last Days of the War on Drugs* is beautifully wrought: lively, humorous, and poignant. And it's a compelling case for why the drug war must end, yesterday." —**Norman Stamper, former chief, Seattle Police Department**

"In this energetic and thought-proving book, Hari harnesses the power of the personal narrative to reveal the true causes and consequences of the war on drugs." —**David Nutt, former chief scientific advisor on drugs to the British government**

"This book is an entertainment, a great character study and page-turning storytelling all rolled into one very sophisticated and compelling cry for social justice." —**Stephen Downing, former deputy chief, LAPD**

Chasing the Scream

The First and Last Days of the War on Drugs

JOHANN HARI

BLOOMSBURY

NEW YORK · LONDON · OXFORD · NEW DELHI · SYDNEY

Bloomsbury USA
An imprint of Bloomsbury Publishing Plc

1385 Broadway	50 Bedford Square
New York	London
NY 10018	WC1B 3DP
USA	UK

www.bloomsbury.com

BLOOMSBURY and the Diana logo are trademarks of Bloomsbury Publishing Plc

First published 2015
This paperback edition published 2016

ISBN: HB: 978-1-62040-890-2
ePub: 978-1-62040-892-6
PB: 978-1-62040-891-9

Library of Congress Cataloging-in-Publication Data
Hari, Johann.
Chasing the scream : the first and last days of the war on drugs
/ Johann Hari.—First U.S. edition. pages cm
Includes bibliographical references and index.
ISBN 978-1-62040-890-2 (hardback)
1. Drug control—United States—History. 2. Drug traffic—
United States—History. I. Title. HV5825.H234 2015
363.450973—dc23
2014021633

2 4 6 8 10 9 7 5 3 1

Typeset by Hewer Text UK Ltd, Edinburgh
Printed and bound in USA by Berryville Graphics Inc., Berryville, Virginia

To find out more about our authors and books visit www.bloomsbury.com. Here you will find extracts, author interviews, details of forthcoming events, and the option to sign up for our newsletters.

Bloomsbury books may be purchased for business or promotional use. For information on bulk purchases please contact Macmillan Corporate and Premium Sales Department at specialmarkets@macmillan.com.

For Josh, Aaron, Ben, and Erin

Note: The audio of the quotes from this book that were spoken directly to the author can be heard in full at www.chasingthescream.com—you can follow along there and hear the voices of all the people from the book while you read.

Contents

Part IV: The Temple

Part V: Peace

Introduction

Almost one hundred years after the start of the war on drugs, I found myself stuck on one of its more minor battlefields. In the suburbs of North London, one of my closest relatives had been rock-bottoming on cocaine again, while my ex-boyfriend was ending his long East London romance with heroin and picking up a crack pipe instead. I was watching all this with some distance, in part because I had been swallowing fistfuls of fat white narcolepsy pills for years. I am not narcoleptic. Many years before, I had read that if you take them, you can write in long manic weeks without pause and without rest, and it worked—I was wired.

All this felt like home to me. One of my earliest memories is of trying to wake one of my relatives from a drugged slump, and not being able to. Ever since, I have been oddly drawn to addicts and recovering addicts—they feel like my tribe, my group, my people. But now, for the first time, I was beginning to wonder if I had become an addict myself. My long drugged writing binges would stop only when I collapsed with exhaustion, and I wouldn't be able to wake for days. I realized one morning that I must have been starting to look a little like the relative I had been trying to wake up, all those years before.

I had been taught how to respond—by my government, and by my culture—when you find yourself in this situation. It is with a war. We all know the script: it is etched onto your subconscious, like the correct direction to look when you cross the street. Treat drug users and addicts as criminals. Repress them. Shame them. Coerce them into stopping. This is the prevailing view in almost every country in the world. For years, I had been publicly arguing against this strategy. I wrote newspaper articles and appeared on television to argue that punishing and shaming drug users only makes them worse—and creates a blizzard of other problems for the society. I argued instead for a second strategy— legalize drugs stage by stage, and use the money we currently spend on punishing addicts to fund compassionate care instead.

But as I stared at these people I loved through my own drugged glaze, a small part of me wondered if I really meant what I had been saying. The voices in my mind were like a howling drill sergeant in an old Vietnam War movie, shrieking abuse at the recruits. You are an idiot to do this. This is shameful. You are a fool for not stopping. Somebody should prevent you. You should be punished.

So even as I criticized the drug war with my words, I was often waging it in my head. I can't say I was evenly divided—my rational mind always favored reform—but this internal conflict wouldn't stop.

I had been looking for a way out of this chemical-stained stalemate for years—and then one morning, a thought came to me. You and the people you love are just tiny smudges on a much larger canvas. If you stay where you are—focused only on the shape of your own little smudges, this year like last year and the year before—you will never understand more than you do now. But what if you found a way to step back and look, for once, at the entire painting?

I scribbled down some questions that had puzzled me for years. Why did the drug war start, and why does it continue? Why can some people use drugs without any problems, while others can't? What really causes addiction? What happens if you choose a radically different policy? I decided to go on a journey across the front lines of the war on drugs to find the answers.

So I packed up my apartment, flushed my last remaining pills down the toilet, and set off. I knew this war had begun in the United States, although at that point I didn't know when, or how. I arrived in New York City with a list of names of experts in this field. It is a good thing, I know now, that I didn't book a return ticket. I didn't realize it on that first day, but this journey would end up taking me across nine countries and thirty thousand miles, and it would last for three years.

On the road, I found the stories of people I could not have imagined at the start—people who taught me the answers to the questions I had been wrestling with for so long. A transsexual crack dealer in Brooklyn who wanted to know who killed his mother. A nurse in Ciudad Juárez marching through the desert searching for her daughter. A child smuggled out of the Budapest ghetto during the Holocaust who grew up to uncover the real causes of addiction. A junkie leading an uprising in Vancouver. A serial killer in a cage in Texas. A Portuguese doctor who led his country to decriminalize all drugs, from cannabis to crack. A scientist in Los Angeles who had been feeding hallucinogens to a mongoose, just to see what would happen.

They—and many others—were my teachers.

I was startled by what I learned from them. It turns out that many of our most basic assumptions about this subject are wrong. Drugs are not what we think they are. Drug addiction is not what we have been told it is. The drug war is not what our politicians have sold it as for one hundred years and counting. And there is a very different story out there waiting for us when we are ready to hear it—one that should leave us thrumming with hope.

PART I

Mount Rushmore

CHAPTER 1

The Black Hand

As I waited in the drowsy neon-lit customs line at JFK, I tried to remember precisely when the war on drugs started. In some vague way, I had a sense that it must have been with Richard Nixon in the 1970s, when the phrase was first widely used. Or was it with Ronald Reagan in the 1980s, when "Just Say No" seemed to become the second national anthem?

But when I started to travel around New York City interviewing experts on drug policy, I began to get a sense that this whole story had, in fact, begun long before. The pledge to wage "relentless warfare" on drugs was, I found, first made in the 1930s, by a man who has been largely forgotten today—yet he did more than any other individual to create the drug world we now live in. I learned there are vast forgotten piles of this man's paperwork at Penn State University—his diary, his letters, all his files—so I headed there on a Greyhound bus, and began to read through everything I could find by and about Harry Anslinger. Only then did I begin to see who he really was—and what he means for us all.

In those files, I learned that at the birth of the war on drugs, there were three people who could be seen as its founding figures: if there was a Mount Rushmore for drug prohibition, it is their faces who would be carved into its mountainside, staring impassively back, slowly eroding. I chased the information about them across many more archives, and to the last remaining people to remember them. Now, three years later, after all I have learned, I find myself picturing these founding figures as they were when the drug war clouds first began to gather—as kids, scattered across the United States, not knowing what was about to hit them, or what they would achieve. That is where, it seems to me, this story begins.

~

In 1904, a twelve-year-old boy was visiting his neighbor's farmhouse in the cornfields of western Pennsylvania when he heard a scream. It was coming from somewhere above him. This sound—desperate, aching—made him confused. What was going on? Why would a grown woman howl like an animal?

Her husband ran down the stairs and gave the boy a set of hurried instructions: Take my horse and cart into the town as fast as you can. Pick up a package from the pharmacy. Bring it here. Do it now.

The boy lashed at the horses, because he was certain that if he failed, he would return to find a corpse. As soon as he flopped through the door and handed over the bag of drugs, the farmer ran to his wife. Her screaming stopped, and she was calm. But the boy would not be calm about this—not ever again.

"I never forgot those screams," he wrote years later. From that moment on, he was convinced there was a group of people walking among us who may look and sound normal, but who could at any moment become "emotional, hysterical, degenerate, mentally deficient and vicious" if they were allowed contact with the great unhinging agent: drugs.

When he grew into a man, this boy was going to draw together some of the deepest fears in American culture—of racial minorities, of intoxication, of losing control—and channel them into a global war to prevent those screams. It would cause many screams in turn. They can be heard in almost every city on earth tonight.

This is how Harry Anslinger entered the drug war.

~

On a different afternoon a few years earlier, on the Upper East Side of Manhattan, a wealthy Orthodox Jewish trader walked in on a scene that he could not understand. His three-year-old son was standing over his sleeping older brother holding a knife, ready to stab him. "Why, my son, why?" the trader asked. The little boy said that he hated his brother.

The boy was going to hate a lot of people in his life—almost everyone, in fact. He would later declare that "the majority of the human race are dubs and dumbbells and have rotten judgment and no brains." He would plunge his knife into many people, as soon as he had gained enough wealth and power to get other people to wield the weapon. Normally a man with his personality type would end up in prison, but this little boy didn't. He was handed an industry where his capacity for violence was not just rewarded, but required: the new market for illegal drugs in North America. When he was finally shot—separated by twenty blocks, countless killings, and many millions of dollars from his sleeping brother on that night—he was a free man.

This is how Arnold Rothstein entered the drug war.

~

On yet another afternoon, in 1920, a six-year-old girl lay on the floor of a brothel in Baltimore listening to jazz records. Her mother was convinced this music was the work of Satan and wouldn't let her hear a note of it at home, so the child offered to perform small cleaning tasks for the madam of the local whorehouse on one condition: instead of being paid a nickel like the other kids, she would take her pay on this floor, in rapt hours left alone to listen. It gave her a feeling she couldn't describe—and she was determined, one day, to create this feeling in other people.

Even after she was raped, and after she was pimped, and after she started to inject heroin to take away the pain, this music would still be there waiting for her.

This is how Billie Holiday entered the drug war.

~

When Harry and Arnold and Billie were born, drugs were freely available throughout the world. You could go to any American pharmacy and buy products made from the same ingredients as heroin and cocaine. The most popular cough mixtures in the United States contained opiates, a new soft drink called Coca-Cola was made from the same plant as snortable cocaine, and over in Britain, the classiest department stores sold heroin tins for society women.

But they lived at a time when American culture was looking for an outlet for its swelling tide of anxiety—a real, physical object it could destroy, in the hope that this would destroy its fear of a world that was changing more rapidly than their parents and grandparents could ever have imagined. It settled on these chemicals. In 1914—a century ago—they resolved: Destroy them. Wipe them from the earth. Set yourself free.

As this decision was made, Harry and Arnold and Billie found themselves scattered across that first battlefield, and pressed into combat.

∼

When Billie Holiday stood on stage, her hair was pulled back tightly, her
face was round and shining in the lights, and her voice was scratched
with pain. It was on one of these nights, in 1939, that she started to sing
a song that would become iconic:

> Southern trees bear a strange fruit,
> Blood on the leaves and blood at the root.

Before, black women had—with very few exceptions—been allowed
on stage only as beaming caricatures, stripped of all real feeling. But now,
here, she was Lady Day, a black woman expressing grief and fury at the
mass murder of her brothers in the South—their battered bodies hanging
from the trees.

"It was extremely brave, when you think about it," her goddaughter
Lorraine Feather told me. At that time, "every song was about love. You
simply did not have a piece of music being performed at some hotel
that was about the killing of people—about such a sordid and cruel fact.
It was not done. Ever." And to have an African American woman doing
such a song? About lynching? But Billie did it because the song "seemed
to spell out all the things that had killed" her father, Clarence, in the
South.

The audience listened, hushed. Many years later, this moment would
be called "the beginning of the civil rights movement." Lady Day was
ordered by the authorities to stop singing this song. She refused.

Her harassment by Harry's Federal Bureau of Narcotics began the next
day. Before long, he would play a crucial role in killing her.

∼

From his first day in office, Harry Anslinger had a problem, and everybody knew it. He had just been appointed head of the Federal Bureau of
Narcotics—a tiny agency, buried in the gray bowels of the Treasury
Department in Washington, D.C.—and it seemed to be on the brink of
being abolished. This was the old Department of Prohibition, but prohibition had been abolished and his men needed a new role, fast. As he
looked over his new staff just a few years before his pursuit of Billie began,

he saw a sunken army who had spent fourteen years waging war on alcohol only to see alcohol win, and win big. These men were notoriously corrupt and crooked—but now Harry was supposed to whip them into a force capable of wiping drugs from the United States forever.

And that was only the first obstacle. Many drugs, including marijuana, were still legal, and the Supreme Court had recently ruled that people addicted to harder drugs should be dealt with by doctors, not bang-'em-up men like Harry. And then—almost before he had settled into his office chair—Harry's budget was slashed by $700,000. What was the point of this department, this position, this work? It seemed his new kingdom of drug prohibition could crumble into bureaucratic history at any moment.

Within a few years, the stress of trying to hold this together and creating a role for himself would make all of Harry's hair fall out and leave him looking, according to his staff, like a wrestler printed in primary colors on a fading poster.

Harry believed that the response to being dealt a weak hand should always be to dramatically raise the stakes. He pledged to eradicate all drugs, everywhere—and within thirty years, he succeeded in turning this crumbling department, with these disheartened men, into the headquarters for a global war that would last for a hundred years and counting. He could do it because he was a bureaucratic genius—and, even more crucially, because there was a deep strain in American culture that was waiting for a man like him, with a sure and certain answer to their questions about chemicals.

Ever since that day in his neighbor's farmhouse, Harry had known that he wanted to lead the charge to wipe drugs from the earth—but nobody imagined that, from where he started, he could ever do it, never mind so quickly. His dad was a Swiss hairdresser who had fled his home in the mountains to avoid military conscription and eventually washed up in Pennsylvania, where he had nine kids. He couldn't afford much schooling for them, so when the eighth child, Harry, was fourteen, he was forced to go out to work on the railroad. He was a determined boy, and he insisted on working for money in the afternoons and evenings so he could keep going to school every morning.

But it was in his paid work that Harry got his greatest education; there, laying the train tracks for the state of Pennsylvania, he got his first glimpse of something dark and hidden—and it would become his second lifelong obsession. It was his task to supervise a large number of recent Sicilian immigrants. Sometimes, he wrote, he heard them talking darkly in hushed asides about something called a "Black Hand."

Harry recorded their thoughts in the style of the pulp fiction thrillers he was obsessed with. You didn't mention it in front of strangers. You didn't mention it even in front of your family unless you had to. But it could destroy you with one swipe. What could this Black Hand be? Nobody would tell.

But one morning, Harry found one of his work crew—an Italian man named Giovanni—bleeding in a ditch. He had been shot multiple times. When Giovanni woke up in the hospital, Harry was there, ready to hear what had happened, but the workman was too terrified to speak. Anslinger spent hours assuring him that he could keep him and his family safe.

Finally, Giovanni spoke. He said he was being forced to pay protection money by a man called "Big Mouth Sam," one of the thugs belonging to a group called the Mafia that had come to the United States from Sicily and remained hidden amidst the Italian immigrants. The Mafia, Giovanni told Harry, were engaged in all sorts of crimes, and people on the railroad were being charged a "terror tax"—you gave the Mafia money or else you ended up in a hospital bed like this, or worse.

Anslinger went to confront Big Mouth Sam—a "squat, black-haired and ox-shouldered" immigrant—and said, "If Giovanni dies, I'm going to see to it that you hang. Do you understand that?" Big Mouth tried to reply, but Harry insisted: "And if he lives and you ever bother him again, or any of my men, or try to shake any of them down any more, I'll kill you with my own hands."

After that, Anslinger became obsessed with the Mafia, at a time when most Americans refused to believe it even existed. This is hard for us to understand today, but the official position of every official in U.S. law enforcement until the 1960s—from J. Edgar Hoover on down—was that the Mafia was a preposterous conspiracy theory, no more real than the Loch Ness Monster. They reacted the way we would now if a law enforcement agent preached Trutherism, or Birtherism, or the belief that Freemasons are secretly manipulating world events: with bafflement at the idea that anyone could believe something so silly.

But Harry had glimpsed the Mafia in the flesh, and he was convinced that if he followed the trail from Big Mouth Sam to the thugs above him and the thugs above them, he would be led to a vast global web, and perhaps even to an "invisible world-wide government" secretly controlling events. He soon started keeping every scrap of information he could find on the Mafia, no matter how small or how trivial the source. He snipped small stories from pulp magazines and stored them away: one day, he thought, he would use this information.

As soon as the First World War started, Harry tried to sign up for the military, but he was blind in one eye—his brother had hit him with a rock years before—and was turned down. But since he spoke fluent German, he was offered a position as a diplomatic agent in Europe, and before long he was traveling on a boat to London, through a fog that had left the British Isles invisible and lost. From there, he traveled on to Hamburg and The Hague, where his job was to ferret out information from local diplomats and to deal with local Americans in trouble. Several discharged American sailors were brought to him to be shipped home because they had become addicted to heroin. Harry stared into their skeletal faces and found that the hatred he felt as a small boy was only swelling. This, he promised himself, would be stopped.

At the very end of the war, as it was becoming clear to everyone that the Germans had lost, Harry was sent on his most important mission so far: to take a secret message to the defeated German dictator. The way he later told the story, Harry was dispatched to the small Dutch town of Amerongen, where the Kaiser was holed up in a castle and planning to abdicate. Anslinger's job was to pose as a German official and convey a message from President Woodrow Wilson: Don't do it. The United States wanted the Kaiser to retain the imperial throne, to prevent the rise of the "revolution, strikes and chaos" it feared would follow from his sudden departure.

The Dutch guards at the gates of the castle ordered Harry to show his credentials. "Show me *your* credentials," he snapped back in his fiercest German. Frightened, assuming he was one of the Kaiser's men, they let him through.

Anslinger managed to get the message through—but it was too late. The decision had been made. The Kaiser quit. For the rest of his life, Anslinger believed that if he had gotten the president's plea through only a little earlier, "a decent peace might have been written, forestalling any chance for a future Hitler gaining power, or a Second World War erupting." It was the first time Harry felt that the future of civilization hung on his actions, but it would not be the last.

He traveled across a Europe in rubble. "The sight of a large city in ruins, without a house seen standing, creates a feeling that is hard to describe," he wrote in his diary. Bombed bridges lay as wreckage. Factories were either destroyed entirely, or had all their machinery ripped from them, and often dumped along the roadsides, twisted and useless, like metal ghosts of the time before. There were enormous shell-holes, and acres of barbed wire. Whatever you imagined before, he wrote, "magnify the imagination by twenty times."

But what shook Harry most was the effect of the war not on the buildings but on the people. They seemed to have lost all sense of order. Starving, they had begun to riot; the cavalry had been sent to charge against them, and entire streets were on fire. Harry was standing in a hotel lobby in Berlin when Socialist revolutionaries suddenly fired their machine guns into the lobby, and blood from a bystander splattered onto his hands. Civilization, he was beginning to conclude, was as fragile as the personality of that farmer's wife back in Altoona. It could break. After this, and for the rest of his life, Harry retained a deep sense that American society could collapse into wreckage just as quickly as Europe's had.

In 1926, he was redeployed from the gray wreckage of Europe to the blue-watered island of the Bahamas, but Harry was not a man looking for a reason to relax. This was the height of alcohol prohibition: Americans wanted to drink, and smugglers wanted to sell to them, so whisky was washing through these islands like water. Harry was outraged. The bootleggers were West Indian and Central American, and he believed they were filled with "loathsome and contagious diseases" that would spread to anyone foolish enough to drink the booze they handled.

"Just give me a high-powered rifle. I'll stop the bastards," one of Harry's colleagues said, and in this spirit, Harry announced to his bosses that there was a way to make prohibition work: Use maximum force. Send the navy to hunt down smugglers along the coasts of America. Ban the sale of alcohol for medical purposes. Massively increase prison sentences for alcohol dealers until they were all locked up. Wage war on booze until it was only a memory.

In just a few years, Harry made the leap from being a competent if frustrated prohibition agent in the Bahamas to running a Washington, D.C., department. How did he do it? It's hard to tell, but it must have helped that he married a young woman named Martha Denniston who was from one of the richest families in America, the Mellons. The treasury secretary, Andrew Mellon, was now a close relative—and the prohibition department was part of the Treasury itself.

~

From the moment he took charge of the bureau, Harry was aware of the weakness of his new position. A war on narcotics alone—cocaine and heroin, outlawed in 1914—wasn't enough. They were used only by a tiny minority, and you couldn't keep an entire department alive on such small crumbs. He needed more.

With this in mind, he had begun noticing stories in the newspapers that intrigued him. They had headlines like the one in the July 6, 1927, edition of the *New York Times*: MEXICAN FAMILY GO INSANE. It explained: "A widow and her four children have been driven insane by eating the Marihuana plant, according to doctors who say there is no hope of saving the children's lives and that the mother will be insane for the rest of her life." The mother had no money to buy food, so she decided to eat some marijuana plants that had been growing in their garden. Soon after, "neighbors, hearing outbursts of crazed laughter, rushed to the house to find the entire family insane."

Harry had long dismissed cannabis as a nuisance that would only distract him from the drugs he really wanted to fight. He insisted it was not addictive, and stated "there is probably no more absurd fallacy" than the claim that it caused violent crime.

But almost overnight, he began to argue the opposite position. Why? He believed the two most-feared groups in the United States—Mexican immigrants and African Americans—were taking the drug much more than white people, and he presented the House Committee on Appropriations with a nightmarish vision of where this could lead. He had been told, he said, of "colored students at the University of Minn[esota] partying with female students (white) and getting their sympathy with stories of racial persecution. Result: pregnancy." This was the first hint of much more to come.

He wrote to thirty scientific experts asking a series of questions about marijuana. Twenty-nine of them wrote back saying it would be wrong to ban it, and that it was being widely misrepresented in the press. Anslinger decided to ignore them and quoted instead the one expert who believed it was a great evil that had to be eradicated.

On this basis, Harry warned the public about what happens when you smoke this weed. First, you will fall into "a delirious rage." Then you will be gripped by "dreams . . . of an erotic character." Then you will "lose the power of connected thought." Finally, you will reach the inevitable end point: "Insanity." You could easily get stoned and go out and kill a person, and it would all be over before you even realized you had left your room, he said, because marijuana "turns man into a wild beast." Indeed, "if the hideous monster Frankenstein came face to face with the monster Marijuana, he would drop dead of fright."

A doctor called Michael V. Ball got in touch with Harry to counter this view, saying he had used hemp extract as a medical student and it only made him sleepy. He suspected that the claims circulating about the drug couldn't possibly be true. Maybe, he said, cannabis does drive people crazy in a tiny number of cases, but his hunch was that anybody reacting that way probably had an underlying mental health problem already. He implored Anslinger to fund proper lab studies so they could find out the truth.

Anslinger wrote back firmly. "The marihuana evil can no longer be temporized with," he explained, and he would fund no independent science, then or ever.

For years, doctors kept approaching him with evidence that he was wrong, and he began to snap, telling them they were "treading on danger- ous ground" and should watch their mouths. Instead, he wrote to police officers across the country commanding them to find him cases where marijuana had caused people to kill—and the stories started to roll in.

The defining case for Harry, and for America, was of a young man named Victor Lacata. He was a twenty-one-year-old Florida boy known in his neighborhood as "a sane, rather quiet young man" until—the story went—the day he smoked cannabis. He then entered a "marihuana dream" in which he believed he was being attacked by men who would cut off his arms, so he struck back, seizing an axe and hacking his mother, father, two brothers, and sister to pieces.

The press, at Harry's prompting, made Lacata's story famous. If your son smoked marijuana, people came to believe, he, too, could hack you to pieces. Anslinger was not the originator of these arguments—they had actually been widespread in Mexico in the late nineteenth century, where it was pervasively believed that marijuana made you "loco." Nor was he the only one pushing them in the United States—the press loved these stories, especially the mass media owned by William Randolph Hearst. But for the first time, Anslinger gave them the backing of a government department that would broadcast them to the nation at full volume, with an official government stamp saying they were true. From the clouds of cannabis smoke, he warned, there were Victor Lacatas rising all around us.

The warnings worked. People began to clamor for the Bureau of Narcotics to be given more money to save them from this terrifying threat. Harry's problem—the fragility of his new empire—was starting to ease.

Many years later, the law professor John Kaplan went back to look into the medical files for Victor Lacata. The psychiatrists who examined him said he had long suffered from "acute and chronic" insanity. His family was full of people who suffered from similarly extreme mental health problems—three had been committed to insane asylums—and the local police had tried for a year before the killings to get Lacata committed to a mental hospital, but his parents insisted they wanted to look after him at home. The examining psychiatrists thought his cannabis use was so irrelevant that it wasn't even mentioned in his files.

But Anslinger had his story now. He announced on a famous radio address: "Parents beware! Your children . . . are being introduced to a new danger in the form of a drugged cigarette, marijuana. Young [people] are slaves to this narcotic, continuing addiction until they deteriorate mentally, become insane, [and] turn to violent crime and murder."

Harry was sticking to this story whatever he was told—in part because, while he was asserting against a wall of skepticism that marijuana drove you mad, he was discovering something incredible. Everybody had mocked him when he said the Mafia existed. Where's your evidence? they asked, witheringly. But now, through his agents, Anslinger was uncovering proof that the Mafia not only existed, but was bigger than anyone had imagined. He was building up a scrapbook containing the names of details of eight hundred mafiosi operating in the continental United States. His raids were proving him right, but the authorities still refused to believe him, preferring to look away, awkwardly. Some were corrupt; some simply didn't want to disturb their 100 percent clean-up records by taking on such a difficult and messy crusade; and some were frightened. When the police chief of New Orleans, David Hennessy, started to dig too deeply into the Mafia, he was murdered.

Anslinger began to believe all his hunches would turn out like this. He only had to defy the "experts" and keep pursuing his instinct until, finally, he would be shown to be more right than anyone could have predicted.

He ramped up his campaign. The most frightening effect of marijuana, Harry warned, was on blacks. It made them forget the appropriate racial barriers—and unleashed their lust for white women. Of course, everyone spoke about race differently in the 1930s, but the intensity of Harry's views shocked people even then, and when it was revealed he'd referred to a suspect in an official memo as a "nigger," Senator Joseph P. Guffey of Anslinger's home state of Pennsylvania demanded his resignation. Later, when one of his very few black agents, William B. Davis, complained about being called a "nigger" by Harry's men, Anslinger sacked him.

Harry soon started treating all his critics this way. When the American Medical Association issued a report debunking some of his more over-heated claims, he announced that any of his agents caught with a copy would be immediately fired. Then, when he found out a professor named Alfred Lindesmith was arguing that addicts need to be treated with compassion and care, Harry instructed his men to falsely warn Lindesmith's university that he was associated with a "criminal organization," had him wiretapped, and sent a team to tell him to shut up. Harry couldn't control the flow of drugs, but he was discovering he could control the flow of ideas—and it was not only scientists Harry believed he had to silence.

It was clear from Harry's writings that he was obsessed with Billie Holiday, and I sensed there might be a deeper story there. So I tracked down everyone who was still alive who had known Billie, to ask them about this, and one of them—her godson, Bevan Dufty—explained that his mother had been Billie's best friend, and she believed Billie was in effect killed by the authorities. He had the remaining scraps of her writings on this in his attic, where they had been unseen for years. Would you like, he asked, to see them? When I put them together with Harry's files, what her friends had told me, and the work of her biographers, I began to see this story more clearly.

Jazz was the opposite of everything Harry Anslinger believed in. It is improvised, and relaxed, and free-form. It follows its own rhythm. Worst of all, it is a mongrel music made up of European, Caribbean, and African echoes, all mating on American shores. To Anslinger, this was musical anarchy, and evidence of a recurrence of the primitive impulses that lurk in black people, waiting to emerge. "It sounded," his internal memos said, "like the jungles in the dead of night." Another memo warned that "unbelievably ancient indecent rites of the East Indies are resurrected" in this black man's music. The lives of the jazzmen, he said, "reek of filth."

His agents reported back to him that "many among the jazzmen think they are playing magnificently when under the influence of marihuana but they are actually becoming hopelessly confused and playing horribly."

The Bureau believed that marijuana slowed down your perception of time dramatically, and this was why jazz music sounded so freakish—the musicians were literally living at a different, inhuman rhythm. "Music hath charms," their memos say, "but not this music." Indeed, Harry took jazz as yet more proof that marijuana drives people insane. For example, the song "That Funny Reefer Man" contains the line "Any time he gets a notion, he can walk across the ocean." Harry's agents warned: "He does think that."

Anslinger looked out over a scene filled with men like Charlie Parker, Louis Armstrong, and Thelonious Monk, and—as the journalist Larry Sloman recorded—he longed to see them all behind bars. He wrote to all the agents he had sent to follow them, and instructed: "Please prepare all cases in your jurisdiction involving musicians in violation of the marijuana laws. We will have a great national round-up arrest of all such persons on a single day. I will let you know what day." His advice on drug raids to his men was always "Shoot first."

He reassured congressmen that his crackdown would affect not "the good musicians, but the jazz type." But when Harry came for them, the jazz world would have one weapon that saved them: its absolute solidarity. Anslinger's men could find almost no one among them who was willing to snitch, and whenever one of them was busted, they all chipped in to bail him out.

In the end, the Treasury Department told Anslinger he was wasting his time taking on a community that couldn't be fractured, so he scaled down his focus until it settled like a laser on a single target—perhaps the greatest female jazz vocalist there ever was.

Billie Holiday was born a few months after the Harrison Act, the first law banning cocaine and heroin, and it would become her lifelong twin. Not long after Billie's birth, her nineteen-year-old mother, Sadie, became a prostitute, while her seventeen-year-old father vanished. He later died of pneumonia in the South because he couldn't find a hospital that would treat a black man.

Billie brought herself up on the streets of Baltimore, alone, defiant. It was the last city without a sewer system in the United States, and she spent her childhood among clouds of stinking smoke from all the burning shit. Her cold slum district was known as Pigtown, and many people lived in shacks. Every day, little Billie would wash and clean her great-grandmother and listen to stories from her youth, when she had been a slave on a Virginia plantation.

Billie soon learned there were lots of places she couldn't go because she was black. One store that sold hot dogs would let her in if nobody was looking but gave her hell if she tried to eat inside, in case anybody saw. She knew in her gut this was wrong and had to change, and she made a promise to herself: "I just plain decided one day I wasn't going to do anything or say anything unless I meant it. Not 'Please, sir.' Nor 'Thank you, ma'am.' Nothing. Unless I meant it. You have to be poor and black to know how many times you can get knocked in the head for trying to do something as simple as that." This promise would reshape her life—and her attitude toward Harry.

When she was ten, one of her neighbors—a man in his forties named Wilbert Rich—turned up and explained that he had been sent by her mother to take Billie to her. He took her to a house and told her to wait. She sat and waited, but her mother didn't come; as night fell, Billie said she was drowsy. The man offered her a bed. When she lay down on it, he pinned her down and raped her.

She screamed and clawed at the man, howling for help, and somebody must have heard, because the police arrived. When they barged in, the officers decided at once what was going on. Billie, they declared, was a whore who had tricked this poor man. She was shut away in a cell for two days. Months later, Wilbert Rich was punished with three months in prison, while Billie was punished with a year in a reform school.

The nuns who ran the walled-in, sealed-off punishment center looked at the child and concluded she was bad and needed the firm thwack of discipline. Billie kept spitting their attempts at control right back at them—so they decided they needed to "teach her a lesson." They took her to a room that was empty except for a dead body, slammed the door shut behind her, and left her there overnight. Billie hammered on the doors until her hands bled, but nobody came.

When she escaped—out of the convent, and Baltimore—she was determined to find her mother, who was last heard from in Harlem. When she arrived on the bus into a freezing winter, she stumbled to the last address she had been given, only to find it was a brothel. Her mother worked there for a pittance and had no way to keep her. Before long, Billie was thrown out, and she was so hungry she could barely breathe without it hurting. There was, Billie came to believe, only one solution. A madam offered her a 50 percent cut for having sex with strangers. She was fourteen years old.

Before long, Billie had her own pimp. He was a violent, cursing thug named Louis McKay, who was going to break her ribs and beat her till she bled. He was also—perhaps more crucially—going to meet Harry Anslinger many years later, and work with him. Within a few years, Billie's mother was telling her to marry Louis: he was, she said, such a nice man.

Billie was caught prostituting by the police, and once again, instead of rescuing her from being pimped and raped, they punished her. She was sent to prison on Welfare Island, and once she got out, she started to seek out the hardest and most head-blasting chemicals she could. At first her favorite was White Lightning, a toxic brew containing 70-proof alcohol, and as she got older, she tried to stun her grief with harder and harder drugs. One night, a white boy from Dallas called Speck showed her how to inject herself with heroin. You just heat up the heroin in a spoon and inject it straight into your veins. When Billie wasn't drunk or high, she sank into a black rock of depression and was so shy she could barely speak. She would still wake in the night screaming, remembering her rape and imprisonment. "I got a habit, and I know it's no good," she told a friend, "but it's the one thing that makes me know there's a person called Billie Holiday. I am Billie Holiday."

But then she discovered something else. One day, starving, she walked a dozen blocks in Harlem, asking in every drinking hole if they had any work for her, and she was rejected everywhere. Finally she walked into a place called the Log Cabin and explained she could work as a dancer, but when she tried a few moves, it was obvious she wasn't good enough. Desperate, she told the owner maybe she could sing. He pointed her toward an old piano man in the corner and told her to give him a song. As she sang "Trav'llin' All Alone," the customers put down their drinks and listened. By the time she finished her next song, "Body and Soul," there were tears running down their cheeks.

She sang a moment behind the beat and lived a moment ahead of it. One New Year's Eve, a sailor saw her being served in a bar and asked: "When did you start serving nigger bitches?" She stabbed a bottle into his face. Another time in another bar, a group of soldiers and sailors started stubbing out their cigarettes on her mink coat. She handed the mink coat to a friend to hold, picked up a diamond-shaped ashtray, and laid the sailors out flat.

Yet when it came to the men in her life, this impulse to defend herself bled away. Louis McKay graduated from being her pimp to being her "manager" and husband: he stole almost all her money. After her greatest performance at Carnegie Hall, he greeted her by punching her so hard in the face she was sent flying. Her story was about to crash into Harry Anslinger's. He had been, it turned out, watching her very carefully.

~

Harry had heard whispers that this rising black star was using heroin, so he assigned an agent named Jimmy Fletcher to track her every move. Harry hated to hire black agents, but if he sent white guys into Harlem and Baltimore, they stood out straight away. Jimmy Fletcher was the answer. His job was to bust his own people, but Anslinger was insistent that no black man in his Bureau could ever become a white man's boss. Jimmy was allowed through the door at the Bureau, but never up the stairs. He was and would remain an "archive man"—a street agent whose job was to figure out who was selling, who was supplying, and who should be busted. He would carry large amounts of drugs with him, and he was allowed to deal drugs himself so he could gain the confidence of the people he was secretly plotting to arrest.

Many agents in this position would shoot heroin with their clients, to "prove" they weren't cops. We don't know whether Jimmy joined in, but we do know he had no pity for addicts: "I never knew a victim," he said. "You victimize yourself by becoming a junkie."

He first saw Billie in her brother-in-law's apartment, where she was drinking enough booze to stun a horse and hoovering up vast quantities of cocaine. The next time he saw her, it was in a brothel in Harlem, doing exactly the same. Billie's greatest talent, after singing, was swearing—if she called you a "motherfucker," it was a great compliment. We don't know the first time Billie called Jimmy a motherfucker, but she soon spotted this man who was hanging around, watching her, and she grew to like him.

When Jimmy was sent to raid her, he knocked at the door pretending he had a telegram to deliver. Her biographer Julia Blackburn studied the only remaining interview with Jimmy Fletcher—now lost by the archives handling it—and she wrote about what he remembered in detail.

"Stick it under the door!" she yelled.

"It's too big to go under the door!" he snapped back.

She let him in. She was alone. Jimmy felt uncomfortable.

"Billie, why don't you make a short case of this and, if you've got anything, why don't you turn it over to us?" he asked. "Then we won't be searching around, pulling out your clothes and everything. So why don't you do that?" But Jimmy's partner arrived and sent for a policewoman to conduct a body search.

"You don't have to do that. I'll strip," Billie said. "All I want to say is—will you search me and let me go? All that policewoman is going to do is look up my pussy."

She stripped and stood there, and then she pissed in front of them, defying them to watch.

~

When Billie sang "Loverman, where can you be?" she wasn't crying for a man—she was crying for heroin. But when she found out her friends in the jazz world were using the same drug, she begged them to stop. Never imitate me, she cried. Never do this.

She kept trying to quit. She would get her friends to shut her away in their houses for days on end while she went through withdrawal. As she ran back to her dealers, she cursed herself as "No Guts Holiday." Why couldn't she stop? "It's tough enough coming off when you've got some-body who loves you and trusts you and believes in you," she wrote. "I didn't have anybody." Actually, she said, that's not quite right. She had Anslinger's agents, "betting their time, their shoe leather, and their money that they would get me. Nobody can live like that."

The morning he first raided her, Jimmy took Billie to one side and promised to talk to Anslinger personally for her. "I don't want you to lose your job," he said.

Not long after, he ran into her in a bar and they talked for hours, with her pet Chihuahua, Moochy, by her side. Then, one night, at Club Ebony, they ended up dancing together—Billie Holiday and Anslinger's agent, swaying together to the music.

"And I had so many close conversations with her, about so many things," he would remember years later. "She was the type who would make anyone sympathetic because she was the loving type." The man Anslinger sent to track and bust Billie Holiday had, it seems, fallen in love with her. Confronted with a real addict, up close, the hatred fell away.

~

But Anslinger was going to be given a break on Billie, one he got nowhere else in the jazz world. Billie had got used to turning up at gigs so badly beaten by Louis McKay they had to tape up her ribs before pushing her onstage. She was too afraid to go to the police—but finally she was brave enough to cut him off.

"How come I got to take this from this bitch here? This low class bitch?" McKay raged. "If I got a whore, I got some money from her or I don't have nothing to do with the bitch. I don't want no cunt." He had heard that Harry Anslinger wanted information on her, and he was intrigued. "She's been getting away with too much shit," MacKay said, adding he wanted "Holiday's ass in the gutter in the East River." That, it seems, was the clincher. "I got enough to finish her off," he had pledged. "I'm going to do her up so goddam bad she going to remember as long as she live." He traveled to D.C. to see Harry, and he agreed to set her up.

When Billie was busted again, she was put on trial. She stood before the court looking pale and stunned. "It was called 'The United States of America versus Billie Holiday,'" she said, "and that's just the way it felt." She refused to weep on the stand. She told the judge she didn't want any sympathy. She just wanted to be sent to a hospital so she could kick the drugs and get well. Please, she said to the judge, "I want the cure."

She was sentenced instead to a year in a West Virginia prison, where she was forced to go cold turkey and work during the days in a pigsty, among other places. In all her time behind bars, she did not sing a note. Years later, when her autobiography was published, Billie tracked Jimmy Fletcher down and sent him a signed copy. She had written inside it: "Most federal agents are nice people. They've got a dirty job to do and they have to do it. Some of the nicer ones have feelings enough to hate themselves sometime for what they have to do . . . Maybe they would have been kinder to me if they'd been nasty; then I wouldn't have trusted them enough to believe what they told me." She was right: Jimmy never stopped feeling guilty for what he'd done to Lady Day. "Billie 'paid her debt' to society," one of her friends wrote, "but society never paid its debt to her."

～

Now, as a former convict, she was stripped of her cabaret performer's license, on the grounds that listening to her might harm the morals of the public. This meant she wasn't allowed to sing anywhere that alcohol was served—which included all the jazz clubs in the United States.

"How do you best act cruelly?" her friend Yolande Bavan asked me in 2013. "It's to take something that's the dearest thing to that person away from them." Billie had been able to survive everything—but this? "You despair because you have no control. You can't do the thing that is a passion and that you made your livelihood at, and that has brought joy to people all over the world," Bavan says. Billie was finally silenced. She had no money to look after herself or to eat properly. She couldn't even rent an apartment in her own name.

One night, Billie fell over drunk, and her friend Greer Johnson found her sobbing on the floor.

"Baby, fuck it! Honest to Christ, I'm never going to sing again no more."

"What the hell do you think you can do if you don't sing?" Greer asked, according to Julia Blackburn.

"I don't give a fuck!"

"Fine! And then what will you do, Billie?"

She muttered: "I'll sing again."

"You're damn right you will!"

Another of her friends kept telling her she could save enough money to retire to a house with a garden where she could have babies. "Do you think I can? Do you think I can do it?" she asked incredulously. She dreamed of getting a big farm somewhere and turning it into a home for orphaned children, where she'd run the kitchen herself. Sometimes, she would go to visit her baby godson, Bevan Dufty, at his family's apartment on Ninety-Fourth Street, and she would suckle him. Although she had no milk, it seemed to reassure her. "Bitch, this is my baby," she would tell his mother, laughing.

The only other way she could soothe herself was by returning to childhood habits of her own. She would lie in bed all day reading Superman comics and chuckling. One day, she went out with a teenage friend to Central Park. They fed LSD to the horses and then took a ride. The cabbie was puzzled: Why wouldn't the horses follow their normal route? Billie cackled with laughter from her carriage.

But when she was forced to interact with people, she was becoming more and more paranoid. If Jimmy Fletcher had been one of Them, who else was? She believed—correctly, it turns out—that some of the people around her were informing on her to Anslinger's army. "You didn't know who to trust," her friend Yolande Bavan told me. "So-called friends— were they friends? What were they?" Everywhere she went, there were agents asking about her, demanding details.

She began to push away even her few remaining friends, because she was terrified the police would plant drugs on them, too—and that was the last thing she wanted for the people she loved.

~

One day, Harry Anslinger was told that there were also white women, just as famous as Billie, who had drug problems—but he responded to them rather differently. He called Judy Garland, another heroin addict, in to see him. They had a friendly chat, in which he advised her to take longer vacations between pictures, and he wrote to her studio, assuring them she didn't have a drug problem at all. When he discovered that a Washington society hostess he knew—"a beautiful, gracious lady," he noted—had an illegal drug addiction, he explained he couldn't possibly arrest her because "it would destroy . . . the unblemished reputation of one of the nation's most honored families." He helped her to wean herself off her addiction slowly, without the law becoming involved.

As I sat in his archives, reading over the piles of fading papers that survive from the launch of the drug war, there was one thing I found hardest to grasp at first.

The arguments we hear today for the drug war are that we must protect teenagers from drugs, and prevent addiction in general. We assume, looking back, that these were the reasons this war was launched in the first place. But they were not. They crop up only occasionally, as asides. The main reason given for banning drugs—the reason obsessing the men who launched this war—was that the blacks, Mexicans, and Chinese were using these chemicals, forgetting their place, and menacing white people.

It took me a while to see that the contrast between the racism directed at Billie and the compassion offered to addicted white stars like Judy Garland was not some weird misfiring of the drug war—it was part of the point.

Harry told the public that "the increase [in drug addiction] is practically 100 percent among Negro people," which he stressed was terrifying because already "the Negro population . . . accounts for 10 percent of the total population, but 60 percent of the addicts." He could wage the drug war—he could do what he did—only because he was responding to a fear in the American people. You can be a great surfer, but you still need a great wave. Harry's wave came in the form of a race panic.

In the run-up to the passing of the Harrison Act, the *New York Times* ran a story typical of the time. The headline was: NEGRO COCAINE "FIENDS" NEW SOUTHERN MENACE. It described a North Carolina police chief who "was informed that a hitherto inoffensive negro, with whom he was well-acquainted, was 'running amuck' in a cocaine frenzy [and] had attempted to stab a storekeeper . . . Knowing he must kill this man or be killed himself, the Chief drew his revolver, placed the muzzle over the negro's heart, and fired—'intending to kill him right quick,' as the officer tells it, but the shot did not even stagger the man." Cocaine was, it was widely claimed in the press at this time, turning blacks into superhuman hulks who could take bullets to the heart without flinching. It was the official reason why the police across the South increased the caliber of their guns.

One medical expert put it bluntly: "The cocaine nigger," he warned, "sure is hard to kill."

Many white Americans did not want to accept that black Americans might be rebelling because they had lives like Billie Holiday's—locked into Pigtowns and banned from developing their talents. It was more comforting to believe that a white powder was the cause of black anger, and that getting rid of the white powder would render black Americans docile and on their knees once again. (The history of this would be traced years later in Michelle Alexander's remarkable book *The New Jim Crow*.)

But there was another racial group that also had to be kept down, Harry believed. In the mid-nineteenth century, Chinese immigrants had begun to flow into the United States, and they were now competing with white people for jobs and opportunities.

Worse still, Harry believed they were competing for white women. He warned that with their "own special Oriental ruthlessness," the Chinese had developed "a liking for the charms of Caucasian girls . . . from good families." They lured these white girls into their "opium dens"—a tradition they had brought from their home country—got the girls hooked, and then forced them into acts of "unspeakable sexual depravity" for the rest of their lives. Anslinger described their brothels in great detail: how the white girls removed their clothes slowly, the "panties" they revealed, how slowly they kissed the Chinese, and what came next . . .

Once the Chinese dealers got you hooked on opiates, they would laugh in your face and reveal the real reason they sell junk: it was their way of making sure that "the yellow race would rule the world." "They were too wise, they urged, to attempt to win in battle, but they would win by wits; would strike at the white race through 'dope' and when the time was ripe would command the world," explained a senior judge.

At first, ordinary citizens had taken matters into their own hands against this Yellow Peril. In Los Angeles, twenty-one Chinese people were shot, hanged, or burned alive by white mobs, while in San Francisco, officials tried to forcibly move everyone in Chinatown into an area reserved for pig farms and other businesses that were designated as dirty and disease-ridden, until the courts ruled the policy was unconstitutional. So the authorities did the next best thing: they launched mass raids on Chinese homes and businesses, saying it was time to stop their opium use. The agents built a bonfire of opium-smoking equipment with flames "shooting 30 feet into the air," as one observer put it: "The choking smoke spread its heavy mantle over Chinatown like a pall upon the dead." The Harrison Act followed soon after.

Harry Anslinger did not create these underlying trends. His genius wasn't for invention: it was for presenting his agents as the hand that would steady all these cultural tremblings. He knew that to secure his bureau's future, he needed a high-profile victory, over intoxication and over the blacks, and so he turned back to Billie Holiday.

To finish her off, he called for his toughest agent—a man who was at no risk of falling in love with her, or anyone else.

~

The Japanese man couldn't breathe. Colonel George White—a vastly obese white slab of a man—had his hands tightened around his throat, and he was not letting go. It was the last the Japanese man ever saw. Once it was all over, White told the authorities he strangled this "Jap" because he believed he was a spy. But privately, he told his friends he didn't really know if his victim was a spy at all, and he didn't care. "I have a lot of friends who are murderers," he bragged years later, and "I had very good times in their company." He boasted to his friends that he kept a photo of the man he had throttled hanging on the wall of his apartment, always watching him. So as he got to work on Billie, Colonel White was watched by his last victim, and this made him happy.

He was Harry Anslinger's favorite agent, and when he looked over Holiday's files, he declared her to be "a very attractive customer," because the Bureau was "at a loose end" and could do with the opportunity "to kick her over."

White had been a journalist in San Francisco in the 1930s until he applied to join the Federal Bureau of Narcotics. The personality test given to all applicants on Anslinger's orders found that he was a sadist. He quickly rose through the bureau's ranks. He became a sensation as the first and only white man ever to infiltrate a Chinese drug gang, and he even learned to speak in Mandarin so he could chant their oaths with them. In his downtime, he would go swimming in the filthy waters of New York City's Hudson River, as if daring it to poison him.

He was especially angered that this black woman didn't know her place. "She flaunted her way of living, with her fancy coats and fancy automobiles and her jewelry and her gowns," he complained. "She was the big lady wherever she went."

When he came for her on a rainy day at the Mark Twain Hotel in San Francisco without a search warrant, Billie was sitting in white silk pajamas in her room. This was one of the few places she could still perform, and she badly needed the money. She insisted to the police that she had been clean for over a year. White's men declared they had found opium stashed in a wastepaper basket next to a side room and the kit for shooting heroin in the room, and they charged her with possession. But when the details were looked at later, there seemed to be something odd: a wastepaper basket seems an improbable place to keep a stash, and the kit for shooting heroin was never entered into evidence by the cops—they said they left it at the scene. When journalists asked White about this, he blustered; his reply, they noted, "appeared a little defensive."

That night, White came to Billie's show at the Café Society Uptown, and he requested his favorite songs. She never lost faith in her music's ability to capture and persuade. "They'll remember me," she said, "when all this is gone, and they've finished badgering me." George White did not agree. "I did not think much of Ms Holiday's performance," he told her manager sternly.

Billie insisted the junk had been planted in her room by White, and she immediately offered to go into a clinic to be monitored: she would experience no withdrawal symptoms, she said, and that would prove she was clean and being framed. She checked herself in at a cost of one thousand dollars, and she didn't so much as shiver.

George White, it turns out, had a long history of planting drugs on women. He was fond of pretending to be an artist and luring women to an apartment in Greenwich Village where he would spike their drinks with LSD to see what would happen. One of his victims was a young actress who happened to live in his building, while another was a pretty blond waitress in a bar. After she failed to show any sexual interest in him, he drugged her to see if that would change. "I toiled whole-heartedly in the vineyards because it was fun, fun, fun," White boasted. "Where else [but in the Bureau of Narcotics] could a red-blooded American boy lie, kill, cheat, steal, rape and pillage with the sanction and blessing of the All-Highest?" He may well have been high when he busted Billie for getting high.

The prosecution of Billie went ahead. "The hounding and the pressure drove me," she wrote, "to think of trying the final solution, death." Her best friend said it caused Billie "enough anxieties to kill a horse." At the trial, a jury of twelve ordinary citizens heard all the evidence. They sided with Billie against Anslinger and White, and found her not guilty. Nonetheless, "she had slipped from the peak of her fame," Harry Anslinger wrote. "Her voice was cracking."

~

In the years after Billie's trial, many other singers were too afraid of being harassed by the authorities to perform "Strange Fruit." But Billie Holiday refused to stop. No matter what they did to her, she sang her song.

"She was," her friend Annie Ross told me, "as strong as she could be." To the end, Billie Holiday kept the promise she had made to herself back in Baltimore when she was a little girl. She didn't bow her head to anyone.

~

When Billie was forty-four years old, a young musician named Frankie Freedom was serving her a bowl of oatmeal and custard in his apartment when she suddenly collapsed. She was taken to the Knickerbocker Hospital in Manhattan and made to wait for an hour and a half on a stretcher, and they said she was a drug addict and turned her away. One of the ambulance drivers recognized her, so she ended up in a public ward of New York City's Metropolitan Hospital. As soon as they took her off oxygen, she lit a cigarette.

"Some damnbody is always trying to embalm me," she said, but the doctors came back and explained she had an array of very serious illnesses: she was emaciated because she had not been eating; she had cirrhosis of the liver because of chronic drinking; she had cardiac and respiratory problems due to chronic smoking; and she had several leg ulcers caused by starting to inject street heroin once again. They said she was unlikely to survive for long—but Harry wasn't done with her yet. "You watch, baby," Billie warned from her tiny gray hospital room. "They are going to arrest me in this damn bed."

Narcotics agents were sent to her hospital bed and said they had found less than one-eighth of an ounce of heroin in a tinfoil envelope. They claimed it was hanging on a nail on the wall, six feet from the bottom of her bed—a spot Billie was incapable of reaching. They summoned a grand jury to indict her, telling her that unless she disclosed her dealer, they would take her straight to prison. They confiscated her comic books, radio, record player, flowers, chocolates, and magazines, handcuffed her to the bed, and stationed two policemen at the door. They had orders to forbid any visitors from coming in without a written permit, and her friends were told there was no way to see her. Her friend Maely Dufty screamed at them that it was against the law to arrest somebody who was on the critical list. They explained that the problem had been solved: they had taken her off the critical list.

So now, on top of the cirrhosis of the liver, Billie went into heroin withdrawal, alone. A doctor was brought into the hospital at the insistence of her friends to prescribe methadone. She was given it for ten days and began to recover: she put on weight and looked better. But then the methadone was suddenly stopped, and she began to sicken again. When finally a friend was allowed in to see her, Billie told her in a panic: "They're going to kill me. They're going to kill me in there. Don't let them." The police threw the friend out. "I had very high hopes that she would be able to come out of it alive," another friend, Alice Vrbsky, told the BBC, until all this happened. "It was the last straw."

One day, her pimp-husband Louis MacKay turned up at the hospital—after informing on her—and ostentatiously read the Twenty-Third Psalm over her bed. It turned out he wanted her to sign over the rights to her autobiography to him, the last thing she still controlled. She pretended to be unconscious. As soon as he was gone, she opened her eyes. "I've always been a religious bitch," she said, "but if that dirty motherfucker believes in God, I'm thinking it over."

On the street outside the hospital, protesters gathered, led by a Harlem pastor named the Reverend Eugene Callender. They held up signs reading "Let Lady Live." Callender had built a clinic for heroin addicts in his church, and he pleaded for Billie to be allowed to go there to be nursed back to health. His reasoning was simple, he told me in 2013: addicts, he said, "are human beings, just like you and me." Punishment makes them sicker; compassion can make them well. Harry and his men refused. They fingerprinted Billie on her hospital bed. They took a mug shot of her on her hospital bed. They grilled her on her hospital bed without letting her talk to a lawyer.

Billie didn't blame Anslinger's agents as individuals; she blamed the drug war itself—because it forced the police to treat ill people like criminals. "Imagine if the government chased sick people with diabetes, put a tax on insulin and drove it into the black market, told doctors they couldn't treat them," she wrote in her memoir, "then sent them to jail. If we did that, everyone would know we were crazy. Yet we do practically the same thing every day in the week to sick people hooked on drugs."

Still, some part of Billie Holiday believed she had done something evil, with her drug use, and with her life. She told people she would rather die than go back to prison, but she was terrified that she would burn in hell—just as her mother had said she would all those years before, when she was a little girl lying on the brothel floor, listening to Louis Armstrong's music and letting it carry her out of Baltimore. "She was exhausted," one of her friends told me. "She didn't want to go through it no more."

And so, when she died on this bed, with police officers at the door to protect the public from her, she looked—as another of her friends told the BBC—"as if she had been torn from life violently." She had fifteen fifty-dollar bills strapped to her leg. It was all she had left. She was intending to give it to the nurses who had looked after her, to thank them.

Her best friend, Maely Dufty, insisted to anyone who would listen that Billie had been effectively murdered by a conspiracy to break her, orchestrated by the narcotics police—but what could she do? At Billie's funeral, there were swarms of police cars, because they feared their actions against her would trigger a riot. In his eulogy for her, the Reverend Eugene Callender told me he had said: "We should not be here. This young lady was gifted by her creator with tremendous talent . . . She should have lived to be at least eighty years old."

The Federal Bureau of Narcotics saw it differently. "For her," Harry wrote with satisfaction, "there would be no more 'Good Morning Heartache.'"

∼

It is easy to judge Harry Anslinger. But if we are honest, I suspect that everybody who has ever loved an addict—everybody who has ever been an addict—has this impulse in them somewhere. Destroy the addiction. Kill the addiction. Throttle it with violence. Harry Anslinger is our own darkest impulses, given a government department and a license to kill.

As I researched this book, I traveled a long way from the farm fields of Pennsylvania—but at every step, I began to feel I was chasing the scream that terrified little Harry Anslinger all those years ago, as it echoed out across the world.

In his private files, Harry kept a poem that had been sent in by an admiring member of the public, addressed directly to him. It defined for Harry his mission in life. Until the day that "the Great Judge proclaims: / 'The last addict's died,'" the poem said, "Then—not till then—may you be retired."

CHAPTER 2

Sunshine and Weaklings

In Harry Anslinger's files I began to notice a few names that he raged against repeatedly, as monsters who were trying to sabotage his work and spread drugs throughout America. This intrigued me. Who were these people? Who, for example, were Edward Williams and Henry Smith Williams?

I began to follow a paper trail through file folders, old court records, and yellowing books, and I uncovered a story that, as far I can tell, has been almost entirely forgotten for more than sixty years now—yet it has the power to transform how we see this whole war.

The drug war was born in the United States—but so was the resistance to it. Right at the start, there were people who saw that the drug war was not what we were being told. It was something else entirely.

Harry Anslinger wanted to make sure we would never put these pieces together.

∼

In the sunshine of Los Angeles, there was a doctor in the early 1930s named Henry Smith Williams, with a long, unsmiling face. He wore small wire-framed glasses through which he peered down on the world and at almost everyone in it. This doctor shared all of Harry Anslinger's hatreds. He said that addicts were "weaklings" who should never have been brought into the world and wrote that "the idea that every human life has genuine value . . . and therefore is something to be treasured, is an absurd banality. The world would be far better off if forty percent of its inhabitants had never been born." In his view, drugs led only to destruction, and nobody should take them, ever.

But sometimes, as a historical trend is forming, there is one person who can see what it will mean for humanity, way ahead of everyone else—and sometimes, these prophets come in the most unlikely form.

Henry Smith Williams was about to announce in a detailed new book that he had made a remarkable discovery, one he believed would make this new war on drugs untenable. While Harry Anslinger was raging against the Mafia in public, he was, in fact, secretly working for them. The drug war had been created, Henry said, for one reason and one reason alone. The Mafia paid Harry Anslinger to launch his crusade because they wanted the drug market all to themselves. It was the scam of the century. And it was about, at last, to be exposed.

The long road that led Henry to this conviction began one day in 1931 when a man shivered into the clinic run by Henry's brother, Edward Williams. He was suffering all the obvious symptoms of heroin withdrawal, so he was in the right place: Edward was the one of the most distinguished experts on opiate addiction in the world. "The man is a wreck, at the verge of collapse," Henry wrote. "He is deathly pale. Sweat pours from his skin. He is all a tremor. His life seems threatened."

Both brothers had seen people like this in their offices for many years. Henry believed, in his Social Darwinist way, that they were weaklings who had survived only because they had been stupidly coddled by society; in a state of nature, they would have died to make way for stronger men with better genes. Yet Edward couldn't bear to see their suffering— not when he knew there was a way to stop their pain. That is why he had helped to set up this clinic—and why he was about to be ruined.

"Can the doctor do nothing? Oh yes, the doctor knows just what should be done," he explained. "He knows that he has but to write a few words on the prescription blank that lies at his elbow, and the patient, tottering to the nearest drug store, will receive the remedy that would restore him miraculously to a semblance of normality and the actuality of physical and mental comfort." He can provide a legal prescription for the drug to which the patient has become addicted. It will not damage his body: all doctors agree that pure opiates do no harm to the flesh or the organs. The patient, after taking the drug, will become calm. He will be able to function again. He will be able to work, or support a family, or love.

So Edward Williams wrote the prescription. He had done it many times, and he was confident he had the law on his side. He was given even more confidence when the Supreme Court ruled in 1925 that the Harrison Act didn't give the government the authority to punish doctors who believed it was in the best interests of their addicted patients to prescribe them heroin.

But on this particular day in 1931, the addict was not what he seemed. He was, in fact, working for Harry Anslinger, as one of a flock of "stool pigeons" the Bureau was sending out across the country to trick doctors. They were desperate addicts tossed a few dollars by the bureau to con doctors into treating them. Once the prescription was written, the police burst in to the room, and Edward Williams was busted, alongside some twenty thousand other doctors across the country, in one of the biggest legal assaults on doctors in American history.

Most of the people the bureau had picked on up to now—addicts and African Americans—were in no position to fight back. But Henry Smith Williams was one of the most respected medical authorities in the United States. He was said to know more about the chemistry and biology of the blood cells than any other man in America, and he had written a thirty-one-volume history of science and many entries in the Encyclopedia Britannica, all in his spare time left over from treating more than ten thousand patients. So in the aftermath of his brother's arrest, Henry started to investigate—and he uncovered something he didn't expect.

~

As he watched his brother's career being destroyed by the police, Henry remembered something that now seemed to him, for the first time, to be significant.

Before it became a crime to sell drugs, he had many patients who used them—but things had been very different then. They had bought their opiates, including morphine and heroin, at a low price from their local pharmacist. They were sold in bottles as "remedies" or "little helpers," for everything from a chest infection to the blues. One of the most popular was called "Mrs. Winslow's Soothing Syrup," of which each ounce you bought contained 65 milligrams of pure morphine. The vast majority of people who bought them, he recalled, used them without a problem. Most people, even addicts, used them in low doses.

"No one thought of the use of these medicines as having any moral significance," he explained. One famous campaigner against alcohol was addicted to morphine, and nobody thought this was odd or hypocritical. There were many women who used opiates in the form of "syrups" every day who, he said, "would have gone on their hands and knees to pray for a lost soul had they seen cigarette stains on the fingers of a daughter."

Just as a large majority of drinkers did not become alcoholics, a large majority of users of these products did not become drug addicts. They used opiates as "props for the unstable nervous system," like a person who drinks wine at the end of a stressful day at work.

A small number did get hooked—but even among the addicted, the vast majority continued to work and maintain relatively normal lives. An official government study found that before drug prohibition properly kicked in, three quarters of self-described addicts (not just users— addicts) had steady and respectable jobs. Some 22 percent of addicts were wealthy, while only 6 percent were poor. They were more sedate as a result of their addiction, and although it would have been better for them to stop, they were rarely out of control or criminal. But in 1914, the Harrison Act was passed, and then Anslinger arrived sixteen years later to rapidly ratchet it up.

Doctors saw the results of the policy changes. "Here were tens of thousands of people, in every walk of life, frantically craving drugs that they could in no legal way secure," Henry wrote. "They craved the drugs, as a man dying of thirst craves water. They must have the drugs at any hazard, at any cost. Can you imagine that situation, and suppose that the drugs will not be supplied? . . . [The lawmakers] must have known that their Edict, if enforced, was the clear equivalent of an order to create an illicit drug industry. They must have known that they were in effect ordering a company of drug smugglers into existence."

The drug dealer could now charge extortionate prices. In the pharmacies, morphine had cost two or three cents a grain; the criminal gangs charged a dollar. The addicts paid whatever they were told to pay.

The world we recognize now—where addicts are often forced to become criminals, in a desperate scramble to feed their habit from gangsters—was being created, for the first time. The Williams brothers had watched as Anslinger's department created two crime waves. First, it created an army of gangsters to smuggle drugs into the country and sell them to addicts. In other words: while Harry Anslinger claimed to be fighting the Mafia, he was in fact transferring a massive and highly profitable industry into their exclusive control.

Second, by driving up the cost of drugs by more than a thousand percent, the new policies meant addicts were forced to commit crime to get their next fix. "How was the average addict—revealed by the official census as an average person—to secure ten or fifteen dollars a day to pay for the drug he imperatively needed?" Henry Smith Williams asked. "Can you guess the answer? The addict could not get such a sum by ordinary means. Then he must get it by dubious means—he must beg, borrow, forge, steal." The men, he wrote, usually became thieves; the women often became prostitutes.

"The United States government, as represented by its [anti-drug] officers," Henry explained, had just become "the greatest and most potent maker of criminals in any recent century." And every time Harry Anslinger created new drug criminals, he created new reasons for his department to be saved—and to grow.

~

The road to Edward Huntington Williams's arrest had begun when he became slowly convinced that there was a better way to respond to the problem of drug addiction—one that was already perfectly legal.

When the Harrison Act banning heroin and cocaine was written in 1914, it contained a very clear and deliberately designed loophole. It said that doctors, vets, and dentists had the right to continue giving out these drugs as they saw fit—and that addicts should be dealt with compassionately in this way. Yet the loophole was tossed onto the trash heap of history, as if it didn't exist—until Edward Williams decided to dig it out and act on it. He helped to build a free clinic for addicts, and he volunteered his own time there. He wrote his prescriptions for whoever needed them. And he waited to see the results.

Even he was surprised by what he saw. Patients who had come in as unemployed physical wrecks were able, slowly and steadily, to go back to work, support their families, and look after themselves again, just as they had before drugs were criminalized. The order and calm that had existed before narcotics prohibition started to return to their neighborhoods. The mayor of Los Angeles came out and celebrated the clinic as a great gift to the city, and the local federal prosecutor announced that these clinics accomplished "more good . . . in one day than all the prosecutions in one month."

Thousands of miles away, the Federal Bureau of Narcotics was furious. Harry kept picturing the addicts he had seen in his childhood, and in

Europe, and he wanted to stop this contagion from spreading. Or did he—as Henry Smith Williams was beginning to suspect—have darker motives?

Harry said that building clinics for heroin addicts was like providing "department stores for kleptomaniacs" where they could steal whatever they wanted. The tabloid newspapers, after briefings from the bureau, savaged the clinics as dens of sin, and the stool pigeons began their flight. In Portland, Oregon, a doctor stood in his clinic as Anslinger's men forcibly shut its doors and asked them pleadingly, was there anything he could legally do to help all these addicts? "Yeah, sure: there's plenty you can do," the agent told him. "Run the whole bunch of them down to the ocean and kick 'em in. They'll make fair fish food. That's all any of them are good for."

After the clinic in Los Angeles closed and doctors like Edward Williams were busted, almost all the addicts lost their jobs and were reduced once again to constant scrambling for the money for a fix. They fell into crime and homelessness, and dozens of them died. The bureau was defying the clear ruling of the Supreme Court that the Harrison Act allowed doctors to prescribe to addicts, but "the Supreme Court has no army to enforce its decisions," the press noted with a shrug.

Some twenty thousand doctors were charged with violating the Harrison Act alongside Edward Williams, and 95 percent were convicted. Most were charged massive fines, but some faced five years in prison for each and every prescription written. In many places, horrified juries refused to convict, because they could see the doctors were only treating the sick as best they could. But Anslinger's crackdown continued with full force.

Harry wanted Edward Williams to be broken more than any other doctor, because he was widely respected and many people listened to him. "The moral effect of his conviction," Anslinger wrote, "will most certainly result in greater circumspection." You only have to destroy a few doctors to silence the rest. Go for the top. Maximum intimidation. This was always Harry's way. "Anybody that came out with any academic work that could be critical of him, his Bureau, or his philosophy, had to go to prison," Howard Diller, one of his agents, said later. "Or be beheaded."

∼

As he watched the birth of the drug war, Henry Smith Williams—cold, chilly, arrogant—felt a war breaking out within himself. Part of him believed addicts were the result of barbaric genes left over from cavemen, and the sooner they died off, the better. But he was also seeing the faces of the individual human beings who were being broken. When he saw the work of Anslinger in the world, he began to question the Anslinger in his own heart.

He went to meet Harry Anslinger in Washington, D.C., to plead for his brother's reputation and freedom. Harry was now confronted with one of his victims face-to-face, perhaps for the first time. He offered no defense of himself, and he put forward none of the arguments he proclaimed so loudly elsewhere. He backed off. He said that he "could not discover that the Bureau had any case against Dr. Williams, and could not understand why such a man had been attacked." He put all the blame on his Los Angeles representative, a big redheaded agent named Chris Hanson. Yet after Williams was gone, Anslinger privately jeered at him, saying that Henry Smith Williams was suffering from "hysteria."

At the trial, every single one of the seventeen doctors who testified supported Edward Williams, yet he was found guilty of violating the Harrison Act—in effect, of being a drug dealer—and sentenced to a year on federal probation. This ensured he would never again write a prescription for an addict—nor would any other doctor in the United States for generations to come. "Doctors," Harry boasted, now "cannot treat addicts even if they wish to."

Harry's own agents began to quit in disgust. One of them, William G. Walker, said: "If anyone could see the suffering of these poor devils . . . they would understand why we should have a change."

One doctor—stripped of his power to prescribe—decided he had to stop this cruelty once and for all. He traveled to Washington, D.C., with a gun stuffed into his coat. He was determined to walk into Harry Anslinger's office and kill him. He stood outside Harry's office until he was finally allowed in. Anslinger offered to take the doctor's coat—and, as he reached for it, snatched the gun. Harry boasted later that even if the doctor had taken a shot at him, he would have "made a sieve out of him" by firing first.

None of this gave Harry pause. The doctors were so emotional, Harry insisted, because they were corrupt. Don't be fooled: they only wanted the money from drug addicts' prescriptions. They were missing the hard cash, he said, and nothing more. Besides, he said, he had proof that his way worked. Since the bureau's crackdown began, the number of addicts had fallen dramatically, to just twenty thousand in the whole country. Years later, a historian named David Courtwright put in a Freedom of

Information request to find out how this figure was calculated—and found that it was simply made up. The Treasury Department's top officials had privately said it was "absolutely worthless."

~

Back in Los Angeles, after a long period of digging, Henry Smith Williams was finally ready to make his announcement—one he believed would change the course of the twentieth century, and finally end this "American Inquisition." In 1938, he published a book titled *Drug Addicts Are Human Beings*, laying out his evidence that the entire policy of drug prohibition in America was a gigantic racket—running right up to and including the bald man in Washington, D.C., directing the "crackdown." Harry, he maintained, was taking his instructions from the Mafia.

If you want to know how this scam works, he explained, you need to look at the story of Chris Hanson. He was a thickset man in his sixties, with bright red hair and a strangely smooth and youthful face, known to everyone as Big Chris. He was Harry's bureau chief in California, and he masterminded the mass round-up of doctors there, including Edward Williams.

And we now know why he did it, wrote Henry Smith Williams. Not long after he shut down the clinic in Los Angeles, it was proven in court that Big Chris was secretly working for a notorious Chinese drug dealer named Woo Sing. He was taking bushels of cash from the drug dealers, and in turn he was doing their bidding. The dealers paid Big Chris to shut down the heroin clinics. They wanted him to do it.

I had to read through these files several times before I realized the significance of this accusation. At the start of the drug war, the man who launched the drug crackdown in California did it because he was paid to—*by the drug dealers themselves*. They wanted the drug war. They wanted it so badly, they would pay to speed it up.

Henry Smith Williams urged the public to ask: Why would gangsters pay the cops to enforce the drug laws harder? The answer, he said, was right in front of our eyes. Drug prohibition put the entire narcotics industry into their hands. Once the clinics were closed, every single addict became a potential customer and cash cow.

Since his brother's clinic had been shut down by the Federal Bureau of Narcotics following bribes from the Mafia, Smith Williams reasoned that that must be what was happening at the national level, too. Anslinger must be in their pay: if the drug gangs win from Anslinger's policies, and nobody else does, the only explanation is that he is one of them.

Henry Smith Williams was, it turns out, wrong on this one crucial detail. There is no evidence that Anslinger ever worked for the Mafia, and it's fair to assume it would have emerged by now if he had. Anslinger really believed he was the sworn enemy of the drug gangs, even as they were paying his officers to enact his policies. Henry Smith Williams assumed that Anslinger—and prohibition—were rational, like him. They were not. They are responses to fear, and panic. And nobody, when they are panicking, can see the logical flaws in their thought.

Harry worked very hard to keep the country in a state of panic on the subject of drugs so that nobody would ever again see these logical contradictions. Whenever people did point them out, he had them silenced. He had to make sure there was no room for doubt—in his own head, or in the country—and no alternative for Americans to turn to.

～

Henry Smith Williams was never the same after these experiences. Before, he saw the majority of human beings as feeble dimwits who barely deserve life. But he started to argue that humans didn't have to be engaged in a brutal Darwinian war of survival after all; instead, we can choose kindness in place of crushing the weak.

He spent his remaining years setting up a group to campaign for an end to the drug war, but Anslinger's men wrote to everyone who expressed an interest in it, warning them it was a "criminal organization" that was "in trouble with Uncle Sam." Henry Smith Williams died in 1940. *Drug Addicts Are Human Beings* remained out of print and largely forgotten for the rest of Anslinger's life, and ours.

The book contained a prediction. If this drug war continues, Henry Smith Williams wrote, there will be a five-billion-dollar drug smuggling industry in the United States in fifty years' time. He was right almost to the exact year.

The story of the Williams brothers, and all the doctors who were crushed alongside them, was so successfully wiped from America's collective memory that by the 1960s, Anslinger could say in public that doctors had always been his allies in the drug war. "I'd like to see," he told a journalist, "the doctor who claims he was treated in anything but the kindliest fashion."

CHAPTER 3

The Barrel of Harry's Gun

While Harry Anslinger was shutting down all the alternatives to the drug war in the United States, across the rest of the world, drugs were still being sold legally. Over the next few decades, this began to end—and by the 1960s, they were banned everywhere.

At first, I assumed this was because every country had its own local fears and its own local Anslingers—but then I started to notice something odd in Anslinger's archives, and I didn't understand it.

In his letters, he was issuing orders all over the world—including to my country, Britain. He acted as the first "drug czar" not just for the United States, but for the world. How? I started trying to figure out the story of how Harry took his war global—and pushed his views into the laws of everyone reading this book, wherever you are.

~

Once the doctors were whipped into line, there was one thing left that puzzled Harry. He was doing all the right things. He was cracking down on addicts and doctors and dealers. He held up one city in particular as a model for the whole world of how to wipe out drugs, because it adopted every single piece of hard-line legalization he demanded. That city was Baltimore. Yet something, it seemed, wasn't working. Baltimore was—inexplicably—not becoming a drug-free paradise. Harry said there was only one possible explanation. Just as he had glimpsed the

Mafia secretly operating beneath the surface of American society, he now believed he could see another, even more evil force secretly manipulating events.

The Communists, he declared, were clearly flooding America with drugs, as part of a "cold, calculated, ruthless, systematic plan to undermine" America. Testifying before Congress, he gave details of a tide of "Communist heroin" flowing from the paddies of China straight into the veins of white Americans. Why would the Chinese do this? They wanted to weaken the white man—and to "build a fifth column within the United States," an army of addicts who would "be willing to pay with treason for their drugs." Now, Harry warned sternly, every addict was not only a criminal and a thug. He was also a potential Communist traitor.

His agents told him none of these claims were true. One of them later gave an interview in which he said: "There was no evidence for Anslinger's accusations, but that never stopped him." But once again, Harry had tapped into the deepest fears of his time and ensured that they ran right through his department, swelling his budget as they went. Whatever America was afraid of—blacks, poor people, Communists—he showed how the only way to deal with the fear was to deal with drugs, his way.

By conjuring this Communist conspiracy into existence in the 1950s, Harry found a way to turn his failure into a reason to *escalate* the war. Drug prohibition *would* work—but only if it was being done by everyone, all over the world. So he traveled to the United Nations with a set of instructions for humanity: Do what we have done. Wage war on drugs. Or else. Of all Harry's acts, this was the most consequential for us today.

~

He stayed in one of the best hotels in Geneva, and he would stare at the representatives of smaller, weaker countries and growl his orders. But just as Billie Holiday was refusing to bow her head, many countries were refusing to bow theirs. Thailand, for example, flatly refused to ban opium smoking, on the grounds that it was a long-standing tradition in their country, and less harmful than prohibition. So Harry started to twist arms. One of his key lieutenants, Charles Siragusa, boasted: "I found that a casual mention of the possibility of shutting off our foreign aid programs, dropped in the proper quarters, brought grudging permission for our operations almost immediately." Later, leaders were threatened with being cut off from selling any of their countries' goods to the United States.

Whenever any representative of another country tried to explain to him why these policies weren't right for them, Anslinger snapped: "I've made up my mind—don't confuse me with the facts."

And so Thailand caved. Britain caved. Everyone—under threat—caved in the end. The United States was now the most powerful country in the world, and nobody dared defy them for long. Some were more willing than others. Pretty much every country has its own minority group, like African Americans, whom it wants to keep down. For many, it was a good excuse. And pretty much every country had this latent desire to punish addicts. "The world belongs to the strong," Harry believed. "It always has and it always will." The result is that we are all still stuck at the end of the barrel of Harry Anslinger's gun.

~

But something else was frightening Harry—something much closer to home. From the start of his period at the bureau, he was finding that his thoughts were spiraling off into strange, disordered directions. His private files started to warn in frantic tones that addicts were "contagious," and that any one of us could be infected if they were not immediately "quarantined." And then, quite suddenly, Harry disappeared from the bureau for months.

Although nobody was told at the time, Harry in fact had a mental breakdown and had to be hospitalized. When he returned, his paranoia only seemed to have grown. He saw enemies and plots and secret attempts to control the entire world around every corner.

At times, as I read through Harry's ever-stranger arguments, I wondered: How could a man like this have persuaded so many people? But the answers were lying there, waiting for me, in the piles of letters he received from members of the public, from senators, and from presidents. They wanted to be persuaded. They wanted easy answers to complex fears. It's tempting to feel superior—to condescend to these people—but I suspect this impulse is there in all of us. The public wanted to be told that these deep, complex problems—race, inequality, geopolitics—came down to a few powders and pills, and if these powders and pills could be wiped from the world, these problems would disappear.

It is a natural human instinct to turn our fears into symbols, and destroy the symbols, in the hope that it will destroy the fear. It is a logic that keeps recurring throughout human history, from the Crusades to the witch hunts to the present day. It's hard to sit with a complex problem, such as the human urge to get intoxicated, and accept that it will always be with us, and will always cause some problems (as well as some pleasures). It is much more appealing to be told a different message—that it can be ended. That all these problems can be over, if only we listen, and follow.

~

After Harry finally retired from running the bureau—with a little nudge from JFK—they discovered something odd about Harry's paranoia. It turns out it had been pointed in every direction except where it would have been deserved—at his own department. Immediately after he finally stood down, an investigation by a special team from the Internal Revenue Service found that the bureau was not free from corruption, leading historian John McWilliams to claim that, "the bureau itself was actually the major source of supply and protector of heroin in the United States."

Anslinger had been too busy chasing doctors, jazz singers, addicts, and Chinese dragons to see there were drug dealers in front of him all along.

But no matter. Harry had won. By the time he left office as the only man ever to run a U.S. security agency longer than J. Edgar Hoover, nobody was suggesting disbanding the Federal Bureau of Narcotics anymore. It was an essential part of the government machine.

Years later, in 1970, *Playboy* magazine arranged a roundtable debate of the drug laws and invited him to take part. For the first time since he sat down with Henry Smith Williams in the 1930s, Harry Anslinger was forced to defend his arguments against articulate opponents. They included the psychiatrist Dr. Joel Fort, the lawyer Joseph Oteri, and the poet laureate of narcotics, William Burroughs.

This time, Harry did not run away from defending his views, as he had with Henry Smith Williams. He went on the attack. "A person under the influence of marijuana," he declared, "can get so violent that it takes about five policemen to hold him down." He said there is "proof that continued use of hashish results in commitment to mental hospitals."

Before, he would have been greeted with a respectful silence. Not now. When asked for evidence for these claims, he talked about the Indian psychiatrist Dr. Isaac Chopra, "who has stated flatly and unequivocally that Cannabis drugs lead to psychosis."

"I got Dr. Chopra on the stand in Boston, under cross-examination," Oteri replied, "and he admitted his studies did not involve a valid scientific sample and didn't really connect marijuana and insanity in any cause and effect fashion." Anslinger had no response.

His opponents offered studies, facts, figures about how prohibition had not worked. Anslinger kept coming back with anecdotes, almost always sexual: "I can tell you about a case in a fraternity house where they were having a weekend party. On a dare, one of the girls took a sugar cube in which there was a drop of LSD. She was out for two days and during that time she was raped by a number of the fraternity boys."

The other people around the table seemed nonplussed, as sexy stories adapted from the pages of 1930s pulp fiction bumped up against valid scientific studies. It's as if a Mickey Spillane detective had wandered into a medical seminar and started telling the doctors they were talking bunk because one time he'd followed a blond dame down an alleyway.

Anslinger started to try to compete with their world of factual claims, saying: "I challenge you to name one doctor who has reported a beneficial effect of marijuana, outside of the backward areas of the world." He was immediately answered with names: Dr. Lloyd J. Thompson, professor of psychiatry at Bowman Gray School of Medicine, and George T. Stocking, one of Britain's leading psychiatrists. Again, Anslinger had no response. This kept happening in a strange fox-trot of debunking. Anslinger asserted; the experts rebutted; Anslinger fell silent.

When feeling met fact, he was stumped. And then Anslinger snapped. He started calling everybody at the table around him "utterly monstrous" and said they were talking "vicious tripe" and must have a "disordered mind." Then he compared them to Adolf Hitler, and finally spluttered: "We've been hearing some of the most ridiculous statements that have ever been made."

As I sat amid boxes and boxes of Harry's papers—all that remains of him, except for a global war—I found something sad about this scene. He was clearly an old man in pain, both from the angina he had developed and from no longer having the power to silence this conversation. Still, he tried, raising the rhetorical stakes to claim that the people who disagree with him will cause the death of America: "History is strewn," he said, "with the bones of nations that have tolerated moral laxity and hedonism."

Dr. Fort looked over at Anslinger's vast bald head and replied. "You have led this country to treat scientific questions," he said, "the way such matters were handled in the Middle Ages." Dr. Henry Smith Williams had said this at the beginning of Anslinger's long career; now another doctor was standing before him saying precisely the same thing, as Harry Anslinger offered his last recorded words.

CHAPTER 4

The Bullet at the Birth

As I dug deeper, I realized there was a hole in the story of the start of the drug war—a large and cavernous one. It is possible to piece together how this all began through the eyes of the cops, the doctors, and the addicts. But as I read on, I found they were all obsessed with a fourth force—the new army of drug dealers that was emerging all around them. I wanted to know their stories, and how they saw the world. But drug dealers don't keep records. There is no National Heroin Dealers' Archive to consult. For a long time, no matter how hard I looked, it seemed that this was a tale that could never be retrieved. Their memories died with the people who knew them, and they are all gone now.

But then I found out there was one exception. The first man to really see the potential of drug dealing in America was a gangster named Arnold Rothstein—and I slowly realized it was possible to piece him back together in quite a lot of detail. He was so egotistical he actually invited journalists to write about him—and he was so powerful he didn't worry about the police reading it. He owned them. There have been a number of biographies written of him, and even more important, I found out that after he died, his wife wrote a detailed memoir of her life with him, explaining exactly what he was like, in lush novelistic detail.

There was only one problem. Every copy of his wife's memoir seemed to have disappeared. Even the copy at the New York Public Library had vanished sometime in the 1970s. I eventually tracked down what seems to be the only remaining copy, in the Library of Congress, so I sat there in the shadow of the Senate and tried to reconstruct him piece by piece. This is the story I found—of how Arnold taught the world to deal drugs.

～

In the mid-1920s, Arnold Rothstein would stand on a street corner by the flickering neon crush of Times Square, waiting for someone—anyone—who owed him money to walk by.

The streets of the city were thick with people in hock to Rothstein, and—like Anslinger—he could make people afraid just by looking at them. At first glance, though, it was harder to see why. He was 5 feet 7, pale and baby-faced, with small, feminine hands. He never fidgeted, or drank, or raised a fist. He refused even to chew gum. He was sober and smart to the last thread of his perfectly tailored suits, but everybody in New York City knew that Rothstein could have you killed just by snapping his fingers—and that he had bought so many NYPD cops and politicians that he would never be punished for it.

Rothstein's wife, a Broadway chorus girl named Carolyn, had a habit of driving past, and she would call out to him. But she, too, was afraid. Later, she would write:

> Often on my way home in a car, I would have myself driven slowly up Broadway, past Forty-seventh to Fiftieth street. It might be a cold night, or a rainy one. Or it might be snowing. But more often than not, Arnold would be there. I would ask him to come home. He would shake his head and say: "I'm waiting to see someone to collect from" . . . He would stay out in all kinds of weather to collect small sums, even amounts as low as fifty dollars. Yet, he might have made thousands that same day. The amounts, it always seemed to me, were not what counted so much with Arnold, as the percentages. He was playing with chips, and the chips must show a profit.

It was the height of the Jazz Age, and Arnold Rothstein was the most feared man in New York City. After he had shaken down enough cash from people for the day, he would sit until long after dawn in Lindy's, a café in the throng of Times Square, and orchestrate his network of fraud, theft, and extortion. At the tables around him were the members of the Manhattan underworld and overworld huddled together: actors and songwriters, boxers and their managers, columnists and Communists, cops and criminals. Carolyn said it was like a "water hole in the jungle where beasts of prey and their natural enemies gather under a very real, but invisible, flag of truce for refreshment."

On one of these nights, at a table nearby, two men were writing a musical whose main characters were based on Arnold and Carolyn; they were going to call it *Guys and Dolls*. The musical would be funny. Arnold, though, was not; when he laughed, everybody thought it was strangely artificial. "I learned that when he laughed the laughter was a surface demonstration, a combination of the movement of face muscles synchronized with a sound, counterfeiting, but not partaking of, hilarity," Carolyn recalled years later.

But to us, Arnold matters most for just one reason. He was about to be handed the biggest black market in history.

~

Nobody could understand how Arnold got this way. His father—who had witnessed his toddler son standing over his sleeping brother with a knife—was one of the most beloved men in Manhattan's Jewish community. Avraham Rothstein's family had fled vicious anti-Jewish mobs in Russia for the Lower East Side in the 1880s; Avraham started out sewing caps, then worked his way up in the garment trade and eventually became a wealthy cotton goods dealer. If you had a problem in the Orthodox Jewish community, you'd come to him, and he would adjudicate: he was so scrupulously fair they called him "Abe the Just."

They would call his son a lot of things, but never "just."

Even as a small boy, Arnold had one marked quality beyond his coldness: an astonishing ability with mathematics. He could manipulate numbers and odds in a way that startled people. From the age of twelve, he knew that his father wouldn't dream of carrying cash from the setting of the sun on Friday night to the end of the Sabbath the next day, so Arnold stole the money from his wallet, played craps, and won so often and so big he could always replace the cash without anyone's noticing. By the time he ran away from home at seventeen to be a traveling salesman, Arnold knew he could crack card games better than anyone else.

He was starting to regard himself as a superman, far above the dumb herd, explaining later: "There are two million fools to one brainy man." He was the brainy man, and he was going to get his due from the fools.

And the Brain—as he now insisted on being called—soon discovered the greatest truth of gambling: the only way to win every time is to own the casino. So he set up a series of underground gambling dens across New York City, and when they got busted, one after another, he invented the "floating" craps game: a never-ending craps shoot that skipped from shadowy venue to dusky basement across the island. He carried the cash on him, up to a hundred thousand dollars at a time, and he obsessively counted the money, by hand, again and again. He had a tactile relationship with cash. The crinkle of banknotes was his music and his muse. He took no pleasure from the games themselves, only the end result; even after years spent at racetracks, he couldn't tell one horse from another. He knew only their statistics, and the cash that would whir his way at the end.

No matter how much money he had, Rothstein always believed he was behind and had to find a way to make more. When he first met his future wife, Carolyn, at a friend's party, he said he was a sporting man. "I thought that a sporting man was one who hunted and shot," she wrote. "It wasn't until later that I learned all a sporting man hunted was a victim with money, and all he shot was craps." On the night of their wedding, he told her he would need to pawn her engagement ring to free up funds, and she handed it over without complaining.

He guarded his money without a smile. One day, a gambler Rothstein knew called him long distance. He said he was broke and desperately needed five hundred dollars to get back to New York and back in the game.

"I can't hear you," Arnold said into the phone. The gambler kept repeating his request. "I can't hear you," Arnold repeated. The caller fiddled with his phone until the operator interrupted:

"But Mr. Rothstein, I can hear him distinctly," she said.

"All right," Arnold replied, "then you give it to him," and hung up.

He was used to rigging bets. "I knew my limitations when I was fifteen years old, and since that time I never played any game with a man I knew I couldn't beat," he said. At the racetrack, he would pay jockeys to throw the race, and gradually, year by year, he took this to a higher level. The bets got bigger and his winnings got more improbable, until he finally reached the biggest, most watched, most adrenaline-soaked game in America: the World Series. Fifty million Americans were following the result in 1919 when, against all the odds and every prediction, the Cincinnati Reds beat the far-and-away favorites, the White Sox. Long after the gasps were silent and the stadium was full only of echoes, the reason emerged: Rothstein had paid eight White Sox players to throw the match. All eight players were charged with fraud—and all were mysteriously acquitted.

In accounts of Arnold's story, I found that word appearing again and again: "mysteriously."

A man like Arnold Rothstein would always have been able to ferret out some criminal opportunity, but Arnold was handed two of the largest industries in America, tax-free. He immediately spotted that the prohibition of booze and drugs was the biggest lottery win for gangsters in history. There will always be large numbers of people who want to get drunk or high, and if they can't do it legally, they will do it illegally.

"Prohibition is going to last a long time and then one day it'll be abandoned," Rothstein told his associates. "But it's going to be with us for quite a while, that's for sure. I can see that more and more people are going to ignore the law . . . and we can make a fortune meeting this need."

Under prohibition, dealers were starting to discover, you can sell whatever crap you want: Who's going to complain to the police that they were poisoned by your illicit booze? Outbreaks of mass alcohol poisoning spread across America: in one incident alone, five hundred people were permanently crippled in Wichita, Kansas. But the market for illegal alcohol would live on for thirteen years, and then Franklin Roosevelt—desperate for new sources of tax revenue—would make it legal again in 1933. The greater gift, Rothstein saw, was in the market for drugs. They, surely, would stay banned far into the future.

At first the street peddlers had controlled the trade, and they got their supply in one of two ways: by staging heists of legal opiates as they were delivered to hospitals, or by ordering in bulk from legal suppliers in Mexico or Canada under fake company names. In 1922, Congress cracked down on this. Rothstein saw that these small-time crooks were missing the bigger opportunity anyway: this, he concluded, was a task for industrial manufacturing and industrial-scale smuggling. He sent his men to buy in bulk in Europe, where factories could still legally make heroin, shipped it over, and then distributed it to street sellers across New York and beyond.

For his system to work, Rothstein had to invent the modern drug gang. There had been gangs in New York City for generations, but they were small-time hoodlums who spent most of their energy beating each other up. Arnold's gangs were as disciplined as military units, and he made sure they had only one passion: the bottom line. That is how, by the mid-1920s, Rothstein and his new species of New York gang controlled the entire trade in heroin and cocaine on the Eastern seaboard of the United States.

~

We need to freeze the frame here for a moment, as Arnold stands by Times Square in the afternoon of the Jazz Age, looking for people who owe him money. At this moment, the heroin clinics are being shut down by the Federal Bureau of Narcotics across the United States. This is a hinge point in history. It is the moment when the control of drugs is transferred to the most dangerous people. As the result of the Harrison Act and its subsequent hard-line interpretation by Harry's bureau, it is passing from Henry Smith Williams and his colleagues to Arnold Rothstein and his thugs. It wasn't by the law of nature. It was by political decree.

~

When it came to addicts, Rothstein was as repulsed as Anslinger. The day he found one of his associates sucking on an opium pipe, he threw him out. But it's not hard to see why Arnold stuck with his new trade. The *World* newspaper reported: "For every $1000 spent in purchasing opium, smuggling it into the country and dispensing it, those at the top of the pyramid collect $6000 or more in profit." Arnold soon discovered that when you control the massive revenue offered by the drug industry, individual police and politicians are easy to buy. His profit margins were so vast he could outbid the salaries cops earned from the state. "The police," a journalist wrote in 1929, "were as gracious to him as they were to a police commissioner." This is why every time Arnold Rothstein was caught committing violence, the charges "mysteriously" vanished.

Arnold tamed the police with an approach that, years later, would be distilled by his successors, the Mexican drug cartels, into a single elegant phrase: *plata o plomo*. Silver or lead. Take our bribe, or take a bullet. Every now and then, there would be a police officer who refused to accept these ground rules. When two detectives, John Walsh and Josh McLaughlin, broke into one of Rothstein's illegal dens one night, he shot at them, suspecting they were robbers. The judge dismissed the case. A journalist asked: What's "a little pistol practice with policemen as targets" when you are Arnold Rothstein?

He did to law enforcement what he did to the World Series: he turned it into a performance the watching public believed was real, when it was in fact a puppet show. Enough of the players on the field worked for him to guarantee his success every time.

But no matter how rich he got, he lived exactly the same, eating at Lindy's late into every night. There was only one luxury he allowed himself. He paid a dentist to remove every one of his teeth, and insert shiny white ones in their place.

~

At some point, Arnold began to kill. This is where the camera lens of history becomes misted up and it gets harder to see what really happened. For obvious reasons, nobody recorded the names and details of Arnold's victims. We can only infer that they existed through hints here and there. Everyone—even hardcore gangsters—was terrified of him; we know you don't get that reputation only through wisecracks. There is only one of Rothstein's likely victims whose name is traceable now. The biographer David Pietrusza was able to dig it up—and that is because the victim was the third richest man in the world.

One day, Arnold met in a hotel on East Forty-Second Street with Captain Alfred Lowenstein, a financier so rich that when the Germans seized Belgium during World War One, Lowenstein reputedly offered to buy it back with his own cash. With Rothstein, the captain signed the biggest drug deal in history up to that point, a plan to mass-market a range of opiates to a growing new market. Soon after making the pact, he got on his private plane and flew to Europe.

When the plane landed, Captain Lowenstein was not on board. The staff said he had gone to the toilet and not come back. The *New York Times* reported that "it was practically impossible to open such a door if the plane were flying at ordinary cruising speed." Presumably, whatever Rothstein got in the deal up front, he kept.

As I pieced together Arnold's story in the shadow of the Capitol, I kept thinking of all the dry sociology studies I had been reading about the drug war—and they began to make sense. They explain that when a popular product is criminalized, it does not disappear. Instead, criminals start to control the supply and sale of the product. They have to get it into the country, transport it to where it's wanted, and sell it on the street. At every stage, their product is vulnerable. If somebody comes along and steals it, they can't go to the police or the courts to get it back. So they can only defend their property one way: by violence.

But you don't want to be having a shoot-out every day—that's no way to run a business. So you have to establish a reputation: a reputation for being terrifying. People must believe that you are so violent and brutal that they are too afraid to even try to pick a fight with you. You can only establish that reputation with attention-grabbing acts of brutality.

The American sociologist Philippe Bourgois would give this process a name: "a culture of terror." But the first person to notice and begin to articulate this dynamic was a half-drunk, nicotine-encrusted tabloid journalist, Donald Henderson Clarke, whose beat was to hang out in bars, from Midtown to the Bowery, with Rothstein and his fellow thugs.

It is hard, he wrote, to convey "the fear with which Rothstein was regarded. Get in bad with a Police Commissioner, or a District Attorney, or a Governor, or anyone like that and you could figure out with a fair degree of certainty what might happen to you on the basis of what you had done. Get in bad with Arnold Rothstein, and all the figuring in the world wouldn't get you anywhere. It's true that nothing might happen to you but Fear. But that's an awful calamity to come upon any man."

Arnold's men sprayed bullets across the city with the cheerful abandon of wedding guests tossing confetti. One of his chief henchmen, Jack "Legs" Diamond, was on the receiving end of so much return fire he was nicknamed "the human ammunition dump for the underworld." But Rothstein and his men seemed always to come out on top, and as a result, nobody dared to cross them. One day, Arnold was on the subway when some anonymous pickpocket silently stole his pearl stickpin, the only personal adornment he had ever loved. Over dinner, with his mirthless laugh, he explained to some other gangsters how he'd been robbed: "Me, the wiseguy. What do you think of that?"

The next day, a package arrived at his house. It contained the stickpin and a note reading, "The guy who took it didn't know who you were."

∿

While Arnold spread his terror, his wife, Carolyn, was virtually a prisoner in his house. He forbade her from going out after 6:00 P.M., or to be contacted by anyone. He said it was because the police were constantly watching. He controlled everything about her: he ordered her not to bob her hair, saying she would "lose all dignity" if she did. At night, she recalled in her memoir, she would sit up listening to the roulette wheel from the underground gambling parlor her husband ran across the street. She could figure out if the house was winning by listening to whether the croupier was speedily raking in the chips or more slowly counting them out.

As she waited up for him, the fragment of a memory from years ago kept coming back to Carolyn. When she was a dancer, she had cha-cha'd all over the country in a comedy show called *The Chorus Lady*. Once, on a train chugging through Pennsylvania—or maybe Kansas, she forgot the precise location—she had seen a long lazy row of country houses lit only by the flickering kerosene lamps inside. She tried to picture the lives of the people inside: calm and cool and safe.

Arnold came home every morning around five or six and immediately indulged his only addiction: glugging quarts of milk and eating trays of cakes in a frenzy. A giant leather screen hung in front of the windows to block the light. He woke at three in the afternoon and always groaned the same thing: "I don't feel well." He had a headache, or indigestion—his repressed way, perhaps, of dealing with what he must have known: that he could be killed at any moment.

He always promised Carolyn he would get out once he had enough, but she slowly realized there would never be enough for him. Besides, if he let go of the reins of violence for even a moment, he would be killed by the Rothstein wannabes jostling in the alleys of Broadway. Any sign of weakness would mean a bullet in an alleyway. "It's too late. I can't do it," he told her. "I've gotten into it, and I can't get out of it."

He had always been freakishly fearless. One day, a gunman shoved a revolver into his stomach and demanded he hand over five hundred dollars. "When you get five hundred dollars out of me you'll need it to pay your funeral expenses with," he said. "Now think that over." Yet beginning around 1926, something happened to Rothstein, and for the first time in his life, he seemed afraid. He was told that there was a serious threat to his life, and not long after, a man roughly the same height and appearance as Rothstein left his building. He was met by two gun-toting men who told him to get into their car. It was only after they had taken the man several blocks that they cursed: "We got the wrong man."

One night not long after that, Arnold woke Carolyn up, ashen-faced.

"I've just had a terrible experience," he said. He had arrived at their apartment building and tried the door, but it was locked. "I rang the bell and knew it was sounding because I could hear it. Then I saw the elevator man lying on the couch. I thought he was bound and gagged." Arnold ran several blocks to find a policeman—but when they returned, the door opened easily. Nothing was wrong.

Everything was in its place, except Arnold's nerve. He was losing it.

In 1927, a car he used was found riddled with machine gun bullets as it waited for him outside the Hotel Fairfield on West Seventy-Second Street. Not long after that, Carolyn asked for a divorce. He knew what was coming—and so, in the end, it did. Arnold Rothstein was forty-seven years old when he staggered into the service entrance of the Park Central Hotel on Fifty-Sixth Street at 10:50 P.M. on November 5, 1928. The Brain had taken a bullet to the gut.

"Get me a taxi," he said. When the cops came instead and asked who did it, he mumbled: "If I live, I'll tend to it; if I die, the gang will."

It took him more than a day to die, in a hospital in Bedford-Stuyvesant in Brooklyn. As he lay there semicomatose, his lawyer and his mistress, a twenty-seven-year-old chorus girl (another one) named Inez Norton, "guided" his hand to write a new will. They thought they would inherit a fortune, but in fact, once his endless shuffling of money was picked apart, it turned out Arnold's massive running debts exceeded his assets, and his lawyer and mistress got nothing. As it happened, Rothstein had taken out a fresh life $50,000 insurance policy the Saturday before. The check hadn't reached the company: the payment was never made.

The police didn't want to investigate the murder—they didn't want to lift the lid and unleash on themselves all the criminal and official forces swirling around Rothstein's corpse. "It was as if no one, lawman or criminal wanted to be close to this murder in any way," Rothstein's biographer, Nick Tosches, wrote. Eventually, a rival gambler named George McManus was charged with the murder, but he was acquitted by the jury. From then, Tosches says, "until today, the mystery has grown. Speculation has run and roamed wildly in a desire to identify not only the hand that pulled the trigger, but also the interplay of hidden forces that controlled the hand."

It was only a year after I first learned about this, on the streets of the deadliest city in the world, Ciudad Juárez, that I realized the significance of that moment.

This was the bullet at the birth of drug prohibition, and nobody knows where it came from, even now. It is like the bullet that claimed the Archduke Ferdinand at the start of the First World War: the first shot in a global massacre.

Rothstein's domination of the East Coast drug trade shattered as that trigger was pulled—from that moment on, drug dealers would be engaged in a constant conflict to control the distribution of drugs.

The drug war analyst Charles Bowden says there are in reality two drug wars going on: there is the war on drugs, where the state wages war on the users and addicts, and then there is the war for drugs, where the criminals fight each other to control the trade.

The war for drugs was launched in earnest in the Park Central Hotel in Manhattan as Arnold Rothstein lay bleeding.

There would be many more bullets, but I was going to learn on my journey that Arnold Rothstein has not yet died. Every time he is killed, a harder and more vicious version of him emerges to fill the space provided by prohibition for a global criminal industry. Arnold Rothstein is the start of a lineup of criminals that runs through the Crips and the Bloods and Pablo Escobar to Chapo Guzman—each more vicious because he was strong enough to kill the last. As Harry Anslinger wrote in 1961: "One group rose to power over the corpses of another." It is Darwinian evolution armed with a machine gun and a baggie of crack.

And I was going to see that, like Rothstein, Harry Anslinger is reincarnated in ever-tougher forms, too. Before this war is over, his successors were going to be deploying gunships along the coasts of America, imprisoning more people than any other society in human history, and spraying poisons from the air across foreign countries thousands of miles away from home to kill their drug crops. The key players in the war continue to be either Anslingers or Rothsteins—the prohibitionist and the gangster, locked together in a tango unto the far horizon. The policy of prohibition summoned these characters into existence, because it needs them. So long as it lives, they live.

The scream that tore through Harry Anslinger, the bullet that tore through Arnold Rothstein, and the laws that tore through Edward Williams's medical practice—they are part of all our lives, whether we have a direct relationship to illegal drugs or not.

To see how that came to be, seventy years later I traveled from city to city and realized I had come to understand these dynamics best through the stories of three people.

One was trying to be Arnold Rothstein.

One was trying to be Harry Anslinger.

And one was sitting outside on her porch, playing with a doll.

PART II

Ghosts

CHAPTER 5

Souls of Mischief

I closed the files on Harry and Arnold and Billie and resolved to find myself a drug dealer. I wanted to see how the dynamics set in train by these men so long ago were playing out today, not only in academic papers or in polemics about the drug war but on the actual street corners of New York City, where Arnold fought and Billie died. The scraps left to history can only get you so far. It was time for me to watch the drug war's history unfold in real time.

A friend of mine who works in drug policy reform in New York gave me the number of a person called Chino Hardin. Go meet him, he said. Nobody can explain it better.

I first met Chino outside a diner in Greenwich Village. He walked into my life smoking, and he has been smoking almost continuously ever since. His hair was tied back tightly, and a bright bandana covered his head. He was wearing a big baggy sweater with the Incredible Hulk on it: he was waving his big green fist at the world. His voice, I noticed, was deep and husky.

We took our seats in the diner and Chino watched me carefully as I told him what I wanted to know—how drug dealing works from the inside. I couldn't tell if he was suspicious or anxious, but I was aware he was sizing me up. And then he said to me, quite abruptly, as if he had made a decision: "I grew up in East Flatbush, Brooklyn . . . I was born in Kings County Hospital, down the road from my house." And from that starting point, in interview after interview, we talked through the story of his life. We would continue talking about it for three years and counting.

I found out later that Chino was transitioning to living as a man, and considering gender reassignment surgery. At his request, I refer to him throughout this book with masculine pronouns—even though he was regarded as a woman by the people around him and by the legal system for most of this time period—because he always felt, inside, that he was male.

On that first afternoon, I noted that Chino spoke very fast and in a rhythm, as though there was always a beat behind him that I couldn't quite hear. But after a while, I felt I began to hear the beat. It was one of many things Chino has taught me.

~

Almost seventy years after Arnold Rothstein stood on his street corner in New York City waiting for a pile of cash to walk on by, Chino had, he explained, been doing just the same. Like him, he scared people just by being there. He had a pit bull by his side, and gold fangs attached to his teeth. His hair was pulled back into a baseball cap, and in the brim he had stashed little baggies of crack. Hidden nearby, in a trashcan, he kept his gun, a 9 mm Smith and Wesson. He had a crew called the Souls of Mischief, and they did what he said, when he said. He was fourteen years old.

"Are you holding?" his customers would ask as they drove up.

"Yeah, I'm holding," he would reply.

He stood at the junction of East Thirty-Eighth Street and Church Avenue in East Flatbush, a slum stretch of Brooklyn. The brand names of Manhattan vanish this far out, leaving only small businesses with names like Michael's Prime Meats, White Sheep Laundry, and endless 99-cent stores, broken only by evangelical churches promising the path to salvation. The houses must have looked new and glossy when they first rose in the 1950s, but they seemed to have been slowly sighing back into the earth ever since.

Chino's crack came in white slivers that looked like chips of soap. At first, he stashed them in his mouth, but they made his cheeks and tongue go numb. Then he held them in his hand, but they started to dissolve, and nobody wanted to buy that. So he learned you had to get creative. He sometimes stuck them under a nearby parked car, attached to a magnet.

Later, he got a collar for his pit bull, Rocky, and kept the crack in his collar—"so Rocky sold crack, too," he laughed. But on that day—and the endless days like it—they were in his cap and up for sale.

There was once only one Arnold Rothstein in New York City. In the seven decades of escalating warfare ever since, there has come to be an Arnold Rothstein on every block in every poor neighborhood in America. The fragmentation that began with the bullet to Rothstein's gut had continued to this block in Brooklyn on this day.

Chino went out onto his corner selling whether it snowed or rained or the sun shone down. It was the only route to riches he could see in this neighborhood—and the only way to be safe. He knew that would seem strange to outsiders; how does becoming a gangster make you safe? But looking out over his block as a kid, he concluded that in East Flatbush, in the crosshairs of both the war on drugs and the war for drugs, you have to feed, or you will be food.

You could see the Souls of Mischief on the corner—Chino and four of his homies, all boys. Chino was the unquestioned top dog. When Chino said move, they moved. When Chino said go, they'd go. They were entirely obedient. They watched his anger and aggression with awe, as if he was not a person but an electrical storm with skin.

Even then, he dressed as a boy and acted like a boy. They called him Jason. They knew he was "biologically" a woman at that point but they treated him as a man, and he was careful to be twice as brave just to underline it. He never told his crew to do anything he wouldn't do himself: he would always get his hands dirty with you. If the crew had to attack, he would be at the front. And sometimes it was necessary to attack.

Their crew was part of a wider network called Brooklyn's Most Wanted, who controlled the Thirties in Flatbush. He got his drugs from Peter, a guy in his twenties from Chino's block, and he answered to him. Peter first approached him when Chino was thirteen, asking if he wanted to make a lot of cash. He explained: you take the bags, you work the corner, you keep up to $500 a week. After that, everybody knew he was under Peter's protection. You couldn't touch him without retaliation from Peter, and he was one of the three or four biggest dealers between Utica and Flatbush. It meant Chino had power, and respect, and a name, and as much freedom from fear as he would ever get.

And money. He would spend the money on going to the movies, treating his friends, buying clothes he would wear only once. And he spent a lot of time at Coney Island, riding the Cyclone, or playing Mortal Kombat.

To protect this way of life, you have to be terrifying. As we learned under Rothstein, you can't go to the police to protect your property or your trade. You have to defend it yourself, with guns and testosterone. If you ever crack and show some flicker of compassion, he tells me years later, *everybody's going to fucking rob you . . . They'll just move in on your turf, take over your block, do whatever they want to you. You have to be fucked up to survive in this fucked-up paradigm . . . You got to be violent to not have violence done to you . . . You set examples. You make examples out of people. Some of them are completely justified and called for. A lot of them are not."*

So the crew shot at trees, shot in the air, killed animals. Sometimes Chino would shoot in the direction of people—rival crews he needed to scare shitless. He will tell me that his bullets never hit them. He will also tell me there are things he can never tell anyone.

Sometimes the gun jammed and everyone else was too frightened to unjam it. Not Chino. "I would cock that bitch back," he says, "let that bullet come out, put it back in the clip and put the clip back in." Two of their rival gangs were called the Autobots and the Decepticons, after the Transformer toys that were popular at the time, and that they still played with. These child soldiers lived in a mental landscape they constructed from scraps of TV cartoons, hip-hop, and a policy decision that handed them a crucial place on the delivery line for one of the biggest industries in the world.

One time, some older men arrived on the block to try to claim it as theirs. Chino remembers it this way: "We had some cats come through . . . some older cats . . . we welcomed them, smoked with them, laughed with them. Basically, they were trying to son us [that is, treat them like kids— like their sons]—tell us what to do as if we didn't have our own set. Some altercation happened between them and one of my soldiers, and before you know it, we was beating their ass . . . We jumped them . . . and beat the shit out of them. We hit them with bottles, garbage cans, and we let them run out of the neighborhood and told them to never come back." About this need to defend his teenage crew against older aggressors, he says: "It's almost like in the animal kingdom—it's no different in terms of how our minds are . . . They thought they were the bigger, older lions . . . but we're not necessarily lions, we're like packs of hyenas. If you're going to play by animal kingdom rules, you got to know the right animal."

This violence was taken for granted in the neighborhood. "If you don't hear a gunshot," one resident told a reporter in 1993, "you're amazed at the quiet."

It wasn't only rival gangs that Chino had to discipline with violence—it was his own soldiers. His number two, his right hand, was named Smokie, a Jamaican boy from his block. One day Smokie started a fight with some Crips—one of the main gangs in the United States—outside Chino's house because he wanted to establish that this was unequivocally their turf: they owned it, and they commanded respect on it.

"Who the fuck is that talking loud on my block?" he demanded of them.

"Yo . . . you just grew the fuck up," they spat, taunting him.

Suddenly, Chino saw Smokie had picked a fight he couldn't win; they were getting into his face and they outnumbered him, so he had to step in—only to find he had created a situation where "I can't be diplomatic . . . that would be a sign of fucking weakness."

He told Smokie to take his knife and go slash them, to prove nobody could mess with this crew or their trade. But they just laughed at the knife. They snatched the gold chain from his neck, and Smokie lost his nerve, and ran.

Chino knew that this situation was potentially fatal for his crew and its reputation. If they could humiliate his number two, the next step would be to humiliate him and take his patch. He would be left with nothing. Carolyn Rothstein said about Arnold: "He never failed to fashion a punishment for the one who had offended against his omniscience." He must do the same. His pit bull was growling at them, but the dog couldn't do much—Rocky had all the heart, but not a lot of the equipment. They were smelling fear.

Chino pulled a knife. He had to show them—in a slash—that he would use it if he needed to.

Suddenly, he got sucker punched, and everything went woozy.

But he had made his point: His crew wouldn't just run in the face of threats. They would fight, even when it was a girl up against two guys.

But now Chino had to deal with Smokie. He had pulled the crew into danger and then vanished. When he skulked toward Chino after it was all over, he claimed he had run to get a gun to defend them—but Chino couldn't make allowances for cowardice, not here. The crew took him to the 235 Park nearby, a grassy patch, and poured water on his shirt.

Then Chino took off his belt, and he lashed Smokie, thirty-one times.

That was the standard first phase of punishment for cowardice. Then he had to embark on the second phase. He had to go find the opposing set and slash one of them. Smokie staggered off—but something went wrong. He didn't slash a rival. Terrorized and half-crazed and hyped, he looked for anyone he could attack—and he slashed an old man in a store, which isn't what Chino wanted at all. Soon he was back in prison. Chino was furious: the point he needed to be made was that his set was strong and nobody should ever try and fuck with them or take their drugs or mock their status. By attacking an old person, he says, he "actually made us look weaker."

That was the careful balance of terror he had to negotiate every day. For Chino, the war on drugs was not a metaphor. It was a battlefield onto which he woke and on which he slept. He explains: "I can live with you breaking my heart, but I can't live with you making other people think I'm weak. I literally can't live with that . . . [because then] they come for me."

~

I would leave my meetings about Chino and pore over academic studies and explanations of the drug market, trying to see how this fitted into the story he was telling me.

Slowly I began to see the patterns underlying it. When we hear about "drug-related violence," we picture somebody getting high and killing people. We think the violence is the product of the drugs. But in fact, it turns out this is only a tiny sliver of the violence. The vast majority is like Chino's violence—to establish, protect, and defend drug territory in an illegal market, and to build a name for being consistently terrifying so nobody tries to take your property or turf.

Professor Paul Goldstein of the University of Illinois conducted a detailed study in which he and his team looked at every killing identified as "drug-related" in New York City in 1986. It turned out 7.5 percent of the killings took place after a person took drugs and their behavior seemed to change. Some 2 percent were the result of addicts trying to steal to feed their habit and it going wrong. And more than three quar-ters—the vast majority—were like Chino's attacks. They weren't caused by drugs, any more than Al Capone's killings were caused by alcohol. They were, Goldstein showed, caused by prohibition.

Just as the war on alcohol created armed gangs fighting to control the booze trade, the war on drugs has created armed gangs fighting and kill-ing to control the drug trade. The National Youth Gang Center has discovered that youth gangs like the Souls of Mischief are responsible for between 23 and 45 percent of all drugs sales in the United States.

I discussed this one afternoon with Chino, and he nodded. He explained the gang didn't exist only to sell drugs, but "it gives the gang way more power. You have access to money and resources to buy guns, to be extravagant, to actualize the persona of being a big shot. The clothes, the jewelry." The gang—and the violence required to be in it—is made far more attractive by the fact it controls one of the few profitable industries in the neighborhood.

But when he was sixteen, Chino began to break one of the cardinal rules of dealing, one made famous by Biggie Smalls: Don't get high on your own supply. To understand, I had to go back with him, to the start of his story.

~

Chino had always, he told me, been puzzled by one thing about his mother. Since she was openly a lesbian, how did she end up becoming pregnant—and by a cop, the species of man she had good reason to loathe the most?

He found out the answer when he was thirteen. He explained his confusion to his aunt, Rose, who then offered, coldly, a story. In 1980, Chino's mother, Deborah, was raped by his father, Victor. Deborah was a black crack addict. Victor was a white NYPD officer, there to arrest her. So Chino is a child of the drug war in the purest sense. He was conceived on one of its battlefields.

Chino had already known the vague outlines of his mother's life. He constructed a story that strung together his own fragmented memories of her and the hushed conversations he overheard from his relatives. Deborah was abandoned by her biological mother in the hospital as soon as she was born—perhaps because her mother was herself a drug addict, soon to be sent to prison. The baby was adopted by a distant relative, Lucille Hardin, an old and old-school Southern black woman who had come to New York from South Carolina and earned her living making brassieres. Mrs. Hardin didn't talk much about her childhood in the segregated South, except to say proudly that she never said "yes'm" to any white man, and that she worked on the assembly lines in World War Two to save her country.

Lucille Hardin raised Deborah as her own child, adoring her and spoiling her as if she were a little doll. But the word in the family was that at some point in her adolescence, Deborah was kidnapped by a group of men and gang-raped. She was never quite the same again. Nobody seems to know the details of it, or when she started soothing the pain it caused with the jab of a needle and the numbing of heroin. Mrs. Hardin paid for Deborah to go to rehab a few times, but nothing worked for long. She was sunk far enough into addiction to catch the first wave of crack in the early 1980s.

Deborah would break in and take anything she could to get her next fix from the local gangsters. Her adopted mother would frequently have to call the police on her. It was on one occasion, when Deborah was twenty-two and in her mother's house, that Victor showed up.

Long after, Chino will describe this, the night of his conception, with a controlled anger. Cops could rape with impunity "because who's going to believe a drug addict, right? Who's going to believe somebody who's addicted to a substance and will do anything to get that substance, including lie? Who's going to believe somebody who's been in and out of prison the majority of their adult life?"

He came into the room that had been Deborah's all her life and was going to be Chino's for all of his childhood, too. Nobody knows now what took place next. Rose told Chino it was a rape, because that is what Deborah told her. Years later, Chino will wonder: "Maybe—I don't know. I totally think he raped my mother. But I also think that—maybe—some prostitution stuff happened. Or [she] traded freedom for sex." Was that common then? "It's common now," he says in 2012.

Deborah went into labor in a bar. Chino was born with a severe blood disorder, in a hospital a few blocks away from where Arnold Rothstein died. He weighed only a few pounds, and he had a thin layer of skin over his eyes. The doctors said this was the result of his mother's drug use during pregnancy, and they thought he was blind and would be mentally disabled.

Just as her mother had abandoned her, Deborah immediately abandoned Chino—and the same Mrs. Hardin, now in her sixties, took in the baby and raised him, too, as her own. She was a strict grandmother: she had grown up in a place and time when disobedient kids were told to go to the woods to find a branch to be beaten with. It was called "picking your switch." But, at the same time, she was an old woman, and her powers to discipline, or to understand this new little child, were fading.

Chino called Mrs. Hardin "Ma." Every now and then, he was taken to a strange place to see Deborah. He saw only that she was a short, wiry woman who wore men's clothes and had a smile just like Chino's. Deborah, he says later, "was my biological mother [and] only in that sense." Some part of Deborah never forgot her child, and longed for him.

One day, she turned up in Flatbush and took the toddler Chino away by the hand, so he could be hers, for once. They hid out for days, not telling anyone where they were. It was a motel. The police arrived. They said they were looking "for Victor's daughter."

All those years, it turned out, Victor had kept an eye on his child from a distance, and when he heard Chino had been kidnapped, his colleagues rallied to find the kid.

Years later, Deborah snatched him again. When I spoke to him about it, Chino remembered playing in a dollhouse with a little girl and eating chips, when—suddenly—a woman Deborah owed money to took him by the hand to another room. Chino saw a blade with brass knuckles on it. It is only years later that Chino would realize where they were: in a crack house. Out of nowhere the woman was trying to insert this blade into Chino's vagina. Chino managed to hit her with some toys and scream as loud as he could. Deborah appeared and saw what was happening. Deborah and her friend dragged the woman onto the roof of the crack house. They began to beat her as hard as they could. "I don't know if she lived or not," Chino will remember, "but I remember a lot of blood, and the woman not moving anymore."

His little eight-year-old self felt happy. It was a moment when his mother most appeared to love him.

Deborah appeared every now and then in Chino's life after that, but infrequently, in manic jags. Why did she keep circling back? "I think her circumstances didn't allow her love for me to ever fruitfully grow," Chino speculates. "The seedling hatched, it pulled out [of] the ground, but it never bore any fruit."

He always wanted boys' toys, especially GI Joes. He only liked the toy oven he had been given because he could melt the GI Joes' heads in it. "My grandmother had to beat me into a dress," he remembers. From about eight years old, he pushed his hair up, demanded to be called Jason, and put socks down his underwear. His grandmother asked him why, and he said that "being a girl sucks. And in my life, it did suck."

Deborah was the first person ever to punch Chino in the face. When he was twelve, Chino found his mother sleeping in a bush behind the house, and he was embarrassed and angered—anybody could see her, homeless, openly gay, filthy—and so he turned the hose on her. He figured he had enough time between Deborah getting up and him getting back into the house, but he miscalculated—so Deborah "lumps me up like Mike Tyson," as he put it.

Chino learned to lash out first whenever his mother appeared: he threw a pot at her out of a window once and cracked Deborah's head open. He threw scissors out the window and opened up Deborah's finger, so the next day she caught Chino after school, and beat him again. And yet sometimes Chino went looking for Deborah, in the park, on the benches, or on the corner where she would be looking for business, because Chino wanted her. Usually, she was nowhere to be found.

Around this time, across the United States, a new blood-borne disease was being uncovered. People were staggering into hospitals and collapsing. It was causing strange symptoms, as if it was a sudden, rapidly killing cancer.

Scientists quickly realized the people in most danger were gay men and injecting drug users who shared needles. They recommended handing out clean needles as a matter of urgency. The Scottish city of Glasgow—which had a massive drug injection problem—became one of the first in the world to do this. As a result, fewer than 2 percent of their injectors became HIV positive. In New York City, they refused to do it.

So by 1992, 50 percent of the city's injectors were HIV positive—including Deborah. When the authorities finally relented, it brought down new infections by 75 percent. It was too late for this story. Indeed, the people who tried to get Deborah and all the users like her clean needles were threatened with arrest.

As an adult, Chino would have about ten memories of Deborah. Half were violent and despairing, half were good. One time she turned up and stole Chino's back-to-school clothes so she could sell them. They went skating once. They went to Coney Island once and got on the Cyclone and Deborah held his head the whole time. They went to see a movie—the Tina Turner biopic *What's Love Got to Do with It?* Another time she talked Chino through how they were related, and who her own biological mother was. Somewhere along the way, Deborah told him that she was HIV positive, but Chino didn't quite understand what that meant.

One time, when he was twelve, Chino went to see Deborah in a psychiatric unit. He brought her a knish, her favorite food. Deborah obsessively asked Chino who he was having sex with. Chino explained he wasn't having sex with anyone, but Deborah kept asking, insistent. Looking back on this, Chino would realize she was trying to give him all the guidance she could, on the tiny range of subjects on which she felt able to dispense advice, knowing time was short.

The last time Deborah came home from her stints in and out of jail, she announced she had found Jesus, and she was wearing a dress. Chino couldn't remember ever seeing her in a dress before. She had a boyfriend, a real jerk, whom Chino hated—but he was at least reassured to see that his mother was, for the first time in Chino's life, undrugged.

It didn't last long. One day Chino came home and his mother was frantically searching the house, looking in strange places, for something unnamed, unseen. She believed something was hidden inside the radiator. She was due to take Chino to the movies, but she was clearly in a crack frenzy—and soon she ran out of the house screaming, vanishing down the street. Chino started to run after her, but then thought to himself: "I'm not going to fucking run after her. I'm tired of looking for her. If she goes, she goes."

Later that night, there was a call from the hospital. Chino and Mrs. Hardin went to see her. The body in the bed, stuffed with tubes, looked incomprehensible to Chino. Deborah's tiny body had blown up as if she had already been filled with embalming fluid. Her face and hands were distended and misshapen. The nurses said Deborah had been trying to rob a woman on the bus, and when the police arrived to arrest her, they beat her. But her liver was already destroyed and she had water on the brain. Deborah would never wake up again. She was thirty-three years old. At the funeral, Deborah's boyfriend sneered at Chino. "So," he said, "you'll cry for her now?"

Not long after, Chino found his corner, and started selling his crack. And three years after that, when he was sixteen, he would smoke it for the first time. "I wanted to know," he would say to me years later, "what she chose over me."

~

Chino was first put into a jumpsuit and caged when he was thirteen. He was sent to Spofford Juvenile Detention Facility in the Bronx as punishment for his violent "street shit" against other teenagers, which he carried out because "the dealing puts me in positions where my default emotion is anger and my default position is retaliation."

The paint was peeling on the walls. There was a stench of mold in the air. There was no fresh air anywhere—it was almost hard to breathe. Nobody asked if he was okay. Nobody tried to talk to him about why he was there. Their manner wasn't cold or aggressive: it was utterly indifferent. The staff looked at the kids as objects on a loading line that it was their job to briefly inspect. As Chino puts it, instead of bottles or sneakers, this loading line happens to hold humans. Do you have any medical conditions? Are you sexually active? Next.

In this child prison, you could watch TV, watch TV, or watch TV. Oh—or you could play Spades. Chino remembers: "To say I felt alone would be an understatement. I felt like an animal . . . When you go to prison, the one thing you got to check at the door is not your wallet or your jewelry. It's your humanity."

He was being taught, in stages, that life is a series of shakedowns and shoot-outs, punctuated by boredom.

In prison, "being humane can get you fucking hurt . . . Simple shit like, [if] you're home in the world and somebody knocks on your door and says, 'Can I borrow some toothpaste, a cup of sugar?' you're like—why not? It's fucking sugar. Who cares? Take the whole fucking thing . . . You don't do that shit in jail . . . You can't do that shit. That just opens up the door for a lot of bullshit . . . People thinking you're a punk and they can just take from you. It's called friendly extortion. It's like . . . 'I know you want to give me that, right? I know you want to give me a pack of cigarettes.' That's me threatening you without saying—Unless you give me that, I'm going to punch you in the face . . . [But] I was scared . . . as a child, because that's what I was—of the unknown, of what the next day would bring."

In one cell, when he was sixteen, he decided this story had to end. He couldn't take it. He couldn't take the slow process of morphing into his mother, of erasing himself from existence day by day.

Better to do it in one sudden fall.

He made a noose out of his shoelaces. He double-tied them so they would slip down nicely but not slip out.

He tied them to the top of the bar.

He jumped.

And there was all this fucking slack, hanging down, saving him, and he thought—I am such a fuck-up, I can't even get this shit right. He tried again when he was out—he overdosed on sleeping pills, twice—but they pumped his stomach and put him back on the street.

～

Rikers Island is a vast concrete fortress in the East River, suspended in water between Queens and the Bronx. More than fourteen thousand people are warehoused in its stone cells, and it became a second home to Chino and his crew, as it has to generations of teenagers from his neighborhood. But something strange was happening—his drug charges kept disappearing. He was arrested and charged, but the paperwork seemed to vanish. "If you look at my criminal record on its face," Chino says, "I got let out of the back door of the courthouse a lot, without even seeing a judge. I got let go from the precinct. I had charges that you cannot believe they still let me go."

He was certainly beating the odds. If you are a part-time street dealer in the District of Columbia—a place with similar demographics and drug use to East Brooklyn—you have a 22 percent chance of being jailed for each year you work. But Chino had been dealing for nearly a decade without being imprisoned for these offenses: he always got busted for other crimes. Some of his crew began to suspect he was a snitch, but if he had been, sooner or later the evidence would have come out at trial, and it never did. Chino was puzzled—why them and not him?

Gradually, Chino believed he had figured out what was really going on. Victor had come looking for him when he was a child. Victor had sent his colleagues to find him when he was kidnapped by Deborah. And now that he was a teenager, Victor was—Chino became convinced—still watching over him from a distance, getting his colleagues to "lose" his drug charges down the back of their filing cabinets.

Is this evidence of more police corruption—or does Chino want so much to believe that his rapist-father loves him, despite everything, that he is seeing his hand in the random glitches and failings of a bureaucratic criminal justice system?

He only ever met Victor once. When Chino was in his teens, one of his cousins told him Victor wanted to see him, and he named the corner of Nostrand and Church in Brooklyn, and a time. Victor wheeled toward him. He had, Chino discovered, been shot years before, and was now a paraplegic. His first thought was—Wow, he wears his hair just like mine, in a ponytail. Then he noticed his dad was wearing cut-off leather gloves, just like his mother used to. But he didn't want to hear what Victor had to say.

"What do you want?" he asked him.

"I want to get to know you."

"You should have thought about that before you raped my mother and before you walked out of my life," he replied.

His conversation was rambling. Victor said that his mother was very top-heavy, like Chino. He said his two sons had died in a plane crash. He seemed half crazy. Chino explained: "From the way he approached me, it's almost like we had a relationship," like he knew him, like they had been talking all along. Chino didn't want to know. He walked away.

A few years later, somebody told him Victor had died. He didn't go to the funeral.

But for Chino, in East Flatbush at fifteen, he was discovering newer and bolder crimes. Now that he had formed his crew to sell crack, they found they worked well together and could push it further: prohibition functioned for him as a gateway drug to robbery and assault. In prison, they were constantly learning about new crimes and new techniques and graduating from this university back onto the streets. They robbed boats in the harbor, taking flare guns and cool Nautica jackets. They tried to get the boats to start up, and whenever this happened, Chino would laugh and say, "So if we get it started, where the fuck are we going? But okay." They stole cars. They beat people up.

Chino's best friend at this time, Jason Santiago, tells me that being a gangsta was "emotional armor" for Chino. With a gun and Tupac blaring behind you, "you're untouchable, so you can't be hurt." There is, he says, a doubleness to this gangsta front. You need to appear tough so other people don't fuck with you. But you also need to be tough to convince yourself you can walk onto an urban battlefield every day and survive.

Chino did everything the boys did—and that included taking girl-friends. "I had to make sure they saw me at all times as an equal, and as a dude and not a chick. I think I did that for my safety as well," he would recall. "The more they saw me like them, the less likely I was to be abused, or to have to fucking kill somebody." If he didn't establish this reputation, "I would probably have been raped. Killed. Or imprisoned."

He defied anyone to criticize him for being a lesbian—which is how he was seen at the time. Apart from a few stray comments on the street, they were too afraid to do it.

As Chino guided me through his world, I kept thinking about the parts of ghetto culture that seem irrational and bizarre to outsiders—the obsession with territory, the constant demand for "respect." And I began to think maybe they are not so irrational. You have no recourse to the law to protect your most valuable pieces of property—your drug supply—so you have to make damn sure people show you respect and stay out of your territory. The demand for respect, I began to see, is the only way this economy can function. If enough of the local economy is run by these rules, they come to dominate the neighborhood, even the people who manage to stay out of the drug trade.

One of Chino's homies, a guy nicknamed File, had links to a gang in Newport, Virginia, who needed new suppliers. They drove out there to negotiate, and it was there—far from home—that Chino made the decision to try crack.

"It did exactly what I was already doing when I was toting guns and being crazy, which was the heart—it was a pure physical thing," he remembers. "It was like the heart, boom boom boom . . . You're definitely hyped . . . It only lasts for five minutes. Then you need another hit and another hit and before you know it you've been up for four fucking days, and looking horrible, and things that used to be a lot more important in your life—like bathing and brushing your teeth and, oh I don't know, eating become less and less important than chasing it." He says, "That was it—I was on a crack mission."

That first time, he kept going and was high for a week, and he knows he must have nodded off a few times, but there was no bedtime, no REM sleep, no rest—and crack, so much crack, and strippers, and prostitutes, all piling into this hotel room, and now there is a party rolling and ripping through it and Chino does what the men do—he fucks the hoes, he rolls, he smokes.

Arnold Rothstein was a psychopath. He found it easy to play the role prohibition had handed him as the amoral terrorizer. Chino said to me one afternoon: "I'm pretty sure people will read this and think, damn, Chino had borderline sociopathic tendencies." But as he tried to play the role prohibition required of him, Chino found something awkward and unwanted breaking through. It disrupted his ability to carry out his function in the drug delivery chain. It was empathy. One day, the mother of one of his crew approached them and asked to buy crack. Chino recalls: "Seeing the look in my boy's face when his mom came to buy from us . . . It wasn't like a look of embarrassment. It was a look of hurt. Sometimes you can see the hurt on somebody." He said later: "It's hard to not feel compassion for somebody . . . We are born with compassion . . . What breaks loose is my ability to feel not just what's happening to me, but what is happening to someone else."

They sold her the crack. But it's hard to be Arnold Rothstein with a conscience.

The more the pain of what he was doing intruded into his consciousness, the more he jabbed it away with violence, or drugs. Chino wasn't a psychopath, but the prohibition system we have created required him to be one to play his role in it. So he drugged himself into psychosis.

$\sim$

But prison had not been entirely a waste of time for Chino. A fellow prisoner taught him how to steal cars in Spofford, and when he was then caught for that and sent back to prison, he learned how to be a Blood and ascend to a whole new level of gangsterism.

At first, the other inmates assumed Chino was Hispanic. In some lights, he looked black; in some, Native American; but the Latina gangs tried to recruit him because he looked most like them. But he couldn't speak Spanish or relate to their world.

That's when a girl called L.A. approached Chino and told him he could be Blooded in—if he was prepared to work for it. Chino discovered the Bloods were a gang who originated on the West Coast out of the wreckage of the Black Panther Party and its revolutionary goals. The Bloods were "the bastards of the party," a nickname so pervasive there's even a movie with that title. To become a Blood he had to learn this history and all their ethical codes, which are written down like laws. You don't steal from your supplier. You don't drop a dime (that is, talk to the police) if you get caught. You don't do fucked-up shit when you are flagging—that is, when you are wearing your official Blood colors.

If you break these rules, there are very clear punishments, from lashes to death.

Once he learned the codes, nine Bloodettes crowded into a cell to watch Chino take the oath. It began with the words: "Blood is 410 percent gangster." Now he was Blooded, he had an extra layer of protection. From this day on, when he was locked up and severed from his crew, he had all the other crewless Bloods in the prison watching his back.

It was here, in these cells, that Chino first fell in love. When Chino saw a girl named Nicole, he felt a crazy lust but could only express it with aggression and loathing: he had learned from his mother that that's what love is. He went to Nicole's cell and told her the head of her set was a faggot who was being raped in the ass, and that Chino was going to kill her. He made shooting noises. Then, one day, Chino got word that his girlfriend out on the streets, in the free world, had been raped. There was nothing that Chino could do from his cell to protect her, and he was distraught. Nicole came to see him and told him she was sorry to hear about what happened. Chino couldn't believe—after all he had done to her—that she was being so kind. "That literally changed me," Chino recalls. "That one act of human compassion . . . I went into her cell and started talking to her. And all my shit stopped."

Nicole was released and they lost touch, but something about the experience stays with Chino.

But neither the Bloods nor the discovery of love could protect him from the people who seemed, from where he was standing, to be the toughest gang of all—the corrections officers. On the Island, one officer, whenever he saw Chino, started taunting him—you want to be a man, he said, but you'll never be a man. You're just a dyke. Chino cursed back: "Why you so afraid of me, yo? Is it because you're not really a man?"

The officer was especially incensed when Chino started going out with one of the most beautiful women on the island, a stripper who I will call—to protect her identity—Dee. (This is one of only three places where a name has been altered in this book; the other two are indicated in the text later.) He had learned to love with Nicole, and now it seemed to be coming more easily to him. He could do this. He could care. It incensed the officer. So one day he grabbed Dee, pulled her into a facilities cupboard, and fucked her. There was nothing Chino or Dee could do.

I was skeptical about this story when Chino first related it to me, but then I started doing some digging. A few years after the incident Chino was describing, an in-depth investigation by the federal government into the complex where men are held found that there was a "deep-seated culture of violence" towards teenagers, with a "staggering" number of injuries. They didn't look at the part of the prison complex where Chino was held, but said that these problems "may exist in equal measure" there.

One day, Chino couldn't contain his anger any more. He approached the rapist-officer and told him he was a fucking coward who preyed on the weak, and if he'd had the nerve to try to drag him into the broom closet, he'd have been the one getting fucked. Later, in a revenge swipe, he had Chino locked in solitary confinement. "There are many things you can do to a human—you can physically hurt them, you can spiritually pain them, but the most cruel and unusual way is to isolate [them from] all other human contact," he says. "It's just too much—especially when you have so many demons . . . That lasted forever." He found himself slipping into a fantasy world where he imagined he was rich, and free.

Dumped back outside onto the streets, angrier than ever, Chino started leaning on crack more and more. His friend Jason said when he was using it, Chino was "just not there. Like the lights are on, somebody put the radio on, but there's nobody at home . . . It wasn't like crazy, running around the street, stripping naked . . . [He was] subdued, maybe just a little off. It just seemed robotic. Almost like the soul was turned off. The emotion wasn't within reach." What Chino got out of it, Jason says, was "emotional numbness," a state where he "did not seem to be able to access emotion . . . During that time, Chino was almost always in a lot of emotional pain . . . [He was] being kicked in and out of [his] house [by his grandmother], dealing day to day with not being wanted by your family."

The next few years passed in a crack blur. He knew there was more violence with his crew, more dealing, more prison, and a lot of watching TV. He started using heroin. It made things slow down when he needed them to. One of the few things that gave him hope was watching the Oliver Stone movie *Natural Born Killers*. "I feel like it's the first movie I've ever seen where the bad guys get away," he said. "The bad guys always die at the end of the movie, unless you're a Freddy or Jason type. Whereas if you're just regular people murdering motherfuckers you always get yours in the end." But here, for once, "the bad guys had some kids and did their happily ever after."

One day, he woke up and realized he was so thin "I looked like a fucking Calvin Klein commercial. I couldn't take it anymore." He could feel Deborah's fate waiting for him. He began to see "it's like my mother was in a constant battle [with] her trauma, who she is, who she wants to be. All the time. Her demons were way deeper than drugs. Way deeper than prison. I don't know what they were. They were her demons. I'm pretty sure I carry some from her, and now they're mine."

He decided to quit all drugs except weed in one single swoop. He went to stay with a friend who nursed him through the shakes, wiped up his vomit, and brought him glasses of water. Now "there is no more numbness to be had," he said.

And so—flooded with feeling, violent torrents of feeling—he started to learn and read and think. He began to ask: Had his life been shaped by a policy decision that didn't have to be made, and didn't have to continue?

∼

Chino was standing on a New York street corner once again, pacing nervously, and sweating a little. In front of him, there was a crowd of over a thousand people, and standing next to him was a member of the House of Representatives. We were in Foley Square, in lower Manhattan, on a spring day in 2012. Chino gave the word and everybody, including me, marched behind him to One Police Plaza, the headquarters for the New York Police Department. He walked determinedly, alone, his eyes focused on the middle distance. When we arrived, words erupted from him, through a throat covered with a tattoo of the Egyptian wind-sun god rising.

"We're not demanding anything that's alien," he said. "We want justice . . . Not just on the Upper West Side, but in Brownsville, Brooklyn, too! Not just in City Hall, but in Jamaica, Queens! . . . Now statistically we know who smokes marijuana at higher rates. They don't look like me. They don't look like you. They look like [Michael] Bloomberg [then the mayor of New York]. But they don't face the collateral consequences of being deported, of having your housing taken, your financial aid stripped."

The crowd started to chant with him.

"No justice!" said Chino.

"No peace!" they replied. And it echoed out across the police plaza, across to the Department of Justice: "No justice!" "No peace!"

He called this protest "a Tale of Two Cities." Everybody gathered here knew the raw fact that drug use is evenly distributed throughout New York City—in fact, the evidence suggests white people are slightly more likely to use and sell drugs—but in his neighborhood there is crackdown, violence, and warfare, while in the richer, paler neighborhoods there is freedom and rehab for the few who fall through the cracks. Harry Anslinger's priorities and prejudices are still in place.

"Our communities are the one that are targeted," he said to the crowd. "Our communities are the ones that are locked up and sent to bookings so that they"—he gestured toward police HQ—"can get overtime, because we know that it's about money, because apparently if it don't make dollars in New York City, it don't make sense." The demonstration ended with the protesters—white, black, and brown in equal measure—sitting down and peacefully blockading the police building.

Chino left to lead a class he took every week for young teenagers who were trying to stay out of gang life in the South Bronx. We jumped into a yellow cab and sped through Manhattan, pulling up outside a sign that said "No Exit." Behind it, in a library, there were teenagers waiting for him. They had been growing up on the same drug war battlefields as Chino.

"I don't like people," a fifteen-year-old girl said. "I barely leave my house . . . I just stick to myself." She saw a boy get shot in the chin a few years back, she mentioned, almost casually. Her body language was turned inward, as if she were trying to shut herself down. Chino sat with her, listening intently. Next to her, a teenage boy reacted differently: "I feel I could kill somebody if I had to," he said, with a smile full of swagger, and sadness.

~

Until he was twenty-one, Chino regarded the drug laws as a force of nature, as uncontrollable and irrevocable as the weather. But then gradually, in stages, over time, he uncovered something that was buried with Henry Smith Williams but keeps stubbornly rising in the minds of people—that, as he puts it, "there's nothing natural about this."

The last time Chino got out of Rikers, he was surprised he had lived to be twenty-one. He didn't expect it, nor did many of the people in his life. He was looking for a job that didn't involve breaking rocks or flipping burgers when he heard about a summer internship at a local community group that was calling for an end to the seemingly inexorable building of prisons across New York State. He thought it was perfect for his girlfriend at the time, so he called up to get the details for her and started chatting to the staff on the phone—and they offered the internship to Chino on the spot.

There, and in the years that followed, he began to read about the origins of the drug laws and punishments in America—and discovered something that surprised him. It began to occur to him over time that his story, Deborah's story, Victor's story—it didn't have to happen this way. It wasn't inevitable. What if it doesn't have to keep playing out, generation after generation? What if there is another way?

On Chino's block back in East Flatbush when he was a kid, there were no alcohol dealers selling Jack Daniel's or Budweiser with a 9 mm Smith and Wesson at their side. Yet this happened—this exact process—when alcohol was prohibited in the 1920s. The government fought a war on alcohol, and this led inexorably to gangs tooling up, creating a culture of terror, and slaughtering as they went. I spent weeks reading over the histories of alcohol prohibition, and there it was—this story, repeating right through history. When the government war on alcohol stopped, the gangster war for alcohol stopped. All that violence—the violence produced by prohibition—ended. That's why today, it is impossible to imagine gun-toting kids selling Heineken shooting kids on the next block for selling Corona Extra. The head of Budweiser does not send hit men to kill the head of Coors.

Chino begins to conclude there wouldn't have been "the same culture of violence—absolutely not" if other drugs were brought back into the legal economy. "It wouldn't be such an extreme culture of violence—a continuous culture of violence."

There will always be some people who are violent and disturbed and sadistic—but human beings respond to incentives. In Chino's neighborhood, the financial incentives for a kid like him were to step up the violence and the sadism—because if he did, he would have a piece of one of the biggest and most profitable industries in America, and if he didn't, he would be shut out and left in poverty. He says: "A human is capable of anything if you're in fucked up situations. You'd never drink your piss, but try not drinking anything for twenty days."

As he explained this, I started to think of so much of the academic research I had been poring through. Professor Jeffrey Miron of Harvard University has shown that the murder rate has dramatically increased twice in U.S. history—and both times were during periods when prohibition was dramatically stepped up. The first is from 1920 to 1933, when alcohol was criminalized. The second is from 1970 to 1990, when the prohibition of drugs was dramatically escalated. In both periods, people like Chino responded to the incentives to be terrifying and to kill, in order to control an illegal trade. By the mid-1980s, the Nobel Prize–winning economist and right-wing icon Milton Friedman calculated that it caused an additional ten thousand murders a year in the United States. That's the equivalent of more than three 9/11s every single year. Professor Miron argues this is an underestimate. Take the drug trade away from criminals, he calculates, and it would reduce the homicide rate in the United States by between 25 and 75 percent.

Chino saw what the effects of taking drugs away from gangsters could be in his own life. In his early twenties, as he began to walk away from being a gangster, he decreed that his crew wasn't going to sell cocaine or crack or heroin anymore. That decision had a pretty rapid effect. "Our members dwindled . . . because we didn't have" resources, he explained. His crew couldn't buy fancy consumer goods or weapons anymore, because they didn't have the cash. Several of them started to get legit jobs. Take away the drugs—transfer them somewhere else—and the gang and the terror it perpetrates largely fizzle out.

But the role of the drug war went deeper into Chino's story than that—to its very start. In the midst of all this violence—gang-on-gang, gang-on-police, police-on-gang, police-on-anyone-in-gang-areas—the rape of an addict like Deborah became something that passed unpunished. It was "not only normalized," Chino said, "but accepted. And accepted in such an insidious way that it's almost overlooked . . . There's no level of humanity that it's acceptable for these people to be treated" with. Instead, they are viewed "in this very degrading, almost animalistic way . . . It's not just there's no sense of justice—[there's] no sense they need justice. They're so far down on the human level that justice doesn't even apply to them. That's one of the most tremendous impacts in the drug war."

That is the question Chino found hardest as he rethought the drug war, the one that ate away at him. If a different drug policy had been in place, would his mother be alive today?

"I firmly believe," Chino says, "that, while I don't know intricate details of how it would be different, she would probably be alive . . . Maybe she would have dealt with her trauma as a patient, like she should've. Maybe I wouldn't have been a product of rape." This is one reason why he now believes "we need to approach drug addiction not as a criminal justice situation but more as a public health situation." Yet he found it hard to sit with this thought. I asked him in 2012—when Chino was about to turn the age Deborah was when she died—if he was angry with his mother.

"I think so," he said, "even though I constantly try to make peace with it. I do. It's kind of hard to be angry with someone that's dead, right? But it's hard not to be when you only have about ten memories and five of them are fucked up. You know what I'm saying? I don't have much goodness to reflect on. The only thing I can say is that—she could've had an abortion. I was a rape baby . . . She chose to bring me into the world. That speaks to a lot. Everything else was demons and drugs and shit that got in the way."

Chino chain-smoked as we talked about Deborah. "I'm under no illusions that she would've been a great mom even if she wasn't on drugs. I think she would've been a great dad, though," he said between puffs, laughing. "Interestingly enough, I'm not mad that she busted my face open and stuff like that. I'm mad that she didn't stick around. I'm mad that I didn't get to watch her change or help her. At this stage in my life, if she was still alive and she was using drugs, we would find an answer to that problem, one way or another. And I know that's easier to say because that possibility's not here, but I hold on to it. I wrap myself in it like a blanket."

Through his girlfriend, Chino recently met a woman called Miss Cynthia, who is in her late fifties, the age Deborah would be now if she had lived. She, too, has lost decades to heroin and crack and to the scramble to get them from gangsters. She, too, is HIV positive. She has been clean now for eighteen months. Chino went to her Narcotics Anonymous anniversary meeting with her recently, and he said to Miss Cynthia's children: "I know you love the fact that your mother's clean and I know you probably still have horrible memories of things that she's done, or didn't do, while she was addicted. But you're fortunate. Because you've gotten to see something that I will never get to see—and that's your mother get clean. So hold dear to that." When I hear Chino talking on the phone to Miss Cynthia, I notice that he has started calling her "Ma."

Once his war was over, Chino had a name tattooed on his chest. "Deborah," it says, in slanting letters.

And on the opposite side of his body, he had inked another name, one that surprises me: Victor.

"In many ways, he was a victim as well," he says carefully. "It's rape . . . He had to be a victim at some level in [his] life to have the ability to commit such an atrocious act, or the inability to see it's an atrocious act. I feel more sorry for him than angry. Do I think what he did was fucked up? Absolutely. But it's kind of hard to contextualize that because as much as it's fucked up, it produced me . . . Do I not want to be born? I want to be born. But not in such a horrible way."

Armed with this new insight into the drug war, Chino became one of the leaders of the No More Youth Jails Coalition. When he started to talk about this to me, his voice changed, and suddenly he sounded like he had skipped from a Spike Lee movie to a policy wonkathon scripted by Aaron Sorkin. New York City, he explained, had committed to shut down Spofford—where he was imprisoned as a thirteen-year-old—and build two new state-of-the-art facilities. Instead, they built the new facilities and reopened Spofford and announced plans for even more youth jails—"even though they were operating between 79 and 81 percent under capacity . . . and at a cost of $64.6 million that was in the capital budget . . . and that didn't entail what it would cost to operate. It was just the extra hundred jail cells." Despite all that money, "the recidivism rate was over 80 percent . . . as opposed to an alternative to incarceration program, the chances are they might not come back, and it's cheaper."

For two and a half years, he organized marches and lobbying and ceaseless public pressure. He built a coalition of all the groups working in this field, using the management skills he had learned out on the street. He stood up and told legislators and journalists what it is really like in there, to be thirteen and caged. And at the end of it, there was an announcement. The expansion of youth jails was halted in New York State. "Spofford," Chino explains, "is closed."

"It feels good. It feels really good," he said. "But now . . ." He shook his head. "It still feels good to have a successful campaign," but "it makes me realize how much more work there is to be done. For every little win that we get on the social justice side . . . it's a drop in the fucking ocean . . . So while it feels good, it's also daunting." He looked at me, and then looked away.

～

Now Chino loves to go camping, way out, in the middle of nowhere.

He has a recurring daydream about being dropped in the wilderness, alone, and finding out if he could survive.

～

"You've got to understand—this happens all the time," says Kyung Ji "Kate" Rhee, who has worked with Chino for ten years and with kids in this area for even longer. "I honestly don't think it's that exceptional," she says about Chino's experiences. "I'm not mitigating the pain that she went through. It's just that this is happening on a scope and scale that the general public has no idea about . . . The disconnect is immense . . . We are ten minutes away from Brooklyn Heights," she says, and shakes her head. "It's a different world."

As I traveled from country to country, I started to realize that this story—of a street dealer—is only the story of the first layer of violence and criminality caused by transferring the drug trade into the illegal economy.

Beyond Chino Hardin, there is another layer of gangsters controlling the neighborhood.

Beyond them is a network of smugglers who transported the drugs from the U.S. border to New York.

Beyond them is a mule who carried them across the border.

Beyond them is a gang controlling the transit through Mexico, or Thailand, or Equatorial Guinea.

Beyond them is a gang controlling the production in Colombia, or Afghanistan.

Beyond them is a farmer growing the opium or coca.

And at every level, there is a war on drugs, a war for drugs, and a culture of terror, all created by prohibition. I started to think of Chino, and all he has been through, as only one exploded and discarded shell, left behind on a global battlefield.

CHAPTER 6

Hard to Be Harry

Two groups fight this war out with sweat and guns every night. One is Chino's side. The other is the police. As I spent time with Chino, I found myself wondering—How does all this look to the other army in this war? To find out, I interviewed sixteen current or former law enforcement officials, from the Swiss mountains to the U.S.-Mexico border—but there was one I kept coming back to, again and again, over three years, because I could never quite understand her.

I first met Leigh Maddox around the same time I met Chino, in a restaurant in Manhattan, not far from where Occupy Wall Street had just erupted. Our meeting was arranged by an organization called Law Enforcement Against Prohibition (LEAP). As she came into the restaurant, I saw she was a slender woman in her fifties with brown hair, but she walked with the confidence of a person who is used to flashing a badge and making arrests.

No matter how well I got to know her later, Leigh always made me picture the Heather Locklear character in the 1980s TV series *T. J. Hooker*: I always half expected her to suddenly tell me to duck so she could take a shot at some villain she had spotted at the other end of the room. She ordered a glass of wine, and started to tell me her memories of life on the front line of the drug war.

∼

At the beginning of the twenty-first century, Leigh Maddox was standing on the I-95, the long stretch of highway that leads into Baltimore. She was a police captain with long hair and a short temper. Her men were waging the war on drugs by pulling over cars and hunting through them for contraband. Leigh had been busting people for drug possession like this for years. Her cops had clear orders: Go for numbers. Get the maximum possible arrests. Don't worry about how severe the offense is. If a person is found with any drugs at all, even the tiniest roach, bust them. She was Anslinger's dream girl made flesh.

Her officers all knew they could seize the property of anyone they arrested for drug offenses to be auctioned off, with much of the proceeds—usually 80 percent—going straight back into the local police budget. "So if you stop a car [and search it and find], say, four million [dollars in cash]—not unusual—shit, that's good," Leigh said.

Drugs were flowing so fast into Baltimore that hauling out users was like throwing your rod into a crammed commercial fishery. Her police force had taken all the measures Anslinger could never push through in his lifetime and put them into practice. Every night, army-style SWAT teams using the latest military equipment were smashing their way across the state. The prisons were crammed with people serving the harshest possible sentences. The streets were militarized. Harry's old instruction—"Shoot first!"—was believed to be the unofficial motto of the state's cops by many of the people who lived here.

But for Leigh, the fight was, by this point, about much more than that. She ended up here for a very personal reason.

Leigh first met Lisa Renee Taylor in gym class when they were thirteen years old, and they almost immediately became best friends. They looked so alike—both brunettes and slim—that a few years later they were able to share a fake ID to buy booze because nobody could tell them apart. They smoked weed and partied together and shared everything. Even their names sounded similar. Leigh comes from a strict military family—her dad was a lieutenant colonel in the U.S. Navy. She left home when she was eighteen to marry a jerk, mainly to anger her parents—but when she did it, Lisa was there as her maid of honor, just as she was always there for her.

While Lisa studied chemistry at Salisbury State University, Leigh was working as a cocktail waitress and a pizza delivery girl, but they stayed in constant contact. In June, during Lisa's first year at college, the girls met up in Ocean City, and they spent the day on the beach, talking and tanning. Lisa wore a white one-piece swimsuit with the stomach cut out; Leigh wore a similar black-and-gold number. A couple of photographers came up to them on the sand and told them they could be models—a cheesy pickup line but one that made them laugh. But Lisa, lovesick for her new boyfriend John, decided she just had to see him and couldn't wait. She didn't have a car and she didn't have the money for a bus, so she decided to hitchhike to his place in New Jersey.

Late the next day, Leigh got a call from Lisa's sister. She hadn't heard from her. Oh, there's nothing to worry about, Leigh said—she's only gone to see John.

The next day, Leigh received a knock at her back door. It was hot and she had no air-conditioning. Through the door she could see the silhouette of John standing there. "Leigh, she never made it to New Jersey," he said.

The police came and asked some questions and concluded that Lisa had run away. Leigh told them it was impossible—she had left her makeup bag behind, and "girls don't run away without their makeup bag." But they refused to investigate. The murder investigator assured Leigh "she'll pop up sooner or later."

She didn't. The summer passed, and nobody heard from Lisa. Leigh prayed a lot, and told God if He got Lisa out of this, she would dedicate her life to doing good. She marched up the steps of the state police barracks and demanded an application to join. One evening, she was working as a cocktail waitress at the Sheraton Hotel in Bloomsbury while her application was being processed when she saw a headline on the TV news. "Body of missing woman found," it said. "My whole life stopped," Leigh would say, years later, "and all these people were still partying and having a good old time, and I was just standing there."

Once she graduated from the police academy, she climbed to the third floor of the Salisbury state police barracks where the files were kept and forced herself to read every document on Lisa and look at every photograph of her, to try to find out what really happened.

Lisa had stopped by her mom's house and asked for some money, and they'd had some kind of argument, so she started to walk back to her dorm room a mile away. She never made it. She ran into a drug gang—a group of at least ten young men. Lisa was sexually assaulted by all of them, and at the end of it, she was stabbed thirteen times and left for dead in a wooded area directly across the street from the university. Years later, after Leigh had worked in policing for a long time, she would come to believe this gang was bonding itself together—establishing its reputation for terror—with a gang rape, as part of its initiation rites.

The woman living in the house across the street from the university couldn't understand why her dog had been barking incessantly all summer. Lisa had lain there all season rotting, and animals started eating her. When they found her body, her ankle was missing. Only one person was ever arrested and charged.

So Leigh became a state trooper to honor Lisa. Nobody had a better reason to hate the drug gangs than she did. Nobody was more determined to stop them.

~

A few years later, the Ku Klux Klan was marching through Elkton, a town of fifteen thousand people in rural Maryland. The men in white hoods were at the front, with sixty supporters in train, chanting, "Hey hey! Ho ho! Niggers have got to go!" Antiracist campaigners who turned up to counter-demonstrate were jeering and hurling objects like batteries at them and yelling abuse, but the Klan kept on going. And in the middle of the march, there was a proud Klanswoman in her white hood—Leigh Maddox.

She had been helping to plan their marches and their picnics and recruiting people in the street for a year now. Near her, in another neat white hood, was the head of this Klan chapter's chief henchman, a man who had committed murder twenty years before and been let off when he pled insanity. Leigh continued marching, through a hail of batteries.

Her bosses told her that women couldn't infiltrate the Klan because it's too dangerous. But she insisted. She explained that she believed they were burning crosses outside the homes of African Americans in Elkton and threatening violence against them, so the police need somebody in there. Eventually, because she insisted for so long, her bosses gave in. But for Leigh, it was doubly risky, because she was going home from the Klan rallies to her black boyfriend.

Her undercover Klan name was Rosa Leigh. Women rarely turned up at Klan rallies alone, so she had to invent a boyfriend who was living far away and couldn't be with her. She was forced to find something to talk to these people about, so she burrowed hard to find something good about them, or at least something she shared. One of the Klansmen knew a lot about plants, and she liked nature, so they discussed that. Another liked Coors Light—she isn't much of a beer person, but she imagined that if she were . . . Yes, this was hard going.

But she was gathering intelligence that was vital to the safety of black people in this town. One day, in broad daylight, two of the Klansmen were driving through Elkton when a black guy pulled up next to them at an intersection with a white girl next to him. Her comrades from the Klan grabbed a length of lead pipe, dragged him from the vehicle, and beat him close to death. Leigh was able to identify them from the witness reports, so they were taken off the streets. And this went on. She was able to tell the police which vehicles to stop on their way to the rally that would contain illegal guns, drugs, and who was driving under the influence. She was giving intelligence almost in real time.

The Klan soon began to panic. Is there a snitch? How else could the police know this much? Which one of you motherfuckers is telling the cops everything?

After one Klan meeting, the men asked "Rosa Leigh" to stay behind and accused her. Outright. Of being a cop. Leigh knew these were felons and psychopaths with a history of violence and killing. She felt sick. All she could do to have a chance of surviving was to lash out.

"You are a bunch of goddamn motherfuckers," she yelled. "I can't believe that after all this time and all I've done for this organization you would dare question my loyalty . . . I'm beginning to think you guys are a bunch of losers. I don't even know why I hang out with you." They started to insist. We want to see your house. We need to see your grandparents. Leigh had to think fast. "You guys want to come down see my house? Seriously? You wanna come down see my grandmother on a Sunday without notice? You know how ill my grandmother is, and you guys are not exactly the kinda guys she would want me to bring around!"

But they insisted. She had to agree. There was no choice.

"Fine, fine," she said. She told them to follow her car—and then sped away faster than she had ever driven in her life.

Leigh would always know she made a difference in Elkton, getting violent racists put away. Thanks to her, fewer Americans were terrorized.

It wasn't easy being a female cop in those days, but Leigh was proving she had balls, and she had some crucial allies. She drove the ninety miles to work every morning talking to her colleague Ed Toatley, a goateed African American undercover narcotics agent who had grown up just outside Baltimore. He was head of the union, and he stood up to the encrusted sexism on the force as Leigh rose higher and higher, cracking a series of glass ceilings.

Yet the work Leigh was most driven by was taking on the drug gangs. This was what got her out of bed in the morning. She was sure that her roadside stops and drug busts were disrupting the supply routes through Maryland—and this meant there would be fewer gangsters, fewer addicts, less violence, and less misery in the world.

This is one of the most important facts about Leigh, and one that it would be easy for somebody like me—with the politics that I have—to ignore.

Leigh's support for the drug war was an act of compassion. She genuinely believed that she was making the world a better place by protecting people from drugs and drug gangs. She is a kind and decent person, and that is what drove her to fight the drug war.

She pictured Lisa, and fought for her.

~

Yet all over the United States—all over the world—police officers were noticing something strange. If you arrest a large number of rapists, the amount of rape goes down. If you arrest a large number of violent racists, the number of violent racist attacks goes down. But if you arrest a large number of drug dealers, drug dealing doesn't go down.

Another police officer, Michael Levine, was learning this lesson for himself. As he made clear when I interviewed him in 2011, as with Leigh, the drug war was personal for him. His brother died of a heroin overdose in Harlem in the 1950s. His son was a cop murdered by a drug addict in the 1980s. So when he was told to go to one of the most notorious drug-selling corners in Manhattan—near the top of Ninety-Second Street—and "clean up that damned corner, once and for all," he was delighted. In a long surveillance operation, his team identified a hundred likely street dealers within fifty feet who work from the moment the sun falls to the moment the sun rises. Within two weeks, he had busted around 80 percent of them.

He was satisfied, and for a couple of days, there was less drug activity. But within a week, everything was back to normal, "as if we had never been there," as Levine puts it in his writing. Why? Because "as every dealer knows, if he is arrested, there are hundreds right behind him ready to take his place." He asked himself: "If all those cops and agents couldn't get this one corner clean, what is the purpose of this whole damned drug war?"

~

Back on the roads running into Baltimore, Leigh was discovering something that was going to change her life. It was even worse than Levine suspected. It's not just that arresting dealers doesn't cause any reduction in crime. Whenever her force arrested gang members, it appeared to actually cause an *increase* in violence, especially homicides. At first this puzzled her, but it was a persistent pattern.

Why would arresting drug dealers cause a rise in murders? Gradually, she began to see the answer. "So what happens is we take out the guy at the top," Leigh explains, so "now, nobody's in charge, and [so the gangs] battle it out to see who's going to be in charge."

As I try to understand this, I imagine if Chino had been put away for a really long stretch, or killed. The demand for drugs in Flatbush would not be reduced. There would still, every day, be people turning up on his corner in search of drugs. So there would either have been a war within Souls of Mischief to see who would be the new top dog, or a rival gang— like the older men whom they drove out that day—would have sensed weakness and swept in to fight for control of the patch. In the fighting or the crossfire, it's easy to see how there would be killing.

Is that right? Is this why every crackdown triggers a turf war? I went away and read through the studies, trying to discover if what Leigh witnessed is part of a wider pattern. Professor Jeffrey Miron of Harvard University has studied the murder statistics and found that "statistical analysis shows consistently that higher [police] enforcement [against drug dealers] is associated with higher homicide, even controlling for other factors." This effect is confirmed in many other studies.

So Leigh was beginning to realize that while she went into this job determined to reduce murder, she was in fact increasing it. She wanted to bust the drug gangs, but in fact she was empowering them.

In her heart she suspected this had been the case for years—but she tried to avoid seeing it for as long as she could, until one night she was left with no choice.

~

One job in policing is, everyone told me, pretty consistently the toughest gig. Ed Toatley—the union head who championed Leigh as she rose through the force—had to pretend, every day, to be a drug dealer among drug dealers.

Back in the 1950s, Harry Anslinger had described what it takes to do this job. An undercover agent, he said, "must be a better actor than an

Academy Award winner, quick on his feet, even faster with his hands, and ten times as fast with his mind . . . one slip—one false word—could cost his life."

When they were being honest with themselves, Leigh and Ed admitted they were both adrenaline junkies. "There's nothing like knowing you almost died [and] spending the next half hour saying—'but I didn't!'" Leigh told me, laughing. So she wasn't surprised when, on the morning of October 30, 2000, Ed told Leigh how excited he was—he had finally been given the order to take out a midlevel dealer he'd been tracking for six months. He was given a pile of cash to head to Washington, D.C., buy a kilo of cocaine, and do the bust. "This is like the pinnacle of my career," he said.

That night, Leigh got a call from the duty sergeant. He was brief. As Ed handed over the three thousand dollars, the twenty-four-year-old dealer didn't hand him cocaine. He shot him straight in the head. "I didn't give it a second thought," he said later in court.

A few minutes later, as she was hurrying to the hospital, her major called her. "Leigh, this is Mike," he said, and all she could say was: "Who the fuck is Mike?" She couldn't process anything. When she arrived at the emergency room, more than a hundred police officers were there. Ed was the head of the union and a popular man. As soon as they heard, they all came. One of them put his hand on Leigh's shoulder and said, "Leigh, man—he's gone." Her chief appeared and said: "This is going to be hard, but you got to be strong for the troops—they need your leadership right now."

The cops were waiting in line to see Ed's body, and Leigh joined them. His head was wrapped in an improvised turban to keep his brains from spilling out. His body was still warm and soft when she touched it.

Years from that day, Leigh would explain in a speech: "As I rested my hand on his chest, I said a prayer—for his family, his friends, and for myself. And as I did so, I felt the presence of every police officer who had lost [their] lives to the war on drugs. I felt the presence of my dear friend Lisa and every other victim caught in the crossfire of our failed policies. I felt them in that darkened hospital room with me. Their spirits were careening down from the walls. Their spirits were jeering and mocking me. Justice? Justice? What is this of your justice? It was," she says, "my Damascus moment."

～

Leigh tried to get back to work, but this time she knew too much. It is hard to be Harry Anslinger with your eyes and your mind open.

She had believed that by fighting the drug war, she was crushing the drug gangs that had killed her two closest friends. Now she began to see that her work in fact kept them in business and made them more deadly. The lesson of ending alcohol prohibition, she had come to believe, is that there is a way to actually stop this violence: legalize and regulate the drug trade.

After he was told about the killing, Ed's five-year-old son Daniel insisted on leaving the hallway light on at night, so "Daddy could find his way home."

While Leigh was studying for a law degree at night, another part of the drug war was slowly becoming clear to her. The shaft of light she had allowed in was illuminating more than she expected.

She knew that drug use and drug selling are engaged in by all the racial groups in America—hell, she smoked marijuana herself as a teen. But that's not who she was arresting and imprisoning. The 1993 National Household Survey on Drug Abuse found that 19 percent of drug dealers were African American, but they made up 64 percent of the arrests for it. Largely as a result of this disparity, there was an outcome that was more startling still. In 1993, in the death throes of apartheid, South Africa imprisoned 853 black men per hundred thousand in the population. The United States imprisons 4,919 black men per hundred thousand (versus only 943 white men). So because of the drug war and the way it is enforced, a black man was far more likely to be jailed in the Land of the Free than in the most notorious white supremacist society in the world.

Indeed, at any given time, 40 to 50 percent of black men between the ages of fifteen and thirty-five are in jail, on probation, or have a warrant out for their arrest, overwhelmingly for drug offenses.

It's easy to assume that Harry Anslinger's prejudices at the birth of the drug war were just a product of their time, long since discarded. Leigh was discovering they are not. The race panics that drove the early drug war have not burned out.

But here, again, I was forced by Leigh—and by the facts—to see that this is not a simple story, with straightforward heroes and villains.

I was inclined to assume that this hugely disproportionate rate of arrest of black men is due to naked racism on the part of cops. But Leigh is not a racist. We know this because she risked her life to expose violent racism. And most of her colleagues, she said with confidence, were not racist, and they would have been appalled if any of their colleagues made racist statements. Yet Leigh was—as she would see later—acting as part of a racist machine, against her own intentions.

Around this time, other police officers across the United States were trying to figure out how this works, too. Matthew Fogg is one of the most decorated police officers in the United States, responsible for tracking down more than three hundred of the most-wanted felons in the country—from murderers to rapists to child molesters. But he was bewildered as to why his force only ever goes to black neighborhoods to bust people for drugs. He went to see his boss to suggest they start mounting similar raids in white neighborhoods.

He explained in a speech that his superior officer told him: "Fogg, you know you're right they are using drugs there [but] you know what? If we go out and we start targeting those individuals, they know judges, they know lawyers, they know politicians, they know all of the big folks in government. If we start targeting them, and their children, you know what's going to happen? We're going to get a phone call and they're going to shut us down. You know that, Fogg? You know what's going to happen? There goes your overtime. There's the money that *you're* making. So let's just go after the weakest link. Let's go after those who can't afford the attorneys, those who we can lock up."

I kept trying to understand this dynamic, and the more cops I met—people who were not racist, but had produced a racist outcome—the more it came into focus. More than 50 percent of Americans have breached the drug laws. Where a law is that widely broken, you can't possibly enforce it against every lawbreaker. The legal system would collapse under the weight of it. So you go after the people who are least able to resist, to argue back, to appeal—the poorest and most disliked groups. In the United States, they are black and Hispanic people, with a smattering of poor whites. You have pressure on you from above to get results. There has to be a certain number of busts, day after day, week after week. So you go after the weak. It's not like you are framing them—they are, in fact, breaking the law. You keep targeting the weak. And you try not to see the wider picture.

But then, for some people, it becomes inescapable.

Leigh started to ask herself: How can you continue with this? But she felt an intense loyalty to her fellow officers, whom she knew to be good people. They were being increasingly sued by the American Civil Liberties Union—often personally—and her reflex was to defend them. These were the men she had faced gunfire with for years. How could she walk off the battlefield?

We humans are good at suppressing our epiphanies, especially when our salaries and our friendships depend on it. She knew that a big chunk of her police department's budget ran on the money they got from seizing drug suspects' property. What would happen to all their jobs if that were taken away from the cops? She deliberately kept herself so busy that "I just didn't have any time to think about it."

As she explained this to me, I realized that for Chino and for Leigh, all the incentives laid out by prohibition were to keep on fighting their wars and shooting their guns and ignoring their doubts.

But on I-95, Leigh began to see the act of pulling over a car to search it in a new way. Once, she saw this scene as a soldier in a just war approaching the enemy. Now she sees it as a meeting of people who are surrounded by ghosts. As he approaches the car, the police officer has ranged behind him the ghosts of all the cops he has known, "all the funerals he's been to, all the people who've been killed in traffic stops—because it's a lot," she says. And then "there's also this poor black kid" in the car. Sitting in the passenger seats behind him are his ghosts—all of his relatives and friends who have been killed in police raids or vanished into the American prison system.

Neither can see the other side's ghosts. They can only hate.

~

One day, Leigh discovered she was not alone. A friend told her about a group called Law Enforcement Against Prohibition (LEAP), an organization of cops and judges and prison officers fighting to end the drug war so they can bankrupt the drug gangs. She was intrigued. She needed to find an answer to a question that was plaguing her: What had been the practical effect of all the policing she has done over the years?

She decided to venture out into the drug war zones of Baltimore, not in uniform this time, but as a civilian. She looked at the kids in the city, and talked with them. She discovered "they are growing up in war zones. There's no doubt about it." There were prohibition-related killings almost every night, and "the kids see it. All the kids know this. It traumatizes you to a point you can't begin to imagine."

But perhaps most important, once you have been busted for a drug offense—at   fifteen   or   seventeen   or   twenty—you   are   virtually unemployable for the rest of your life. You will never work again. You will be barred from receiving student loans. You will be evicted from public housing. You will be barred from even *visiting* public housing. "Say your mother lives in public housing, and you get arrested for possession, and you go visit her," Leigh says. "If the housing authority find out you've been there [they will say] you've violated the lease and they'll kick [the whole family] out." I kept meeting people like this across the United States—second-class citizens, stripped even of the vote, because at some point in the past, they possessed drugs.

Leigh was amazed to uncover all this. She explains: "When I was a police officer nobody ever trained me on the collateral consequences of marijuana arrests. I had no idea . . . It's not something they're made aware of. It's—go out and get numbers. Do your job."

Just as Jimmy Fletcher—the agent sent by Harry Anslinger to break Billie Holiday—never forgave himself for what he ended up doing to her, Leigh Maddox never forgave herself for what she had done to all the kids she arrested over the years. It was not enough, Leigh decided, for her to say she's sorry. You have to make amends. So she completed her retraining as a lawyer, quit her job as a cop, and started providing services in Baltimore to help the very people she had been busting and breaking before. She set up a low-cost legal clinic called Just Advice, where she and her students fight to have the arrest records of accused drug offenders expunged any way they can. She writes to universities imploring them to provide access to scholarships to students with drug convictions. She defends drug users in court. This is Leigh's life now.

It sounds like a neat ending to her story, but Leigh is more downbeat and humble than that. She can't say, in all honesty, that she has found any redemption for herself, she tells me. No—because she keeps meeting "the people you can't help [under prohibition]. The guy who comes in and he's forty-five years old . . . and he has his criminal record with him and he wants to get it expunged and [all you can say is] 'Sorry . . . you're out of luck' . . . To see that kind of distress in their eyes." She is up against a legal system in which even a famously liberal judge like Justice Thurgood Marshall would openly brag: "If it's a dope case, I won't even read the petition. I ain't giving no break to no drug dealer."

In 2011, Leigh drove to the city where Harry Anslinger launched this war long before—Washington, D.C. Not far from the old Federal Bureau of Narcotics building, she delivered a speech.

"To those who urge the United States not to wave the white flag of surrender, I say—what white flag?" she asked. "Your white flag is now a red flag . . . A red flag, sullied and stinking from countless deaths of good guys and bad guys and simple people caught up in the crossfire."

CHAPTER 7

Mushrooms

Without really thinking about it, I guess I have always assumed that the people who die in the drug war are those who choose to enter it—dealers and users and cops. But I soon found out there is another category all together. In Baltimore, I learned, they call them "mushrooms."

～

Tiffany Smith was playing on the sidewalk as the light faded on a hot July night in West Baltimore in 1991. She was playing with her doll, Kelly, and her best friend, Quinyetta. They were outside Quinyetta's house, where they were going to have a sleepover. Her parents were watching from the porch.

The *Baltimore Sun* recorded the details in the days that followed. It had been a fun day. They had been singing and clapping at a block party, then they danced along to antidrug songs performed by the group Parents, Students Moving Against Drugs, and now this: sitting up in the heat with her doll and her friend. Tiffany's hair was tied into pigtails. In a few weeks, she was going to be seven years old.

Except she wasn't. We don't know if Tiffany saw the two young men at the corner. We don't know if Tiffany knew what a "drug turf war" is. We don't know if she heard the gunshot.

～

Unlike Chino and Leigh and all the other people in this book, Tiffany didn't get to formulate a position on the drug war. I got a message through to her parents. They didn't want to talk.

～

They call them mushrooms because they can pop up anywhere.

They renamed the block where she died Tiffany Square. Today, it is a place where dealers openly sell drugs.

PART III

Angels

CHAPTER 8

State of Shame

By the summer of 2012, I had been working on this book for a year, and I felt like I was trapped in a strange recurring dream in which I caught a glimpse of Harry Anslinger and Arnold Rothstein fleeing out the door every time I arrived at a drug war battlefield.

I watched as Chino and Leigh tried to be Anslinger and Rothstein, and failed—but I kept hearing about people across the world who had in fact succeeded in becoming these founding fathers, and then went further than they ever dreamed. They had, I realized, taken the darkest impulses I found and feared within myself and our culture—to repress addictive urges with violence; to crush, in the belief you will conquer—and followed them literally. I needed, I knew, to go looking for those men. I wanted to understand them. They might hold the key.

So I booked a ticket to Arizona, and within a few days, I was marching with a chain gang of meth addicts in the desert—all arranged by Harry Anslinger's personal disciple. Then I booked a flight to Texas and found myself in a bare prison cell, talking through reinforced glass to a young man who has sawed off heads for the great-grandchildren of Arnold Rothstein. Then I headed into the deadliest city in the world, to track a dead woman's dream.

~

The female chain gang meets at five o'clock every weekday morning, just as the sun is starting to rise over the Arizona desert. The women emerge unfed from the tents, surrounded by barbed wire, as they are ordered to put on T-shirts that display to the world why they are here. I WAS A DRUG ADDICT, it says in bold black letters you can read from a distance. I watch as they clamber into their striped uniforms, their limbs flailing with hunger and exhaustion. Then they put on leg-irons. Then the guards order them to begin their chant.

> *Everywhere we go*
> *People want to know*
> *Who we are*
> *So we tell them*
> *We are the chain gang*
> *The only female chain gang.*

They have to stamp their boots and jangle their chains in rhythm to the song, as though they are the chorus line in some dystopian Broadway musical. And so their march out into the desert heat begins.

Some days they are made to bury dead bodies. Today, they clamber into a bus. They are being taken, they are told, to a parched, trash-strewn traffic island in the 110-degree heat and ordered to collect trash, in front of signs urging people to vote for the politician who has pioneered this particular form of punishment.

The women try to get out of the bus but keep tumbling into each other as the chains catch their feet. They always apologize, in small voices, as the other women hold them up. When they step out into the sun, the women are shoved a bottle of sunscreen. The expiration date on the bottle, I notice, is 2009—three years earlier. It comes out as a thick paste.

One girl is free of the chains. It is her job to nail into place a sign that says CAUTION! SHERIFF'S CHAIN GANG AT WORK! and to fetch water for women when they are on the brink of collapse. Gabba is a pale, bony nineteen-year-old Italian American. As I follow her around, she tells me that she was thrown out by her parents as a teenager and started using heroin. "It was my escape," she says, looking down.

I can see Candice staggering around, looking fazed. She is a blond woman in her twenties with an inflamed red face that looks as if it is being slowly eaten by something. It is bleeding where she has scratched it too hard. The doctors have told her it is an allergic reaction to the bleach they use in the tents, she says, but there is no alternative for her. Her story comes out, like the other women's, in a matter-of-fact monotone—it's nothing special here. She ran away from her family when she was fourteen and joined the carnival, and she started using meth there. "It was the best thing I ever had in my life—it made the bad feelings go away," she told me, scratching. "I'm afraid to get released because I don't know what I'm going to do. It numbs all the bad feelings. It makes me not feel anything." Like everyone else, Candice is sweating constantly in this heat, and the salt in her sweat is making the rash burn.

The other T-shirts the women are forced to wear say I AM BREAKING THE NEED FOR WEED, CLEAN(ING) AND SOBER, and METH USER. Michelle, an older former meth user, says to me as she collects rubbish awkwardly: "A lot of people didn't have a lot of dignity to begin with, to come here, and what they did have is taken away. Everything ... [is] about humiliating us until there's nothing left." A few hours after she tells me this, when she has been in the desert sun all this time covered only with out-of-date paste, Michelle starts vomiting and shaking, and has to be held up by the rest of the chain.

The day before, when I mentioned Harry Anslinger's name to the man who invented this chain gang—along with a slew of other ways to punish addicts—his face beamed big and wide.

"Oh, wow! You're amazing!" he exclaimed. "It's amazing that you remember that man!" He had Harry's signature on his wall, staring down at him as he worked. To him, Anslinger was a hero, a role model, the man who started it all. He kept repeating Anslinger's name in our conversation as though stroking a purring cat: "When you go back to Anslinger—you got a good guy here!"

Harry Anslinger employed Joe Arpaio in 1957 to be an agent in the Federal Bureau of Narcotics, and he rose through the bureau over decades. Since 1993, he has been the elected sheriff of Maricopa County, Arizona. He was eighty when I met him, and about to be elected to his sixth consecutive term. His Stetson, his shining lawman's badge, and his sneer have become national symbols of a particular kind of funhouse-mirror Americana, and his hefty chunk of Arizona, home to nearly four million people, is now Harry Anslinger's last great laboratory. Sheriff Joe has built a jail that he refers to publicly as his "concentration camp," and presidential candidates flock here during election campaigns, emerging full of praise. Anslinger said addicts were "lepers" who needed to be "quarantined," and so Arpaio has built a leper colony for them in the desert.

I watch Gabba and Candice and Michelle and their fellow addicts march back into it in lockstep. Again, they have to chant:

> *We're in a state of shame*
> *Couldn't get our lives straight*
> *We're headed back to intake*
> *We're here without our kids*
> *We lost our hope*
> *We gave up dope.*

The women look at me while they chant, then look away quickly. They have been ordered to look only at the back of the head of the person in front of them on the chain.

It takes a moment for me to register what they are singing now. The guards have also ordered them to chant warnings that they will be given electric shocks if they dare to talk back:

> *We're in stripes*
> *They're in brown* [meaning the guards]
> *We walk in chains with them close by*
> *We dare not run, we dare not hide*
> *Don't you dare give them no lip*
> *'Cause they got tasers on their hip.*

This isn't an idle chant: in the jails and prisons of Arizona, several inmates have been tasered to death. As we stumble back into the bus and then back into the prison, the women are unshackled and strip-searched to see if they have any drugs in their vaginas or anuses.

They live in tents that Arpaio got the military to donate for nothing. Many of the tents are from the Korean War. At night, you can hear the low scuttle of scorpions and the squeak of mice venturing out from the nearby trash dump. In the winter, it is freezing. In the summer, the heat hits you like an unimaginably vast hairdryer pointed at your face. Inside the tents, the temperature hits 140 degrees. The women go into the shower fully dressed to get soaked and then go lie on their beds. It takes an hour and then you are bone-dry again, but that, at least, is an hour in which you feel some relief.

The first time I enter Tent City, the prisoners crowd around me, trying desperately to explain what is happening.

"This is hell!" one of them shrieks. They are given two meals a day, costing fifteen cents each. It is referred to by guards and inmates as "slop"—a brownish gloop of unspecified meat that Arpaio boasted to a reporter contained "rotten" lumps, and costs at most 40 cents a meal. People from the outside can give you money to buy small items from the commissary, like potato chips, but there are plenty of inmates who have nobody willing or able to give them money, so they live in a state of constant hunger. The prisoners are never allowed to touch their visitors: it all has to be done by video. Your children can be brought into a visiting room, but you will be handcuffed to the table and not allowed to touch them in any way, no matter what age they are. Even when the child cries "Momma, Momma" and asks for a hug, the prisoner cannot reach out, and has to watch her child crying, helpless. The guards, the women say, openly mock and abuse them: "They think it's funny," one woman says, "to see us down. To see us without our children." Another tells me: "It's like they're trained to be brutal."

As I walk through the tents a cacophony hits me from all around—a diabetic twenty-year-old, imprisoned for drinking alcohol, saying he's not being given his insulin; frightened cries from everywhere about being dispatched to some place called the Hole.

The next day, I return to take down more details—but something has changed. The prisoners who hurried to me yesterday, full of pain, face away from me now. When I approach them in the tents, they are mute, and simply shake their heads. I walk from one to another: they all refuse to talk, and when I keep asking, they try to shoo me away. The cacophony has been replaced by a perfect silence. One woman grabs at me as I pass and says that she's sorry she can't talk to me but she'd like to shake my hand. As she does, I realize she is passing me a tiny folded note.

I open it later. "If I speak the truth to you I will go to the Hole and it's awful, you have nothing. Please understand, I'd like to talk to you but I can't. They are watching us," it says. "We all got in trouble yesterday after you left. Please don't let no-one see this note."

I assume I will get no more information from Tent City. But—to my surprise—when I ask to see the Hole, the officers agree to show me. Everybody gives it this name, including the guards, although technically it is called an Isolation Unit. As I walk through the tents into the concrete heart of the prison itself, I see the Hole consists of a series of tiny concrete solitary cells laid out in rows, on two different levels. The cell doors have a tiny slit in them, and as the guards unlock them, eyes peer out. When they see an outsider, they immediately start yelling for help, and their voices have a cracked quality, as though their throats are too narrow to let out their words. They are not allowed to communicate with the guards: they have to put anything they have to say in writing and slide it under the door. They are trying to talk to me.

The first thing that hits me as I approach these eyes is the stink, literally, of shit: it is so overwhelming it makes me retch.

The inmates let me peer past them into the cells. There is a steel bunk bed that would fit a ten-year-old child, and that's it. No radio; no life. The prisoners inside cannot see the sun or the sky or another human face. Some inmates are given a cellmate, and even though they can barely move with another person in there and have to shit in front of each other, they consider themselves lucky.

As an inhabitant of the Hole, you get one hour out of your cell to take a shower and stretch your legs; you can't communicate during that hour, and no phone calls are permitted. This is where you go if you break one of the rules Sheriff Joe has laid down, or if one of the guards takes a dislike to you. For example, he has banned cigarettes, so a woman is here, for a month, for being found with one.

In one of the cells, on the top level in the corner, a woman is screaming—hysterically, poundingly, her voice like a car alarm in the night. I can't make out what she is saying except for scattered words, but then I am told who it is: a young woman from Saudi Arabia. Strangely, she is the one person I spoke to the day I arrived who said something positive about Tent City. "It's making me not want to come back," she said. "Do you know what I mean? That's why they're hard on us. People can bitch all they want but that's why they're hard on us." She is trying to tell me something now. The guards surround her cell. They tell me I can't speak to her and that they have phoned a doctor.

The other women shout to me that somebody tried to commit suicide here last night. "We heard the whole thing," one of them says. "She said to the DO [Directing Officer, through the slit in her cell door] 'Take the razor away,' but the DO didn't listen . . . [Then later] we heard the DO say 'Holy shit.'" The girl has been taken to the medical unit by the time I arrive. They say I can't speak to her.

This use of solitary confinement is a standard punishment in American prisons. Not long before this, a mentally disabled man in another Arizona prison called Mark Tucker was kept in solitary for so many years, with his pleas for a cellmate refused, that he eventually set himself on fire. In the hospital, with 80 percent of his body burned, he was informed that the

Department of Corrections was charging him $1.8 million to pay for the medical care to treat his injuries.

In an office away from the tents, in the middle of the prison complex, I find a psychologist named Jorge de la Torre. His job is to provide some counseling for the women here. He has a weary air about him, as if he has misplaced something and can't quite find it. Some 90 percent of the inmates, he tells me, "are here because of a drug-related problem," and virtually all of them are from traumatized backgrounds. "They grow up with no alternatives," he says. "They start with family problems they cannot manage." At any given time, Jorge can treat one in a hundred of the prisoners. The rest are left with the guards and the Hole.

There is a properly built air-conditioned prison near Tent City, but Joe Arpaio has thrown these prisoners out of it and turned it into an animal shelter. Now dogs and cats relax in cool rooms while addicts ache in the heat and dust storms outside. The animals, he believes, deserve it.

∼

When I explain Tent City to the people I sit next to on Greyhound buses as I travel across the country, they say this must be a freakish outlier—a ghoulish parody of the wider prison network. But the more I traveled, the more former prisoners I met, and the more studies I read, it slowly became clear to me that this is in fact quite typical of how addicts are treated across the United States and around the world.

I keep looking at the statistics. The United States now imprisons more people for drug offenses than Western European nations imprison for all crimes combined. No human society has ever before imprisoned this high a proportion of its population. It is now so large that if all U.S. prisoners were detained in one place, they would rank as the thirty-fifth most populous state of the Union.

From the liberal state of New York to the liberal state of California, the jailing and torture of addicts is routine. To pick just one kind: the Justice Department estimates that 216,000 people are raped in these prisons every year. (This is the number of rape victims, not the number of rapes—that is far higher.) As the writer Christopher Glazek has pointed out, this means that the United States is almost certainly the first society in human history where more men have been raped than women. The rape of Chino's mother was not, it turns out, an unusual event in the war on drugs—and it happens to both genders.

Nor is the United States alone. In China, addicts are often sent to hard labor camps, where they are forced to do backbreaking manual work as punishment. In Russia, Thailand, much of South America . . . the list goes on. This is all standard. Europe is slightly softer—and one ray of light has broken through, as I would see later.

Sheriff Joe Arpaio is the corporate logo for this cruelty, but there is a whole range of cheap products lined up behind him, and they are bought by everyone. The drug war has turned the United States into a shining tent city on a hill, inspiring the world to imitation.

~

As I tried to understand what is really happening to drug users in Arizona, I talked with the handful of people who are working on improving prisoners' rights in the state, including Donna Leone Hamm, the head of a group called Middle Ground Prison Reform.

I asked her one of my standard questions: What in your work, over the years, has most shocked you?

She started to reel off a long list—and around the middle of her litany, she referred in passing to a case where a woman was cooked in a cage, before continuing on.

Sorry, Donna, I said—can we go back a moment? Tell me about the woman who was cooked in the cage.

Donna sent me to the archives—and the archives sent me on a journey across the United States, to discover who this woman really was.

~

Prisoner Number 109416 woke up in her cell in Perryville State Prison Complex, Arizona, and said she felt suicidal.

She was a small blond woman in her forties with rotted teeth and sunken cheeks whose thoughts often dissolved into a long stream of paranoid incoherence. She was here because a year ago, a man had approached her on the street in Phoenix and said he would give her a bag of meth if she gave him a blowjob. She said yes, and so she was detained close to death row prisoners. All her life, she had been periodically caged, either for being addicted to drugs, or for selling her body to get them.

She was taken to see Dr. Susan Kaz, who was on duty in the prison that day. It was on the prisoner's files that she had been diagnosed with bipolar disorder and was so badly mentally incapacitated that the courts had appointed a guardian to look after her interests. When 109416 was put in the Hole in Tent City, she had swallowed a razor blade because—as her former cellmate, Juliana Philips, said—"she wanted to talk. Nobody would talk to her, and the guards treated her like shit. She just wanted a friend." But the doctor concluded that 109416 was being manipulative and just trying to get herself moved into another, less restrictive cell.

So the guards took 109416 and put her in an outdoor cage in the desert. The cage was uncovered with the sun raging down. There was nothing in it: no water, no bench, no bed. It was 106 degrees.

They are supposed to use this cage for a maximum of two hours per prisoner, but in practice, people are sometimes left there much longer. The cage was in direct sight of the guards. The prisoner asked for water. The guards mocked her for requesting it. One guard would later say the prisoner was "spacey, all she cared about was coffee and cigarettes." Another would agree she was "not all there."

The prisoner shat herself. Nobody came to clean up the mess.

The hours passed in the cage. 109416 was getting hotter and hotter and starting to burn up. She was screaming. The guards would say later her shouting "was something about Jay-Z and Beyoncé conspiring to kill her."

At some point, she collapsed, covered in her own shit. With her face against the floor of the desert, it sustained first-degree burns, as if she was in a fire. Sixteen different guards had the opportunity to do something. None of them responded.

Here the story diverges. The guards claim they told her: "Don't lay down on the ground, it is too hot!" But the prisoners say one of the guards was asked: "Did Powell really pass out when you tried to see her?" and he replied: "Yeah, it was the funniest thing. You should have seen it."

Watching from a few stories up, the prisoners could see something terrible was happening. "We said—that girl's been laying there a long time not moving. We saw guards walk past and nobody stopped," her former cellmate Juliana Philips tells me. "She was just laying there. Who's gonna take a nap on the cement in the sun in polyester and no shade?"

After the guards finally called an ambulance, the paramedics tried to take her temperature. Their thermometers only go to 108 degrees: she was that hot, or hotter still. Her internal organs had cooked, as if in an oven.

At the hospital, they were legally required to call her court-appointed legal guardian before making medical decisions. They didn't. The decision was made by the prison authorities and the hospital authorities. She died, just before midnight.

The autopsy found that her body was badly burned. Her eyeballs were, it was later explained, "as dry as parchment."

Three prison officers were fired soon after the incident. No prison officer involved ever faced charges. The guards never spoke to the media. In the transcripts of the interviews that were conducted for the official investigation with some of the guards on duty, they deny mocking her as she was dying.

This is her story as I found it in the records of the investigation into her death. The person in charge of this prison is not Joe Arpaio. This prison is run by the state, not the county: this way of treating addicts is much wider than him. It is statewide, and nationwide, and planetwide. One of the men in charge of this particular prison, and those like it across Arizona, was Chuck Ryan, who worked all his life in the Arizona Department of Corrections, except for one interlude, when he was a consultant for the Bush administration on how to handle the prison system in Iraq, a period that culminated in the Abu Ghraib scandal.

Nobody knew much about prisoner number 109416. She was due to be buried in a pauper's grave at the prison until Donna's charity stepped in. She was stripped of an identity in death, just as she was stripped of an identity in the cage. But in 2012, I was able—with the help of the Arizona prisoners' rights campaigner Peggy Plews—to track down Richard Husman, the ex-boyfriend who fathered 109416's son, to Springfield, Missouri. We sit in a bar, and I hear his story. To him, she was Marcia Powell.

Richard is a huge man with tattoos of flame covering his chunky bulked-out arms, so it seems a little incongruous at first that he arrived clutching in his hand the picture of a child. He laid it in front of me. I put next to it all the records I have been able to find of Marcia—police interviews, court records, the accounts of her death. Together, we began to stitch together the story of who she was.

Marcia lived with her biological mother, he said, until she was about three. After that, she spent three years in foster care until she was finally adopted. Something went wrong with the family who adopted her in California. She would never say what, but her adopted mother, as Richard put it, "kicked her out when she was thirteen and she'd been on the run ever since."

She had nowhere to go but the beach. She was sleeping on the sand because it's warm, and nobody can throw you out. But your stuff is always stolen, you have to wash in the bathroom at McDonald's (and only if you are lucky), and you are afraid all the time that other people will, Richard says, "rape you, beat you up, kill you." After that, she always had "the paranoia—when you don't have a home you're paranoid. She had no education, she had no school." About life on the beach, he says: "Think about it. That's hard. You can't go to Burger King to go to work. You got to prostitute." She probably became a child prostitute at this point, like Billie Holiday, and tried to snort and shoot the pain away.

Marcia needed protection. The only people she met who offered it were the Hell's Angels—the drug-dealing motorbike gang who couriered coke across the highways of America. Richard thought they used her to transport drugs because a pretty young white girl doesn't attract much attention. So she became a "house mouse"—one of the women who travels with them and skivvies for them, cleaning their bikes and their homes. A female friend of Richard's, who came along to the interview, said that in that life, "you're a slave. You're nothing . . . when you're a biker chick . . . and once you get in, it's kind of a Mafia deal. Once you get in, you may as well leave the country and hide because they will kill you. They will kill you because you know too much."

So what was in it for Marcia to be a house mouse? Richard says: "A safe place to sleep. And food. And drugs. Place to shower. Ain't got to worry about people kicking in the door because there's a guy with a gun at the door." Marcia's man in the Angels was a much older guy called Conrad Kurz, who "was kind of strict to her. He was a Nazi . . . a full-fledged Nazi." His home was filled with swastikas and Hitlerian flags. He "kept a pretty good leash on her," Richard says, until they had a baby girl, Eureka, and the baby was taken away by the authorities in Arizona, presumably because Marcia had developed a drug addiction. Conrad couldn't take the loss of his child. One day, he shot himself in the head in the shower.

Richard met her when he pulled up on his motorcycle at a truck stop when they were both in their early thirties. He, too, is an Angel. "That's why she stopped me—because I had the fastest bike in town . . . She liked to go fast," he says. He immediately liked her: she cooked him pork chops, and he loved the way she even made a fully cooked breakfast—egg and sausages—for his dog. They went gold panning—they rode up to the lakes to look for chunks of gold. "We'd do that for weekends at a time," he says. Marcia loved being outside, in the water. It was where she was happiest.

They decided to settle down in Missouri. "I worked the railroad for a year. We had a house, I had a car," he says. He managed to get Marcia to give up all drugs except weed. She started to do normal things. She mowed the lawn. She watched TV. She planted flowers. She started to draw flowers, too. "She was so happy to be stable," he says. "I always got her stable." But she decided she wanted to go back to Arizona for her daughter, Eureka: she couldn't just leave her out there, without her mother.

When Marcia got back to Arizona, she discovered she had an outstand-ing warrant for having 1.5 grams of marijuana—two joints. The police busted her and she received her first conviction and was sentenced to a year under house arrest. When he looks back over her life, Richard believes this was the turning point, when her stability was pulled down again. She had been okay for a year, but now, after her arrest, Marcia's paranoia returned with a vengeance. One day, when it was extremely hot out, she flew into a terror and ran off down the street barefoot, and she got third-degree burns on her soles. They had to take skin from her back to graft in its place.

As he said this, I found myself thinking of the last time Billie Holiday got clean—and George White came to stalk her, because of her past.

Marcia and Richard had a son together, Ritchie. She relapsed after the arrest and kept getting arrested now. Richard says it should have been clear to the authorities that "she was an addict . . . Addiction can be overcome with proper help. It ain't a jail thing." He believes the solution was to get her into "a mental hospital—that's probably what would have helped her. Get her whatever she needs—Xanax, morphine, to get her chemical imbalance right . . . Get her on the right meds. Show her some respect. Give her some working skills. Get her a GED so when she comes out she has a place, like a woman's shelter, [can] get a job . . . Give her respect, that's how it's supposed to be." He believes "if you're calm and cool and know you've got a life ahead of you that's going up the steps . . . if you know you're going up in the world, you're going to stay going up in the world." Instead, she kept being kicked down the steps by the criminal justice system. One day, she disappeared into a police car, and he never saw her again.

Richard eventually got together with another woman, and took Ritchie back to live with her and her kids in Missouri, where the boy would often ask about his mother. Then one day, ten years later, Richard came home to find the house on fire. He only found out later what happened: his stepson had raped and murdered Ritchie and his entire family and burned down their home. He tells me about this in broken fragments, as if it is too painful to explain clearly. He pushes in front of me newspaper reports of the deaths, which have the same baffled tone. He says the kid just went crazy one day, and murdered them all.

Richard doesn't know whether Marcia ever found out that her son had died. She had another year to live. He hopes she didn't.

In the arrest reports for Marcia Powell, you can hear her voice. In 1996, she gave a blowjob to a man in an alleyway in Phoenix and a pass-ing thirteen-year-old boy happened to get a glimpse of it. The police charged her with sexual indecency to a minor—a charge normally leveled against pedophiles. The police wrote down her babble, in a tone that sounds mocking. She said she had been asked to give a blowjob to a man but "life would not permit it. We couldn't do it because of a jolt which is a life we conquered." She then offered to have sex with the officers arresting her because "there was a nationwide emergency! John's in trouble! Visa! Army, Navy, Air Force, Marines, Special Forces, National Guard!" But then, suddenly, she was sane again, and sad. The report says she argued "she is not really a bad person, did not 'hurt the kid or anything,' and is not a menace to society because she 'loves people,' is teaching love while in jail, and is 'not a total waste of time.'"

Richard looks at these reports when I hand them to him and reads for a moment. Then he says simply: "I miss her."

In prison, looking out across the desert, Marcia would talk dreamily about nature. "She was a pagan in her beliefs—she believed that the trees had the same DNA that we did," one of her former cellmates, Juliana Philips, tells me. Marcia would say "that everything out there has a soul and is our brother. We contaminate the water, people can't drink the water. We can drink bottled water but our squirrels and cows and dogs and cats and buffalo can't drink that—they still have to be poisoned."

Later, Rich tells me: "If Arizona hadn't stuck her in jail for 1.5 grams of usable marijuana, we'd be in Illinois living high [that is, well]. I'd be twenty years with the railroad. We had a nice house there, a huge yard. She'd be a mom. Kids raised. Ritchie would have been eighteen now. My kids might still be alive. Just because of a little bullshit." Perhaps this is only a comforting myth he uses to deal with his pain, since Marcia had such deep-seated problems; but perhaps it is true. Perhaps that conviction did kick her out of the only trough of stability she ever found.

For Richard it seems to hurt most that as she lay dying, "they're making fun of her. For being ill." Richard hands me a photograph of Ritchie, and asks if I can arrange for it to be put with Marcia's grave. "So she knows she wasn't a criminal." Because, he says, "she made angels."

Many of the prison guards who put Marcia Powell in an exposed cage in the desert and ignored her screams are still at work today.

CHAPTER 9

Bart Simpson and the Angel of Juárez

An eight-foot-tall angel stood on the sidewalk in Ciudad Juárez with his vast feathery wings bristling in the breeze and his silver skin glistening in the light, as he stared down at yet another corpse. It is—it was—a twenty-year-old man. He had been walking on the street next to his house in this city, the most dangerous in the world, when the gunmen arrived. The angel could see the bullet wounds, and the puddle of blood, and the weeping when two of his relatives arrived. The angel was carrying a sign. It was addressed to the murderers—the people who had massacred more than sixty thousand people like this in Mexico in just five years. It addressed them by name. Chapo Guzman, the drug lord. The Zetas, the craziest of his rivals. The police. The army.

TIME IS SHORT, the sign said. SEEK FORGIVENESS.

Juan Manuel Olguín grew up in Ciudad Juárez, the Mexican city that sits across the border from the Texan city of El Paso, as the drug war was turning it into the deadliest place on the planet. I met him some time after he had stood over that corpse, on a Thursday night in 2012, in Juárez, when he was wearing his wings.

I had been reading the figures on Mexico's drug war for years, but they didn't make much sense to me. I knew the best estimate was—I'll repeat the number—that sixty thousand people had been killed in five years. That 90 percent of the cocaine used in the United States passed through here every year. That Mexican drug cartels make between $19 and $29 billion every year from U.S. drug sales alone. But the human stories I heard were so extreme I couldn't make any connection with them. They seemed to all focus on such unimaginable sadism—beheadings posted on YouTube, or pregnant women carved up with bottles—that it seemed unreal.

That is why, one morning in July, I walked into Ciudad Juárez from the United States over the thin brown trickle of the Rio Grande. The bridge was backed up with cars and squeegee merchants. Women sat on the ground, begging in two languages. The Mexican border agents didn't check anything I brought in. They waved me through with an unsmiling nod.

One of the first things I saw was a sign. HISTORIC DOWNTOWN TOUR OF JUÁREZ, it said, directing me to the sites to that were famous when this was one of the great party towns of North America. This is where Billie Holiday came to get hitched and get wasted, and she was only one of millions of Americans who wanted the same Juárez buzz. But that route has, I saw, now been papered over with posters. HAVE YOU SEEN HER? the plastered signs say, above images of one young woman or another, smiling at a party, in the time before. One of them, in red lipstick and a multicolored scarf, caught my eye. This is all there is to see now in Juárez—the absences. The tourist attractions have all been shuttered or burned down.

My fixer, Julián Cardona—the Reuters correspondent for Juárez— drove me around the city as I tried to get a feel for where I was. It soon became clear that if Rothstein's Manhattan was a vertical city reaching for the skies, this is a horizontal city scrambling for the desert. Its city center looks like any North American nowhere town, where a twenty-four-hour Wendy's squats next to a mall where the theme from *Titanic* plays in a pan-pipes version as people buy enormous flatscreen televisions. But as you follow the fat eight-lane highways for miles out of town, the city thins, and the malls turn into burned-out husks of stores and rusty shantytowns. Just when you think you have hit the edge of Juárez, you find another rash of homes and stores, before finally the sand dunes win.

But before Juárez petered out, I had arranged to meet the angels.

When he was eleven, Juan started to watch his friends vanish into the Juárez drug trade. This is the most important smuggling route into the United States, and the gangs were at war to control it. The cartels prefer kids: they don't understand death, so they are less afraid. Juan's best friend joined for the cash and the sense that, finally, he was part of something.

Juan, in a fog of hormones, considered joining a cartel himself. He would have money, at last. He would be able to support his family, which was sunk in alcoholism and drug addiction. But with people being slaughtered all around him, with houses being burned and shops being abandoned on every corner, he made a different choice. He told me that at the age of sixteen, "I decided to become an angel."

At first, when the murders began, people would run in panic from the death scenes. Then it changed. They started to stop and stare. Then it changed again. They would just walk on by. As if it was normal. As if it was nothing. Because in Juárez, it was. People were training themselves not to see, to dismember the part of them that sees the dismembering.

But Juan and his teenage friends refused to live in a city where murder was ignored. Even though every adult who spoke out against the cartels, the army, or the police had been killed, he and a group who met at his church decided to go to the murder scenes to protest. They built angel costumes with great two-meter wings made from plastic and feathers. They covered themselves with sparkling silver paint and stood on a tall stool. The long shining robes hang down over both their body and the stool, so the angel looks like a giant, as though he has just descended from heaven. It is hard to describe what this looks like: it is almost unreal, like a hallucination. These kids make signs directly challenging the most brutal murderers on earth, and they hold them aloft at the very spot where these men have just done their killing.

On the night I met Juan, after a summer storm, he was about to go to stand by another roadside at midnight to hold up his signs. He invited me to come along. Two young girls perched behind him, holding on to his wings so the wind wouldn't blow him backward. People in the cars that hurried past looked astonished, and bewildered, and frightened.

"I am not afraid. If I get killed, or whatever happens to me, it's because I'm doing something good for the city," Juan tells me. "I tell my mother to be proud of me if something happens." He and his friends have been betrayed by the generation leading the drug war, he believes: "We want to show them, by example, that we want a better society."

Most people in Juárez are amazed the angels have not been shot. They will tell you, wearily, that it is only a matter of time.

Arnold Rothstein dreamed of a New York City where the rule of law had been hollowed out and the only true rulers were criminals like him. He wanted to establish power by force, and buy the remaining broken slivers of the state piece by piece until he could use them, too, as weapons.

He never got to realize his dream. His bullet hit too soon. But his dream did come to pass.

I wanted to know what this meant, for real people, in their real lives. This is the part of the drug war most remote from my world, back in the stability of London. Yet I was beginning to feel we were all enmeshed together—the subjects of the drug war, and its logic—in a long, densely connected global chain. The impulse to repress, I suspected, had given birth to all this, but I wanted to see how.

I met many people in northern Mexico who shared their stories with me, but in the end, I came to understand what has happened there best through the tale of three teenagers. They were an angel, a killer, and a girl in love.

⌢

Just as Chino had explained to me what life is like inside a street gang, I wanted to understand what life is like inside a cartel, but I kept being told this was impossible. The cartels kill anyone who talks to outsiders. These are the most paranoid and secretive people in the world. And then, one day, I learned about one person—the only one to ever make it out and keep talking.

I wrote to the Texas Prison Service. After a long wait, I was told I had half an hour. Once I arrived in the middle of Tyler County in rural Texas—a huge mess of concrete and barbed wire—a guard smiled at me. I like your accent, she said, in deep Texan—you can have as much time as you want. I was guided through the prison by another guard until I was in a wide gray room and there was only glass in front of me. On the other side of the glass were tiny white cells.

The guard said: "I'm going to be around here in the area, because I can't leave you by yourself," and then she left.

At the back of one of the cells, a door opened, and he walked in, small and lithe. He looked like a nerd who should be presenting his science project to me. The only thing undermining this look was his eye tattoo—a bright-colored flame, dominating his face.

"So what's going on?" he said, looking me up and down. Before I could say anything, he said: "First of all—what do you know about me? . . . That's what I want to know."

He had a low voice. I said—I know you are here because, from the age of thirteen, you were a member of the Zetas. He nodded.

I asked Rosalio if I could put a little recorder between us. There was a hole in the glass, and the recorder sat there, with its red light on. He began to talk. After each piece of information he gave me, he asked nervously what I thought of him, and whether I would make him sound good. He was almost pleading. He had been alone for a very long time, in solitary confinement. We talked for over four hours. This is his story as I can patch it together from what he told me and from the other evidence of his crimes in the public record.

$\sim$

In 2005, Rosalio Reta was at summer camp, like all the other American teenagers his age—a short Texan fifteen-year-old with spiky hair, nicknamed "Bart" because he looked like a less yellow Bart Simpson and loved to skateboard. He was also into the Power Rangers, alternative pop, and Nintendo 64, especially The Legend of Zelda and Donkey Kong. At camp in that particular year, he was learning useful skills, ones he would remember for the rest of his life. Except at this camp, you don't learn how to canoe, or sing in a chorus, or make a log fire.

He remembered the techniques he learned there well. Take beheading, for example. "There's times I've seen it they've done it with a saw," he told me through the prison glass. "Blood everywhere. When they start going they hit the jugular and—" he snaps his fingers—"[it's] everywhere . . . They put the head right there. The head still moves, makes faces and everything. I think the nerves, you can see inside, the bone, everything's moving. It's like they've got worms. I've seen it move, when it's on the ground. If he's making a screaming face, it stays like that sometimes. Sometimes it slacks off."

This camp was deep in the mountains of Mexico, and Rosalio was there for six months, slowly being turned into a human weapon. "They just teach you everything. Everything you learn at a military camp," he says. "How to shoot, how to coordinate . . . All kinds of explosives, handguns, rifles, hand-to-hand combat." The camp's slogan is "If I retreat, kill me." He used these skills to murder more people than he can count. He committed industrial killings, threw hand grenades into crowded nightclubs, and shot a man in front of his toddler son and pregnant wife.

A few years before his trip to camp, the United States government—determined to achieve Harry Anslinger's mission of spreading the drug war to every country on earth—had decided to train an elite force within Mexico to win the war on drugs. The United States brought them to Fort Bragg to provide the best training, intelligence, and military equipment from America's 7th Special Forces Group. Their motto was "Not even death will stop us." Once it was over and they had learned all they could and received all the weapons they wanted, these expensively trained men went home and defected, en masse, to work for the Gulf Cartel. These breakaways called themselves the Zetas. It would be as if the Navy Seals defected from the U.S. Army to help the Crips take over Los Angeles— and succeeded.

Rosalio's hometown, the dusty desert of Laredo in Texas, is right across the border from Nuevo Laredo in Mexico. He tells me: "Every cartel wants that route. It's one of the biggest places of crossing from country to country . . . It's a big commercial place. So everybody wants it . . . That's what everybody's fighting for: that I-35." If your cartel controls that interstate highway, you control the flow of billions of dollars. If your enemies control it, they can strip you of your livelihood. That is a recipe for a war.

There are two different stories of how Rosalio became a Zeta. There is the story he told when he first talked to the police when he was sixteen, and then there is the story he told me when he was twenty-three. I have no way of knowing which of these is more accurate—so I have laid them out here, for you to judge.

We know this much for sure: He grew up in a house made of wood that was propped up on cinder blocks. His mother was a hairdresser. His father was an undocumented immigrant who worked on construction sites. They had ten children. Laredo is one of the poorest parts of the United States—a border town where, as he has said, "if you're not a cop, you're a drug dealer. If you're not a drug dealer, you work for a cartel. That's all there is down there." He said another time: "A lot of people here [in the United States] want to be an attorney, a lawyer, a judge, a firefighter, a policeman. Over there [on the U.S.-Mexico border] they worship the Zetas. The little kids [say] 'I want to be a Zeta when I grow up.'"

But he insists: "I wasn't, like, poor poor poor. My mom and dad both worked, we had stuff to eat every day. We were normal. We were a family." He had two best friends he spent all his time with: Jesse and Gabriel. They played football, hung out by the lake, played video games. All through his childhood, he skipped back and forth over the border. Sodas and candies are cheaper in Nuevo Laredo, so he would often head there with his friends. And as an adolescent, there are nightclubs there that will let you in as young as thirteen, so he and Jesse and Gabriel spent more time there. Here's where the story splits, for a moment.

When Rosalio was first questioned by the police, he had spent three years immersed in Zeta life, a world where the culture of terror has been taken to its most extreme variant yet. In the tapes he looks hyped with this hatred, smirking and strutting and half-expecting the cops to be impressed by his boasts of mass murder. He tells them that at thirteen, he started hanging out at a nightclub in Nuevo Laredo and heard whispers of a man who had it all: Miguel Treviño. He came from nothing to be number two in the Zetas. Like Arnold Rothstein, he was an unassuming, almost anonymous-looking man: five feet eight, a teetotaler, drug-free, dressed in blue jeans and Walmart T-shirts. But he was the king of the town—he controlled the drug trade, the military, the police, everything. Rosalio wanted what he had. He met him and offered to prove his loyalty. Whatever it took.

Then there's a different story about how it all started. He told me his friend had an older brother who worked for the cartels, and one day they went to eat in Nuevo Laredo. The brother received a call and said he had to go to deal with some business—so Rosalio hid himself in the back of his truck. He was curious. He wanted to know what it looked like. When they arrived, he discovered he was at one of the ranches used by Miguel Treviño to carry out his business—and he saw too much.

Here's where the stories converge again. In both versions, the ranch was a typical Zeta workspace. There were about thirty people tied up. On one side, "they put them in an oil drum and they just burn them burn them burn them and there's just ashes left." On the other side, they were being "cut to pieces." The Zetas usually torture members of other gangs, or anyone who irks them, to find out "safe houses, routes, who they work for . . . About what they do, who they working for, what is he doing?" before the killing starts. After they are dead, "they burn the bodies by [making] *guiso* [the Spanish word for stew]—throw 'em in there . . . and poke at the body until it dissolves."

This is where Rosalio carried out his first killing. "I didn't look at him in the face," he says. "He was tied up . . . He was kneeling down, tied up behind his back and his feet . . . They were all crying, begging, saying don't kill me. Everybody. Some of them weren't even saying anything. They knew they were going to get killed. Everyone was there to be killed."

He took the gun and shot the man in the head. He would never find out who he was.

The first Rosalio, emerging blinking from the Zeta light, told the cops he loved this experience: "I thought I was Superman. I loved doing it, killing that first person. They tried to take the gun away, but it was like taking candy from a kid." He said from then on, "there were others to do it, but I would volunteer. It was like a James Bond game . . . Anyone can do it, but not everyone wants to. Some are weak in the mind and cannot carry it in their conscience. Others sleep as peacefully as fish." He added: "I like what I do. I don't deny it."

The second Rosalio, in the monochrome of the Texas prison system, says this was crazed babble, offered up in a moment of mania "because after a long while, I was safe. I was alive. I actually made it from Mexico alive. And the majority of everybody around me is dead. Everybody I really cared for, that I grew up with, is dead already. I was alive. I made it alive. After having been this close to being killed . . ."

No, he says, he didn't enjoy it. He started killing on that day because he realized that once he had seen the ranch, they wouldn't let him walk away as a witness. He had to either die, or become a participant. From that moment on, "you're forced to do what they want. You have to do it, whether you want it or not. You're forced to do it. If you don't do it, they kill you. It's just plain and simple. You kill or you get killed."

And that's it. That bullet made him a Zeta and blocked all the exits. "Whether you go in willingly or forcibly," he says, "once you're in, you're in . . . It's a done deal," and, "whether I like it or not, these people molded me into one of their soldiers, doing their deeds."

That account was confirmed, years later, by the U.S. police investigation. Rosalio is a very rare example of somebody who peers into the heart of the Mexican drug cartels and makes it out alive. For three years, he was working directly for Miguel Treviño. For long stretches, he was one of the paramilitary posse living with him in safe houses, by his side, killing on his orders. Treviño and his fellow Zetas refer to kids like Rosalio and Jesse and Gabriel by a name: the Expendables.

"It happened so quick, since that first day. From there, everything went"—Rosalio makes a *pppppft* sound. "That's when I knew I had stepped over the border already—I was in a different world."

He didn't tell his parents, because he was convinced if he did, they would be killed. He didn't tell anyone.

When I met him, he wouldn't even say Treviño's name for a long time. He tells me: "It's better you don't even talk about him." He repeats it: "It's better if you don't even talk about him . . . He don't have any limits. That's why a lot of people don't even talk about him. Especially in Mexico. They're afraid of even saying his name over there."

But haltingly, in fragments, he painted a picture of a man who, like Rothstein, thought only of money, and would do anything to get it. While the violence was more extreme, it followed the same logic demanded by prohibition. He captured the market by violence and maintained it by terror. His killing was never random, even as it was psychotic. It was all geared, Rosalio explained, toward "intimidation. For the rival cartels. Trying to behead them on videos, so they can know they mean business. That they ain't playing around."

He was absorbing the same rules Chino learned on his block, cast onto a more extreme canvas. You have to be so terrifying nobody will ever try to fuck with you. For Brownsville teenagers that means whipping and shooting. For Nuevo Laredo teenagers that means beheading and burning. Rosalio was ordered to embark on a string of targeted killings—of rival cartels, and of anybody who got in the Zetas' way.

From day to day, "you never know what they're going to do. They might want to torture somebody to death today, or they might drown him today, they might hang him today, or they're going to cut him to pieces and burn him alive. You never know what they're going to do. It depends what they feel like doing." He added: "Everything was always the same. They killed people on a daily basis. There's not a day that goes by [that] they don't kill someone. That they don't torture someone. That they don't burn someone alive . . . That's your daily routine. That's what they do for a living." When he was sent to kill a person, "I don't know the person who was in front of me. I don't know what they had done. Anything." He just knew to make sure they died.

The cartels send messages written in human flesh. They have a system of signals known to everyone. If you betray the cartel, they'll shoot you in the neck. If you talk too much, they'll shoot you in the mouth. If you are a spy, they'll shoot you in the ear. Each body is a billboard, advertising that your cartel is the most vicious.

His friends, Jesse and Gabriel, started to work with him for the Zetas. He won't say how this started, but the police investigation—and their subsequent fates—confirm their involvement is real. Did he introduce them? Did he bring them in? It's not clear. But it was becoming obvious to everyone that, as he said, "it's not a game anymore."

"We have to stay up a lot of time—sometimes a week, a week and a half," he explained. "Almost two weeks. No sleep. And everybody used to do cocaine so they so they used to give us that . . . We had to go from one place to another, so we couldn't sleep." At some point, Gabriel had eyeballs tattooed on his eyelids, so it looked as if he was always awake, always watching. Which you had to be if you wanted to be safe. In the house with Treviño, "there's a lot of people they have taking care of the place—lookouts and everything. They see some rivals or anything, they call all groups to a shoot-out." Everybody was afraid of everybody else. After a while, "I couldn't trust them," he says. "I'd just stay to myself. You never know if one of them might try to kill you, from the back. I've seen it happen so many times. It's a lot of people over there when you're working for them, if somebody doesn't like you, you at the wrong place, they sneak up on you and kill you. The same people you're working with."

Everybody knew "all [Treviño] has to say is"—he snaps his fingers—"kill him. That's all he has to do. Just give the order and I'm gone."

He called his mother every now and then to let her know he was still alive. He didn't tell her what he was doing.

The worst nightmares aren't where you are killed; they are where you are a killer.

But in the midst of the terror, there were treats. "They were throwing around money, everything you wanted. Everything." Treviño held raffles. He put everybody's name in a cup, and the winner—Rosalio!—got a brand-new Mercedes. There were girls whenever you wanted them, and coke. Rosalio was paid $500 a week as a retainer, and much more for big hits: $375,000 for killing one of Chapo Guzman's associates, at the age of fifteen. Forgetting his story about being forced from the start for a moment, Rosalio told me that when the treats began, "you didn't have to do anything then and there. But once they lured you in, it was a trap." Then he seemed to realize what he had said and added quickly that he was talking about his friends, but not himself: he was forced, he insists, he was forced.

Sometimes, they lived in a fancy safe house back over the border in Laredo. Gabriel spent all his time there with his girlfriend. Rosalio and Jesse would ride around their old neighborhoods and play by the lake, as they used to. Why, I asked Rosalio, did the cartels use American teenagers and not Mexicans? "Because of the easy access to both sides of the border," he says. But what's the advantage to that if they're killing people in Mexico? What would you do in the United States for them? "I don't want to talk about that. There's a lot of things I'd just rather not talk about."

Later, as I listened again and again to the recording of this interview, I found myself returning to the work of Philippe Bourgois, the French sociologist whose writing helped me to understand Chino's story. Under prohibition, he explains, if you are the first to abandon a moral restraint, you gain a competitive advantage over your rivals, and get to control more of the drug market. So the Expendables are sent to butcher not just rival cartel members, but their relatives.

On a wiretap, a conversation between Rosalio and Gabriel was recorded. Gabriel described kidnapping two teenagers who were the cousins of a rival. "They died on their own from the beating," he said. "They just died. They just died and shit. You should have been there. You should have seen Pancho, dude. He was crying like a faggot—'No, man, I'm your friend.' 'What friend, you son of a bitch? Shut your mouth!' And *poom!* I grabbed a fucking bottle and *slash!* I slit his whole fucking belly. And *poom!* He was bleeding. I grabbed a little cup and *poom!* The little cup! *Poom! Poom!* I filled it with blood and *poom!* . . . And then I went to the other faggot and *slash!* I slit him with the same thing." Rosalio laughed. The local cops disposed of the bodies for Gabriel.

He said later: "I've killed men while they were tied and bound, but there is no thrill, no excitement in that for me. I prefer to stalk my targets, hunt them down, and then, after I know their moves front to back, I sneak up on 'em, look 'em in the eyes, and pull the trigger—now that's a rush."

If you are the first to kill your rivals' relatives, including their pregnant women, you get a brief competitive advantage: people are more scared of your cartel and they will cede more of the drug market to you. Then every cartel does it: it becomes part of standard practice. If you are the first to behead people, you get a brief competitive advantage. Then every cartel does it. If you are the first to behead people on camera and post it on YouTube, you get a brief competitive advantage. Then every cartel does it. If you are the first to mount people's heads on pikes and display them in public, you gain a brief competitive advantage. Then every cartel does it. If you are the first to behead a person, cut off his face, and sew it onto a soccer ball, you get a brief competitive advantage. And on it goes.

Prohibition, Bourgois explains in his writing, creates a system in which the most insane and sadistic violence has a sane and functional logic. It is required. It is rewarded.

In the midst of all this killing, Rosalio and his friends were never once worried about the police, or being caught by them. Why? Rosalio started to notice something strange about Treviño from the first day he worked for him. Carolyn Rothstein said that her husband Arnold would often argue that "probably the best job in public life for which he was fitted was that of Police Commissioner of New York." Treviño has achieved it.

Wherever they went in Mexico, Rosalio observed that the police worked for Treviño: "There's no police now . . . Everything was under his control. Military. Police. Everything." He bribed them—he drove everywhere with two million dollars in cash, in case any impromptu payments were necessary. And where that didn't work, "they know if they mess something up [like a drug-smuggling route] they're going to get killed, so they just stay out of the way." Indeed, "sometimes the police escort you to do an assassination . . . The same police kidnaps a person and takes them to the cartel." Treviño's associates went right to the top of the Mexican state: "They might be working for the president by day, and by night they're working for the cartels."

Why have these drug gangs been able to capture Mexico, when drug gangs in the United States can't? As I tried to understand this, I started to picture prohibited drugs as a river being redirected to wash across a town. If a river washes into a skyscraper, it might erode the walls and break some windows. But if it washes into a wooden house, it will wash it away entirely. In Mexico, the foundations of law and democracy are made of wood—it was governed by one semidictatorial party for seven decades until 2000, so a culture of feeling that the law is something citizens write together and should obey together has not yet properly developed. And the river is flowing much faster and it is carrying much more water relative to its surroundings: in Juárez, it is believed that 60 to 70 percent of the economy runs on laundered drug money, while drug money represents a vastly smaller fraction of the U.S. economy.

Nothing can withstand this force.

Rosalio was in the woods. He could see that, even though he couldn't see much else. One eye was swollen shut; he could only see a little through the swelling in the other.

And his throat was bleeding.

Treviño's men had tried to slice it open. They cut him up, all over. He will have the scars from this attack covering his body for the rest of his life.

So Rosalio was running.

There are, once again, two stories about how Rosalio got here, to these woods and this throat cutting.

The first story—advanced by the U.S. television documentary *Nothing Personal*—is that after training him to be a killer, the cartels lost control of him. He was running off Treviño's leash and killing freelance. They sent him to kill a cartel rival in Monterrey and instead he threw a grenade into a nightclub, killing four people and wounding twenty-four. The cartels' sadism is unimaginably vicious, but it always has a purpose. If you simply go Jeffrey Dahmer on them, if you are spraying your sadism randomly instead of focusing it where they tell you to, that's a distraction they don't need and won't tolerate.

The second story was offered by Rosalio himself. After three years, "I couldn't keep on living with these people telling me what to do, who to kill, where to go, how to sleep, how to go about myself. I can't live my whole life like that. I can't live in fear of them saying people [will be] killing me. I had to stop it one way or another." In the past, he had seen people get shot by rival gangs and then put out to pasture, allowed out of the life. So he said that in a moment of desperation, he decided, at the age of sixteen, to shoot himself.

He pulled up his trouser leg and showed me the wound. It was large and angry. Some of the nerves were destroyed: he can't feel much there. After pulling the trigger, he said, he shot himself with Novocain and cleaned the wound up, with the skills he had learned at the training camp. "I was missing a big old chunk of meat so I had somebody help me close it and I sewed it up the best I could. I cleaned it, took some antibiotics." On the first day, he didn't feel much. "But the second day—" He sucked his teeth.

It didn't work. "They made me sew my bullet wound up and nurse myself," he said. Not long after, they sent him on another job, to the nightclub in Monterrey. But he couldn't do it. He couldn't kill anymore. He had had enough. "I was tired of that lifestyle," he says. "I wanted to be left alone." That, he says, is the reason they turned on him.

He wouldn't say how he got away from the throat cutters. Even after he was arrested, he doesn't seem to have boasted about that. "Nobody knows what went on," he said. "Nobody knows. I just—I had to fight for my life. I'm not going to let anybody kill me."

But what could he do then? He knew that in Mexico, the Zetas would find him, sooner or later, and they would do to him precisely what he had done to so many people over the preceding three years. So he called the American police in Laredo and said he had information for them. He was back in the United States within forty-eight hours. "I didn't want to die, I didn't want my family to die, for a mistake that was made when I was thirteen years old," he says. "I didn't get caught. I turned myself in . . . Ain't nobody caught me, no cops went into arrest me. I turned myself in. I just wanted all this to stop . . . I don't want to live that life anymore. I couldn't keep on going like that."

He made the right call. Years later, as court evidence, Rosalio would see the pictures of what Treviño's men did to his best friend Jesse not long after Rosalio fled. "Holes everywhere. He got stabbed all over the place. Neck, head, face, chest, arms, all over his neck, face, and he had a hole right here in his head." Rosalio looked genuinely moved when he described the images, perhaps for the first time in our conversation.

"He was still a human being," he says. "He was still my brother."

Rosalio is now serving two consecutive life sentences in a prison camp in rural Texas for killings he carried out on that side of the border. He will be released when he is in his eighties, if he lives that long. It is unlikely. After I passed through the barbed wire and metal detectors to see him, the prison guard told me cheerfully that "it would be nothing for them [the Zetas] to be able to reach out and put a hit on him inside prison."

A year before I met him, two other prisoners seized Rosalio and stabbed him three times in the back and once in the head. He showed me the scars. His body, I realize now, has a complex topography, where each wound or mess of scar tissue marks a different part of his life. His ripped flesh is a history of the drug war all by itself. He believes they tried to kill him because one of his victims was a member of their prison gang, and so they are obliged to avenge him. Now, for his own safety, he lives in "administrative segregation." The guard tells me it "is kinda like solitary, except we don't call it solitary." Rosalio explained: "You're in a room twenty-four seven. Can't go out anywhere. There's nothing I can do . . . Just in a single cell. By yourself. I've been like that for a year already." He can't make phone calls or talk to anyone. "The way I'm treated right now—sometimes I think I shoulda let them kill me," he said.

He will probably live like this for the rest of his life, entombed from the rest of humanity. He is convinced the cartels could kill his family now. His family, and anyone who comes into contact with him.

"What makes you think they're not going to get you?" he said, peering at me. "You want to sit here and say [what] they can't do—they can do anything they want. You don't know the reach people got. You don't know what kind of contacts they got. You don't know who they got on their payroll. You haven't lived that life. I have. I know what these people are capable of doing. I know how far they'll go just to kill somebody. I lived that life. Not you."

He thinks obsessively about that day, when he was thirteen, and made that decision to pull that trigger. He will freely admit to and discuss almost everything he did for the Zetas, but he spends more than four hours trying to convince me, in a pleading, pained voice, that his account of that moment is true, and he was forced.

I realize now I should have told him: It's not that moment that sealed your fate. It's the moment when the drug war was launched, long ago. I don't know if he would have understood.

Clearly, Rosalio was a disturbed adolescent, and would have been, whatever our drug policies. But it was the war for drugs that took his adolescent disturbance and gave him huge cash incentives to cultivate it, enlarge it, and live off it. It said: Murder, and we will shower you with money and cars and women. It gave him paramilitary training to carry out those murders as efficiently as possible. And it hollowed out the Mexican police force so he could continue those murders without fear of arrest.

"Everybody around me is dead now," Rosalio said to me, less, I think, in a tone of self-pity than of shock. "Everybody I used to hang around with—they're all dead. There's not even a handful of us that are alive."

A few months after I met Rosalio, when I was back in New York, it was reported in the international press that Miguel Treviño had risen, through slaughter, to become number one in the Zetas. And then, a few months after that, it was reported that Miguel Treviño had been captured by the Mexican police in Nuevo Laredo—almost certainly because they were paid by a rival drug gang to take him out.

Nobody doubts that another gangster now controls the routes through Mexico into the United States, and nobody doubts he has a fresh batch of expendable child soldiers to defend him.

CHAPTER 10

Marisela's Long March

Rosalio's story was so gruesome that I was sure it couldn't possibly capture the day-to-day life of most Mexicans in the middle of the drug war. He was—as he says—a soldier. Soldiers take part in violence. I kept asking myself: What is life like for the noncombatants? What is normal life like? All these people I could see buying burgers in Wendy's and flatscreen TVs in the mall in Juárez—clearly they weren't working for the Zetas. I wanted to know how living in the middle of all this killing affected them.

As I talked to people all over Juárez, I slowly began to glimpse the answer, but it really became clear to me only when I began to investigate a story of a girl who fell in love, and a mother who went looking for her. I learned it—as will become clear as the story progresses—by tracking down the people who knew them, and by reading through the records from the time.

At first, this will seem like it is a story from a different book, because it focuses on people who have nothing to do with drugs or drug dealing. But in fact it is the closest I came—and the closest, I believe, that I can bring you—to understanding how the drug war has reshaped the psyche of Mexico, and the many other countries on the supply route.

~

Rubi Fraire was on a vacation with her big Mexican family in Jalisco. They all stopped off in a diner where the roof was made of palm leaves and a sleepy river rolled past. She was eleven years old—a sarcastic, slightly plump little girl who was always quipping. Her mother, Marisela, was on a rare break from her endless whirl of work. She was a nurse in the local hospital, and when she clocked off from that job, she sold necklaces and chains and rings. It was exhausting, but she believed in working hard for her family more than anything: she was saving up to buy a shop.

Marisela counted her kids back into the car and—in a moment the family would later remember as like a scene in *Home Alone*—she must have counted somebody else's kid by mistake. They all clambered in and drove off. All except Rubi.

It was only two hours later that they realized she was not with them. "Where is she?" Marisela gasped. How could this happen? How could she forget her?

They drove back in a panic to the last place they had seen her. They expected Rubi to be in tears—or gone.

They pulled into the diner. Is she . . . ? Where is . . . ?

And there was Rubi. She was laughing. She had made friends with another little girl and she was eating fish.

Rubi's older brother, Juan, asked her if she had been scared. No, she says: "I knew that my mom was coming back for me."

Rubi knew that Marisela would always come back for her, no matter what happened. She was right. What she didn't know was quite how far Marisela would have to go to do that.

~

A few years later, Rubi had a crush. A tall, skinny twenty-two-year-old with sticky-outy ears and an impressive line in hard-man talk turned up at her mother's new carpentry store in Ciudad Juárez asking for a job.

"Please help me out, I don't have money to buy food for my little girl," Sergio said. "I'll do anything that needs to be done. Give me a job at least for a couple of days."

Marisela was feeling softhearted, so she made Sergio a carpentry assistant. Soon, her daughter was hanging around him all the time. She was fourteen, and impressed by his tall tales of being a DJ for a radio station, of being fired because he slept with the owner's daughter, and of owning an AK-47. By now, Rubi had developed fast. She was curvy and precociously beautiful.

We don't know when they first become involved. He got a tattoo with Rubi's name on it, and started telling her that her mother didn't love her.

Why is she on your back for not doing well at school, if she really cares about you?

And one morning, Rubi was gone. The police refused to go get her. A few months later, Marisela found her, pregnant, and they became friends again—but Rubi ran back to Sergio each night.

Just beyond the frame of this small domestic drama, their city was starting to look like the set of the *Saw* movies. Chopped-up bodies were being found all over the streets of Juárez. Decapitated corpses hung from the traffic overpasses with signs from the cartels declaring they were in charge now. But this had nothing to do with Marisela and her family. Like most people in Juárez, they looked away and tried to get on with their lives. What else could they do?

One day, Rubi's big brother, Juan, turned up to redecorate the flat where Rubi lived, and he was puzzled by what he found. The furniture was gone. The place was empty. There was only one thing: a note from Rubi. It said that she was having a lot of problems with Sergio because Marisela kept criticizing him, and they were going away to find a new life, free of her, far away.

Rubi had run off before. She always came back.

Christmas came. Rubi didn't call.

New Year's Eve came, and still Rubi didn't call.

Marisela was puzzled. There had been no fight before she vanished, not this time. Where was she? She decided to visit Sergio's mother to see if she knew. When she arrived, she saw something that startled her. It was Rubi's baby. He was with Sergio. But there was no Rubi.

Sergio said Rubi had abandoned them both. To Marisela, this was inconceivable. She could leave Sergio, yes, but her own baby? She looked again at Rubi's letter, and she had a fear: What if she hadn't written it? What if it was faked?

When she returned shortly after to visit her grandson, she found Sergio had vanished and taken the baby with him. Marisela and her eldest son, Juan, decided to print up flyers of Sergio's face and leaflet his neighborhood, Fronteriza Baja, asking people to come forward if they'd seen either of them.

But nothing came of it.

Then, after two weeks, there was a call. It was a teenager named Angel.

"I need to talk to you—I'm going to tell you something real hard," he said. "I don't want to talk because I'm scared. [But] I have a family member [who] is missing also. I know how you are feeling. I know the feeling you have when you are looking for somebody and you can't find them."

When Marisela met Angel, he was shaking. She had to drive him far out of the neighborhood before he was able to form the words he had to say.

Months before, he had been hanging out in his 'hood when Sergio drove up to a group of them and said he needed help. He had to remove some furniture from his house, and there was some quick money in it if they'd help him, so a posse of them—Sergio's brother Andy, Angel, and a ten-year-old boy—went back there. And when they did, they saw Rubi. Her head had been smashed in. She was dead. The kids didn't want to get involved in this. Sergio became furious. If you don't help me fix this, he announced, I'll kill you all.

So they rolled up Rubi's body and put it in the truck. Sergio drove off with the ten-year-old boy. And Angel had had to live with what he'd seen ever since.

Marisela and Juan didn't know what to make of this. The kid seemed plausible. But they didn't want to believe it. She begged Angel to come to the police with her. Finally, terrified, he agreed. The police wrote it up, but still nothing happened.

She turned up at the police station every day now, demanding to know: "So what are we going to do today" to find Sergio? "What's the next step?" She virtually moved into the police station as a one-woman pressure group. But even now, the police were shrugging. Sergio has vanished: What can we do?

At this point, Marisela made a decision. If the police wouldn't do their job, she would do it. She would become a detective. In the middle of the killing fields of Ciudad Juárez, she was going to become a freelance police force of one.

She trawled the mountains around the city, looking hour after hour for Rubi's corpse. Then she headed back to Sergio's neighborhood to hand out flyers. Finally, one day, a woman told Marisela she knew where Sergio was. I can't disclose the details of who this woman was, because it might get her killed. But she told Marisela that Sergio was in Fresnillo sixteen hours from Juárez, and gave Marisela his landline number. She took it to the police and . . . still nothing. They refused to act.

Marisela had been feeling ill for a long time. She assumed it was because of Rubi's disappearance, but her doctors told her she was wrong. She had breast cancer, and she needed a double mastectomy urgently.

At this point, most of us would have given up. Marisela did not.

A few days after the operation, she set off for Fresnillo. She had tubes attached to each breast to drain the fluid and serum that seeped from her into a container.

And then, in Fresnillo, she found him. The local police finally seized Sergio, and he immediately confessed. Yes, he had smashed Rubi's skull. He had set her on fire and tossed her body in the area on the outskirts of the city where the local abattoir dumps the bones and grease from the slaughtered pigs. The police started a search back in Juárez. They were only able to recover one third of her body: her arm, a few parts of her head—not even the skull. Just fragments. There were thirty-six bones in total. The investigators told Marisela that normally, when you are burned, your head explodes through your eyes and your ears, but because Rubi's skull was broken, hers had exploded through the hole in her head.

Marisela believed there must be more of Rubi left than that. She drove with her eldest son Juan to the abattoir dump. There were thousands and thousands of pig bones, and wheelbarrows dumping more all the time. They started to scramble through the bones and the grease, a pump still attached to each of Marisela's breasts. "There were maggots and the smell of death and all these bones—we were going through the bones trying to find one piece of her. Trying to find one piece of her," Rubi's brother, Juan, remembers. "Of course we didn't find anything."

Angel testified at the trial. He described everything he saw, and he explained that Sergio had threatened to kill him if he ever spoke out about it.

One day, Sergio turned to Marisela from the dock and said: "I know that I did a big harm that nobody will be able to repair. She already said that she will not forgive me, but I ask your forgiveness, Marisela, because I know that it was a great harm. And it is true what you said—'Where was God at that moment?' Unfortunately, I didn't know God at that moment, but I had the good chance to find God in jail. I don't have words . . . that's all."

It was obvious he would be convicted—but then everything took a mysterious turn. The judges said they couldn't accept Sergio's confession, because the prosecutor has to be present for a confession to be valid. On these grounds alone, they said there was insufficient evidence, and he was acquitted.

Marisela always believed in doing things the right way. Now, Juan says, "it was like she was betrayed by her own people, because she believed in the authorities." She announced: "These judges have killed my daughter again." Nobody understood why this had happened, but they knew it wasn't unusual: the murder conviction rate in Juarez is just 2 percent.

Angel—the kid who had testified at the trial—was found dead along with his family, just as Sergio had promised.

Marisela started to walk the streets of Juárez with signs demanding justice for Rubi, holding aloft her picture. She called on all the mothers who had missing daughters to leave their homes and join her. All over the country, people who protested were being murdered, but Marisela would not be stopped. And steadily, as they saw her standing up, other mothers began to come out into the streets to join her, holding aloft their own pictures of their own daughters. They walked all day, through the deadliest city in the world, refusing to accept that this is how things would always be. She said in a speech: "It is only a few of us that are gathered here, but there are plenty more waiting at home, crying . . . We ask you: How many more will it be? How many victims? . . . We stand alone in this struggle. Please join and support us." Everywhere they went, people would shout "Keep on going!" and "We're with you!"

She was approached by rival cartel members who said they could deal with Sergio if she wanted. Some of her family were tempted—but Marisela refused. She believed in justice, not violence.

She went to interview everybody who had ever known Sergio, to beg them for information—and finally, somebody gave her an address in Fresno, a city nine hundred miles away.

Almost as soon as she arrived on the block, somebody fired bullets into the air, to scare her off. She refused to run. She rented a house nearby, and then—one day—she saw him, in the street, just as she had expected.

She was perfectly still. She didn't want him dead; she wanted him brought to justice.

Years after this, in a shack in Juárez, I asked her best friend Bertha Alicia Garcia—weren't you afraid? "We are always afraid," she said, "but sometimes, the love of your children is stronger than fear itself."

Marisela called the police and told them everything. They sent three cops, who arrived noisily at the front of the house—while Sergio escaped out the back.

They let him get away. Again.

Was this incompetence? Corruption? Fear?

Marisela tried to follow his trail, asking questions in the surrounding small towns, but this area was totally controlled by the Zetas, and they don't like people asking questions. So Marisela decided to walk from Juárez to Mexico City—a journey of more than a thousand miles—to beg the president himself to act. In terms of distance, this is like walking from Paris to Kosovo, or from Los Angeles to Denver. It was the last option she had left.

So Marisela began her long march through the desert. In this heat, animals burrow into the ground and only come out at sunset. Marisela walked through it all, across sand dunes, and mountains, and dust storms. She had spent her life savings by now. Some days she and the other mothers marching with her went hungry; some days they ate only bread smeared with mayonnaise. They slept where they could. Sometimes people let them into their homes, or allowed them to lie down in their trucks.

The heat on these roads is so intense that it looks as though the tarmac in front of you has melted into shimmering black pools. The dust and the glare were so bad that her son Juan's eyes became infected, and for two days he was blind; he walked holding his mother's shoulder.

It was as if she thought she could outpace her grief. Everybody in the country was watching and asking—If a nurse with no resources and no money can find a murderer, how come the police can't find him, with everything they've got? What is happening to our country?

When after three months of walking she made it to Mexico City, President Calderon refused to see her. In the video clips from this time, you can see her face becoming slowly misshapen by grief.

That is when Marisela heard rumors that started to make it possible to make sense of this whole story. Sergio, she was told, is a Zeta. That is why the police would not touch him. That is why he kept escaping. When Marisela got her final lead on where Sergio was, the police were finally honest with her. "If he's with the Zetas, we're not going to be able to do anything, because they run the state," they told her. "If we do a bust, it's because they allow us to do it. We don't bust people just like that." They were apologetic, but they explained that the Zetas give them money if they serve them and death if they don't.

I found myself thinking back to the start of this war. Arnold Rothstein was allowed to shoot at cops and walk away a free man. The wealth that came from controlling the market in criminalized drugs bought more than fancy fur coats for Carolyn. It bought him a place above and beyond the law. At first, he bought freedom from being prosecuted for the crimes involved in running his drug business. And then it spread from there, buying him immunity for the laws surrounding theft and extortion and murder, like an oil slick that slowly covers the whole society in its goop. This oil slick, I began to see, covers Mexico today.

First the drug dealers bought immunity from the drug laws. Then they bought the law itself. By joining the Zetas somewhere along the line, Sergio had placed himself above the law. This is what the desire to repress drugs has wrought.

But Rubi always knew her mother wouldn't abandon her.

Marisela believed she had one card left to play. Go public. Tell the world everything. She went to the state capitol in Chihuahua City and announced to the world's press everything she had found—that the Zetas now ran the state and could do what they liked.

The governor publicly dismissed her. She had arrived in early December, and she invited the governor to Christmas dinner on the doorstep of the state capitol building, because she wasn't leaving until Sergio was arrested. "What's the government waiting for—that he come and finish me?" she said. "Then let him kill me, but here in front, to see if it makes them ashamed."

This was one of the most tightly policed places in Mexico, guarded by the federal police, the local police, and the military.

But one night, at eight o'clock, the gates to the capitol started to close, and the area suddenly emptied of police and soldiers.

A man approached her now, right in front of the security cameras, in the shadow of the offices of the city police.

He took out a gun. He put the gun to her head. He pulled the trigger.

But the gun didn't go off. Something had jammed. Marisela's brother tried to throw a chair at the hit man; Marisela ran.

The hit man ran after her. As they were both running, he pulled out another gun, and this time, he shot her straight in the head.

On the morning of her funeral, her business was burned down, and a man who resembled Marisela's boyfriend was kidnapped off the street nearby, suffocated to death, and dumped for everyone to see.

Those searching for the disappeared disappear; those seeking justice for the murdered are murdered, until the silence swallows everything. This is all happening in a city with a Walmart and a Pizza Hut and several KFCs.

~

Marisela's eldest son, Juan, made it to the United States. I met him in a city there that he has asked me not to name, for his own safety.

"I just want for you to understand," he said, "who the real victims are in this war. It's not the cartels, it's not the police, but the people coming between [them in] this war." When you picture the seventy thousand dead, don't picture a drug dealer, or a drug user—picture Marisela. She is more representative. And it is all, he says, for nothing. "Since the war started, the cartels have got stronger. The drugs, they won't stop—if you walk the streets of Mexico and the United States, drugs are still selling on the streets, drugs are still in the schools. They haven't stopped anything at all."

"Of course the control of the drugs, the routes, is what gives them the money to pay off cops, military, federal police—everyone," Juan told me. "If you legalize drugs they are going to lose a lot of money." When they legalized alcohol in the United States, lots of gangsters were bankrupted. Would it be similar in Mexico, I ask him, if drugs were legalized? "Of course. There's going to be less sources of money." But he feared that now, the cartels' control is so deep they would simply transfer to other forms of crime.

As he spoke, I found myself thinking back to the start of this war. Harry Anslinger himself wrote in the 1960s: "Prohibition, conceived as a moral attempt to improve the American way of life, would ultimately cast the nation into a turmoil. One cannot help but think in retrospect that Prohibition, by depriving Americans of their 'vices,' only created the avenues through which organized crime gained its firm foothold."

Marisela's other son, Paul, is severely autistic, so he can't fully understand what happened. But when we met, he wanted to show me something. It is Google Maps, on a laptop. He looks obsessively at the house where he lived with Marisela. He says, staring at the screen: "It's dangerous. I can't go back. But my house is fine. Nothing's going to happen. I hope they don't burn it. I hope they don't burn my house. Everything's going to be fine over there." And he smiles, awkwardly, looking away from me.

Difficult questions continued to be asked about the case, and what it revealed about the drug war and corruption in Mexico. In November 2012, the Mexican police surrounded a house in the state of Zacatecas. Four men were shot dead. One of them was Sergio.

It is not what the family wanted. Now there will be no trial, and there will be no opportunity to ask any uncomfortable questions.

～

Before all this happened, back when she was a nurse, Marisela had something she loved to do. She would take a break from looking after her kids and working hard for them, and she would climb onto her motorbike and ride far out into the desert, with the sand and the breeze in her hair.

⁓

As I traveled across Mexico, I kept asking myself—If it is condemning sixty thousand of their countrymen to violent murder and has butchered the rule of law, why is this country fighting the drug war at all?

The most articulate analyst of the drug war I could find is Sandra Rodriguez, a journalist in her early forties. She has remained at her post as chief crime reporter for the Juárez newspaper *El Diario* even as her colleagues are murdered all around her. Over a glass of wine in a friend's apartment in Juárez, I asked her why this was happening to her city, and she said straight off: "Mexico is not deciding this policy . . . This war, this criminalization strategy, is imposed by the U.S. government."

I only really understood what she meant later, when I started researching the history of how this happened.

In the 1930s, Mexico watched its neighbor to the north launch drug prohibition, and they saw that it wouldn't work—so they decided to choose a very different path. In Mexico City, the country's leading expert on drugs was a sober-minded doctor named Leopoldo Salazar Viniegra, who ran a hospital treating drug addicts, so he was considered to be a good person to put in charge of the country's drug policy. The president appointed him chief of the Alcohol and Narcotic Service.

This Mexican started to make the same discoveries as the silenced California doctor Henry Smith Williams, at precisely the same time. He published a fourteen-year study demonstrating that cannabis does not cause psychosis, and talking about the "myth of marijuana," and when it came to other drugs, he explained: "It is impossible to break up the traffic in drugs because of the corruption of the police and also because of the wealth and political influence of some of the traffickers." Unless, that is, you resist the whole idea of the drug war. Keep drugs legal, he said. Have their sale controlled and supplied by the state, so it can regulate their use, purity, and price. This would prevent criminals from controlling the trade and so end drug trafficking and the violence and chaos it causes.

Just as Henry Smith Williams had to be crushed by Anslinger for showing there was a better alternative to prohibition, so did Leopoldo Salazar. Harry started demanding that he be fired. He instructed Mexico's representative at the League of Nations that addicts "were criminals first and addicts afterwards"—and before long, on American orders, he was forced from office.

But Mexico wouldn't surrender its convictions for long: a few years later, it resumed providing narcotics legally to addicts who needed them, in order to smother the new rise of the cartels. Harry responded by immediately cutting off the entire country's supply of opiates for pain relief in its hospitals. Mexicans literally writhed in agony. Mexico now had no choice. Its government started to fight the drug war obediently, and the U.S. Treasury's officials declared: "This is a notable victory for Harry Anslinger." The first step of Marisela's long march was taken on that day.

The U.S. government has approached Mexico with the same threat as the cartels—*plata o plomo*. Silver or lead. We can give you economic "aid" to fight this war, or we can wreck your economy if you don't. Your choice.

What is never an option is to pursue a rational drug policy.

In 2012, not longer after Marisela was killed, Michele Leonhart, the head of the U.S. Drug Enforcement Administration, said that the level of violence and death in Mexico is in fact "a sign of success in the fight against drugs."

~

On one of my final days in Juárez, I was driven out to the sand dunes that lie just beyond the city's sprawl, and I looked back over the flat, semi-abandoned city where Rubi met Sergio, and Marisela found her in the pile of pig bones.

I ran my fingers through the prickly-hot white sand and tried to picture these three teenagers I have learned so much about sitting together at a party in a Mexico that had been allowed to choose drug peace instead of drug war. Lady Gaga is playing in the background. Rubi is texting her mother, laughing. Juan, stripped of his angel wings, is chatting with Rosalio about World of Warcraft. They might, I like to think, have been friends.

PART IV

The Temple

CHAPTER 11

The Grieving Mongoose

Sometimes, after journeying to the front lines of the drug war in Brownsville or in Juárez or in Tent City, I would go back to an anonymous hotel room and ask myself one question. Why? Why are these people being shot or beheaded or cooked? What is the purpose of this war?

I looked again at the official reasons. The United Nations says the war's rationale is to build "a drug-free world—we can do it!" U.S. government officials agree, stressing that "there is no such thing as recreational drug use." So this isn't a war to stop addiction, like that in my family, or teenage drug use. It is a war to stop drug use among all humans, everywhere. All these prohibited chemicals need to be rounded up and removed from the earth. That is what we are fighting for.

I began to see this goal differently after I learned the story of the drunk elephants, the stoned water buffalo, and the grieving mongoose. They were all taught to me by a remarkable scientist in Los Angeles named Professor Ronald K. Siegel.

~

The tropical storm in Hawaii had reduced the mongoose's home to a mess of mud, and lying there, amid the dirt and the water, was the mongoose's mate— dead. Professor Siegel, a silver-haired official adviser to two U.S. presidents and to the World Health Organization, was watching this scene. The mongoose found the corpse, and it made a decision: it wanted to get out of its mind.

Two months before, the professor had planted a powerful hallucinogen called silver morning glory in the pen. The mongooses had all tried it, but they didn't seem to like it: they stumbled around disoriented for a few hours and had stayed away from it ever since. But not now. Stricken with grief, the mongoose began to chew. Before long, it had tuned in and dropped out.

It turns out this wasn't a freak occurrence in the animal kingdom. It is routine. As a young scientific researcher, Siegel had been confidently told by his supervisor that humans were the only species that seek out drugs to use for their own pleasure. But Siegel had seen cats lunging at catnip—which, he knew, contains chemicals that mimic the pheromones in a male tomcat's pee—so, he wondered, could his supervisor really be right? Given the number of species in the world, aren't there others who want to get high, or stoned, or drunk?

This question set him on a path that would take twenty-five years of his life, studying the drug-taking habits of animals from the mongooses of Hawaii to the elephants of South Africa to the grasshoppers of Soviet-occupied Czechoslovakia. It was such an implausible mission that in one marijuana field in Hawaii, he was taken hostage by the local drug dealers, because when he told them he was there to see what happened when mongooses ate marijuana, they thought it was the worst police cover story they had ever heard.

What Ronald K. Siegel discovered seems strange at first. He explains in his book *Intoxication*:

> After sampling the numbing nectar of certain orchids, bees drop to the ground in a temporary stupor, then weave back for more. Birds gorge themselves on inebriating berries, then fly with reckless abandon. Cats eagerly sniff aromatic "pleasure" plants, then play with imaginary objects. Cows that browse special range weeds will twitch, shake, and stumble back to the plants for more. Elephants purposely get drunk off fermented fruits. Snacks of "magic mushrooms" cause monkeys to sit with their heads in their hands in a posture reminiscent of Rodin's Thinker. The pursuit of intoxication by animals seems as purposeless as it is passionate. Many animals engage these plants, or their manufactured allies, despite the danger of toxic or poisonous effects.

Noah's Ark, he found, would have looked a lot like London on a Saturday night. "In every country, in almost every class of animal," Siegel explains, "I found examples of not only the accidental but the intentional use of drugs." In West Bengal, a group of 150 elephants smashed their way into a warehouse and drank a massive amount of moonshine. They got so drunk they went on a rampage and killed five people, as well as demolishing seven concrete buildings. If you give hash to male mice, they become horny and seek out females—but then they find "they can barely crawl over the females, let alone mount them," so after a little while they yawn and start licking their own penises.

In Vietnam, the water buffalo have always shunned the local opium plants. They don't like them. But when the American bombs started to fall all around them during the war, the buffalo left their normal grazing grounds, broke into the opium fields, and began to chew. They would then look a little dizzy and dulled. When they were traumatized, it seems, they wanted—like the mongoose, like us—to escape from their thoughts.

~

I kept returning to the UN pledge to build a drug-free world. There was one fact, above all others, that I kept placing next to it in my mind. It is a fact that seems at first glance both obvious and instinctively wrong. Only 10 percent of drug users have a problem with their substance. Some 90 percent of people who use a drug—the overwhelming majority—are not harmed by it. This figure comes not from a pro-legalization group, but from the United Nations Office on Drug Control, the global coordinator of the drug war. Even William Bennett, the most aggressive drug czar in U.S. history, admits: "Non-addicted users still comprise the vast bulk of our drug-involved population."

This is hard to dispute, yet hard to absorb. If we think about people we know, it seems about right—only a small minority of my friends who drink become alcoholics, and only a small minority of the people I know who use drugs on a night out have become addicts.

But if you think about how we are trained to think about drugs, this seems instinctively wrong, even dangerous. All we see in the public sphere are the casualties. The unharmed 90 percent use in private, and we rarely hear about it or see it. The damaged 10 percent, by contrast, are the only people we ever see using drugs out on the streets. The result is that the harmed 10 percent make up 100 percent of the official picture. It is as if our only picture of drinkers were a homeless person lying in a gutter necking neat gin. This impression is then reinforced with the full power of the state. For example, in 1995, the World Health Organization (WHO) conducted a massive scientific study of cocaine and its effects. They discovered that "experimental and occasional use are by far the most common types of use, and compulsive/dysfunctional [use] is far less common." The U.S. government threatened to cut off funding to the WHO unless they suppressed the report. It has never been published; we know what it says only because it was leaked.

As I write this, I feel uncomfortable. The 10 percent who are harmed are most vivid to me—they are some of the people I love most. And there is another, more complex reason why I feel awkward writing about this. For anybody who suspects that we need to reform the drug laws, there is an easier argument to make, and a harder argument to make.

The easier argument is to say that we all agree drugs are bad—it's just that drug prohibition is even worse. I have made this argument in debates in the past. Prohibition, I said, doesn't stop the problem, it simply piles another series of disasters onto the already-existing disaster of drug use. In this argument, we are all antidrug. The only difference is between prohibitionists who believe the tragedy of drug use can be dealt with by more jail cells in California and more military jeeps on the streets of Juárez, and the reformers who believe the tragedy of drug use can be dealt by moving those funds to educate kids and treat addicts.

There's a lot of truth in this argument. It is where my instincts lie. But—as I try to think through this problem—I have to admit it is only a partial truth.

Here, I think, is the harder, more honest argument. Some drug use causes horrible harm, as I know very well, but the overwhelming majority of people who use prohibited drugs do it because they get something good out of it—a fun night out dancing, the ability to meet a deadline, the chance of a good night's sleep, or insights into parts of their brain they couldn't get to on their own. For them, it's a positive experience, one that makes their lives better. That's why so many of them choose it. They are not suffering from false consciousness, or hubris. They don't need to be stopped from harming themselves, because they are not harming themselves. As the American writer Nick Gillespie puts it: "Far from our drugs controlling us, by and large we control our drugs; as with alcohol, the primary motivation is to enjoy ourselves, not to destroy ourselves . . . There is such a thing as responsible drug use, and it is the norm, not the exception."

So, although it is against my instincts, I realized I couldn't give an honest account of drug use in this book if I talked only about the harm it causes. If I'm serious about this subject, I also have to look at how drug use is deeply widespread—and mostly positive.

~

Professor Siegel's story of buzzing cows and tripping bees is, he believes, a story about us. We are an animal species. As soon as plants began to be eaten by animals for the first time—way back in prehistory, before the first human took his first steps—the plants evolved chemicals to protect themselves from being devoured and destroyed. But these chemicals could, it soon turned out, produce strange effects. In some cases, instead of poisoning the plant's predators, they—quite by accident—altered their consciousness. This is when the pleasure of getting wasted enters history.

All human children experience the impulse early on: it's why when you were little you would spin around and around, or hold your breath to get a head rush. You knew it would make you sick, but your desire to change your consciousness a little—to experience a new and unfamiliar rush—outweighed your aversion to nausea.

There has never been a society in which humans didn't serially seek out these sensations. High in the Andes in 2000 B.C., they were making pipes through which they smoked hallucinogenic herbs. Ovid said drug-induced ecstasy was a divine gift. The Chinese were cultivating opium by A.D. 700. Hallucinogens and chemicals caused by burning cannabis were found in clay pipe fragments from William Shakespeare's house. George Washington insisted that American soldiers be given whiskey every day as part of their rations.

"The ubiquity of drug use is so striking," the physician Andrew Weil concludes, that "it must represent a basic human appetite." Professor Siegel claims the desire to alter our consciousness is "the fourth drive" in all human minds, alongside the desire to eat, drink, and have sex—and it is "biologically inevitable." It provides us with moments of release and relief.

~

Thousands of people were streaming in to a ten-day festival in September where they were planning—after a long burst of hard work—to find some chemical release, relaxation, and revelry. They found drugs passed around the crowd freely, to anybody who wanted them. Everyone who took them soon felt an incredible surge of ecstasy. Then came the vivid, startling hallucinations. You suddenly felt, as one user put it, something that was "new, astonishing, irrational to rational cognition."

Some people came back every year because they loved this experience so much. As the crowd thronged and yelled and sang, it became clear it was an extraordinary mix of human beings. There were farmers who had just finished their harvest, and some of the biggest celebrities around. Their names—over the years—included Sophocles, Aristotle, Plato, and Cicero.

The annual ritual in the Temple at Eleusis, eighteen kilometers northwest of Athens, was a drug party on a vast scale. It happened every year for two thousand years, and anybody who spoke the Greek language was free to come. Harry Anslinger said that drug use represents "nothing less than an assault on the foundations of Western civilization," but here, at the actual foundations of Western civilization, drug use was ritualized and celebrated.

I first discovered this fact by reading the work of the British critic Stuart Walton in a brilliant book called *Out of It*, and then I followed up with some of his sources, which include the work of Professor R. Gordon Wasson, Professor Carl Ruck, and other writers.

Everyone who attended the Eleusinian mysteries was sworn to secrecy about what happened there, so our knowledge is based on scraps of information that were recorded in its final years, as it was being suppressed. We do know that a special cup containing a mysterious chemical brew of hallucinogens would be passed around the crowd, and a scientific study years later seemed to prove it contained a molecular relative of LSD taken from a fungus that infested cereal crops and caused hallucinations. The chemical contents of this cup were carefully guarded for the rest of the year. The drugs were legal—indeed, this drug use was arranged by public officials—and regulated. You could use them, but only in the designated temple for those ten days. One day in 415 B.C., a partygoing general named Alcibiades smuggled some of the mystery drug out and took it home for his friends to use at their parties. Walton writes: "Caught in possession with intent to supply, he was the first drug criminal."

But while it was a crime away from the Temple and other confined spaces, it was a glory within it. According to these accounts, it was Studio 54 spliced with St. Peter's Basilica—revelry with religious reverence.

They believed the drugs brought them closer to the gods, or even made it possible for them to become gods themselves. The classicist Dr. D.C.A. Hillman wrote that the "founding fathers" of the Western world

> were drug users, plain and simple: they grew the stuff, they sold the stuff, and more important, they used the stuff . . . The ancient

> world didn't have a Nancy Reagan, it didn't wage a billion-dollar
> drug war, it didn't imprison people who used drugs, and it didn't
> embrace sobriety as a virtue. It indulged . . . and from this world
> in which drugs were a universally accepted part of life sprang art,
> literature, science, and philosophy . . . The West would not have
> survived without these so-called junkies and drug dealers.

There was some political grumbling for years that women were behaving too freely during their trances, but this annual festival ended only when the drug party crashed into Christianity. The early Christians wanted there to be one route to ecstasy, and one route only—through prayer to their God. You shouldn't feel anything that profound or pleasurable except in our ceremonies at our churches. The first tugs towards prohibition were about power, and purity of belief. If you are going to have one God and one Church, you need to stop experiences that make people feel that they can approach God on their own. It is no coincidence that when new drugs come along, humans often use religious words to describe them, like ecstasy. They are often competing for the same brain space—our sense of awe and joy.

So when the emperor Constantine converted to Christianity and brought the Empire with him, the rituals at the Temple at Eleusis were doomed. They were branded a cult and shut down by force. The new Christianity would promote wine only in tiny sips. Intoxication had to be sparing. This "forcible repression by Christianity," Walton explains, "represents the beginning of systematic repression of the intoxication impulse in the lives of Western citizens."

Yet in every generation after, some humans would try to rebuild their own Temple at Eleusis—in their own minds, and wherever they could clear a space free of local Anslingers.

Harry Anslinger, it turns out, represented a trend running right back to the ancient world.

When Sigmund Freud first suggested that everybody has elaborate sexual fantasies, that it is as natural as breathing, he was dismissed as a pervert and lunatic. People wanted to believe that sexual fantasy was something that happened in other people—filthy people, dirty people. They took the parts of their subconscious that generated these wet dreams and daydreams and projected them onto somebody else, the depraved people Over There, who had to be stopped. Stuart Walton and the philosopher Terence McKenna both write that we are at this stage with our equally universal desire to seek out altered mental states. McKenna explains: "We are discovering that human beings are creatures of chemical habit with the same horrified disbelief as when the Victorians discovered that humans are creatures of sexual fantasy and obsession."

Just as we are rescuing the sex drive from our subconscious and from shame, so we need to take the intoxication drive out into the open where it can breathe. Stuart Walton calls for a whole new field of human knowledge called "intoxicology." He writes: "Intoxication plays, or has played, a part in the lives of virtually everybody who has ever lived . . . To seek to deny it is not only futile; it is a dereliction of an entirely constitutive part of who we are."

~

After twenty-five years of watching stoned mice, drunken elephants, and tripping mongooses, Ronald K. Siegel tells me he suspects he has learned something about this. "We're not so different from the other animal lifeforms on this planet," he says.

When he sees people raging against all drug use, he is puzzled. "They're denying their own chemistry," he says. "The brain produces endorphins. When does it produce endorphins? In stress, and in pain. What are endorphins? They are morphine-like compounds. It's a natural occurrence in the brain that makes them feel good . . . People feel euphoric sometimes. These are chemical changes—the same kind of chemical changes, with the same molecular structures, that these plants [we use to make our drugs] are producing . . . We're all producing the same stuff."

Indeed, he continues, "the experience you have in orgasm is partially chemical—it's a drug. So people deny they want this? Come on! . . . It's fun. It's enjoyable. And it's chemical. That's intoxication." He seems for a moment to think back over all the animals guzzling drugs he has watched over all these years. "I don't see," he says, "any difference in where the chemical came from."

This is in us. It is in our brains. It is part of who we are.

But this leaves us with another mystery. If the drive to get intoxicated is in all of us, and if 90 percent of people can use drugs without becoming addicted, what is happening with the 10 percent who can't? What is different about them? It is a question I had been circling all my life. As I looked for experts who might be able to answer this question, I discovered that a disproportionate number of them seemed to be clustered together—in just a few blocks of the Downtown Eastside of Vancouver, in Canada.

CHAPTER 12

Terminal City

Ever since I was a child, I have been asking myself: What causes addiction? What *is* addiction? I had heard many explanations over the years. It's a moral failing. It's a disease. It's carried in the genes. I believed this was, ultimately, a mystery—but when I arrived in Canada, I learned that a small band of dissident scientists has been uncovering the answers to my questions, almost unnoticed, for several decades now.

Their findings were so radically different from anything I had been told before that it took some time to absorb what they were really saying.

The story of how they came to their discoveries began in the last days of the Holocaust, when a Jewish mother smuggled her baby out of a ghetto.

Judith Lovi awoke from a dream that her parents were being murdered, to find that her breast milk had dried up. Her four-month-old baby, Gabor, was crying. He cried all the time. She had grown up as the daughter of a wealthy doctor, but now she was alone, crammed into a building with over a thousand people, all infested with lice, and there was shit smeared on the floor because the toilets were overflowing.

She knew she was not allowed out onto the streets until the afternoon, because when you were a Jew in the Budapest ghetto in 1944, walking out your door any earlier could get you shot. By then, the only milk she could buy for her baby would be sour.

She had married Andor just a few months ago, but now he was gone.

He had been taken as a forced laborer. He might have been digging ditches for the Hungarian army or he might have been dead. She had no way of knowing. The only reason she woke up in the morning—the only reason she went on—was to look after her son, in the hope she could somehow get him out. But she doubted it. She believed that, at the age of twenty-four, she was going to be killed, along with her child.

Judith was right about her parents: at just about that time, they were being murdered. The last time she had seen them was on a train platform in Budapest. She had wanted to go back to their town with them, but her father told her, by some instinct, not to leave the city. All around them, 80 percent of the country's Jews were being rounded up and exterminated with remarkable efficiency. Her parents and sister were seized after they got home and sent to Auschwitz. As the Red Army troops began to besiege Budapest, the Nazis started taking Jews from the ghetto down to the river and shooting them outright.

Judith called the doctor because she was afraid that Gabor's endless crying meant he was sick. "I'll come, of course," the doctor told her, "but I should tell you—all my Jewish babies are crying."

Many years and many thousands of miles from there, the memory of these infant screams would help Gabor—once he had become a doctor himself—to make a crucial discovery about the nature of addiction. He asked himself: How did the Jewish babies know they were in terrible danger? Why did they scream?

One day, Judith noticed that another woman in the ghetto was being visited by a Christian friend. She thrust Gabor at him and begged: Get him out of here. She gave this anonymous Christian the address of a place outside the ghetto where her friend was hiding, and she begged him to take her child there.

Without her baby, Judith was entirely alone, but she believed he, at least, would survive. Three weeks later, the Russian army liberated Budapest from the Nazis, and she quickly reclaimed her child. A year after that, she found Andor, weighing just ninety pounds and wearing a German army uniform because it was the only clothing he could find. But it turned out his experience—of profound danger, of separation from his mother at a crucial moment—shaped the brain of baby Gabor in ways that would affect him for the rest of his life.

When Gabor was fifteen, his family finally made it out of Europe, to Vancouver, the farthest dot on the map of distant North America. There, Gabor was going to find a different kind of ghetto—and in it, two people who, along with him, would begin to solve the mystery of how you make an addict.

～

I knew what caused addiction before I even left London. We all do. As a culture, we have a story about how addiction works, and it's a good one. It says that some substances are so chemically powerful that if you use them enough, they will hijack your brain. They will change your neurochemistry. They will give you a brain disease. After that, you will need the drug physically. So if you or I or the next ten people you pass on the street were to use an addictive drug every day for the next month, on day thirty, we'd all be addicts. Addiction, then, is the result of repeated exposure to certain very powerful chemicals.

When I looked at the people I love who have become addicts, that is what I believed had happened to them.

This model of addiction had been proven through animal experiments. Put a rat alone in a cage and give it unlimited quantities of cocaine, and nine times out of ten, it will use so much and so compulsively that it will kill itself. Harry Anslinger and Henry Smith Williams agreed on very little, but they did agree on this. Anslinger thought the chemicals hooked you forever so you should be shut away; Smith Williams thought the chemicals hooked you forever so you should be given them by doctors forever. One was cruel and the other compassionate, but they were both sure that chemicals are the cause of the addicts' wound. The fancy term for this is "the pharmaceutical theory of addiction."

I did not realize there was another theory—with very different premises—until I happened across a book called *In the Realm of Hungry Ghosts*, written by Gabor Maté. I found its ideas confusing at first, but then they made me think. I realized then that I had to go to meet this man and get to know him. This account is based on my interviews with him, sitting in on his training sessions, and his writings, and on interviewing his former colleagues and patients.

When I first saw Gabor, it was at one of his training sessions for people who work with addicts. He is a slim man with hollow cheeks. He has olive skin and a low voice in which he speaks quickly, in perfectly formed sentences. There is—I noticed at once—an air of sadness about him. As he guided me through his life, I began to understand why.

～

Gabor had been a successful family doctor for years, he explained to me, when he applied for a job on the Downtown Eastside of Vancouver in 1998. To many people this decision was puzzling. These ten blocks had one of the highest death rates in the developed world. The scene in this neighborhood is notorious to Vancouverites: against every charred or boarded-up building lean glassy-eyed addicts. On a typical day, some are passed out; others are looking around them very fast, as if trying to spot a buzzing insect with a nasty sting.

As I walked around, I tried to picture it as it must have been when Gabor first came here. There is an insistent rhythmic chant on the streets as you walk past dealers: "Rock? Rock?" "Powder?" "Rock? Rock?" "Powder?" Women with hollow faces and painted red lips pace nervously, offering a date to passing cars. Oversized pigeons peck around them.

The glamorous names of the hotels here—the Balmoral, for example, gets its title from a castle belonging to the queen of England—seemed to mock the people who live in the tiny single room occupancies into which the hotels have been carved, in a last gasp, to suck up the thin dust of government housing assistance. Overdose and hepatitis C seem to come with these rooms, the way minibars do in other hotels. The streets were cluttered with bottles of mouthwash and hand sanitizer that had been swigged by alcoholics who wanted the maximum possible intoxication for the lowest possible price. The police appeared periodically to pluck out a person or two to jail, then they vanished. The sea breeze wafted through indifferently.

This neighborhood is the end of the line in the city at the end of the line of North America—the terminus of Terminal City. There is nowhere left on the continent to head after here.

There are ghosts of what the Downtown Eastside used to be in the names of these buildings. On one street there is the Loggers' Social Club, a reminder that this was once the place where workingmen would come after chopping down the forests. The logged trees would be placed on skids and dragged through here to be put on the train to travel across America, so this was known as Skid Row: the first and the original. The men would stay, flush with money, for a month or two of partying, and then vanish again. But there came a time when they had cut down all the trees. The party continued, for a while, as it slowly soured.

The businesses that serviced the loggers vanished one by one. The Woodward's department store used to be the Macy's of Vancouver; by the time Gabor arrived, it had become an echoing concrete husk, and there were men injecting women straight in the jugular vein out in the open air of the alleys. The Vancouver writer Charles Demers explains: "People in Vancouver talk about the Downtown Eastside the way that people throughout the Western world talk about Africa. Some call for apolitical charity and aid; others call for armed intervention. Everyone agrees it's a problem to be dealt with, filled with people who are their own worst enemies and whose lives are a mess."

What good, people wondered, could a doctor do here? But Gabor gave up his practice as a family doctor and went to work with the Portland Hotel Society, a local charity that had begun an experiment that was regarded by the local drug warriors as insane. Routinely in this neighborhood—and across North America—the moment the authorities found out you were an addict, they would throw you out of public housing and cut you off from all social support. Get clean, they would say, or you will never have a home again. Often, even the homeless shelters would then turn you away.

A young nurse named Liz Evans working in the Crisis Psychiatric Unit at the local hospital saw the results of this policy coming through her doors the whole time. She would look across her ward, and see it was full of people who had been forced onto the streets and were only deteriorating further. They were offered a few pills to cope with their disturbance—but nothing to help them deal with the fact their lives had fallen apart.

So she decided to pioneer a totally different approach. Her nonprofit took over a hotel and turned it into a place for the people who could not be housed anywhere else—the most chronic addicts and most severely mentally ill people. Liz was put in charge, with a commitment to the residents that they would never be kicked out or lectured to. Instead, they would be offered a room of their own, and—whenever they wanted it— staff who would sit with them, and listen to them, and try to love them. That was all.

"Our method is—be a human being with other human beings," Liz tells me. "Be there for them. Don't judge. Don't tell them how to live their fricking life. Just be in their life. Be a nice, solid presence. Somebody who isn't going to bow and bend . . . and walk away. Who's not going to abandon them. Who's not going to leave. Who's not going to kick them out."

The almost universal reaction was that this is mad. Surely the addicts will just drink or drug themselves to death faster if you give them a place to do it, with no critical judgment? One doctor told Liz a better solution would be to drop a bomb on the Portland Hotel and kill everyone in it.

But Gabor wanted to be part of this experiment. At the Portland, he was tasked by Liz with doing everything from lancing abscesses to prescribing psychiatric medications. But the core of his work was something more radical. He wanted to listen to the hard-core addicts here—to let them talk about their feelings.

These are people, he soon discovered, who have spent their lives being chased away or chastised. Most of them have never sat down with a person who wanted to listen to their life story sympathetically. Authority figures with questions have, to them, only ever been people who will take something away or inflict pain. Most of the users, then, were critical. They found it hard to believe they were being given a place to live and the offer of help. What's the trick? Where's the scam? When is the crackdown coming?

Gabor was divided between his desire to listen to the addicts and his instinctive revulsion toward them. Out in the chaos of the streets, he thought the addicts looked like ghoulish extras in a Fellini film. Alone in his office, he still felt judgmental at times. Why are they doing this to themselves? Why would somebody be so foolish? "I had a somewhat moralistic attitude towards them," he says.

As he explains in his book, one of the residents who came to talk to Gabor, a thirty-six-year-old man named Carl, began over time to open up. He had spent his childhood shunted from one foster home to another, unwanted. When he got hyperactive, one set of foster parents tied him into a chair in a dark room. When he swore, they poured dishwashing liquid into his mouth. Carl learned from them that you can't ever express your anger without being punished; so when he felt fury, he took out a knife and started cutting into his own foot. As Gabor wrote later, Carl revealed this in a shamed crouch: he expected to be condemned, just as everyone had always condemned him.

Gabor heard a variant of this story over and over again. The addicts had been made to feel disgusting and ashamed all their lives—and only the drug took this sense away. "The first time I did heroin," one woman told him, "it felt like a warm, soft hug."

After a while, Gabor started to see patterns in the psyches of the people at the Portland. As he spoke, I found myself thinking about the addicts I had written about so far in this story: Billie Holiday, Chino's mother Deborah, Marcia Powell cooked in her cage. What did they all have in common? Horribly disturbed childhoods, marked by violence, sexual assault, or both.

Gabor was finding that virtually all his patients fit this description.

And then it occurred to him. Could it be that these hard-core addicts were all terribly damaged *before* they found their drugs? What if the discovery of drugs wasn't the earthquake in their life, but only one of the aftershocks?

Gabor started to pore over a series of scientific studies, and he noticed something striking.

All over the Western world, people are being given very powerful opiates every day, legally. If you have been badly injured in a car crash, or had a hip replacement, or had significant dental surgery, you have probably been given opiates, perhaps for quite a long time. These are pretty much the same opiates taken by Gabor's patients (except yours didn't have the contaminants added by drug dealers). So if the pharmaceutical theory of addiction is right—if the drugs are so chemically powerful they hijack your brain—then it's obvious what should happen. You should, at the end of your treatment, be an addict. When you are discharged from the hospital, you should be looking to score on the streets, because now you need your fix.

Yet you will have noticed something. You didn't become addicted.

You are not alone. The *Canadian Journal of Medicine* reviewed the best academic research into people who had received opiates from doctors following surgery. It found, Gabor writes, that "there was no significant risk of addiction, a finding common to all studies that examine the relationship between addiction and the use of narcotics for pain relief."

This happens in every city every day, and it passes mostly unnoticed.

You can take the same drugs as an addict for long periods of time, and not become addicted at all. And at the same time, you can take no drugs whatsoever—and become just as severe an addict. If that sounds odd, go to any meeting of Gamblers Anonymous in your town this evening. Listen to their stories. Early in this journey, I went to sit in—with the permission of everyone there—on a Gamblers Anonymous meeting at the Problem Gambling Center in Las Vegas. I found—just like you will—that they were indistinguishable from those of alcoholics or heroin addicts in their essentials. But you don't inject a deck of cards into your veins; you don't snort a roulette wheel.

How can we begin to make sense of this? After thinking about it deeply, Gabor came to suspect that it means, as he told me, "nothing is addictive in itself. It's always a combination of a potentially addictive substance or behavior and a susceptible individual. So the question we need to keep asking is—What creates the susceptibility?"

Since the drug alone can't explain the addiction, there is clearly an additional ingredient, or several—things that are present in some people but not in others.

Gabor began to read about a group of American scientists who had carried out something called the Adverse Childhood Experiences Study. It is the most detailed research ever conducted into the long-term effects of early childhood trauma. It looked at ten different terrible things that can happen to a kid, from physical abuse to sexual abuse to the death of a parent, to track how it shapes that child over their lifetime.

These scientists discovered that for each traumatic event that happened to a child, they were two to four times more likely to grow up to be an addicted adult. Nearly two-thirds of injection drug use, they found, is the product of childhood trauma. This is a correlation so strong the scientists said it is "of an order of magnitude rarely seen in epidemiology or public health." It means that child abuse is as likely to cause drug addiction as obesity is to cause heart disease.

Another long-term study, published in *American Psychologist*, followed kids from the age of five until they were eighteen, to figure out how much the quality of your parenting while a child affects your drug use as you get older. When the children were still small, the scientists gave them a task to carry out with their parents—like piling up building blocks—and then they watched how well the parents helped and encouraged them through a one-way mirror. They wrote down which kids had parents who were loving and supportive, and which had parents who were disengaged or nasty to them. It turned out the kids whose parents had been either indifferent or cruel were dramatically more likely to heavily use drugs than the others. They had grown up, they found, less able to form loving relationships, and so they felt more angry and distressed and impulsive a lot of the time.

If we can figure out at the age of five which kids are going to be addicts and which ones aren't, that tells us something fundamental about drug addiction. "Their relative maladjustment," the study found, "precedes the initiation of drug use." Indeed, "Problem drug use is a symptom, not a cause, of personal and social maladjustment."

This is one reason why Dr Vincent Felitti—one of the key figures in the Adverse Childhood Experiences Survey—concluded, as Gabor writes, that "the basic cause of addiction is predominantly experience-dependent during childhood, and not substance-dependent. The current conception of addiction is ill-founded." This fact forces us to radically reconsider many of the stories we are told about drug epidemics—including, I was to learn later, the prescription drug epidemic in the United States.

~

Back in Harlem, many years before, Billie Holiday had said: "I don't know much about psychology and all that, but I do know that there are things that can happen to you during early childhood which can influence your whole life."

Even Harry Anslinger had noticed the connection with addiction. Addicts, he noted, often "grow up in homes that are not homes, with parents that are not parents, [so] they seek escape. Girl or boy, this is a familiar pattern."

~

But why would childhood trauma make you so much more likely to grow into an addicted adult? I sit for hours, day after day, with Liz Evans, the nurse who established the Portland Hotel Society. She has spent over twenty years sitting with the most hard-core addicts on the Downtown Eastside. She talks to them, and holds them, and sits up all through the night with them. She asked herself this question more times than she can count. And then, finally, in a café, she told me about one night, about a year after she started at the Portland, when she fully made the connection.

One of the Portland's residents at that time was an aboriginal woman whom I will call Hannah, because Liz asked me not to use her real name. (This is one of only three places in this book where I have changed a detail to protect somebody's identity; all are indicated in the text.) She was a tiny thirty-eight-year-old, chronically addicted to heroin and alcohol, and every morning she would stumble down into the hotel lobby, vomit into the trash can, and then stagger out to sell her body for her next fix. Hannah was drawn to violent men who would beat the shit out of her, and she would often fly into drunken rages and hurl things out her window. One day, she threw an entire bike down onto the street.

Liz refused to throw her out. Instead, she had Plexiglas screwed onto her window so she couldn't open it.

Liz had read Hannah's files, dating back to when she was a child. She had been removed from her reservation and, like a lot of Native American (or First Nations, as they are known in Canada) kids, shunted from one foster family to another. The police eventually found her, emaciated, locked in a room, where it turned out she had been shut away from the age of seven to eleven, fed nothing but a liquid diet, because one of her foster families had claimed she had a disease and this was the only cure. She tried to cut her own throat for the first time when she was thirteen. Liz would try to bring up the subject of her childhood with her sometimes, but Hannah would only say it "wasn't great," and then move on.

One night, Hannah came back to the Portland shaking, with blood seeping from a blow to her head. "I remember picking her up and holding her in my arms like a little child" and walking her to her room, Liz told me. Hannah stammered that she had been beaten and raped. "And I remember just listening to her say to me, over and over again, 'It's my fault. I deserve this. It's my fault. I'm a bad person.'" And on the little table beside Hannah, there was her alcohol, and her heroin, and a needle. And Liz—who has never wanted to use drugs—looked at them and looked at Hannah and thought: "Which of these things on your bedside table can I give you to take your pain away?"

"And that was the moment I understood what addiction did for people," she tells me. "It was like, in an instant, I made a connection to those black moments in my life where I felt that way . . . when I wanted to die, when I felt that I was a bad person." The survivors of childhood trauma are often left with that sense of self-hatred all their lives, Liz saw now, and that is why so many of them turn to the strongest anesthetic they can find. It's not a spasm of irrationality. It meets a need. It takes away the pain, for a while.

As Liz told me this, I thought about how fiercely critical I had been of the people I love for their addictions over the years, and I realized I was crying.

Long before, one of Billie Holiday's friends, Memry Midgett, told an interviewer: "The reason for her being an addict was because she had a tremendously poor threshold of pain." Another of her friends, Michelle Wallace, said: "People think sometimes people use drugs because they're bad or evil. Sometimes . . . the softest people use drugs, because they can't take the pain."

This helps, I realize, to explain the previously mysterious gap between the 10 percent of drug users who sink into addiction and the 90 percent who don't. A man named Bud Osborn, who was helped to recover from his heroin addiction by Gabor, tells me: "The childhood trauma makes you feel bad about everything. Bad about your family, bad about life," he said. "And then when you take drugs, they make you feel good about your life, about yourself, about being in the world . . . [People] wonder—why do [addicts] keep doing it? Because it makes them feel good, and the rest of their life doesn't make them feel good."

~

Some people, after absorbing all this, would develop an idealized or sanitized picture of addicts. This was not an option at the Portland Hotel Society.

Gabor was often spat at and told to fuck off. The staff there have had shit—literal shit—flung into their faces. One of Gabor's patients, Ralph, was a middle-aged coke addict with a dyed Mohawk and a Hitler mustache. He was a Nazi, and he taunted Gabor by muttering *"Arbeit macht frei."* When Gabor explained his grandfather died in a death camp where those words were displayed over the gates, Ralph said his grandfather had it coming.

Sometimes Gabor snapped. One day he said to me, "I'm lancing an abscess on somebody and [the patient] keeps attacking me verbally and I totally lose it. In the end, I'm waving this bloody scalpel around. I wasn't hurting anybody with it, but emotionally I lost it. That happened a number of times. In those moments you don't think—you just emote. Frustration. Anger. Judgment."

He understood how these emotions intrude on the public debate about addicts because even he, after all he has uncovered, couldn't scour them out of himself. But, he added, "Once I calmed down, shame comes into it, and I want to apologize."

Some days, Ralph was quiet and reflective and recited passages of Goethe's poetry to Gabor. The next week, he was back to muttering "Heil Hitler."

~

Gabor felt there was much more to investigate about addiction, but he was distracted by something he didn't like to discuss. He hid it from everyone, even his wife.

Quite often, he would be in the middle of his medical duties when he would feel an overpowering urge. It was a compulsion that forced him to drop everything. He would rush to music stores and compulsively spend hundreds of dollars on CDs. Usually, he didn't even listen to them: he simply stashed them. This might sound harmless, until you hear that he was in the middle of delivering a baby one time when he felt the compulsion and had to run away to binge on CD buying. When his kids were still small, he abandoned them in public places to rush away to buy music. Why was he doing this? He didn't understand it. He only knew that, as he would write later, "I lose myself when caught in one of my addictive spirals. Gradually I feel an ebbing of moral strength and experience myself as hollow. Emptiness stares out from behind my eyes." At times, it made him feel blackly depressed; at times he felt suicidal.

Yet once Gabor learned that there was a connection between traumatic early childhoods and compulsive behaviors, he began to think about what the doctor told his mother all those years ago: "All my Jewish babies are crying."

The babies obviously couldn't know that a genocide was taking place, but they did know, on some level, that their mothers were distraught and not able to meet their needs. His own mother, he says, "was stressed, depressed. She said the only reason she got out of bed was to look after me. So I saved her life. It's a hell of a responsibility for a four-month-old, to save his mother's life . . . She carried tremendous pain . . . tremendous grief, and as an infant, you absorb all that." So he developed differently from a baby whose mother was able to offer calm and consistent love. Now, as an adult, he found himself unable to control himself at moments of stress. For him, the outlet was to buy music. He realized that when he was a small child, there was one thing that relaxed his mother, and so, in turn, relaxed him. She would listen to music. Now it was the thing he tried to buy and hoard, as if it held the secret key to being calm.

He saw a similar dynamic at the Portland, only the residents' experiences were "not like my childhood. They're much worse," he tells me. "While the historical circumstances might be more horrifying in my case, the actual personal experience was far more traumatic in the case of my clients." He says this is "because I wasn't traumatized by my parents' psychological dysfunctions . . . The trauma I sustained was the trauma they sustained . . . It came from the outside. But once my parents were united, we had a stable family life. I was not abused . . . It's nothing like being sexually abused by your father or your mother. It's nothing like being ignored by your addicted parents who are out carousing while you are left alone."

Gabor's trauma was mild, so his addiction was mild: he can bear to be present in the world most of the time. His patients' trauma was extreme, so their addiction is extreme: they can bear to be present in the world very little of the time. But—crucially—in both cases, something had gone askew, he explains, "before the use of mind-altering substances begins."

~

I find myself walking in circles through the Downtown Eastside after one of my conversations with Gabor, past addicts who are half collapsed on the street. They are wearing the exaggerated stage makeup of the street prostitute, or hawking drugs or random items they have discovered in dumpsters—old VHS tapes and half-broken shoes. They shout and holler, at me, and at the world.

I picture the look of judgment on the faces of people who stumble into this neighborhood by mistake. I can see them now. The people from stable families, who glance at addicts and shake their heads and say, "I would never do that to myself." I feel an urge stop them and wave Gabor's statistics in their face and say—Don't you see? You wouldn't do this to yourself because you don't have to. You never had to learn to cope with more pain than you could bear. You might as well look at somebody who had their legs amputated in a car crash and declare: "Well, I would never have *my* legs cut off." No. You haven't been in a car crash. These addicts— they have been in car crashes of the soul.

And then, just as I am rehearsing this self-righteous lecture in my mind, I notice that I, too, am hurrying past the street addicts, with a look on my face that seems a lot like—what? Fear? Disgust? Superiority? Recognition?

~

All this information had been available in scattered sources before Gabor began to write about it. But, he told me, "What absolutely surprised me was that all this information hadn't been brought together before. Nobody had brought together childhood trauma, brain development, and the stories of the addicts that we work with, to provide a coherent theory of addiction."

But—as Gabor is the first to point out—even with these discoveries, our picture is still incomplete. It plainly cannot be the case that all addicts were treated appallingly as kids. It is an important factor in addiction— but it is not enough. As Gabor worked at the Portland, not far away, on another part of the Downtown Eastside, another man was working, a professor named Bruce Alexander. He agreed with Gabor's analysis about childhood trauma, but he was trying to answer this further question.

Some people do not have traumatic childhoods, yet they still become addicts. What, he wanted to know, is going on with them?

~

As I sat with Gabor over dinner in a Greek restaurant near the end of my time with him, I kept thinking: How should the facts he has uncovered change the way we think about the drug war?

He has shown that the core of addiction doesn't lie in what you swallow or inject—it's in the pain you feel in your head. Yet we have built a system that thinks we will stop addicts by *increasing* their pain. "If I had to design a system that was intended to keep people addicted, I'd design exactly the system that we have right now," Gabor would tell me. "I'd attack people, and ostracize them." He has seen that "the more you stress people, the more they're going to use. The more you de-stress people, the less they're going to use. So to create a system where you ostracize and marginalize and criminalize people, and force them to live in poverty with disease, you are basically guaranteeing they will stay at it."

"If negative consequences led people to transformation then I wouldn't have a single patient left," he says, "because they've experienced every negative consequence in the book. Being jailed. Being beaten up. Being traumatized. Being hurt. HIV. Hepatitis C. Poverty." Gabor looks at me, his eyes sagging a little, as if picturing it all. "What haven't they suffered yet?"

But what if we replaced this war on addicts with a war on the causes of addiction?

Gabor says that since child neglect and abuse is a major cause of addiction, if we were serious about reducing the number of addicts, we would start "at the first prenatal visit, because already the stresses on the pregnant woman will have an impact on the potentially addictive propensity of the child." We would identify the mothers who are most stressed and least able to cope, and we would give them extensive care and support and coaching in how to properly bond with their child.

Then, after birth, we would keep carefully identifying mothers who are having problems bonding with their babies and offer them wrap-around care. We would be highly vigilant for the parents who still can't provide a safe home, or who become abusive, and find an alternative loving home for the child if we had to. These are approaches that would, over time, reduce addiction, instead of deepening it, as our current strategy does. Of course, services to help mothers and vulnerable kids already exist in all developed societies, but outside Scandinavia, they are usually threadbare and chronically underfunded. Wouldn't it be better to spend our money on rescuing kids before they become addicts than on jailing them after we have failed?

Of all the ideas I have heard, this seems to me to be the one that would have been most likely to save the life of Chino's mother, and Marcia Powell, and Billie Holiday. It sounds persuasive, I tell Gabor. But what about once an adult addict has already been created? What can we do for them?

For the last ten years of her life, Hannah—the addict who had been removed from her reservation and then starved in a room for three years as a girl—lived in her own suite at the Portland Hotel Society, where she was surrounded by people like Liz and Gabor who listened to her and reassured her she would never be cast out again.

Liz helped her to find the family she had left behind on the reservation all those years ago. Her family came to visit her in her own room at the Portland, and she cooked for them, and she felt proud. When Hannah would fall into her furies and call herself a worthless junkie, Liz said to her: "You are an amazing human being . . . You show more resilience and tenacity and strength than any person I know . . . You're strong. You're beautiful. Can you tell yourself today you did an amazing job surviving?"

Hannah never stopped seeking out abusive relationships, and she never stopped drinking, although over time she did transfer from heroin to methadone. She had contracted the HIV virus back when there were no needle exchanges in the city, and so she died in the hotel of AIDS at the age of forty-eight. Because of the Portland, she did not die alone. She was surrounded by people who loved her and admired her.

To the prohibitionists, Hannah is a failure, because she continued using drugs. To the Portland, she was a success, because she knew she was loved.

~

One day, a very senior government minister came to visit the safe injection rooms, and to meet the addicts. He asked Liz: "What percentage of people who use this place would you consider to be write-offs?"

She paused and looked at him, trying to figure out how to tell him that the answer is none.

CHAPTER 13

Batman's Bad Call

Bruce Alexander received his first lesson about addiction from Batman. As a small kid, he grew up on a series of military bases of the United States, where his father was a training officer. One day, he was reading a comic in which a group of crooks beat up a junkie while Batman hid behind a building, watching, impassive.

"Dad," Bruce asked, "why would Batman just stand there while they're beating this junkie to a pulp? Isn't it Batman's job to stop criminals?"

"Well, really, no one cares if they beat a junkie to a pulp," his dad replied, "because they're worthless human beings."

Bruce believed it. Yet as an adult, on the streets of the Downtown Eastside, he was going to make two of the most important breakthroughs about addiction in the twentieth century—ones that would overturn everything we have been taught.

I first heard about Bruce years ago when I was studying psychology at Cambridge University, and I read about an experiment he had conducted on rats. At first, it sounded quirky and intriguing, nothing more—but I found that his experiment kept coming into my mind at unexpected moments for years and years. It was only when I decided to begin this journey into the drug war that I resolved to dig deeper.

I met Bruce in the café on the first floor of the library in Downtown Eastside. It is a Spartan place with hard chairs and track lighting, and almost everybody there that fall day seemed to be homeless addicts, warming themselves with weak coffee. Bruce looked a little incongruous there at first: he is a genial gray-haired man in his sixties who looks like both the professor he is, and the Canadian he has become. He wore a smart sweater and a friendly smile. Soon, it became clear to me that my first-glance impression was wrong: he does belong here. Not long after we started talking, we were interrupted by an addict who has known him for years—and knew about his work and what it meant for her. After she had gone, he began—then, and over several subsequent interviews—to tell me the story of his experiment. It was going to change how I thought— about addiction, about some of the people closest to me, and about the world.

~

In the early 1970s, Bruce was a young professor of psychology at Simon Fraser University in British Columbia, Canada. He was told by the faculty to teach a course called Social Issues that nobody else wanted to bother with. He knew the biggest social issues of the day were the Vietnam War and heroin addiction, and he couldn't go to Saigon, so he went to the Downtown Eastside. He headed there wearily, to learn just enough to explain it to his students, and no more. The same parade of addicts that Gabor would see years later passed before him on the streets, and he thought of them just as Batman taught him to—as zombies whose minds have contracted to the single drooling dimension of their drug.

Since Bruce was trained in family therapy, he figured that the best way to bring himself up to speed would be to provide counseling to addicts at a local treatment agency.

One of his first patients was Santa Claus. Every Christmas, this man was employed at the local shopping mall, where he would arrive in a helicopter, climb down a rope ladder, ho-ho-ho at the local children, use some smack backstage, and then promise to grant their wishes. Bruce persuaded Santa Claus to invite his parents in for family therapy, since behind the beard and the reindeer, he was only twenty-three. The parents were terrified their son would die; the son felt he couldn't stop. And one day, they were discussing his work as a smacked-out Santa, and they all began to laugh helplessly.

Something about this pricked at Bruce. He had been taught to believe addicts were incapable of self-reflection—yet this young man could see the absurdity of his situation clearly. There was a humanity in this laughter that Bruce had not expected to hear.

He continued to interview addicts in depth. Like Gabor, he could see that childhood trauma was a crucial factor. But he was also discovering facts that were deeply confusing to him and, at first glance, to everyone.

There were big chunks of time in the 1970s in which the Canadian police managed to blockade the port of Vancouver so successfully that no heroin was getting into the city at all. We know this because the police tested the "heroin" being sold on the streets and found it actually contained zero percent of the drug: it was all filler and contaminants. So the war on drugs was, for some significant stretches, being won here.

It is obvious what should have happened during these heroin droughts. The heroin addicts should all have been plunged into physical withdrawal, writhing in agony, and then, weeks later, they should have woken up to find they were freed from their physical dependency.

But Bruce was seeing something really weird instead. There was no heroin in the city—but all the heroin addicts were carrying on almost exactly as before. They were still scrambling desperately to raise the money—robbing or prostituting—to buy this empty cocktail. They weren't in agonizing withdrawal. They weren't getting gut-wrenchingly sick. They thought the "heroin" they were buying was weak, to be sure, and they were topping it up with heavier drinking or more Valium. But the core of their addiction didn't seem to be affected. Nothing had changed.

This wasn't some freak event: a similar effect was being seen in other North American cities where heroin was successfully blockaded for a while, either by police action or by strikes on the docks that prevented anything being unloaded.

This is perplexing. You can get rid of the drug—yet the drug addiction continues in pretty much the same way. What could possibly be happening here?

∼

Bruce went back and taught his students that drug addiction must have much less to do with the actual chemicals than we commonly assume. They had—like all of us—been told that one of the worst aspects of heroin addiction is the fierce and unbearable sickness of physical withdrawal. Henry Smith Williams believed this process was so harrowing it could kill you. But Bruce saw addicts in withdrawal all the time—and their symptoms were often minor: at worst, like a bad flu. This is so contrary to what we are told that it seems impossible, but doctors now very broadly agree it is the case. The real pain of withdrawal is the return of all the psychological pain that you were trying to put to sleep with heroin in the first place.

Bruce often invited addicts from the Downtown Eastside to come to address his students, and one day an addict explained his life story and then took questions from them.

"Our professor," one of the class members asked, "has said withdrawal symptoms are not really bad at all. They're really not like the way they're depicted in the media and in films. Is that true?"

"Well, he says they're not very serious, eh?" the addict replied. "Says they don't make you crawl on the wall and climb up by your finger-nails? . . . Well, I wonder if you've noticed that I'm in withdrawal right now."

He was. He was a little bit sniffly and sweaty. That's all.

The medical researchers John Ball and Carl Chambers studied the medical literature between 1875 and 1968 and found that nobody had died of heroin withdrawal alone in that time. The only people who can be killed by withdrawal, it turns out, are people who are already very weak: withdrawal helped to kill Billie Holiday when she was terribly sick with liver disease, for example, in the same way that ordinary flu can kill a ninety-five-year-old.

In another class, when Bruce was making his point that chemicals can't be the primary cause of addiction, a student raised his hand.

"This is bullshit," he said, "because we know why people take heroin. They take heroin because it captures their brain once they've taken it . . . and the proof is these rat studies which show that's true."

As I said earlier, the strongest evidence for the pharmaceutical theory of addiction had, for years, been a series of experiments on rats. A famous advertisement that ran on U.S. TV in the 1980s, paid for by the Partnership for a Drug-Free America, explained it best. It shows a rat in close-up lick-ing at a water bottle, as the narrator says: "Only one drug is so addictive, nine out of ten laboratory rats will use it. And use it. And use it. Until dead. It's called cocaine. And it can do the same thing to you." The rat runs about manically, then—as promised by the scary music—drops dead. Similar rat experiments had been run to prove the addictiveness of heroin and other drugs.

But when Bruce looked at these experiments, he noticed something. These rats had been put in an empty cage. They were all alone, with no toys, and no activities, and no friends. There was nothing for them to do but to take the drug.

What, he wondered, if the experiment was run differently? With a few of his colleagues, he built two sets of homes for laboratory rats. In the first home, they lived as they had in the original experiments, in solitary confinement, isolated except for their fix. But then he built a second home: a paradise for rats. Within its plywood walls, it contained everything a rat could want—there were wheels and colored balls and the best food, and other rats to hang out with and have sex with.

He called it Rat Park. In these experiments, both sets of rats had access to a pair of drinking bottles. The first bottle contained only water. The other bottle contained morphine—an opiate that rats process in a similar way to humans and that behaves just like heroin when it enters their brains. At the end of each day, Bruce or a member of his team would weigh the bottles to see how much the rats had chosen to take opiates, and how much they had chosen to stay sober.

What they discovered was startling. It turned out that the rats in isolated cages used up to 25 milligrams of morphine a day, as in the earlier experiments. But the rats in the happy cages used hardly any morphine at all—less than 5 milligrams. "These guys [in Rat Park] have a complete total twenty-four-hour supply" of morphine, Bruce said, "and they don't use it." They don't kill themselves. They choose to spend their lives doing other things.

So the old experiments were, it seemed, wrong. It isn't the drug that causes the harmful behavior—it's the environment. An isolated rat will almost always become a junkie. A rat with a good life almost never will, no matter how many drugs you make available to him. As Bruce put it: he was realizing that addiction isn't a disease. Addiction is an adaptation. It's not you—it's the cage you live in.

⁓

Bruce and his colleagues kept tweaking the experiment, to see just how much your environment shapes your chemical compulsions.

He took a set of rats and made them drink the morphine solution for fifty-seven days, in their cage, alone. If drugs can hijack your brain, that will definitely do it. Then he put these junkies into Rat Park. Would they carry on using compulsively, even when their environment improved? Had the drug taken them over?

In Rat Park, the junkie rats seemed to have some twitches of withdrawal—but quite quickly, they stopped drinking the morphine. A happy social environment, it seemed, freed them of their addiction. In Rat Park,

Bruce writes, "nothing that we tried instilled a strong appetite for morphine or produced anything that looked to us like addiction."

~

Bruce naturally wanted to know if this applied to humans. Oddly enough, a large-scale human experiment along similar lines was being carried out shortly before. It was called the Vietnam War.

Out in Southeast Asia, using heroin was "as common as chewing gum" among U.S. soldiers, as *Time* magazine reported at the time. This wasn't just journalistic hyperbole: some 20 percent of U.S. soldiers had become addicted to heroin there, according to a study published in the *Archives of General Psychiatry* later cited by many writers. This meant there were more heroin addicts serving in the U.S. Army than there were back home in the United States. The American military had cracked down hard on marijuana smoking among its troops, sending in pot-sniffing dogs and staging mass arrests, and so huge numbers of men—unable to face that level of pressure without a relaxant—had transferred to smack, which sniffer dogs can't snuffle out. Senator Robert Steele of Connecticut came home from the jungles ashen-faced to explain: "The soldier going to South Vietnam today runs a far greater risk of becoming a heroin addict than a combat casualty."

Many people in the United States were understandably terrified. The war was going to end sooner or later, and at that point the streets of America were going to swell with an unprecedented number of junkies. They believed the pharmaceutical theory of addiction—so this was the only outcome that made any sense. Their brains and bodies were being hijacked by the drug, so, as Senator Harold Hughes of Iowa warned: "Within a matter of months in our large cities, the Capone era of the '20s may look like a Sunday school picnic by comparison."

The war ended. The addicts came home. And something nobody expected took place. The study in the *Archives of General Psychiatry*—and the experiences people could see all across the country—show that 95 percent of them, within a year, simply stopped. The addicts who received drug treatment and rehab were no more likely to stop than those who received no treatment at all. A tiny number of vets did carry on shooting up. They turned out either to have had unstable childhoods, or to have been addicts before they went.

If you believe the theory that drugs hijack your brain and turn you into a chemical slave—the theory on which the war on drugs has been based since Anslinger—then this makes no sense. But there is another explanation. As the writer Dan Baum puts it: "Take a man out of a pestilential jungle where people he can't see are trying to kill him for reasons he doesn't understand, and—surprise!—his need to shoot smack goes away."

After learning all this, Bruce was beginning to develop a theory—one that radically contradicted our earlier understanding of addiction but seemed to him the only way to explain all this evidence. If your environment is like Rat Park—a safe, happy community with lots of healthy bonds and pleasurable things to do—you will not be especially vulnerable to addiction. If your environment is like the rat cages—where you feel alone, powerless and purposeless—you will be.

As Bruce explains this to me, I find myself picturing the Hole back in Tent City in the Arizona desert. In order to punish addicts, the drug warriors have in fact built the very conditions that will be most likely to produce and deepen addiction.

~

So, Bruce believes, the gap between the 90 percent who use drugs without its causing a problem and the 10 percent who can't isn't set in concrete. It's the product of social circumstances—and it can change as social circumstances change.

The rats in solitary confinement and the soldiers in Vietnam weren't being "hijacked" by the chemicals at hand. They were trying to cope with being dislocated from everything that gave their lives meaning and pleasure. The world around them had become an unbearable place to be—so when they couldn't get out of it physically, they decided to get out of it mentally. Later, when they could get back to a meaningful life, they felt no more need for the drugs, and they left them behind with surprising ease.

The key to understanding this hidden cause of addiction, Bruce came to believe, was found in one idea above all others—dislocation. Being cut off from meaning. He began to set out his ideas in an extraordinary book called *The Globalization of Addiction*.

He began to piece together why this would be. Human beings evolved in small bands of hunter-gatherers on the savannahs of Africa. The tribe was your only way to survive. If you feel that you have been stripped of a tribe and its rituals you will become deeply unhappy: a human on the savannah who was alone against the world would almost certainly have died. Humans seem to have evolved with a deep need to bond, because it was absolutely essential to staying alive.

Bruce began to look over the history of when addiction has suddenly soared among human beings—and he found it has, time and again, been when these bonds were taken away from people. The native peoples of North America were stripped of their land and their culture— and collapsed into mass alcoholism. The English poor were driven from the land into scary, scattered cities in the eighteenth century—and glugged their way into the Gin Craze. The American inner cities were stripped of their factory jobs and the communities surrounding them in the 1970s and 1980s—and a crack pipe was waiting at the end of the shut-down assembly line. The American rural heartlands saw their markets and subsidies wither in the 1980s and 1990s—and embarked on a meth binge.

So Bruce came to believe, as he put it, that "today's flood of addiction is occurring because our hyperindividualistic, frantic, crisis-ridden society makes most people feel social[ly] or culturally isolated. Chronic isolation causes people to look for relief. They find temporary relief in addiction . . . because [it] allows them to escape their feelings, to deaden their senses—and to experience an addictive lifestyle as a substitute for a full life."

∼

This isn't an argument against Gabor's discoveries. It's a deepening of them. A kid who is neglected or beaten or raped—like Chino's mother, or Billie Holiday—finds it hard to trust people and to form healthy bonds with them, so they often become isolated, like the rats in solitary confinement, and with the same effects.

Professor Peter Cohen, a friend of Bruce's, writes that we should stop using the word "addiction" altogether and shift to a new word: "bonding." Human beings need to bond. It is one of our most primal urges. So if we can't bond with other people, we will find a behavior to bond with, whether it's watching pornography or smoking crack or gambling. If the only bond you can find that gives you relief or meaning is with splayed women on a computer screen or bags of crystal or a roulette wheel, you will return to that bond obsessively.

One recovering heroin and crack addict on the Downtown Eastside, Dean Wilson, put it to me simply. "Addiction," he said, "is a disease of loneliness."

∼

Rat Park seems to fill some of the holes in our understanding of addiction, but at first glance, it still leaves at least one. What about the heroin famines?

Miserable people will seek altered mental states to numb the pain. That much makes sense. But the heroin addicts Bruce was working with on the Downtown Eastside weren't actually taking heroin during the period when the port of Vancouver was successfully blockaded. They weren't altering their mental states in any physical sense—but they carried on with the junkie behavior, injecting empty powders into their arms. Why?

Bruce realizes that in all his months and years interviewing addicts about their lives, they had been telling him the answer all along. "People explained over and over before I got it," Bruce tells me.

Before they became junkies, these young people were sitting in a room alone, cut off from meaning. Most of them could hope at best for a McJob with a shrinking minimum wage—a lifelong burger-flip punctuated by watching TV and scrimping for minor consumer objects. "My job was basically to say—why don't you stop taking drugs?" Bruce says. "And one guy explained to me very beautifully. He said, 'Well, think about that for a minute. What would I do if I stopped taking drugs? Maybe I could get myself a job as a janitor or something like that.'" Compare that, he said, to "what I'm doing right now, which is really exciting. Because I've got friends down here and we do exciting things like rob stores and hang around with hookers." Suddenly you are part of a world where, together with other addicts, you are embarked on a crusade—a constant frenetic crusade to steal enough to buy the drugs, dodge the police, keep out of jail, and stay alive.

If your problem is being chronically starved of social bonds, then part of the solution is to bond with the heroin itself and the relief it gives you. But a bigger part is to bond with the subculture that comes with taking heroin—the tribe of fellow users all embarked on the same mission and facing the same threats and risking death every day with you. It gives you an identity. It gives you a life of highs and lows, instead of relentless monotony. The world stops being indifferent to you, and starts being hostile—which is at least proof that you exist, that you aren't dead already.

The heroin helps users deal with the pain of being unable to form normal bonds with other humans. The heroin subculture *gives* them bonds with other human beings.

This seemed odd and jarring when I first heard it. The life of a street addict is horrific. You can be culled at any moment by a bad batch, hypo-thermia, rape, the police. Like Bruce, I had to keep turning this theory over and over in my mind, and applying it to the addicts I knew, until I saw it.

Remember: when the actual heroin was gone, they carried on acting as heroin addicts. The horrifying fact is that, as Bruce puts it, "it's a lot better to be a junkie than to be nothing at all, and that's the alternative these guys face—being nothing at all." So when the heroin was cut off, "They maintained the essence of their heroin addiction—which is a subculture addiction." When you have been told you are a piece of shit all your life, embracing the identity of being a piece of shit, embracing the other pieces of shit, living openly as a piece of shit—it seems better than being alone.

As one addict told Bruce: "This is a life. It's better than no life."

~

As I listened to Gabor and Bruce, I wanted to be persuaded—but part of me was skeptical. What is the opposite side of the argument here? This isn't what I was taught at school. It is not what most of us believe. No matter how persuasive they seemed, there was still part of me that kept thinking—*obviously* it is the chemicals that cause addiction. It's *common sense.*

The best man to provide a rebuttal, it seemed to me, was Robert DuPont. He is the founder of the National Institute on Drug Abuse (NIDA), which funds 90 percent of all the research into illegal drugs in the world. He is a highly distinguished scientist, and the man who created many of the metaphors that help us to understand drugs today. I tracked him down at the World Federation Against Drugs conference in Stockholm, Sweden. Over two days, I milled among antidrug activists from across the world. DuPont is a tall, thin, genial man from Ohio, and he delivered the knockout speech of the conference—an eloquent rally-ing call for the drug war, summing up a conference that warned that chemicals can hijack your brain and cause chemical slavery.

He agreed to let me put to him some of the possible holes in the theory, and as we spoke, he listened intently. I started by asking how many of the negative effects of drugs he believed are driven by their pharmacological component. He looked at me blankly. "As opposed to . . . ?" And there was a silence.

I mentioned childhood trauma, and isolation. He continued to look blank. "I think the environment is really important," he said—and then named only one environmental factor: whether drugs are legal or not. Drug use must be kept as a crime, or it will explode. I tried to press him on other factors, but this was the only one he would acknowledge.

I was a little thrown by this, and so I asked him a different question. The institute you set up says drugs make the addict into a chemical slave—that the chemicals take you over—but I am trying to figure out how that fits with the studies suggesting that most addicts simply stop. How is that slavery? Frederick Douglass didn't just walk off the plantation one day. DuPont looked quizzical, and thought about this. "Your point is well taken—I've never thought about it quite this way. There's an absolute quality to the slavery of two centuries ago. This," he said, "is more of a nuanced slavery."

We smiled at each other, a little awkwardly. What, I asked, about the other key metaphor promoted by the organization he founded—of a hijacking? Most hijackings don't end with the hostages choosing to walk away from their captors. "Oh, yes," he says. "It's a question of partial hijacking. That's a good point too."

I felt a little baffled. These are the central metaphors on which the standard theory of addiction is built, and this was the most distinguished expert on the matter, speaking at a conference with these ideas at its very heart. But when I asked him the most basic questions about how this relates to the wider environment, he said—in a friendly way—that he's never really thought about them. This is the man who set up the main center for drug research in the world, and it was plain he hadn't actually heard of these alternative theories. He didn't seem to know who Gabor or Bruce were, or what people like them have shown in their studies.

To be fair, later, when I read through the scientific literature, I realized this is not a failing of DuPont's. It seems to be standard for scientists in this field, even the very best. They overwhelmingly focus on biochemistry and the brain. The questions Bruce and Gabor look at—how people use drugs out here on the streets—are ignored. Nobody, I kept being told, wants to fund studies into that.

Why would this be? Professor Carl Hart at Columbia University is one of the leading experts in the world on how drugs affect the brain. He tells me that when you explain these facts to the scientists who have built their careers on the simplistic old ideas about drugs, they effectively say to you: "Look, man—this is my position. Leave me alone." This is what they know. This is what they have built their careers on. If you offer ideas that threaten to eclipse theirs—they just ignore you. I ask Professor Hart: Can our central idea about drugs really be as hollow as that? "Can it be as hollow? I think you have discovered—it is as hollow as that . . . Look at the evidence. It's hollow . . . It's smoke and mirrors."

But why, then, do these ideas persist? Why haven't the scientists with the better and more accurate ideas eclipsed these old theories? Hart tells me bluntly: Almost all the funding for research into illegal drugs is provided by governments waging the drug war—and they only commission research that reinforces the ideas we already have about drugs. All these different theories, with their radical implications—why would governments want to fund those?

Eric Sterling is the lawyer who wrote the drug laws for the United States between 1979 and 1989. When every major drug law was being drafted, he was at the table shaping it into words. When I met him in his Maryland office, he told me that if any government-funded scientist ever produced research suggesting anything beyond the conventional drugs-hijack-brains theory, he knows exactly what would happen. The head of NIDA would be called before a congressional committee and asked if she had gone mad. She might be fired. She would certainly be stopped. All the people conducting the science for NIDA—and remember, that's 90 percent of research on the globe into illegal drugs—know this.

So they steer away from all this evidence and look only at the chemical effects of the drugs themselves. That's not fake—but it's only a small part of the picture. There is a powerful political brake on exploring these deeper truths.

And that, it turns out, is what happened to Bruce. Once the nature of their findings became clear, the money for the Rat Park experiment provided by his university was abruptly cut off, before the team had a chance to investigate many of the questions it raised. Years later, Bruce was told by a senior figure at the University that that was because they found it embarrassing. Something so far outside the conventional understanding of addiction seemed crazy.

To a sober-minded military brat raised in a conservative family, the experience of Rat Park and the heroin famines was startling, and it changed how Bruce saw the world. "It's amazing to discover that something which is so centrally believed is false. It's just false," he said to me.

At first he expected that his findings would blast open the field of addiction science and start a whole slew of investigations into how it really works. He was ready for "a ticker tape parade," he says. Instead, all his findings were disregarded, as if they had never happened. "That evidence like this can be so completely disregarded—it's amazing," he says. "I suppose you could say it's poisoned my entire outlook on life."

Nobody has ever received funding to replicate the Rat Park experiment.

⁓

As I walked the streets of Vancouver trying to digest all this, I began to think again about the very beginning of this story, and I saw something I had not seen before.

There were three questions I had never understood. Why did the drug war begin when it did, in the early twentieth century? Why were people so receptive to Harry Anslinger's message? And once it was clear that it was having the opposite effect to the one that was intended—that it was increasing addiction and supercharging crime—why was it intensified, rather than abandoned?

I think Bruce Alexander's breakthrough may hold the answer.

"Human beings only become addicted when they cannot find anything better to live for and when they desperately need to fill the emptiness that threatens to destroy them," Bruce explained in a lecture in London in 2011. "The need to fill an inner void is not limited to people who become drug addicts, but afflicts the vast majority of people of the late modern era, to a greater or lesser degree."

A sense of dislocation has been spreading through our societies like a bone cancer throughout the twentieth century. We all feel it: we have become richer, but less connected to one another. Countless studies prove this is more than a hunch, but here's just one: the average number of close friends a person has has been steadily falling. We are increasingly alone, so we are increasingly addicted. "We're talking about learning to deal with the modern age," Bruce believes. The modern world has many incredible benefits, but it also brings with it a source of deep stress that is unique: dislocation. "Being atomized and fragmented and all on [your] own—that's no part of human evolution and it's no part of the evolution of any society," he told me.

And then there is another kicker. At the same time that our bonds with one another have been withering, we are told—incessantly, all day, every day, by a vast advertising-shopping machine—to invest our hopes and dreams in a very different direction: buying and consuming objects. Gabor tells me: "The whole economy is based around appealing to and heightening every false need and desire, for the purpose of selling products. So people are always trying to find satisfaction and fulfillment in products." This is a key reason why, he says, "we live in a highly addicted society." We have separated from one another and turned instead to things for happiness—but things can only ever offer us the thinnest of satisfactions.

This is where the drug war comes in. These processes began in the early twentieth century—and the drug war followed soon after. The drug war wasn't just driven, then, by a race panic. It was driven by an addiction panic—and it had a real cause. But the cause wasn't a growth in drugs. It was a growth in dislocation.

The drug war began when it did because we were afraid of our own addictive impulses, rising all around us because we were so alone. So, like an evangelical preacher who rages against gays because he is afraid of his own desire to have sex with men, are we raging against addicts because we are afraid of our own growing vulnerability to addiction?

～

After I met Bruce for the last time, I sat on a bench in Pigeon Park, a small concrete sprawl on the Downtown Eastside where addicts drink and talk and buy drugs, and tried to understand: How does all this change the way we should think about the drug war now?

Bruce says that at the moment, when we think about recovery from addiction, we see it through only one lens—the individual. We believe the problem is in the addict and she has to sort it out for herself, or in a circle of her fellow addicts.

But this is, he believes, like looking at the rats in the isolated cages and seeing them as morally flawed: it misses the point. He argues we need to refocus our eyes, as if staring at a Magic Eye picture, to see that the problem isn't in them, it's in the culture. Stop thinking only about individual recovery, he argues, and start thinking about "social recovery."

If we think like this, the question we need to answer with our drug policy shifts. It is no longer: How do we stop addiction through threats and force, and scare people away from drugs in the first place? It becomes: How do we start to rebuild a society where we don't feel so alone and afraid, and where we can form healthier bonds? How do we build a society where we look for happiness in one another rather than in consumption?

These are radical questions, with implications far beyond the drug war, and bigger than this book. But they have to be asked. We haven't been able to reduce addiction, it occurs to me, because we have been asking the wrong questions.

Bruce says this dynamic is producing something even darker than the drug war. Cut off from one another, isolated, we are all becoming addicts—and our biggest addiction, as a culture, is buying and consuming stuff we don't need and don't even really want.

We all know deep down it doesn't make us happy, to be endlessly working to buy shiny consumer objects we have seen in advertisements. But we keep doing it, day after day. It in fact occupies most of our time on earth. We could slow down. We could work less and buy less. It would prevent the environment—our habitat—from being systematically destroyed. But we don't do it, because we are isolated in our individual cages. In that environment, the idea of consuming less, in fact, fills us with panic. All this stuff, Bruce believes, is filling the hole where normal human connection should be.

Unless we learn the lesson of Rat Park, Bruce says we will face a worse problem than the drug war. We will find ourselves on a planet trashed by the manic consumption that is, today, our deepest and most destructive addiction.

~

Over the months that I listened repeatedly to the recordings of Bruce and Gabor and tried to tease out what they were telling me, I kept circling back to an obvious question. They convinced me there are significant factors in addiction that have nothing to do with the chemicals themselves. But it would be absurd to say the chemicals play no role at all in, say, cigarette or crack addiction. So how much really is due to the chemicals, and how much is due to the social factors? What's the ratio?

As I read more, I stumbled across—in the work of an amazing scientist called Richard DeGrandpre—an experiment that gives us a quite precise answer, in percentage terms. You may well be taking part in it right now.

When nicotine patches where invented in the early 1990s, public health officials were thrilled. They believed in the theory of addiction that almost everyone believes in: addiction is caused by chemical hooks that are hidden in the drug. You use a drug for a while, and your body starts to crave and need the chemical in a physical way. This isn't hard to grasp. Anybody who has tried to quit caffeine knows that chemical hooks are real: I am trying it as I type this, and my hands are very slightly shaking, my head is aching, and I just snapped at the guy sitting opposite me in the library.

Everyone agrees that cigarette smoking is one of the strongest addictions: it is ranked on pharmaceutical addictiveness scales alongside heroin and cocaine. It is also the deadliest. Smoking tobacco kills 650 out of every hundred thousand people who use it, while using cocaine kills four. And we know for sure what the chemical hook in tobacco is—it's nicotine.

The wonder of nicotine patches, then, is that they can meet a smoker's physical need—the real in-your-gut craving—while bypassing some of the really dangerous effects of smoking tobacco. So if the idea of addiction we all have in our heads is right, nicotine patches will have a very high success rate. Your body is hooked on the chemical; it gets the chemical from the nicotine patch; therefore, you won't need to smoke anymore.

The pharmacology of nicotine patches works just fine—you really are giving smokers the drug they are addicted to. The level of nicotine in your bloodstream doesn't drop if you use them, so that chemical craving is gone. There is just one problem: even with a nicotine patch on, you still want to smoke. The Office of the Surgeon General has found that just 17.7 percent of nicotine patch wearers were able to stop smoking.

How can this be? There's only one explanation: something is going on that is more significant than the chemicals in the drug itself. If solving the craving for the chemical ends 17.7 percent of the addictions in smokers, the other 82.3 percent has to be explained some other way.

Now, 17.7 percent certainly isn't a trivial amount. That's a large number of people with improved lives. It would be foolish and wrong to say the drug has *no* effect. But it would be equally foolish to say what we have been saying for a century—that the chemicals themselves are the *main* cause of drug addiction. That assertion doesn't match the evidence.

This point is worth underscoring. With the most powerful and deadly drug in our culture, the actual chemicals account for only 17.7 percent of the compulsion to use. The rest can only be explained by the factors Gabor and Bruce have discovered.

To make sense of this conclusion I talked to many scientists, and they explained a distinction that really helped me—between physical dependence, and addiction. Physical dependence occurs when your body has become hooked on a chemical, and you will experience some withdrawal symptoms if you stop—I am physically dependent on caffeine, and boy, can I feel it this morning.

But addiction is different. Addiction is the psychological state of feeling you need the drug to give you the sensation of feeling calmer, or manic, or numbed, or whatever it does for you. My coffee withdrawal pains will have totally passed in two days—but two weeks from now, I might feel the urgent need to get my mind focused again, and I will convince myself I can't do it without caffeine. That's not dependence; that's not a chemical hook; that's an addiction. This is a crucial difference. And what goes for a mild and fairly harmless addiction like caffeine goes for a hard-core addiction like meth. That's why you can nurse addicts through their withdrawal pains for weeks and see the chemical hooks slowly pass, only for them to relapse months or years later, even though any chemical craving in the body has long since gone. They are no longer physically dependent—but they are addicted. As a culture, for one hundred years, we have convinced ourselves that a real but fairly small aspect of addiction—physical dependence—is the whole show.

"It's really like," Gabor told me one night, "we're still operating out of Newtonian physics in an age of quantum physics. Newtonian physics is very valuable, of course. It deals with a lot of things—but it doesn't deal with the heart of things."

PART V

Peace

CHAPTER 14

The Drug Addicts' Uprising

As I tried to find my way through the world of the Downtown Eastside, I kept being told—again and again—that it had changed radically in the past decade. This place, everyone said, has been transformed. It is not what it was. It is incalculably better now. I wanted to know how that happened, and when I asked for the explanation, I was told a story, and one name always featured in it: Bud Osborn. He's a poet, people said. He was a homeless addict. He changed this place. They talked about him almost as a mythical figure. You'll understand, they said, when you meet him.

When I called his number, he sounded unwell—and, to my surprise, a hailstorm of negative assumptions hit me. Another junkie, I thought. What change? Why am I bothering? And then I immediately asked myself—Where did that thought come from?

I went to Bud's little apartment, a short walk from the Portland Hotel Society where Gabor had worked, to meet him. He was waiting in the corridor for me. He was a tall man in his sixties with a long mop of gray hair and an unlined, youthful face. He guided me into his lounge through huge piles of books—on poetry, history, jazz—and before long, he was telling me about a day nearly twenty years before, when he was very different, and the Downtown Eastside was very different, and everything seemed hopeless. This is his story as I learned it from him, his friends, and the people he led a rebellion against.

~

Bud felt like he heard nothing but sirens. All through the day, all through the night, every fifteen minutes, the nee-naw-nee-naw of speeding ambulances scratched through his neighborhood, and he would immediately wonder: Is it one of my friends? Which one?

He was a homeless smack addict in his fifties, watching his friends die all around him. By the mid-1990s, Bud's voice was already dry and toneless, as if the emotion had been scraped from it long ago, when one day, near the park, he bumped into a Native American woman named Margaret whom he had known for a few years. He knew that her family had been dying one by one of drug overdoses, like so many of the people around there, and he could see that she was ashen and had to say something to him but didn't quite know how.

He waited for her to speak.

Her cousin, she said, had just overdosed, and when her partner had walked in on her body, he had ripped up the sheets and hanged himself— and it all happened in front of their young child, who was sitting on his cot, watching. She was just on her way to a meeting of the family to figure out who would end up taking the kid, she explained, distantly.

As Margaret talked, Bud thought of what had happened to him as a child, far away in Toledo, Ohio, and he knew now it was about to happen to another kid, and somewhere inside him, there came a voice saying— This has to stop.

But what can I do? Bud asked himself. I'm just a street junkie. I'm nobody.

He looked around him. Nobody else was rebelling. Okay, he thought. If it has to be me, it has to be me.

It was in that thought—and in everything that followed from it—that the first mass rebellion by drug addicts against the system built by Harry Anslinger was born.

~

In the same year that Gabor's mother was handing him to a Christian stranger in the Budapest ghetto, an American pilot named Walton Osborn Senior was around 150 miles away, in a bomber plane high above Vienna. Bullets must have pierced the plane's engine, because it caught fire and crashed to the ground, and Walton was hauled from the smoking wreckage with his legs all smashed up. The people dragging him out were the Austrian peasants who had survived his bombs, and they were armed with pitchforks, determined to lynch him. Nazi officers suddenly pulled up in a jeep and scared them off, and they took Walton to a prisoner of war camp.

We don't know what happened to him there. He would never say. But when he came back to Toledo, Ohio, to get back to his life as a journalist, Walton started drinking, and he never stopped.

Toledo was a sedate middle-class American town where the memories of the war were being meticulously repressed. Walton insisted on driving across America to seek out everybody who had survived the POW camp with him, because they were the only ones who understood. When he was forced to come home, he threw out all their furniture, leaving their home bare and empty, as if he was trying to rebuild the Nazi prison camp in the middle of America. Nobody knew how to cope with an open wound like Walton: he was like a scream in the middle of a dinner party.

To his wife, Patricia, Walton seemed like a drunken impostor of the man who had left for the war, and she couldn't bear it. She was a former model—a tall, slender brunette—and while he lay in bed for days on end, drinking and reading Walt Whitman, she started an affair with another man, to feel she was not alone. When Walton found out, he started screaming and howling and shrieking so violently that his friends were worried that he was going to jump out a window, so they took him to the local jail, where the cops said they'd keep an eye on him as he sobered up. They put him in the cell at the end, and they forgot about him, so Walton ripped his jacket into shreds, made a noose, tied it to the bars, and hanged himself.

The next week, the local newspaper ran a story. These, it said, are "the consequences of flaunting contempt for the moral laws on which our society ultimately rests." It ran a photograph of the widow, labeling her a slut and saying she had driven her husband to kill himself. The story landed on doorsteps across the city, and in that moment, she and her little son, Walton Osborn Junior, were expelled from their middle-class lives. They were forced to live in the local trailer park and then whatever random room they could find for the night, and they spent most days and evenings in one bar or another. His mother needed to drink all the time now, and she would drag her son along to bars and tell him to play. He was the only child there, so he shot balls on the pool table, alone.

Walton Junior—a plump boy with curly blond hair—wanted to know where his dad had gone. His mother told him he was talking nonsense: Your father never returned from the war, she said. You never knew him. "I had actual memories of him," he told me. He remembered his father holding his hand and taking him to the art museum in Toledo, and lifting him up onto a little concrete statue of a rhinoceros, and many other images. So "I thought there was something wrong with me. Something really wrong with me. Mentally. In my perception of reality."

She would often hand him over to people she barely knew and say she'd be back in a few hours, only to vanish for days on end. This confirmed her son in his suspicions: "The fact that my father left one day and never came back, [and] my mother was always leaving [meant] I thought the reason my parents aren't with me is because there's something really wrong with me." Whenever the little boy heard his own name spoken out loud—"Walton"—he felt terrified, but he didn't know why. As he was playing outside once, another kid told him his name wasn't really Walton, it was Bud. It felt like a liberation. From then on, he demanded to be called Bud by everyone, as if that could shake off the ghost of the father he remembered but who he now believed had never existed at all.

His mother often brought men back to their one-room trailer for a few more drinks, and one night, she brought back a man—an actor—to keep on drinking with. He ripped open her blouse and she yelled; he pressed against her, grinning. Bud wanted to protect his mother, so he hurled his little frame at the man, but he was flicked away like an insect. Bud picked himself up and launched himself again—and this time the man threw him very hard against the wall.

"Stay there! Stay there!" his mother screamed. So Bud had to stay there, and watch. "I was there, just trying not to feel. Just not to be aware . . . I sort of shut off," he remembered. Later, he wrote that in that moment, "I vowed I would never again be vulnerable to another human being."

Not long after that, Bud stood on a big stone porch and hurled himself off it, onto the concrete below. He landed on his head. His skull cracked, and he began to bleed. "Either I was imagining in my child's imagination" that it would be okay, he says, "or I just hated the life I was living."

It was after this incident that he discovered a way out. The answer, he believed, must lie in the mystery of words. His ghost-father's profession had been to shape words into stories: they must contain some alchemy, some answer, to what was happening. Bud cut strips of words from the newspaper, hid them in his pocket, and took them out at school break times, to secretly swallow them. "I thought that if I had the words inside me," he says, that they "would reveal their meaning."

As Bud got older, he started to obsessively play sports—baseball, basketball, cross-country, track, anything that would stop him from thinking, "just to get my mind off [the fact that] the house would be in some kind of chaos, [with] people fighting, or else there'd be no one there at all." Even in the middle of the freezing Ohio winters, he would stand for hour after hour on the basketball court alone, shooting hoops. "It was like a trance for me," he says. There was no pleasure in winning. It was the process he craved—the moment when he was not alone with his thoughts.

But he couldn't run all the time. He learned to live in the stationary world by falling into almost hypnotic trances: he would be sitting with people, but he would go somewhere in his head where he couldn't see or hear them, and he was alone, and he was numb. "I was able to shut it out. Disassociation," he says. "You remove your consciousness from what's going on around you." People would often say: "Bud, where are you?" and he would look blankly back. He had started to do it as a small child whenever his mother left. "I thought, if I can just stay long enough in a trance, she'll come back, she'll come back."

The first time he heard about black holes in space, Bud felt he intuitively understood them. "They absorb any light coming near them and crush it. I felt like that in here," he says, jabbing at his insides. "When I first read about a black hole in space I thought—that's how I've always felt. That's exactly [it]."

The trances were one way of erasing himself from existence—but before long he found a better way. When he was fifteen, he took an overdose of aspirin. A police officer came into the hospital as he lay in bed after having his stomach pumped and snapped: "Do you know what you're doing to your mother?" Shortly before he left high school, she told him: Your father did exist. You did know him. And there was a newspaper story you should probably go look up. After that, Bud started drinking "and I drank for oblivion. Just to knock me out."

He went to study journalism at Northwestern University, but he couldn't focus and dropped out. He kept trying to kill himself, but his belief that words could save him remained. He discovered the French poets of the late nineteenth century. Charles Baudelaire and Arthur Rimbaud became his friends and his way out. "I saw their lives were a total mess," he says, but "what they gave me was a reason to live another hour, another day, another week." Their words kept him going. "I decided this is maybe something I can do because I'm so totally fucked up and they're so totally fucked up—[yet] they're able to do something that actually gives something life-enhancing to someone else." He vowed to write poetry every day, no matter what else happened to him. "I thought—poetry is something that can never be taken away from you . . . You can only lose it yourself."

He had a deeper ambition, one he kept to himself and told to nobody. He hoped that one day, he might write one poem that did for another human being what their poetry had done for him.

Bud volunteered for VISTA, one of the antipoverty programs set up by Lyndon Johnson as part of his War on Poverty, before it was replaced by Richard Nixon's War on Drugs. He arrived at his posting in East Harlem a year after rioters had tried to burn it down, and the block he was assigned to—at the very top of Central Park—consisted of five stories of narrow apartments with long, snaking fire escapes, and stoops facing the street that were always thrumming with people. It was no different from the Harlem that Billie Holiday had arrived in forty years before. Bud was told to go and introduce himself to everyone on the block and ask what help they needed. He was taken aback by how many people were crammed into every apartment: when he told one little kid that he shared a house with just three people, the boy was incredulous. He shared an apartment with seventeen.

He was spending his days handing out subway tokens to kids who didn't have enough money to get to school, or taking elderly people to get their first-ever eyeglasses or hearing aids, when he noticed a guy who was always walking up and down the block. He wore a black hat, black shirt, black pants, and sunglasses, whatever the weather.

"Don't have anything to do with him," the residents told him. "Don't talk to him. Don't bother him. He runs the block."

Bud had heard of heroin, because he had read the novel *Naked Lunch* by William Burroughs, but this was the closest he had come to it in the real world. He looked away, but he kept thinking about this man. "I felt like I was being driven inside," he says, "by something—I didn't know what it was."

After he left VISTA, Bud started working in the West Village in one of the first stores ever to sell Jimi Hendrix posters and buttons, and he met a Manhattan poet a few years older called Shelley, and they started to hang out. One night, they went to Shelley's apartment, and some of his friends turned up with some heroin in a little bag.

"I was always wondering—is this the night I walk to the Brooklyn Bridge and just jump off?" Bud remembered.

He laid the heroin out in lines and snorted it through a straw. Soon after, "I just felt this warmth in the pit of my gut that had always been really cold," he says. "When we went outside—it was freezing out, but I felt warm. I was almost floating." That first night he walked around feeling calm and dreamy. He went back to use heroin again soon after, and as he started snorting it regularly, he found "I was able to just go to sleep whenever I wanted to, or stay awake and feel good whenever I wanted to. I had never felt good. Even with all those sports—if I did well in the sport, I didn't feel any better than if I didn't. It was just something to hurl myself into to take up time." But now, "I felt that I didn't want to kill myself anymore. I felt good. I didn't feel like I hated myself. I felt like I was as good as anybody else . . . Just this warmth. Instead of that black, cold hole, I had this warm feeling in there."

Long before he had heard of heroin, Bud had been trying to put himself into a numbed trance, a distant place in his head where he would be freed from his thoughts. Now there was a drug that could take him there, for far longer than he could manage on his own, and he was glad. "I thought—if I have this stuff, I could maybe have a life," he says.

Whenever Bud had tried to have sex before, he thought of seeing his mother being raped, and he couldn't go through with it. Not long after he started using heroin, he was sitting in a bar on the Lower East Side—bars felt more like home to him than anywhere else—when a tall young black woman with long raven-colored hair came up to him. He thought that she was gorgeous, and that he was the most lost man in New York City. She pushed a piece of fried chicken in his face.

"You want a bite of my chicken?" Misty asked.

Bud was probably the only straight man in New York City who would have said this, but he replied: "No thanks, I've already eaten." She walked away, and he thought—oh, Bud, you are a mess.

She came back to him. "Where are you from, anyway?" she asked.

"Ohio."

"Where's *that*?"

She took him that night on the Staten Island Ferry, and on the deck on a summer's night, they embraced. When they got back to her apartment, he was terrified, but he wasn't going to say no.

Misty lit candles and went to get a little wine, and then she put on a record. "It was so beautiful and there was pain in it," Bud says, "and it reached right inside me and the voice was so extraordinary . . . I had never heard a voice like that before."

"Who's that singing?" he asked.

"Don't they have *anything* in Ohio?" she said. "That's Billie Holiday."

And with Misty, and with Billie Holiday playing, he could have sex, and he was happy. He knew "it was an experience from then on I could always hold on to."

Bud received his draft card to go to fight in Vietnam soon after, but there was no way he was going to go to kill innocent Vietnamese people, so he went on the run, back and forth across the country. He was indicted before a federal grand jury and knew he could face five years in prison when he was caught. He was often hiding in little towns where he couldn't find heroin, and when this happened, he quickly became suicidal again. Bud didn't want to be an addict—he knew shooting street heroin was a bad idea, for all the obvious reasons—so he spent five years without using, attending Alcoholics Anonymous meetings every night across America, and he was constantly depressed.

One Christmas Day, he decided to finish the work he began when he was a little boy jumping off his porch, and he took a car and drove it into a wall at sixty miles per hour. The last thing he thought before it hit was, with relief: "I'm dead now."

He woke up to find a surgeon picking pieces of glass out of his face. When he was discharged from the hospital, on crutches, his head swaddled in a turban, he looked around in the numbing Ohio winter and thought: "I can't believe I'm still here. I can't believe I'm still in this." He found himself walking the streets with a hammer hidden in his clothing, searching for somebody to hit over the head, to snatch a couple of dollars for smack. But as he contemplated breaking a skull, he "saw a pitch-black hole open in front of me"—a hole that would crush him—and he couldn't go through with it.

One day he came home and his mother called him. She was being detained in a psychiatric unit—she had been manic for years now—and explained she had an exciting announcement. She was going to run for president. "I think I have a real good chance too," she explained, because she was guaranteed the support of all the mental patients, alcoholics, and drug addicts. She told Bud to think about what cabinet appointment he would like after the election.

"I spent considerable time," he recalled, "trying to decide between secretary of health, education, and welfare." He thought: "In my family, if we didn't count our chickens before they'd hatched, I don't think we'd have been able to do very much counting at all." It would have seemed absurd to him then, but Bud was going to wield real political power, and soon.

He needed to run from the United States and from his urge to use smack. So, not sure what else to do, he headed across the Canadian border, toward the Downtown Eastside—an area he was going to transform.

～

As he stood surrounded by sirens and heard Margaret describe how that little boy had watched his mother overdose and his father hang himself, this story flashed before Bud and he thought—It doesn't have to be this way.

For years, he had heard the drug warriors point to drug overdoses and say: see? This is why we need to crack down. This is why we fight our war. But Bud knew that the drug war doesn't prevent overdoses—it massively increases them. Ethan Nadelmann, one of the leading drug reformers in the United States, had explained: "People overdose because [under prohibition] they don't know if the heroin is 1 percent or 40 percent . . . Just imagine if every time you picked up a bottle of wine, you didn't know whether it was 8 percent alcohol or 80 percent alcohol [or] if every time you took an aspirin, you didn't know if it was 5 milligrams or 500 milligrams."

Even more important, under prohibition, people use their drugs in secret, to make sure the police don't spot them. Bud and his friends would hide in dumpsters across the Downtown Eastside to shoot up—but this meant that if they overdosed, nobody else would spot them, and they would die. Bud looked it up in the library and saw that in European countries that provide addicts with safe rooms where they are watched over by nurses as they use their drugs, deaths from overdose had ended.

But what could Bud do? Who would listen to him? He convened a meeting in a hall provided by the local church, and announced that people inside the Downtown Eastside were going to have to fight for change. Nobody was coming to save them. They would have to save themselves.

At the first meeting, eight or ten people shuffled in, addicts from the street, like him. "They'd be there to see—Are we there, like everyone else, to hustle them somehow? To shoot an angle on them?" Bud recalls. "To make a group out of them and then us keep the money?"

Bud's first moves were very practical. He suggested the addicts patrol the alleyways to spot people who were overdosing and immediately call medical help for anyone who needed it. He invited the local fire department to come and explain to addicts how to perform CPR on an overdose victim so they could keep their friend alive until the ambulance got there.

This was tangible. Everyone could see what it meant, right away. The addicts organized themselves into brigades and started watching one another. In the weeks and months that followed, people who would have been found dead in the morning were spotted in time, and survived. So at the next few meetings, other addicts started to come up with suggestions themselves for how they could save each other. How do we get a safe injecting room? How do we protect the addicted sex workers? Soon the meetings had a hundred people at them, and they had to find a bigger room.

The group decided to turn up at community centers and City Hall meetings where they were having discussions about the need to crack down on The Junkies. They would listen to people talking about how they had to be wiped out or driven away, and then politely stand up and explain—That's us. We are the people you are talking about. How can we answer your fears? How can we be good citizens? There was a look of amazed disgust on people's faces. They had never had a conversation with the people they were raging against. They turned to the addicts and poured their fear and scorn over them—you are filling our children's playgrounds with used syringes in an attempt to hurt them, they'd say. Bud explained they were happy to solve this problem: he arranged a regular patrol of addicts to go and clear away the needles.

People were nonplussed. Are they trying to mess with our heads? Is this a trick?

The addicts started to insist on being at every meeting where drug policy was discussed. They took a slogan from the movements of psychiatric patients who were fighting to be treated decently: "Nothing about us, without us." Their message was: We're here. We're human. We're alive. Don't talk about us as if we are nothing. They began, haltingly, to find a new language to talk about themselves as addicts. We have certain inalienable rights: to stay alive, to stay healthy, to be treated as people. You are taking those rights away from us. We will claim them back.

The mayor of Vancouver was a right-winger named Philip Owen—a rich businessman with sharp suits and sharper solutions. He knew how to deal with this problem: round up all the addicts, he said, and lock them away at the army base at Chilliwack. He dismissed calls for the supervised injection rooms, and the evidence that they had hugely reduced the overdose and AIDS transmission rates in Frankfurt, declaring: "I'm totally and violently opposed." His solution was "twenty-five years, mandatory life sentence" for anyone selling drugs. "Bango, just like that. Just like that. Throw away the key."

This attitude ran right through Vancouver. A senior member of the Vancouver Police Department dismissed addicts as "vampires" and "werewolves." When a serial killer started to murder the mainly addicted sex workers of the Downtown Eastside, the police did virtually nothing for years, effectively allowing him to continue. One policewoman explained to the subsequent inquiry that the attitude among her fellow officers toward these addicts was that "they wouldn't piss on them if they were on fire." Bud went on radio shows and callers told him: "The only good junkie is a dead junkie." One asked: "Why don't they just string barbed wire around the Downtown Eastside and let them inject each other to death?"

In the middle of all this, a killer whale named Finna died in the Vancouver Aquarium, and there was an outburst of Princess Diana–style grief in the city. The deaths of more than a thousand addicts, by contrast, were stirring no response.

Bud believed that it would take a dramatic gesture to jolt the city into seeing his neighborhood differently. So the group he and his friends had formed—now christened the Vancouver Area Network of Drug Users (VANDU)—headed to Oppenheimer Park, one of the great green spaces of the city, and VANDU volunteers along with the staff of the Portland Hotel Society filled it with a thousand plain wooden crosses. Each cross represented a drug user who had died on the Downtown Eastside in the past four years. Their names were written on the crosses in black marker. As the crosses stretched across the neat lawns of Oppenheimer Park, it looked like the graves of the First World War—a great swath of lost love. Bud and his friends sealed off the surrounding streets with wire, and hung a vast banner that declared that these blocks were "killing fields." They handed out leaflets explaining that overdose was the single biggest cause of death at that time in British Columbia for people between the ages of thirty and forty-nine.

The traffic stopped and the streets were still, as if these deaths mattered, as if the loss of a thousand addicts deserved a pause. Gandhi said one of the crucial roles for anyone who wants to change anything is to make the oppression visible—to give it a physical shape.

Bud wrote a poem titled "a thousand crosses in oppenheimer park." It says:

> *a question each one of these thousand crosses puts to each of us*
> *why are we still alive?*

These activists believed that if people knew—if they could see the addicts as human—they would care. Ann Livingstone, Bud's girlfriend at the time of the protests, tells me they were working on the belief that "Canadians are decent people and they don't know what's happening to us and they need to know."

Addicts had been persecuted by prohibition since 1914 and none of them had fought back before. It hadn't seemed possible. Bud wasn't only creating a rebellion; he was creating a language with which addicts could rebel. It happened in Vancouver and nowhere else for a reason: in most cities in the world, if addicts came out in public and declared who they were and began to fight for their rights, they would risk being fired from their jobs, stripped of their welfare, and expelled from their homes. But the Portland Hotel Society—where Gabor and Liz Evans worked—had a policy of housing Vancouver's addicts and refusing to throw them out. These addicts, alone in the world, had safe ground on which to stand.

VANDU built a coffin and started to carry it to every City Hall meeting where drugs were discussed. On it, written in large letters, were the words: WHO WILL BE THE NEXT OVERDOSE VICTIM? They forced the mayor, Philip Owen, to see it, and to see the cost of his policies. They carried a sign, with words echoing right from the start of the drug war: DRUG USERS ARE PEOPLE TOO!

Since Henry Smith Williams was broken, anybody opposing the drug war had entered the debate in a defensive crouch. They had preemptively pleaded—no, no, we are not in favor of drug use, no, no, we are not bad people, no, no, we are not like those dirty junkies. VANDU was different. For the first time, they were putting prohibitionists on the defensive. They were saying: You are the people waging a war. Here are the people you are killing. What are they dying for? Tell us.

For months, Vancouver's officialdom watched this movement puzzled and repelled. After a while, the local health board figured it might be able to muffle this force and prevent it from embarrassing them with its protests by getting Bud to sit on the board for Vancouver—a powerful body that monitors all the health spending in the city and has more resources at its disposal than City Hall. At one meeting after Bud joined, a top health official for the province explained calmly that the AIDS rate—the biggest cause of death among Bud's friends and neighbors—would eventually reach a saturation point in the Downtown Eastside and fall of its own accord, because the addicts would simply die out.

Sitting there, carefully taking notes, Bud slowly realized what was being said. The authorities were nonchalantly declaring that he and his friends would all die, and then the problem would be over.

Bud managed—after a lot of arguing and lobbying—to get some small funding for VANDU from the health board, over the protests of Mayor Owen, and the group's members voted for a detailed agenda. Their first demand was simple: establish a safe, monitored place where people could go to inject their drugs. That would mean they would live, and not die.

Across Vancouver, people were starting to look at the addicts in a different way. These people who had been lying and dying alone were now campaigning together, and often they seemed to have more dignity than the people screaming at them that they should just go away and kill themselves. Many people had believed what Bruce Alexander was taught by Batman and his dad—that addicts didn't care about their lives, or about anything but their next fix. But here they were, organizing to defend themselves and each other.

And the addicts were starting to look at themselves differently. Bud said, "People would work sixty hours a week" at VANDU. "To see people's faces and how they changed—they saw, I have worth, I have value. I'm able to help somebody else. I'm no longer just what they call me in the newspapers." And Bud discovered, as a side effect, something else: "If we're off demonstrating, we're having board meetings deciding what to do, and thinking about what our next actions could be, how is so and so doing, how can we help so and so because he got busted again—all that's taking you away from just being totally fixed on 'I got to get a drug, I got to get a drug, drug drug drug.'"

Ever since he was five years old, Bud had wanted to die. But now, faced with a barrage of abuse saying people like him are better off dead, he was discovering something deep inside himself—the will to live. For the first time in his life, he felt as if he had a home, and a community, and people to fight for.

Bud's story can be read as proof of Gabor's theories that childhood trauma creates addiction, but he can also be seen as proof of Bruce's theories. Back in Toledo, when he stopped taking heroin and drinking alcohol but was still in an empty cage alone, he was chronically suicidal. Now his life was becoming like Rat Park, where he had friends and everything that gives life meaning—and he was finding his desire to use drugs ebbed.

"That's what I wanted—for my spirit to wake up. I didn't just want to stop drugs and feel like shit, feel even worse," Bud says. He wanted to be fully alive as a person making a difference in the world, and now it was happening.

Yet even as the most active members of VANDU were starting to feel better about themselves, people were still dying all around them. "We had twenty-five board members," one of the cofounders, Dean Wilson, says, "because you never knew who was going to be alive at the next meeting." When Bud came out of one health board assembly, he watched a man methodically going through the trash in an overflowing dumpster, and he saw empty syringe packages floating and a pink blouse in a heap. And there were still the sirens, all the time.

When you are confronted with historical forces that seem vastly bigger than you—like a war on your people that has lasted nearly a hundred years—you have two choices. You can accept it as your fate and try to adjust to being a pinball being whacked around a table by the powerful. Or you can band together with other people to become a historical force yourself—one that will eventually overwhelm the forces ranged against you.

Bud chose the second way. He appealed for more and more people to join VANDU. He studied in the library to find out what the official definition of a public health emergency is in Canada, and discovered that Vancouver had never declared one. He started maneuvering for the health board to formally do it—and under his pressure, they finally agreed. This was now, officially, the city's first emergency. Suddenly, VANDU was an international news story, and Bud was interviewed by everyone from the BBC to the *New York Times*. He wrote a poem explaining that "the war on drugs / is a war against hope and compassion and care."

Now that they knew there were addicts at the meetings and that helping them to survive was now an official duty, the city bureaucrats started to talk differently. It's hard to dismiss somebody's death as irrelevant if they are looking you in the face. Bud was able to persuade the health board to provide funding for VANDU, and they established a permanent center in the city—a big old storefront in the heart of the Downtown Eastside. They voted to use their public money to fly in experts from

Switzerland and the Netherlands to explain how those countries had massively reduced the death rate of addicts by abandoning the war on drugs. (I traveled to Switzerland later to see how this worked.)

But still the mayor, Philip Owen, was determined to block all progress. He actually declared a moratorium on all new projects to help addicts—in the middle of the emergency. VANDU cofounder Dean Wilson stood up at a city council meeting, looked him in the eye, and said "It almost seems like you are sentencing us to death . . . One [addict] a day is dying, and if one of you were dying every day—every day you woke up and there was one less person working in City Hall—I tell you, that problem would be solved in two minutes."

Owen stared on, pale, his face drawn, as if he couldn't understand how this was happening. Who *are* these people?

Bud won the City of Vancouver Book Award for a collection of his poetry. Normally, the award is presented by the mayor, but Owen refused to do it. Bud was beginning to despair. He had fought so hard—but the mayor seemed to be an insurmountable barrier.

But then something nobody could have predicted happened. Embarrassed by this endless protest, Mayor Owen decided he had better find out who these addicts were, and how they could be shut up. They were from a different world: he had been a businessman for thirty years, and came from a privileged political dynasty in which his grandfather was the chief constable, and his father the lieutenant governor. He hadn't ever known any addicts, so he decided to walk around the Downtown Eastside incognito, and sit with the addicts, and hear what they had to say.

And this man who had argued that they should all be rounded up and locked away on army bases—this local Anslinger—was amazed.

When he described his memory of it in 2012, he still seemed startled by what he had witnessed. "The stories you hear," he said to me, "blow you away." These people, he found, had had such hard lives. He remembered a fifteen-year-old girl on the streets, and shook his head. They're not malicious, he came to see. They're not bad. They're just broken. So he arranged "an afternoon tea party" for "the most hard-core addicts" and sat and listened to them talk about their lives for hours. "The stories were just unbelievable," Owen repeated, shaking his head again.

Now that addicts were no longer phantasmagorical bogeymen but actual people with real stories, Owen realized he would have to learn more. He met with Milton Friedman, the Nobel Prize–winning economist who was the pope of the neoliberal right, and a leading critic of the drug war. Friedman had grown up under alcohol prohibition in Chicago, where he concluded that prohibition causes more problems than the drug itself. The drug war, he believed, was the ultimate big government program—a criminal waste of money. Owen, who had always been a fiscal conservative, started to look at the cost of the drug war, and said to his fellow conservatives: "You want to balance the budget and get our fiscal health in shape? Let's get realistic."

Mayor Owen knew that politicians were supposed to ignore the facts he had learned and keep pledging endless warfare. But he said: "I just get so sick and tired . . . of bullshit."

He decided he was going to change the way he conducted his public meetings and press conferences about drugs. From now on, sitting on the platform with him, he had the chief of police to answer questions about crime, the medical officers to answer questions about health, and an addict from VANDU to answer questions about drug use and addiction. The mayor admitted he knew nothing about it: Why not have an addict there to provide a firsthand answer? With addicts by his side, he pledged to open the first safe injecting room in North America, to keep his new friends in VANDU alive, as the start of a wave of policies to protect addicts.

"Just think about it," he implored his fellow politicians. "Think about the country. Leave politics at the door."

The more the mayor looked and learned, the more he came to believe the prohibitionist policies were rotten right through. "Let's start by legalizing marijuana, taxing it and putting it under the control of the federal government. It's not rocket science. It's a fairly simple proposal, and it works," he said to me. "Let's start with marijuana. We're not talking about cocaine and heroin, [although] I hope we get there eventually. You got to crawl before you walk . . . Then we'll come to the others and gradually go through the process . . . The evidence is in. The facts are in."

Other politicians told him he was mad—not because of the substance of his policies, but because of the politics. "People said—you're going to get defeated, mucking around with a bunch of no-goods," Owen tells me. In fact, he was reelected at the next two mayoral elections in landslide victories.

When he and I met in a café on the Downtown Eastside, people interrupted us spontaneously to thank him for what he had done.

But for his conservative party, it was all too much. They eventually deselected him for the next mayoral race in favor of a more prohibitionist candidate, who lost. His successor as mayor, Larry Campbell, was a strong supporter of the injection site, now named InSite. I walk there, past Oppenheimer Park where the crosses once spiked through the grass, and I find that on the inside, it looks rather like a hairdresser's. As you enter, you are taken through the lobby, shown to your booth, and given clean needles. You inject yourself, while a friendly trained nurse waits unobtrusively in the background. The booths are small and neat and lit from above. Once you have injected yourself, you can walk through to get medical treatment or counseling or just to talk about your problems. Any time you are ready to stop, there is a detox center right upstairs, with a warm bed waiting for you.

Because of the uprising by VANDU, and a conservative mayor who listened to the facts, opened his heart, and changed his mind, Vancouver now has the most progressive drug policies on the North American continent.

But many people had understandable fears about this experiment. Wouldn't it open the floodgates to even more drug use—and therefore end up with more death, not less? It seemed like common sense. The local business owner Price Vassage reflected the opinion of many people when he warned at the time: "People say drug injection sites are going to save lives because there's all these deaths from drug injections. Bullshit. People die of drug overdoses because they do drugs. If you encourage them to continue to use drugs, there's a greater chance they will have a drug overdose."

In 2012, the results of a decade of changed policies came in.

The average life expectancy on the Downtown Eastside, according to the city's medical health officials, had risen by ten years. One newspaper headline said simply: LIFE-EXPECTANCY JUMP ASTOUNDS. The *Province* newspaper explained: "Medical health officer Dr. John Carsley said it is rare to see such a shift in a population's life expectancy." Some of this improvement is due to the fact that the neighborhood is no longer seen as a disaster zone, so some wealthier, healthier people have started to move in; but the *Globe and Mail* newspaper reported, using figures from the British Columbia coroners' office, that drug-related fatalities were down by 80 percent in this period. To find a rise in life expectancy this drastic, you'd have to look to the end of wars—which is what this is.

Philip Owen smiled at me in his expensive suit and said he was proud to have sacrificed his political career in this cause.

In 2012, the Canadian Supreme Court ruled that drug addicts have a right to life, and that safe injecting rooms are an inherent part of that right and can never be legally shut down. There is no need to fill

Oppenheimer Park with crosses today. The killing fields have emptied. And the addicts did it for themselves.

~

Throughout 2013, Bud kept getting sick. He had a lot of pain in his back—the legacy of his time on the streets, he believed—and finally, in May 2014, he was taken to the hospital, where he was diagnosed with pneumonia. They released him early. The next day, he was found dead in his apartment. He was sixty-six years old.

For his memorial service, the streets of the Downtown Eastside were shut down and sealed off—just as they had been on the day they laid a thousand crosses in Oppenheimer Park. Everyone from homeless street addicts to a member of Parliament read his poems aloud, and VANDU marched through the streets in a parade. There were many people in that crowd who knew they were alive because of the uprising Bud had begun all those years before.

Bud lived long enough to see something he feared he would never witness. Back when he was at the lowest ebb of his addiction, it was the poetry of Rimbaud that kept him alive. He vowed then, he told me, to "write one poem like that for another human being . . . to really connect deeply in their pain and their suffering, in the same way these poets did with me."

A few years before he died, Bud went on a reading tour of high schools in British Columbia, and way up north in a town called Smithers, he read out a poem titled "When I Was Fifteen" about the time he had tried to kill himself. He didn't impose any retrospective wisdom. He tried only to describe truthfully what it had been like for him on that day. He didn't know it yet, but there was a girl in the audience who, a few days before, had taken an overdose, and her parents had responded by telling her she couldn't be unhappy because they gave her everything. Her teacher suggested she come to the poetry reading to take her mind off things.

At the end of the reading, the girl approached Bud. She insisted that the teacher unlock the office and run off a photocopy of the poem; she wasn't leaving without it, she said.

She clutched it as she left, glowing now.

And Bud thought to himself—I stayed alive long enough to keep my promise. I wrote my poem.

CHAPTER 15

Snowfall and Strengthening

After a year and a half of meeting victims of this war and feeling more and more angry and depressed, Vancouver had given me an itchy sense of hope. I had learned from Bud that things could get dramatically better if people organized and demanded it—and I wanted to see more experiments and innovations like his, to discover whether this was a freak result, or a harbinger of how things could be. But as I asked around, it slowly became clear to me that there were almost no positive experiments taking place in the Americas. A few prisons in the United States have slightly more generous addiction treatment programs. A few state governments have tiny programs giving out weaker substitute drugs to the most extreme addicts. That, it seemed, was it.

But I knew that the two European countries I am a citizen of—Britain and Switzerland—had experimented with much more substantial alternatives. It was time, I realized, to come home.

I had a vague memory—learned, I think, from reading Mike Gray's book *Drug Crazy* years ago—that in the early 1990s, in the north of England, there had been an experiment in prescribing heroin, but I knew very little about it. I tracked down the man who had led this experiment, and it turned out he was in exile in New Zealand. I interviewed him by phone and then traveled to Liverpool to find everyone I could who had witnessed what happened there. The story they told me had—I quickly realized—startling echoes of where the story of the drug war had begun, long ago.

⁓

Forty-four years and five thousand miles from the shuttering of the last heroin clinics in California, a man named John Marks walked into a gray little doctor's office in a stretch of the Wirral, in the drizzly north of England, where they used to build ships, and now they built nothing. It was his first day as a psychiatrist there. John was a big, bearded Welshman from the valleys, swathed in smoke from the pipe he puffed on, and with the murk of the River Mersey washing past, he was not optimistic. Like Henry Smith Williams, he was the intellectual son of a doctor, and like him, he thought he frankly had better things to do than waste his energies on addicts in a place like this.

John had come here to crack the mystery of schizophrenia and how it really works, but because he was the new boy, he was given a chore. His colleagues said to him: "You can have all the addicts, John—all the alcoholics and drug addicts."

John knew that there would be plenty of addicts waiting for him, because Merseyside in the 1980s was the site of one of the most charged class wars in British history. Margaret Thatcher's Conservative government had pledged to kick the north of England off what they saw as subsidy-sucking nationalized industries, and her ministers were privately proposing to abandon Liverpool, saying that reviving its economy would be like "trying to make water flow uphill." The people of Merseyside saw their workplaces shuttered, their houses become dilapidated, and their streets set on fire as riots began to rip through the inner cities. Now heroin was spreading in the wake of the flames. John could see that the hopelessness sinking over the region would breed even more addiction, and he sighed.

Every Thursday, a slew of addicts came into the clinic, and it was John's job to write them prescriptions—for heroin. They sat down. They answered a few questions. Then they were given enough heroin to last them until the following Thursday. And that was it. At first, John was bemused, thinking this a bizarre idea. Free heroin for addicts? He had unwittingly inherited the last crease in the legal global drug supply system that Harry Anslinger had never been able to iron out.

⁓

Before my journey home, I believed Britain's war on drugs had been like most of our foreign policy: a cry of "Me too!" in a bad American accent. We jail huge numbers of people, but a little less than the United States. We back the drug wars abroad, but not quite so intensely. It turns out I was a little right and a little wrong. There is one significant area in which we are worse: black men are ten times more likely to be imprisoned for drug offences than white men in Britain, a figure beating both the United States and apartheid South Africa.

This is partly because—just as in the United States—our drug war began in a race panic. As the book *Dope Girls* by Marek Kohn explains, on the twenty-seventh of November 1918, a young white showgirl called Billie Carleton stayed up until five in the morning with her friends in her flat behind the Savoy Hotel, with a large amount of cocaine in front of her. She was found dead later that day. There was a press furor about how two sinister forces were bringing these chemicals into the British Isles— the "sickening crowd of under-sized aliens" who made up the wave of Chinese immigrants, and the "nigger 'musicians'" playing jazz. (They put quotation marks around the word "musician," not the word "nigger.") Drugs were banned to save the country from these racial poisons. After the ban, the *News of the World* reported with relief: EVIL NEGRO CAUGHT, and added "the sacrifice of the souls of white women" would finally stop—and it was all cheered on by the U.S. government, delighted to see that other nations shared its concerns.

But for a long time, there was one loophole. Back when the United States was ordering its doctors to block up all legal supplies of heroin and breaking Henry Smith Williams's brother, doctors in Britain flatly refused to fall into line. They said addicts were ill and that it was immoral to leave them to suffer or die. The British government, unsure of how to proceed, appointed a man called Sir Humphrey Rolleston, a baronet and president of the Royal College of Physicians, to decide what our policy should be. After taking a great deal of evidence, he became convinced that the doctors were right: "Relapse," he found, "sooner or later, appears to be the rule, and permanent cure the exception." So he insisted that doctors be left the leeway to prescribe heroin or not, as they saw fit.

And so for two generations, Henry Smith Williams's policies prevailed in Britain, and nowhere else on earth. The result was that while heroin addiction was swelling into the hundreds of thousands in the United States, the picture in Britain was different. The number of addicts never exceeded a thousand, and, as Mike Gray explains, "the addict population in England remained pretty much as it was—little old ladies, self-medi-cating doctors, chronic pain sufferers, ne'er-do-wells, 'all middle-aged people'—most of them leading otherwise normal lives." British doctors insisted there was such a thing as a "stabilized addict," and they said that when you prescribe, this was the norm rather than the exception.

When Billie Holiday came to London in the 1950s, she was amazed. They "are civilized about it and they have no narcotics problem at all," she explained. "One day America is going to smarten up and do the same thing."

Whenever Anslinger was challenged about this evidence in public, he simply denied the British system existed. His evidence was that they didn't have it in Hong Kong, which he said "is a British city." In private, however, he worked hard to shut down the British system. In 1956, the British health secretary told the House of Commons that, under pressure from the United States, he was going to have to cut off the manufacture of heroin. British doctors were outraged, explaining that "the National Health Service exists for the benefit of the sick and suffering citizen." They would not back down, and Anslinger couldn't crush them the way he did his own country's doctors, and so the policy stayed.

But then, in the 1960s, this system was suddenly ruptured. The British government announced that there had been a catastrophic increase in the number of heroin addicts, because it had gone up from 927 to 2,782. This appeared to be happening for two reasons. The swinging sixties were changing attitudes across the world, prompting more drug experimenta-tion—and it turned out that in London specifically, a handful of doctors in the West End had been effectively selling heroin prescriptions to recre-ational users. So the British government moved closer to the American model—but not all the way. The power to prescribe heroin was kept, but it was restricted to a smaller cadre of psychiatrists.

That's hardly unreasonable, John thought, as he surveyed the addicts who came into his clinic. They were "maybe a few dozen lads, the occasional girl, who came and got their tot of junk . . . Railwayman, bargemen, all walks of life really." He told them to stop using, and they argued back, telling him they needed it. He decided after a few years to shut the program down so he could move on to exploring schizophrenia and manic depression and genuinely interesting conditions. "I found this a bit of a headache," he said to me, "and I had bigger fish to fry."

But as he prepared to do this, there was a directive from Margaret Thatcher's government, inspired by her friend Ronald Reagan's intensified drug war across the Atlantic. Every part of Britain had to show it had an antidrug strategy, it said, and conduct a cost-benefit analysis to show what worked. So John commissioned the academic Dr. Russell Newcombe to look into it. He assumed Newcombe would come back and say these patients were like heroin addicts in the United States, and like heroin addicts everywhere, at least in the cliché—unemployed and unemployable, criminal, with high levels of HIV, and a high death rate.

Except the research found something very different. Newcombe found that none of these addicts had the HIV virus, even though Liverpool was a port city where you would expect it to be rife. Indeed, none of them had the usual problems found among addicts: overdoses, abscesses, disease. They mostly had regular jobs and normal lives.

After receiving this report, John looked again at these patients. There was a man named Sydney, who was "an old Liverpool docker, happily married, lovely couple of kids," John recalled. "He'd been chugging along on his heroin for a couple of decades." He seemed to be living a decent, healthy life. So, in fact, now that John thought of it, did all the people prescribed heroin in his clinic.

But how could this be? Doesn't heroin inherently damage the body? Doesn't it naturally cause abscesses, diseases, and death? All doctors agree that medically pure heroin, injected using clean needles, does not produce these problems. Under prohibition, criminals cut their drugs with whatever similar-looking powders they can find, so they can sell more batches and make more cash. Allan Parry, who worked for the local health authority, saw that patients who didn't have a prescription were injecting smack with "brick dust in it, coffee, crushed bleach crystals, anything." He explained to journalists at the time: "Now you inject cement into your veins, and you don't have to be a medical expert to work out that's going to cause harm."

You could immediately see the difference between the street addicts stumbling into the clinic for help for the first time, and the patients who had been on legal prescriptions for a while. The street addicts would often stagger in with abscesses that looked like hard-boiled eggs rotting under their skin, and with open wounds on their hands and legs that looked, as Parry recalls, "like a pizza of infection. It's mushy, and the cheese you get on it is pus. And it just gets bigger and bigger." A combination of contaminated drugs and dirty needles had given a home to these infections in the addicts' flesh and they "can go right through the bone and out the other side, so you've got a hole going right through you. You have that on both legs and your body's not strong enough—it'll cut right through. You had situations where people were walking and their legs snapped." They often looked like survivors of a war, with amputated limbs and flesh that looked charred and scarred.

The addicts on prescriptions, by contrast, looked like the nurses, or the receptionists, or John himself. You couldn't tell them apart.

Harry Anslinger thought this contamination of drugs was a good thing, because it would discourage people from using. By 1942, he was boasting: "The addict is now using heroin which is over 99 percent adulterated." But Allan Parry saw the effects in this clinic. "These shitty drugs—when you try to inject them they block up [your veins] and they really make a mess of you," he tells me. "The trouble is, with dirty heroin, one vein more or less goes with one hit." Then, "if you damage that vein, you'll try another one, and eventually you work your way around your body looking at what veins you've got and sticking stuff in them," destroying your body as you go.

Faced with this evidence, John Marks was beginning to believe that many "of the harms of drugs are to do with the laws around them, not the drugs themselves." In the clinic, they started to call the infections and abscesses and amputations "drug war wounds." So he "slowly got," he told me, "that this clinic was working wonders" by bypassing criminality and providing safer forms of the drug. John began to wonder: If prescription is so effective, why don't we do it more? If it is preventing people from getting HIV, and injecting poisons into their veins, and dying in the gutters, why not expand it?

He decided to embark on an experiment. He expanded his heroin prescription program from a dozen people to more than four hundred, and with a local pharmacist, he pioneered the prescription of "heroin reefers"— cigarettes soaked in heroin. He also prescribed cocaine, including smokable cocaine, for a small number of people who had become addicted to street crack. He knew that, like alcohol, cocaine is harmful to your health over time, but he explained: "If you were an alcoholic in the Chicago of the 1930s, and had just stolen your grandmother's purse to buy a tot of adulterated methylated spirits at an exorbitant price from Mr. Capone, I would have a clean conscience in prescribing for you a dram of the best Scotch whisky."

The first people to notice an effect were the local police. Inspector Michael Lofts studied 142 heroin and cocaine addicts in the area, and he found that in the eighteen months before getting a prescription from Dr. Marks, they received, on average, 6.88 criminal convictions, mostly for theft and robbery. In the eighteen months afterward, that figure fell to an average of 0.44 criminal convictions. In other words: there was a 93 percent drop in theft and burglary. "You could see them transform in front of your own eyes," Lofts told a newspaper, amazed. "They came in in outrageous condition, stealing daily to pay for illegal drugs; and became, most of them, very amiable, reasonable law-abiding people." It was just as Henry Smith Williams had said, all those years before.

~

One day, a young mother named Julia Scott came into his clinic and explained she had ended up working as a prostitute to support her habit. Confronted with patients like this, John told an interviewer, he was starting to feel "anger. It makes me furious that a group of young able people . . . should suffer from the same death rate as people with small-pox, between 10 and 20 percent. I'm not a bleeding heart, and I don't think there's anything glamorous about drugs; I try to make my clients realize that what they are doing is boring, boring, boring."

He wanted Julia to be bored, not terrified and in danger—so he wrote her a prescription. "I stopped straightaway," she said later to Ed Bradley of CBS's 60 Minutes when they came to report on the Liverpool experiment. "I went back once just to see, and I was almost physically sick just to see these girls doing what I used to do."

Now she was working as a waitress, and able to be a mother to her little girl. As Julia pushed her daughter on a swing, Bradley asked her: "Without that prescription, where do you think you'd be today?"

"I'd probably be dead by now," she said. "I need heroin to live."

~

The changes taking place as John Marks expanded his prescription program weren't limited to his patients. On the streets of the neighborhood, the drug gangs started to recede. John overstated it at the time when he said drug dealing had been totally wiped out—the writer Will Self, reporting on the ground, asked around and learned there were still dealers to be found. But the police said there were far fewer than before—Inspector Lofts explained at the time: "Since the clinics opened, the street heroin dealer has slowly but surely abandoned the streets of Warrington and Widnes." It was as if time was running backward—to the era before the drug war. In a small brick building by the River Mersey, a California dream was being reborn.

But John Marks differed from Henry Smith Williams in one important way. Henry thought that drug addicts would need to be given their prescription for the rest of their lives. That was the part of his story that most disconcerted me. It seemed that the only alternative to the drug war forever was being prescribed a drug forever.

But since then, a discovery had been made about addiction—one that Henry Smith Williams couldn't have foreseen. It was first spotted by a psychologist named Charles Winick, who set up a free clinic for addicted musicians in New York in the 1950s. Winick, like everyone else, used to believe that once you were a heroin addict, you were a heroin addict until you died, but what he found was something very different. "Heroin use was concentrated in the 25 to 39 group, after which it tapered to very little," he wrote. Most addicts simply stopped of their own accord. They "mature out of addiction . . . possibly because the stresses and strains of life are becoming stabilized for them and because the major challenges of adulthood have passed."

This process—the fancy names for it are "maturing out" or "natural recovery"—is not the exception: it's what happens to almost all of the addicts around you. This finding is so striking I had to read about it in slews of studies before I really took it on board: Most addicts will simply stop, whether they are given treatment or not, provided prohibition doesn't kill them first. They usually do so after around ten years of use.

So once John Marks knew this, he came to believe his job was a matter of keeping them alive long enough to recover naturally. That's why every week, the addicts of Widnes turned up at John's office for a meeting, and left with a prescription for smokable heroin or—in a small number of cases, as we will see shortly—cocaine. John explained to the public: "If they're drug takers determined to continue their drug use . . . the choice that I'm being offered, and society is being offered, is drugs from the clinic or drugs from the Mafia."

~

There was one obvious reason why people were worried by John's experiment. If there is no punishment—if you give people drugs for free—surely they will use them more? This was one of Harry Anslinger's most reasonable objections. If you reintroduce prescription, he warned, "drug addicts would multiply unrestrained."

It seems like common sense. But John, by contrast, thought the rate of use would hold steady: If being ostracized by your family, riven with disease, and plunged into poverty didn't affect your decision to use, how would a few free heroin reefers make a difference?

It turns out both sides were wrong. Drug use didn't rise, and it didn't hold steady. It actually fell—including among the people who *weren't* being given a prescription. Research published by John in the *Proceedings of the Royal College of Physicians of Edinburgh* compared Widnes, which had a heroin clinic, to the very similar Liverpool borough of Bootle, which didn't. In Bootle, there were 207.54 drug users per hundred thousand people; in Widnes it was just 15.83—a twelvefold decrease.

But why? Why would prescribing heroin to addicts mean that fewer people became addicts? Dr. Russell Newcombe, working out of John Marks's clinic, discovered what he believes is the explanation.

Imagine you are a street heroin addict. You have to raise a large sum of money every day for your habit: £100 a day for heroin at that time in the Wirral. How are you going to get it? You can rob. You can prostitute. But there is another way, and it's a lot less unpleasant than either of them. You can buy your drugs, take what you need, and then cut the rest with talcum powder and sell it to other people. But to do that, you need to persuade somebody else to take the drugs too. You need to become a salesman, promoting the experience.

So heroin under prohibition becomes, in effect, a pyramid selling scheme. "Insurance companies would love to have salesmen like drug addicts," with that level of motivation, John remarked.

Here's why drug use went into reverse in John Marks's clinic. Prescription, it turns out, kills the pyramid selling scheme, by stripping out the profit motive. You don't have to sell smack to get smack. This explains why when you prescribe heroin, fewer people are recruited to use heroin, and why when you prescribe cocaine, fewer people are recruited to use cocaine.

As Russell Newcombe tells me this, I can't help but think of a weird little twist of history. Harry Anslinger always said drug addiction was infectious. It isn't, in normal circumstances—but the system of prohibition he built makes it so after all.

∼

John Marks was being shouted at. The public meeting was getting nasty, and he was being abused. But it wasn't a right-winger or conservative yelling at him. At this time, Liverpool was run by a Communist group called Militant Tendency, who believed in establishing an immediate socialist revolution in Britain.

John Marks, they declared, was preventing that revolution by tranquilizing the working classes with heroin. The opiate of the masses turned out to be . . . opiates, literally. Marks was blocking Marx.

The father of one of John's patients stood up, and addressed the crowd. "I was a bit puzzled by John giving Jimmy heroin to start with," he said, "because I thought the job was to get him off. But you know what—since he started with this Dr. Marks, we now see him at mealtimes, he sits with us and talks with us, he's even back with his girlfriend, and you know what, lads? He's got an offer of a job next week."

∼

John Marks expected that the news of these results would spur people across the country, and across the world, to do the same. Who would turn down a policy that saves the lives of drug users *and* leads to less drug use *and* causes dealers to gradually disperse?

At last, this ripple effect seemed to have begun. He was asked to set up a bigger version of the Widnes clinic at the Metropolitan Centre in Liverpool, and then it was decided that every health district in the region from Southport in the north to Macclesfield in the east would have a prescribing clinic of its own.

There was a drop in shoplifting so massive that the department store chain Marks and Spencer's publicly praised the policy and decided to sponsor the first World Conference on Harm Reduction and Drug-Taking in Liverpool in 1990. There, one of the police officers inspired by John's experiment, Derek O'Connell, explained: "As police officers, part of our oath of office is to protect life . . . Clearly, we must reach injectors and get them the help that they require, but in the meantime we must try and keep them healthy, for we are their police as well." But John was about to whack into the same wall as Henry Smith Williams.

∼

With a few of his colleagues, John was invited to tour the United States to explain how this policy could save American lives.

Everywhere they went, at the end of the meeting, they were told the same thing—that the Republican congressman Jesse Helms had been pressuring the organizers to shut them down and shut them up. Helms didn't want anybody to interfere with the war on drugs. A few years later, on a CNN phone-in show, a caller thanked him for "everything you've done to help keep down the niggers," and he replied by saluting the camera and saying: "Well, thank you, I think."

After an item about John's clinic was broadcast on one of the top-rated news shows in the United States, *60 Minutes*, in 1991, John was phoned by Bing Spear, the chief inspector of the Drugs Branch of the Home Office.

"We've got a lot of heat from our embassy in Washington," he warned. "They've got on to [the government] saying, 'What's this about somebody in Liverpool giving out crack cocaine? Close it down immediately!'"

The Conservative government decided to "merge" John's clinic with a new health trust, run by evangelical Christians who opposed prescription on principle. The patients panicked, because they knew what being cut off would mean—a return to abscesses and overdoses and scrambling for drugs from gangsters. John was powerless to help them.

The results came quickly. In all the time Dr. Marks had been prescribing, from 1982 to 1995, he never had a drug-related death among his patients. Now Sydney, the Liverpool docker, went back to buying adulterated crap on the streets and died. Julia Scott, who said she would be dead without her prescription, was proved right: she died of an overdose, leaving her daughter without a mother.

Of the 450 patients Marks prescribed to, 20 were dead within six months, and 41 were dead within two years. More lost limbs and caught potentially lethal diseases. They returned to the death rate for addicts under prohibition: 10 to 20 percent, similar to smallpox.

Dr. Russell Newcombe, who had worked in the clinic, tells me the survivors "were immediately forced back onto the street . . . People who had jobs lost them. It split relationships up. People rapidly went back into debt and crime. The average person thrown off John Marks's prescription regime would have been back in acquisitive crime within a month." Whenever he'd see one of them in the street, he'd ask them what they were doing now. "Grafting," they'd say—the local word for stealing to support your habit.

Today, Merseyside is riddled with drug addiction, and drug gangs are killing each other in the war for drugs.

～

John found he was blacklisted within his own country. He ended up literally at the other end of the earth, in Gisborne, the farthest corner of New Zealand, the place from which he told me his side of the story by telephone in 2012.

"I was exiled," John Marks told me. One day, the Royal Astronomical Society asked him to play Galileo at an open day. He had to playact being burned at the stake. His voice softened at the irony. But when I said to him this story made me angry, he replied, flatly: "Whatever gave [you] the idea folk in authority operate according to reason? Your trouble is you're being rational."

And so his story was supposed to go the same way as Henry Smith Williams's. It was supposed to be forgotten. But this time, something was different.

I got on a plane to Geneva, the Swiss city where Harry Anslinger first went to the United Nations to force his vision on the world. It was there, in a sweet twist of history, that his grip was finally being broken. I sat with the woman who—along with others—pioneered this change, and she began to tell me her story. It had been inspired—without him knowing it—by John Marks.

~

The police officer who accompanied Ruth Dreifuss had tears in his eyes. He was taking the future president of Switzerland through an abandoned railway station in Zurich, down by the river. All the local drug addicts had been herded there, like infected cattle.

Ruth had been looking out over scenes like this for years now. A few years before, she had been to the park in Bern that played the same role there. There were girls being openly prostituted out and there were addicts staggering around, out of control, incoherent. There were people injecting themselves "in places you couldn't imagine," she says, because every other vein couldn't be traced, as if it was trying to escape. Above the bustle, dealers were yelling their prices at the top of their voices. As she heard them, Ruth thought of Wall Street brokers, barking on the trading floor. The threat of violence hung over everything as dealers fought for customers.

Most Swiss people had never seen anything like this. The police were not just crying; they were afraid. This was Switzerland in the 1980s and 1990s, but it was an affront to everything the Swiss thought about themselves.

Switzerland has always been the place on earth where it is easiest to pretend nothing ever changes, and everything makes sense. My father is a mountain boy from the Swiss Alps, and in his village, you were raised to believe that the country's last major upset was when Hannibal invaded the mountains with his elephants in 221 B.C. All the country's symbols are about order and cleanliness and permanence. Swiss watches will tick-tock with scientific precision even after a nuclear holocaust. The postcards show the thirty-foot-high cleansing jet of blue water waving out from Lake Geneva into the sky, with the Alps motionless and unchanging in the distance. It is, the Swiss will tell you gravely, a criminal offense to flush your toilet after ten o'clock at night, because it might disturb your neighbors.

But now, Switzerland was watching as drug prohibition created tornadoes in the middle of its pristine clockwork cities. Ruth Dreifuss didn't know it yet as she walked through this scene, but soon she was going to become the first female president of Switzerland and the first Jewish president of Switzerland.

Even more significant, she would become the first president in the world since the 1930s who decided to run not away from drug reform, but toward it. She dedicated her presidency to sitting with addicts, listening to addicts, defending addicts—and getting them a legal supply of their drugs.

I first learned about her when drug policy experts began to say that there was one political leader in the world who really understood what was wrong with the drug war better than anyone else. I wrote to her at once. That's how I found myself, in early 2013, in her apartment, as she chain-smoked and flicked her ash into a big yellow ashtray. She apologized for the smoke. "I am an addict!" she said, and laughed.

～

When Billie Holiday was in prison for heroin possession in the United States, the only people who tried to help her were Swiss. "A wonderful couple in Zurich, Switzerland, sent me a thousand dollars," she wrote, "and a telegram telling me that America would never accept me when I got out, so I should come to them in Europe."

Switzerland is—like all countries—in a constant tussle between its compassion and its cruelty. As that letter was being written, Ruth was at a Swiss school where the other kids would sometimes taunt her, saying that the Jews had assassinated Jesus and would have to be punished forever. Later, Ruth was told that as a woman, she was hysterical and emotional and couldn't be entrusted with the vote. If they ever let her cast a ballot, the country's politicians warned, Switzerland's families would fall apart and the nation would descend into chaos. It was only after she and thousands of others marched and demanded for years that Swiss women were finally enfranchised in 1971. So Ruth Dreifuss had seen how even the most concrete of certainties can fall apart and seem crazy to the next generation.

When Ruth was put in charge of Switzerland's health policy in 1993, there was a corpse waiting in her in-tray. Switzerland had the worst HIV epidemic in Europe, and nobody could see an end to it. This country has no ghettoes where addiction could be hidden away. There are no Us and Them in Swiss chalets: if chaotic drug use is happening, it happens where everyone can see. So she gathered into her office representatives of the country's most despised minorities—gays, prostitutes, and junkies— because she suspected that they held not only the problem but also the solution to the AIDS crisis. She found that sex workers, if you arm them with condoms and information, are actually "very good public health agents. But you have to trust them. You have to accept their job. So prevention begins with respect."

As a socialist, she had always believed that everyone—no matter how seemingly lost—can be empowered if you do it right. But she looked at the drug addicts and asked herself: How?

In the fight against AIDS, Switzerland had already built good needle exchanges, provided safe consumption rooms where addicts could go to take their drugs, and prescribed methadone. Still the disease raged. It turned out that many addicts loathe methadone: they compare it to a flavorless lump of dough when you have a ravenous craving for steak. One day, some of the street doctors Ruth talked to all the time told her that they had been to visit an experiment in Liverpool, England—a program with startling results, even though the ideologues were shutting its doors.

It had been discovered a few years before in Switzerland that there was a clause in Swiss law that allowed heroin to be given to citizens, provided it was part of a scientific experiment. So far that had been done with only a tiny handful of people.

So Ruth said—Okay, we are going to have a really large experiment. We are going to make it much easier for any addict who wants it to get methadone, and for the people who can't cope with that, we will prescribe them heroin. Switzerland has a political system built on consensus. No one official can drive a policy on her own. She needed to persuade her colleagues, and the cantons. So Ruth fought for it. This is an emergency, she explained, and in emergencies, you take dramatic steps.

～

Twenty years later, Ruth Dreifuss lives across the street from one of the heroin-prescribing clinics in Geneva that were made possible by her political battle. At seven in the morning, I hurry past the seagulls squawking on Lake Geneva. It is as dark as midnight, and in the neat little Swiss cafés, men and women in suits are reading newspapers and drinking coffee. Nobody seems bleary-eyed. The Swiss go to bed early, and they wake in the darkness without complaining.

In the white corridor of the heroin clinic, I find a young man with big headphones and an old man in a tweed suit with leather elbow patches sitting in chairs next to each other. They are waiting patiently to shoot up.

The older man follows a nurse into the injecting room, and he emerges a little while later to sit for twenty minutes alone, and then he agrees to talk to me, in a room, to one side. He looks like the secretary of state for a minor Central European nation, with his carefully polished shoes and lined, distinguished face. After we are introduced by the doctors, he says he will tell me his story provided I do not use his real name, because he was admitting to criminal offenses he had carried out before the drug laws were changed. I will call him Jean.

"I was sick, I was dirty," when he first came here, he says. "I was really quite a typical addict." He couldn't concentrate to watch a film for more than a few minutes; he couldn't eat fruit or anything even vaguely greasy, because his digestive system was so curdled by the street contaminants. He had been shooting up for thirty-five years. "When you are using on the street, you feel death already hiding inside you. You can feel it and you can see it," he says. "You have death inside yourself, and death is progressing."

He tried methadone, but it did nothing for him. He still craved heroin all the time. He would wake each morning in a flop-sweat of panic, asking himself: How am I going to get the money I need to buy my smack today? He was trapped in the constant misery-go-round of get money, buy heroin, inject, get money, buy heroin, inject, all day, every day.

"It's not just an addiction. It's a job," he says. He survived only by being involved in drug trafficking—he doesn't want to give the details, except to say that he was a "middleman"—until one day, he heard about the prescription program established by Ruth Dreifuss.

This is the last option in the system for people who cannot be helped any other way. To be eligible, you need to meet three conditions: you have to be over eighteen, you have to have gone through at least two other treatment programs without success, and you have to hand in your driver's license.

"It wasn't easy to accept and see at first," he says. "All addicts are in a total confusion." Suddenly, his constant scrambling for his drugs was taken away, and he had a day ahead of him he had to fill. He tells me patients here "have to reinvent our lives. We have to reinvent the imagination." The heroin program is built around helping the patients to slowly rebuild: to get therapy, to get a home, and to get a job. One of Jean's fellow patients, for example, owns a gas station, while another works in a bank. He discovered that "once you have stability, the speed of events decreases, and you come back into a normal life, and you say—okay, what am I going to do now?"

It's hard to do this, after being addicted for so long, but Jean says "the pain I have now isn't the pain of a sickness. It's the pain of being reborn." For the first time in decades, "I feel well and happy, to have recovered things I had completely forgotten." He has started to eat fruit and watch films and listen to music again. "You can come back," he says, "to reality."

～

Harry Anslinger believed he had spotted the crucial flaw in heroin prescription programs like this. Addicts' bodies gradually develop a tolerance for their drug, so he said they would need higher and higher doses over time to achieve the same effect. "The addict is never satisfied with his dose; he always tries to get more," he explained. He praised two of his officers who laid out what they called the First Law of Addiction: "A person in the condition of opiate addiction, with free access to opiates, will continue in that condition at an accelerated rate of consumption unless the course of addiction is deterred by some extraneous force."

That observation seems to make sense. Yet at this clinic, they tell me, they have discovered something that contradicts it.

If you are an addict here and you want a higher dose of heroin, you can ask for it, and they'll give it to you. So at first, most addicts demand more and more, just as Anslinger and his agents predicted. But within a few months, most addicts stop asking for more and choose, of their own free will, to stabilize their doses.

After that, "most of them want to go always down," explains the psychiatrist here, Dr. Rita Manghi. Jean, for example, started at the clinic taking heroin three times a day—80 mg in the morning, 60 mg in the afternoon, and 80 mg in the evening. Now, he takes only 30 mg in the morning and 40 mg in the evening, and he says, "I'm on the brink of saying to my doctor I don't want any more." He is a typical user here.

Suddenly, the slightly depressing debate at the start of the drug war between Harry Anslinger and Henry Smith Williams—prohibition forever versus prescription forever—seems bogus. But in this clinic, they have discovered that that isn't the real choice. If you give hard-core addicts the option of a safe legal prescription and allow them to control the dose, the vast majority will stabilize and then slowly reduce their drug consumption over time. Prescription isn't an alternative to stopping your drug use. It is—for many people—a path to it.

"This program," Jean says, "gives you the chance to recover the control you have lost," step by step, day by day. A Portuguese psychiatrist who treats people here, Dr. Daniel Martin, tries to explain it to me by giving me a visual image.

Most addicts here, he says, come with an empty glass inside them; when they take heroin, the glass becomes full, but only for a few hours, and then it drains down to nothing again. The purpose of this program is to gradually build a life for the addict so they can put something else into that empty glass: a social network, a job, some daily pleasures. If you can do that, it will mean that even as the heroin drains, you are not left totally empty. Over time, as your life has more in it, the glass will contain more and more, so it will take less and less heroin to fill it up. And in the end, there may be enough within you that you feel full without any heroin at all.

Users can stay on this program for as long as they want, but the average patient will come here for three years, and at the end of that time, only 15 percent are still using every day.

Before, being a heroin addict was violent and thrilling—you were chasing and charging around. In Switzerland today, it is rather dull. It involves sitting in clinics, and being offered cups of tea. The subculture is gone.

After the clinics opened, the people of Switzerland started to notice something. The parks and railway stations that were filled with addicts emptied. Today, children play there once again. The streets became safer. The people on heroin prescriptions carry out 55 percent fewer vehicle thefts and 80 percent fewer muggings and burglaries. This fall in crime was "almost immediate," the most detailed academic study found. The HIV epidemic among drug users stopped. In 1985, some 68 percent of new HIV infections in Switzerland were caused by injection drug use, but by 2009, it was down to approximately 5 percent.

The number of addicts dying every year fell dramatically, the proportion with permanent jobs tripled, and every single one had a home. A third of all addicts who had been on welfare came off it altogether. And just as in Liverpool, the pyramid selling by addicts crumbled to sand: people on the heroin prescription program for a sustained period were 94.7 percent less likely to sell drugs than before their treatment. Jean tells me the drug dealers he used to work for are "completely against this program. They can control people in weak states and make money from them. If I was still in the criminal milieu, they could make me a killer, I would do anything." As he said this, I thought of Chino and Rosalio. "But now? No. I am lost for them."

The program costs thirty-five Swiss francs per patient per day, but it spares the taxpayer from having to spend forty-four francs a day arresting, trying, and convicting the drug user. So when people ask "Why should I pay for this?" the pragmatic Swiss answer is: This doesn't cost you money. It saves you money.

~

But I was still wondering all the time—how did Ruth manage to sell these policies in such a conservative country? My Swiss relatives are often way to the right of the Tea Party—and they are regarded as moderates. This isn't like people opting for drug reform in San Francisco—it's like people opting for drug reform in Lubbock, Texas.

I knew she couldn't have gone over the people's heads, because Switzerland has a system of deep democracy. If you are a Swiss citizen and you don't like a law passed by the parliament, all you have to do is gather fifty thousand signatures, and you will trigger a national referendum on whether it should be struck down entirely. In the late 1990s, a conservative group triggered a national referendum on heroin prescription, and there was a rowdy national debate—or as rowdy as Switzerland ever gets.

Ruth and the many people who agreed with her introduced something to the drug debate that nobody had ever tried anywhere else in the world. Ever since Anslinger, the drug warriors had presented themselves as the forces of order ranged against the chaos that would inevitably be brought by any relaxation in the drug laws. But, in a political jujitsu move, Ruth reversed that argument. Swiss citizens could see now that U.S.-style drug crackdowns had brought chaos to their streets—and after the government provided a legal route to heroin, the chaos vanished. So they argued that the drug war means disorder, while ending the drug war means slowly restoring order.

This argument won. In 1997, some 70 percent of Swiss electors voted to keep the reforms. In 2008, the conservative forces regrouped and called another referendum. The campaign supported by Ruth ran posters of a young mother with her baby, saying: "I want to keep our public parks free of syringes." Another poster showed a couple in their fifties saying: "Thanks to treatment, our son could quit drugs." This time, 68 percent backed the policy. These campaigns showed, in embryo, the case that, I believe, could end prohibition around the world.

They did it to protect and defend not the addicts, but themselves. This is, it occurs to me, a crucial lesson for drug reformers. Those of us who believe in ending the drug war already pretty much have the liberals and leftists on our side. It's the moderates and the conservatives we need to win over—and the way to do it may be heard in a distant yodel from the mountaintops of Switzerland.

∼

One day, Ruth went as president to a heroin clinic in Bern to talk to the addicts there, and among them was one young man—well-dressed and handsome—whom she tried to strike up a conversation with, but he seemed shy, and would barely say a word to her. To her surprise, as she was leaving, he handed her a note, and said she should wait until she was back in her office before reading it.

"Six months ago I was in the streets," he said. "I hated myself, I had lost all respect for myself. I was dirty, I slept outside in the streets and the parks, and [then] I was accepted in the clinic . . . and now I am coming three times a day to receive my heroin. I regained respect." And then he explained that he had been reluctant to talk to her because now he worked for her, in the department she runs.

"When you read such a letter," she says, "you can continue for many years on that."

∼

It's hard, I say to Ruth in her apartment in Geneva one afternoon, to imagine an American president or British prime minister doing what she has done: sitting with addicts, learning their stories, and urging people to help them. "They should," she says. "You have to learn and to see with their own eyes." If she was stuck in an elevator with Barack Obama and

David Cameron, she would tell them: "You are responsible for all of your citizens, and being responsible means protecting them and giving them the means to protect themselves. There is no group that you can abandon."

Yet the same forces that had pressured Britain into locking down John Marks tried to intimidate the Swiss. The International Narcotics Control Board declared: "Anyone who plays with fire loses control over it," and said Switzerland was "send[ing] a disastrous signal to countries in which the drugs were produced." But Ruth Dreifuss was not going to be intimidated by anyone. When the U.S. drug czar, General Barry McCaffrey, visited Europe, he went to the Netherlands and held a press conference at which—like a colonial governor addressing the natives—he berated the Dutch government for their wickedness. He was scheduled to come to Switzerland shortly after. "It was terrible what he said in the Netherlands [about] the cannabis shops," Ruth says.

So she called him and explained: "There will be no press conference in Switzerland. We do not accept [for] you to interfere in our political debate."

Once she left office, Ruth came together with other former heads of state—including President Fernando Henrique Cardoso of Brazil—to set up an organization called the Global Commission on Drug Policy, demanding an end to the global drug war. When I spoke to her, she had recently been to Mexico, Ghana, Budapest, Vilnius, and Italy. Everywhere she goes, she says, she can see that "doubts are rising," and people are eager to hear about the rational alternatives.

It's even harder to imagine, I tell her, a former U.S. president or British prime minister living a minute's walk from a heroin clinic.

"As far as possible, we always wanted to have these places in the center of the city," she says, smoking a cigarette and flicking the ash. "For many reasons. I mean, these people have to come regularly. We can't send them I-don't-know-where. When they have a job it's important they can come during the lunch break or so. It's practical."

And she looks out the window, in the direction of the heroin clinic.

~

After I returned from Switzerland, I enthusiastically jabbered to several Americans about these results and said they should be tried back in the Land of the Free—and they often came back with a response that threw me.

But we already prescribe powerful opiates, they said. We prescribe Oxycontin and Vicodin and other painkillers—and, far from having the effect you are describing, it has caused a disaster. Look, they said, at the headlines any day of the week. More people are becoming addicted every year to prescription drugs that they were given at first for pain relief. More people are overdosing. More people are becoming criminals. More people are transferring to even harder drugs, like heroin. You want more of that?

This narrative was everywhere—including in liberal outlets normally receptive to drug policy reform, like *Rolling Stone*. The conclusion seemed obvious: for some reason, in this country, prescription doesn't reduce problems—it metastasizes them.

This seemed to blast a hole in the case for providing legal access to the most potent drugs in the United States, and I was sent into a spiral of confusion. I looked over the evidence, and these critics seemed to be right. Oxycontin and Vicodin addictions are indeed spreading in the United States, and they are causing more criminality and overdose. The cause, everyone seems to agree, is that doctors have prescribed the drugs too freely.

How could it be, I asked myself, that opiate prescription worked so well in Switzerland but was proving to be a disaster in the United States? Is this just a deep cultural difference? Or is there a flaw in the Swiss model that I'm not seeing?

It was only when I discussed this with Meghan Ralston, an expert on prescription drugs with the Drug Policy Alliance, with Professor Bruce Alexander back in Vancouver, and with Dr. Hal Vorse, a medical doctor who treats prescription drug addicts in Oklahoma City, that I began to understand what was really happening. Between them, these three experts raised three different questions that forced me to see the prescription drug crisis in a radically different light.

The first question that made me think again is: When do the worst problems associated with Oxycontin and Vicodin, the ones you see on the news, start? When do the addicts start to hold up pharmacies to get their next batch, or prostitute themselves, or start overdosing on a massive scale? Meghan Ralston, one of the leading experts on this crisis, explained to me: They don't begin when the drugs are prescribed. They begin when the prescriptions are *cut off*.

The United States, she explained, doesn't have a Swiss-style policy of prescribing Oxycontin or Vicodin or other opiates to addicts. In fact, it has the precisely opposite policy. If I am an American who has developed an Oxycontin addiction, as soon as my doctor realizes I'm an addict, she has to cut me off. She is allowed to prescribe to treat only my physical pain—not my addiction. Indeed, if she prescribes just to meet my addiction, she will face being stripped of her license and up to twenty-five years in jail as a common drug dealer—just like Henry Smith Williams's brother at the birth of the drug war.

That's when, in desperation, I might hold up a pharmacy with a gun, or go and buy unlabeled pills from street dealers. Most of the problems attributed to prescription drugs in the United States, Meghan Ralston says, begin here, when the legal, regulated route to the drug is terminated. Nobody, she explained to me, swallows 80 mg of Oxycontin prescribed by their doctor and goes out to commit a crime, or dies of an overdose. No: it's when the doctor realizes the patient is an addict and cuts them off that all the trouble begins.

This is so different from how the prescription drug crisis has been almost universally reported that it took some time for me to absorb it. It was only when I began to think about it in relation to the last time drugs were sold freely in the United States—before 1914—that I started to understand.

Remember the transformation Henry Smith Williams lived through. Before the ban, almost all opiate users would buy a mild form of the drug at their corner store for a small price. A few did become addicts, and that meant their lives were depleted, in the same way that an alcoholic's life is depleted today. Nobody should dismiss this effect: it is real human suffering. But virtually none of them committed crimes to get their drug, or became wildly out of control, or lost their jobs. Then the legal routes to the drug were cut off—and all the problems we associate with drug addiction began: criminality, prostitution, violence.

The same pattern is playing out today with prescription drugs. If I am a young man with a legal Oxycontin prescription that I am using compulsively to deal with my psychological pain, my life will be depleted, and sluggish, and incomplete. If I am cut off from that prescription—if my own personal 1914 hits me—my life will become disastrous, and I will start acting in all the chaotic ways associated with the prescription drug crisis today. It is when the legal routes are cut off that the worst begins. So, Meghan says, the prescription drug crisis doesn't discredit legalization—it shows the need for it.

But what does "legalization" mean when it comes to prescription drugs? Some people would argue that they should be openly sold, like alcohol—but I think Switzerland's heroin experiment shows a better path forward: you could expand the criteria for prescription. If you can prescribe opiates for back pain, why can't you prescribe them for psychological pain? Imagine if a woman addicted to Oxy in Oklahoma City wasn't abruptly told to stop using, with directions to the nearest Narcotics Anonymous group and a brisk "Good luck." Imagine if, instead, she was told exactly what the patients in Geneva are told: you will be given a safe, legal dose for as long as you need it, and while you receive it, we will give you support and care to help you to rebuild your life, get secure housing, and keep your job.

It seems reasonable to expect that the results would be the same in Vermont or Alabama as they were in Switzerland—that most people would, over time, choose to reduce their dose and eventually give up their drugs as their pain abated.

But that's only the first step: it's the bandage that stops the hemorrhaging. Then you need to have a deeper strategy—one that stops these wounds from forming in the first place. To do that, you need to change the culture so people find life less unbearable. We have to build a society that looks more like Rat Park and less like a rat race. If that sounds like pie in the sky, remember the alternative: addiction outbreaks that only swell, like an Oxy slick forming across the sky.

This leads to the second question: Why did the prescription drug crisis radically accelerate in the past decade? There are two possible explanations. The first is the only one any of us have ever heard. It says that doctors—urged on by the greed of Big Pharma—have been handing out these legal opiates for conditions such as back pain without properly warning their patients about the risk of addiction, and as a result, lots of people are becoming accidentally addicted. You go to the doctor, you take a painkiller believing it'll only deal with your slipped disk, after a few months of taking it, you find that your body needs these chemicals in a very real physical sense—and you can't give them up without going into terrible withdrawal and panic. This is what most people believe has driven this crisis, and it seems like common sense.

But there's a crucial piece of evidence that has been omitted from this picture. As we saw earlier, in hospitals across the West, people are given much more powerful opiates than Oxycontin and Vicodin day in, day out. For example, the diamorphine—heroin—you will be given if you have a knee replacement is a really powerful opiate, agreed by doctors to be around three times more powerful than Oxycontin, and you will often take it for a long time as you recover. Yet—as we saw before, and has been proven beyond doubt—this almost never turns people into addicts. So how could a really powerful opiate cause virtually no addiction when given out by doctors, and an opiate that is three times weaker cause so much?

This suggests we should look at the other possible explanation—a story taught to me by Bruce Alexander back on the streets of the Downtown Eastside. Bruce showed that at any given time, you and I and everyone around us has access to a huge array of chemicals that could drive away our pain for a while, from vodka to valium. Almost all of the time, we leave them on the shelf, unused. So the question is: Why are there sudden moments when large numbers of people, scattered across different bathrooms and barrooms, suddenly pick them up and swallow them compulsively, all at once? The answer doesn't lie in access. It lies in agony. Outbreaks of drug addiction have always taken place, he proved, when there was a sudden rise is isolation and distress—from the gin-soaked slums of London in the eighteenth century to the terrified troops in Vietnam.

This raises the question: Has anything happened in the United States in the past decade that could be the deep driver of the prescription drug crisis? It's not hard to find the answer. The American middle class had been painfully crumbling even before the Great Crash produced the worst economic crisis since the Great Depression. Ordinary Americans are finding themselves flooded with stress and fear. That, Bruce's theory suggests, is why they are leaning more and more heavily on Oxycontin and Vicodin to numb their pain.

This insight puts the prescription drug crisis in a different light. All those stressed-out moms hooked on Vicodin and all those truck drivers hooked on Oxycontin have been seeing their incomes shrink and their abilities to look after their families wither for years as their status and security in American society shrivel away. If Oxy had never been invented, Bruce's evidence suggests, at a moment like this, they would have found something else in their bathroom or liquor cabinet to give them some relief—because in every previous crisis like this, people have found something similar.

It is not that the specific drug plays no effect—clearly it does. Vicodin and Oxycontin do contain chemical hooks, and those do play some role in the addiction. Remember the evidence from earlier, about how just 17 percent of tobacco addiction is caused by the chemical hooks in the drug? Given that tobacco is the most addictive drug, we would expect at most that the chemicals in Oxycontin play—at worst—a similar role in causing Oxycontin addiction. Now, 17 percent is a lot, and doctors should be conscious of it when they are prescribing these drugs to people who could be offered milder painkillers first, with fewer chemical hooks. But whichever way you cut it, 17 percent is still a small part of the effect. Focusing only on this smaller aspect and ignoring the much larger causes is one of the reasons why our responses to this crisis are failing so badly.

∼

Yet even after finding this out, I still had a nagging sense that there was something I was not understanding about the prescription drug crisis. So I researched more, and I kept bumping up against the third question thrown up by this crisis: Why are so many people starting with Oxycontin and Vicodin and ending up using heroin?

This conveyor belt from prescription drugs to more potent stuff has been well documented—nobody can deny it—and at first it seems to refute everything I learned in Switzerland. Indeed, this dynamic is so intense it has become the dominant issue in several states. The crisis is so severe in Vermont, for example, that the governor in 2014 dedicated his entire State of the State address to the surge in heroin use, and it was widely claimed that prescription opiates had been a major cause.

Again, I discovered there are two stories about why this has happened. The first story is that this epidemic proves that the crisis is driven by chemicals. As your body becomes hooked, it clearly needs more and more powerful drugs to hit the same sweet spot. So your Oxy doesn't do it for you anymore, and you turn to heroin. This is what happens when you let the genie of access to drugs out of the bottle—it runs away with you. Again, it sounds reasonable.

But there is another story about what has happened—one that requires you to understand a very different effect of our drug policy. This will sound weird at first—it did to me, at least—but it is a well-proven effect. In fact, if you want to see it in action, you can go to any college football game in the United States, any weekend of the year, and watch it with your own eyes. This effect is called "the iron law of prohibition." To understand it, we have to first go back to the early 1920s, and the reign of Arnold Rothstein, where our story began.

The day before alcohol prohibition was introduced, the most popular drink in the United States was beer, but as soon as alcohol was banned, hard liquor soared from 40 percent of all drinks that were sold to 90 percent. People responded to a change in the law by shifting from a milder drink to a stronger drink. This seems puzzling. Why would a change in the law change people's tastes in alcohol?

It turns out it didn't change their tastes. It changed something else: the range of drinks that were offered to them. The reason is surprisingly simple. One of the best analysts of the drug war, the writer Mike Gray, explains it in his book *Drug Crazy*. When you are smuggling a substance into a country, and transporting it in secret, "you have to put the maximum bang in the smallest possible package," he writes.

Imagine secretly transporting a trunkload of beer across the United States. You will be able to get, say, a hundred people their drink for the night. But load the same trunk with whisky, and you will be able to get a thousand people their drink for the night. So you're going to smuggle the whisky—and when your drinkers come into your speakeasy, that's all that you will be able to offer them, along with even more toxic drinks like Billie Holiday's favorite, White Lightning, a booze so strong that even hard-core alcoholics would turn it down today.

Most people want to get mildly intoxicated. Relatively few of us want to get totally shit-faced. But if no mild intoxicants are available, plenty of people will use a more extreme intoxicant, because it's better than nothing. Prohibition always narrows the market to the most potent possible substance. It's the iron law.

Here's how you can see it for yourself, as I promised before, at a college football game in the United States. As Gray explains: "Students are normally beer drinkers, but since alcohol is prohibited at the stadium, they sneak in a flask and become whisky drinkers." The stadium is a zone of alcohol prohibition—and the college kids end up drinking a much stronger kind of alcohol than they'd prefer, because it's better than nothing.

It works exactly the same way when you ban other drugs. Before drugs were criminalized, the most popular way to consume opiates was through very mild opiate teas, syrups, and wines. The bestselling Mrs. Winslow's Soothing Syrup, for example, contained 0.16 grain of morphine. One wine laced with cocaine—Vin Mariani—was publicly recommended by

Queen Victoria and Pope Leo XIII. The most popular way to consume coca was in teas and soft drinks. But within a few years of the introduction of prohibition, these milder forms of the drug had vanished. They were too bulky to smuggle: even though there was more demand for them, they weren't worth the risk for dealers like Arnold Rothstein. That's when coca tea was replaced by powder cocaine, and Mrs. Winslow's Soothing Syrup was replaced by injectable heroin.

The harder you crack down, the stronger the drugs become. The crackdown on cannabis in the 1970s triggered the rise of skunk and superskunk. The crackdown on powder cocaine in the early 1980s led to the creation of crack, a more compact form of the drug. Many drug users want and prefer the milder forms of their drug—but they can't get them under prohibition, so they are pressed onto harder drugs.

This is where the prescription drug crisis comes in—and we are forced to see it in a radically different light. Almost everyone who is addicted to Oxycontin, and gets cut off by their doctor, wants to carry on using Oxycontin. But under prohibition, it's really hard to get a mild opiate like Oxy, and pretty easy to get a hard opiate like heroin. That's how prohibited markets work: it's the iron law. Dr. Hal Vorse, who treats drug addicts in Oklahoma City, talked me through the economics of it bluntly, as his patients explain it to him day in, day out. On the streets, Oxy is three times more expensive than heroin—way beyond the price range of most addicts. So, he told me, they "switch to heroin, just because of the economics of it."

Just as when all legal routes to alcohol were cut off, beer disappeared and whisky won, when all legal routes to opiates are cut off, Oxy disappears, and heroin prevails. This isn't a law of nature, and it isn't caused by the drug—it is caused by the drug policy we have chosen. After the end of alcohol prohibition, White Lightning vanished—who's even heard of it now?—and beer went back to being America's favorite alcoholic drink. There are heroin addicts all across the United States today who would have stayed happily on Oxy if there had been a legal route to it.

This is worth repeating, because it is so striking, and we hear it so rarely, despite all the evidence. The war on drugs makes it almost impossible for drug users to get milder forms of their drug—and it pushes them inexorably toward harder drugs.

After absorbing all this, I realize we have been told a story about the prescription drug crisis that doesn't graft onto reality. It has been presented to us through the old drug war story—the chemical is to blame, and if only we could eradicate the chemical, we could eradicate the problem.

It is a tempting story, because it is so simple—and allows us to avert our eyes from how much of this problem was created not by pills, but by people. The Swiss heroin experiment, combined with Rat Park, offers us the best answer not only to heroin, but to the prescription drug crisis, too.

~

One afternoon, in the heroin clinic in Geneva, I told one of the psychiatrists there, Dr. Manghi, about how this story had all happened before, long ago, in Los Angeles. Heroin was prescribed; people got better; then it was shut down. Then again, much later, in Liverpool: heroin was prescribed; people got better; then it was shut down. She stroked her wooden necklace, thinking.

"It's like relapse in addiction," she said. "It might look discouraging. But at every relapse, you learn something new."

CHAPTER 16

The Spirit of '74

I had known for years that there was a country where all drugs—from cannabis to crack—were decriminalized in 2001. I wanted to understand what that meant, but I held off from visiting until nearly two years into this journey. I told myself it was because I wanted to end the story on an upbeat note: Here, dear reader, is the solution. But there was also another reason, one that I admitted to myself only in low moments. What if I go to see the alternative, and it doesn't work? What then?

In 2013, I touched down in a sun-washed winter in Portugal to travel through this land of decriminalized drugs. I started by walking the streets of Lisbon for days, and I think I expected to see something different. Boys and girls sauntered hand in hand up and down the seven hills on which this capital city is built, through tiny jagged irrational medieval streets leading nowhere, and through vast straight rational avenidas that stretch to the sea. They sat out in the street drinking coffee and eating more cakes than seems possible for people with such slim waists and slimmer wallets.

The people there live in small brightly colored apartment blocks that stare across the avenidas and alleyways at each other, and from any window you can see into half a dozen homes. Underwear hangs from loosely strung wire to dry, where everyone can see it, unembarrassed, un-English. The people of Lisbon have a relaxed gaze, but it is always present, sipping its coffee, seeing you.

In his anonymous little office in an official building, I met a man named João Goulão. He was wearing a brown suit and a brown tie, and he still spoke in the precise manner of the family doctor he was for so long. He was mild and rather conservative in demeanor—and yet he had led the biggest ever break in Harry Anslinger's global system. He was insistent on sharing credit and deflecting praise, but most people believe he pioneered the transformation here. Over a series of conversations, he—and many other participants in the Portuguese drug revolution—told me how they did it, and why.

~

A nineteen-year-old university student was flicking through a medical textbook in Portugal in 1973 when he found a secret message. It was written on tissue paper. Somebody had slipped it there and then vanished. João Goulão read the message carefully.

It was an underground newspaper, demanding a revolution. João knew if he was found with these words, the secret police would come for him, and he would vanish. He had seen signs across the university campus, demanding the return of students who had been "disappeared." On the rare occasions when people organized a protest, the police unleashed their dogs and their batons, and more people vanished.

A few days later, another student said to João: "Did you find something new in your book?"

"Yes," he said.

"What do you think about it?"

"I think we must be very careful," João replied. But he added: "I enjoyed what I read."

"I can give you more of those papers discreetly if you want."

And so João became a small part of the movement to free Portugal. This is not what his family expected of him. He grew up traveling in the 1950s and 1960s around the silenced interior of the country, moving from place to place through the dry rural heartland of the dictatorship. His father was an engineer whose job was to clear people off their land against their will, to make way for the dams that the government and the electrical companies wanted to build. He was not popular. He carried a gun.

João's family unquestioningly believed the regime propaganda that evil forces were trying to take over the country and destroy everything they knew. Where he grew up, nobody talked about politics beyond a smattering of vague clichés expressing this conviction, muttered to ward off more dangerous thoughts. He had "just a vague [sense] that we had political police [and] that some people were missing. There was no discussion of it. It was a taboo."

Now, after coming to the big city to study, he was learning the truth. At a bus stop, he asked one of his underground comrades about one of the articles he had read in the secret newspaper, and his friend responded by talking loudly about football. João was confused. Later, his friend told him: "Someone from the political police was . . . getting close to us. To listen to our conversation."

João knew something was being prepared—he heard whispers—but he didn't know when it would come.

In the early hours of the morning of the twenty-fifth of April 1974, João's brother-in-law, an officer in the Portuguese army, called his wife with a message that surprised her. We have been plotting a revolution. It is here. We have begun. Tanks were already rolling through Lisbon toward the treasury in the center of the city. The authorities ordered people to stay off the streets, and the radio played only marching music in a constant loop. But João, like tens of thousands of others, headed straight to the town center that morning. It was cold, and the city was holding its breath. João saw a boat on the river pointing its cannons at the Governmental Palace. He saw military columns on the street. In the narrow cavernous roads of Lisbon, the tanks look enormous and outsized, with machine guns pointing outward.

Then there came the moment when João, and all the people standing on the streets alongside him, knew they were not going to be fired at by their country's military—not ever again. The tanks rolling through the city paused when they met with an old lady who was setting up her flower stall. She smiled and gently tossed a single red carnation at the tank commander. By the afternoon, young girls had begun to approach the soldiers and place their own red carnations in the barrels of their guns. It was the moment when the Portuguese people lost their fear. People climbed onto the tanks and danced on them. The dictatorship was over.

In the months that followed, there was an eruption of debates and demonstrations and an unleashing of all the pent-up hopes of decades gone by—a festival of democracy. It was as though the dams his father built all those years had burst, all at once.

And so Portugal was learning a lesson that would flood into this story. Nothing has to stay the same. If a dogma is not working, no matter how strong and immovable it seems, you can cast it aside and start anew.

Two and a half decades later, at the start of the twenty-first century, João helped lead Portugal to do something remarkable, and unprecedented. "It is," he tells me when we meet in 2013, the "result of all the processes that began in '74," the day he saw flowers overwhelm a tyranny.

~

The Algarve stumbled from the sealed-off silence of the dictatorship into a head-banging 24/7 beach party. The southern shores of Portugal are dreamscapes of yellow sand, yellow sun, and blue waters, but they were effectively shut away from the world's tourists by the old regime for fifty years. By the 1980s, however, tourists from across Europe were cooking themselves by day and downing vodka by night on its shores. João was a family doctor by then, and he saw that for a few months of the year, all the locals made pillows of cash and joyfully joined in the sozzled international conga line of tourists, making it the high season in every sense. Then the tourists would go home, and the Algarve would be left empty and jobless.

It created a bipolar region, where collective mania was followed by collective depression. "Of course I saw many people using ecstasy, cocaine, and so on—party drugs—but the big problems of addiction," he explains, "were through heroin." It was by trying to solve this problem that João may have stumbled onto another part of the solution to drug prohibition. This is his story as it was told to me in 2013 by João himself, his colleagues in the Portuguese drug treatment sector, several addicts he has treated, and the news reports about him.

Portugal had, by the 1980s, one of the worst heroin addiction problems in the world. One day, a young musician and poet named Vitor came into João's office. He was "a very intelligent guy," João recalls, "very sensitive, [and] we had big discussions." The young man believed that drugs unleashed his potential to create art. João disagreed, and over time, in the midst of this great national spike in heroin use, he successfully persuaded Vitor to lay down the needle, and he watched him achieve a "wonderful recovery" that served as an example to the people around him.

And then, two years later, Vitor came back to João with a mysterious illness. He died at the age of twenty-three. "It was very tragic," João tells me. "Yesterday, his mother called me, just to wish [me] a good season. Every year, before Christmas, his mother calls me, and she starts crying."

Portugal had virtually no experience with these drugs before this. The

1960s were canceled here by the dictatorship, so the country was starting with a blank slate on drug policy. While the use of drugs like cannabis and cocaine was low by international standards, the use of heroin was off the charts and rising. The government was desperate to respond—and the international prohibitionist playbook was waiting for them. It offered a clear recipe: criminalization, crackdowns, punishment. Portugal adopted it all enthusiastically.

But, to their puzzlement, the problem just kept getting worse. João was seeing more and more heroin addicts in his practice, and more and more AIDS cases. "Heroin use started among marginalized people but then it came to middle classes and even high classes," he says. "At that time it was almost impossible to find one Portuguese family that had no problems inside the family or in the close neighborhood." By the early 1990s, fully one in one hundred people in the country were addicted to smack.

People were scared to come forward for help, even when medical services were offered. Often, addicts stumbled into João's clinic in a desperate state but refused to give their last names or any contact information. They knew there was a war on, and they were the enemy.

"We were out of options," João told one journalist about this period. "We were spending millions and getting nowhere." So he set up the first drug treatment center in the Algarve's history, based on the belief that addicts need help, not contempt. His teams treated hundreds of patients, and they began to observe what works, and what doesn't. So in 1997, he was put in charge of the treatment of addicts for the whole country, and in 1999, he was asked by the government to serve on an independent commission made up of nine doctors and judges, with an impartial academic researcher as the chair, to draw up a comprehensive plan to really deal with the drug problem.

They had free rein to think this problem through, starting from scratch. This meant they could acknowledge some fairly obvious facts that had long been ignored in most countries. The first was that the overwhelming majority of adult drug users had no problem: they used for pleasure and did not become addicts. The authorities, they decided, need not concern themselves with these people, except to offer safety advice. The second point was that when it came to addicts, the country had already tried, João says, the "terroristic" approach pioneered by Anslinger: threaten drug addicts and impose severe pain on them if they continue. In his experience at his clinic, this was "the best way to make them wish to keep using drugs. To deal with it by chaining, by humiliating—it's the best way to make them angry with the system, to not wish to be normal."

They wanted instead to look at the problem in a more sophisticated way. João had seen from all his patients that the addicted person "is always divided between the . . . desire to use drugs, and the desire to stop." Yet the prohibitionist system keeps kicking the recovering addict back to the ground, making it harder for the part of him that wants to walk away from drugs. "It was very frustrating," he says, to see a patient fight really hard to get clean only to hear him say: "What kind of life am I going to have now? I am unprepared, I have no place to go."

So he and his colleagues proposed to build a system based on a radically different notion: they should offer addicts "the possibility of having a new life," and give them "pleasure" instead of pain. His goal as a doctor was always "trying to identify what happened in the past" of an addict that made them find everyday life unbearable, and to help them overcome it by offering compassion and helping them to build a good life as an alternative. Now they were asking: If this is the goal of all good doctors, why can't it be the goal of government policy?

So when the panel reported, it made recommendations based on these insights. It said that "drug users should be treated as full members of society instead of cast out as criminals or other pariahs." Instead of "striv[ing] toward an unachievable perfection such as zero drug use," they would decriminalize all drugs. Choosing to put a chemical into your body should not be a crime, and being addicted should not be a crime. Instead, all the money spent on arresting, trying, and punishing addicts should be transferred to educating kids and helping addicts to recover.

To the astonishment of many people, the Portuguese parliament debated it thoroughly. There was a very senior figure in the government who had a brother addicted to heroin, João took him to visit many places across Europe where drug addicts were treated less cruelly. That politician became one of the great champions of this new approach. The sheer scale of the problem in Portugal meant that it was easier to persuade the public than many people had expected. As João says: "The feeling that a drug addict is a sick person rather than a criminal was already present in the society. People knew—'well, my son is a good guy, he's not a criminal, he's someone who needs help.'"

So in 2001, in Portugal, the persecution of drug users and addicts officially ended. The new law stipulated that recreational drug users "should, above all, not be labeled or marginalized," and addicts should be approached by the state exclusively "to encourage him or her to seek treatment." It was no longer a crime to possess enough drugs for ten days' personal use.

It's important to understand that while it was no longer illegal to use and possess drugs, it was not legal to sell them. To legalize and regulate their sale would have required Portugal to become the first country ever to renounce the UN conventions authored by Anslinger. That is a step that could have triggered sanctions and crackdowns from other countries. This meant that the control of drug trade was still in the hands of armed criminal gangs, but the panel and the parliament felt they were being as bold as they could: no other country had gone this far since the start of drug prohibition.

There were widespread predictions, from parts of the Portuguese right and across the world, that this would trigger a catastrophe. The chief of the Lisbon Drugs Squad, João Figueira, believed there would be "an explosion of consumption [where] lots of people start consuming, and then we lose control of the situation." In the writings of prohibitionists everywhere at this time, there was a clear tone of "Just you wait and see."

In his office, Goulao told me there were two dimensions to Portugal's drug revolution. The panel didn't simply lift the legal penalties and leave people to it. They took the big, lumbering machinery of the drug war and turned it into an equally big, active machine to establish a drug peace. "The big effect of decriminalization," he said, "was to make it possible to develop all the other policies." In the United States, 90 percent of the money spent on drug policy goes to policing and punishment, with 10 percent going to treatment and prevention. In Portugal, the ratio is the exact opposite. Back on Chino's block in Brownsville, Brooklyn, the state spends one million dollars for every five people it arrests and convicts of midlevel drug offenses: that's what it took to get the Souls of Mischief off the streets for a while. What João did in Portugal was to use all that money in a very different way.

He believed that if you removed the stigma and shame caused by making addiction a crime, it would be possible to invite addicts into a welcoming web of care and treatment and support. I wanted that to be true. But was it?

～

Opposite a Santander bank on an overcast day, I find a bare unmarked building, and in one of its hallways, a seventeen-year-old boy with spiky hair, swaddled in a big parka, is waiting. He has just been interviewed by a psychologist for an hour, and now Nuno Capaz—a tall sociologist in his midthirties—is calling him into a small conference room.

The system built by João and his colleagues had a distinction at its heart, between the 90 percent of drug users who have no problem and should be left alone, and the 10 percent who are addicts and need help. They had to figure out a mechanism to sift the addicts from the users. This small room, and the dozens like it across the country, is the solution. It is called the Dissuasion Commission. The police don't go looking for drug users anymore, but if they stumble across you, they will write you a ticket that requires you to come here the next day. The job of the Dissuasion Commission is only to figure out whether you have a drug problem. You can be honest with them, because nothing you say or do here will ever get you a criminal record.

If the interview with the psychologist in the next room reveals that you are a drug user who doesn't have a problem, they will bring you in here, warn you about the risks, tell you how to make your use as safe as possible—don't use alone, for example, in case you have a bad reaction—and send you on your way.

Nuno, who oversees the informal hearings, stresses that the vast majority of the people he sees here are using drugs "just because they like it. They do not have a problem with it, they just do it because it makes them feel good. In those cases they don't actually need treatment [or] imprisonment. They might eventually need to be careful, but they don't need a medical doctor or a jailer or a legal intervention." He tells me, for example, about a typical guy who worked in a bar and used cocaine on the first Saturday of every month without fail—and never on any other day. He loved it; and because he loved it he knew he had to restrict his use tightly so he was able to resist temptation the rest of the time. Nuno tells him: "Be careful. Stick with it. Just do it once a month, in the company of some people who are not doing it, because you might have a seizure." This kind of advice is the end of your contact with the state for nine out of ten people.

I watch as Nuno has a twenty-minute conversation with the teenage boy in his parka, who was found smoking cannabis on the street. Nuno explains that it's bad for your memory and concentration, and that you need both to do well in your studies. The boy agrees, asks for some literature that explains more, and leaves. That's it.

"In a lot of cases of underage people," Nuno tells me once the boy is gone, "what we do is try to reduce the anxiety of the parents. Because the kid was caught with 0.3 grams of hashish, we have parents going, 'He's going to be a drug addict! He's going to ruin the family!' We say—'Let's calm down a bit . . . In the majority of cases he will eventually quit using hashish and he will not use anything else [or] have any psychological and physical problems from it, so let's not make a big deal.' . . . Especially with minors, we have to work more on the mothers and fathers than on the kid, because the kid is much more well-informed than the mothers and fathers."

Nuno continues, "Unless you are very, very unlucky or unless you are trying to be caught," as a nonproblematic user, you won't come back to the Dissuasion Commission, because the police "will not stop you in the street out of nowhere and say, 'Let me see what you have in your pockets.'" The drug users get picked up only when they are using blatantly in public, or when the drugs are found by chance, like in a search of suspects after a street fight. "It'll be very difficult," he says, "for you to be caught" twice. If you are, though, the Commission can level small fines—80 euros is the norm, making it "the most expensive joint the guy ever had, but you could say it's a fairly symbolic thing," Nuno says. If, however, the interview reveals that you are using your drugs dangerously—by, say, sharing needles—they will direct you toward the needle exchanges and other places that will make you safer from disease and death.

When it comes to the 10 percent who are addicts, Nuno's job is to offer "information without judgment" and ferry you toward the services that are there to keep you alive and get you well. "We can't oblige anyone to do anything" when it comes to treatment, he says—but when they are ready for help, it is there right away. "If the person shows up at ten o'clock in the morning," he says, "we can schedule them for one o'clock in the afternoon at the treatment facility in order for them to start the analysis."

From Nuno's office, any addict who wants to stop will be booked, for free, into the Taipas Treatment Center. It is at the edge of a large pink hospital, on yet another hill.

~

Six addicts are lying on a mat in a gym, being gently massaged. Some have their eyes closed; some are looking sideways, with a little smile. These massages help them to cope with the withdrawal pains, one of the nurses tells me, but it has a more important function. It helps them learn how to calm down without a chemical cocktail, often for the first time.

The program here, I am told, is built on João's belief that "using drugs is only a symptom of some suffering, and we have to reach the reasons" that make addicts want to be out of their heads much of the time. "You can stop using drugs for a while, but if you don't solve the problems you have in your mind, things will come back. We have to work [on] the trauma in your life, and only then can you change the way you deal with it."

So this institution is here, as he puts it, to help addicts "to increase their insight, to analyze themselves—helping them to understand themselves [and] the way they react." Over your year and a half being treated here for addiction, the team will try to build a safe, trusting environment where you can do something you have been running away from for years—express your emotions, and tell your story truthfully.

This often starts with basic steps. The recovering addicts play a game based on Pictionary, where they have to make a face that expresses an emotion, such as anger or sadness. At first, many of them refuse: it is too frightening. They can't bear to let these emotions show, even in a game, for a moment. This is one reason why they have needed to be intoxicated for so long: to escape the terror and lack of control that comes with emotions like these.

In another game, they have to let themselves fall backward, knowing the group behind them will catch them as they fall. The addicts find this inconceivable, and they often refuse. They can't trust anyone—but slowly, over time, they learn here that these emotions can be explored, without the need to be chemically numbed. To João, this is what recovery means.

I watch them playing these childlike games, trying to learn how to feel, and I think of the women I left behind at Tent City and in prisons across the United States, who are learning nothing except how to cut off their feelings. I try to picture Chino's mother here, learning to figure out how she feels, at last.

~

But this is—I was going to discover—only the first layer of support for addicts in Portugal, and not the most important.

João believes that addiction is an expression of despair, and the best way to deal with despair is to offer a better life, where the addict doesn't feel the need to anesthetize herself anymore. Giving rewards, rather than making threats, is the path out. Congratulate them. Give them options. Help them build a life.

That was his reasoning behind the second and most important phase of treatment for addicts in Portugal. Once you take those first courageous steps to Taipas or a center like it, the government will prioritize getting you a job with a decent wage, away from the world where you used drugs. "They want to be a part of the society," he tells me. "We can't [tell] them to behave as a normal citizen and deprive them . . . of a role in society: having a job, having work, having a salary." His aim is to give them something to lose.

So the government gives a hefty yearlong tax break to anybody who employs a recovering addict. Almost always, when the year is up, the employer keeps the former addict on in his garage or bakery or shop, because she has turned out to be a good worker.

The last time João moved with his family, he hired a moving company that was established with the help of his department. Ten recovering addicts came together to form a cooperative, and the state lent them the money to buy a truck at a very low interest rate. His wife had been nervous, but the guys did a perfect job, João says with pride. Of course, he adds, in that cooperative of ten, "some of them will relapse," but now "the others are protectors. They will help to deal with that problem. They will insist: go to your doctor, go now, as soon as possible, try to stop again, then you can work with us again. They as a group protect themselves."

This, it occurs to me after we speak, is the precise opposite of the prohibitionist approach. In the drug war, we guarantee addicts will find it almost impossible to work again, by marking them with the scarlet letter of a criminal record. After the drug war, we will make it easier to employ recovering addicts, with subsidies—because we understand this will keep them from relapsing more effectively than the threat of being caged.

~

If, however, you are not ready to move away from using drugs, you will be given a different kind of support.

On a misty Friday morning, I took the subway to a housing project on the edge of Lisbon. The apartments were even more cramped than in the rest of the city, piled on top of each other with brightly colored bricks, like some dystopian Lego model. A large graffitied mural of a rapper I didn't recognize stared at me, as did several women who were hanging out their underwear from their tenth-floor windows. A wispy fog was hanging over the place, so I had to focus hard to see the street names. They were stern: I realized I was wandering along the Avenida Cidade de Bratislava.

At the bottom of the housing project, by a busy road, the mist was clearing, and I could see a plain white van with an open window and a short line of men and women standing in a line, chatting, beside it.

The small white cups they were handed contained methadone. They swallowed it, and then talked to the psychologists and doctors standing there, listening sympathetically. Then they left and got on with their day. João had told me back in his office that with this drug, "you don't feel high but you remain with no suffering for the lack of heroin . . . So you are completely available to work, to study, or whatever. Even to drive a truck—we have several truck drivers on methadone."

I stood with the social workers and listened to their conversations. Their goals were, it quickly became clear, more modest than those of the Taipas Treatment Center. These were the addicts who believed they were not ready to stop, and who were at serious risk of dying of an overdose or of a disease transmitted by dirty needles.

Nuno Biscaia, a psychologist in his midthirties, clearly knew everybody who came here by name, after years of befriending them. I talked to him for hours as the sun came out. A good day at work for him, he said, was when he could persuade one of the addicts he worked with to move from injecting heroin to smoking heroin. I looked at the line of addicts— a tall young man who speaks three languages, a defeated-looking woman in her forties, an angry guy who pulls up on a motorcycle and doesn't want to talk—and wondered how many of them would stay alive if this service was shut down.

Some people argue that you didn't have to decriminalize drugs in Portugal to expand treatment in this way. You could have more treatment, *and* criminalization. It was only standing here, in this line of addicts, that the flaw in this argument became clear to me. These Portuguese addicts were standing in a long line in public, in front of their friends and neighbors and employers. A police car drove past as they were being served; nobody tensed, or even seemed to notice, except me. Would they come forward every morning before everyone to declare themselves criminals?

A few days later, I went out with another team, whose job was to get help to the hardest-to-reach addicts—the people who live on the streets, or in abandoned housing. As we walked through ragged half-houses made of rubble and the battered housing projects, these social workers told me that before João's drug revolution, people ran from them. Now, they run toward them. Addicts come forward, to replace their needles, to chat, to say they are thinking about asking for help. Their reactions were so different from those I had learned under prohibition, I kept being thrown off by them. Can't you see these are the authorities? Run!

I wanted to understand the long-term effects of this approach on individuals—and in Portugal's second-largest city, Oporto, I met a man who seemed to epitomize them.

~

Sergio Rodrigues was sleeping in an abandoned roofless house with only the sky above him in the last days of Portugal's drug war, when he was suddenly woken up.

He was being kicked, hard, again and again, all over his body.

He knew what was happening. All the street addicts in Portugal knew what this was.

It's the police, and they were beating him up, for sport, for fun, because this is a war, and addicts are the enemy. "Get out of here!" they snarled.

Sergio had been an addict for eleven years. He shot up heroin and cocaine five, ten, twenty times a day, however much he could afford, to nuke as much of his consciousness as he could. He had grown up in one of the poorest parts of the city of Oporto, in claustrophobic concrete streets that are a strange mash-up of sixteenth-century buildings and twenty-first-century criminality. In his neighborhood, everybody his age that he knew stood on ancient European cobbles to sell or snort cut Colombian cocaine. All his brothers were street addicts.

He was sixteen when he started, and he didn't see when it would end, but he suspected it would be soon. His friends on the street were dying all around him. Some days he would ask where a friend was, because he hadn't seen him in a while. But in his heart, he would know.

Except, because João had changed the law, a very different group of people was about to come looking for Sergio. João and his panel knew that somebody like Sergio—cut off from society, and terrified of the authorities, after a generation of the drug war—would be hard to reach, so, as part of their policy revolution, they put in place another way to help him. They employed street teams of psychologists to fan out across the country to look in all the old ruined houses and broken crannies where the most hard-core addicts live, and to offer them help. At first, these teams approached modestly, offering clean needles, and collecting the dirty old ones.

Over time, in these exchanges, as they struck up conversations, they

formed relationships. They gave advice on where you should inject yourself to stay as safe as possible, and on how to avoid disease. Then, discreetly,
they started to explain that there was a way out, if you wanted it.

Sometimes they were only planting a seed that would take years to
grow; sometimes people wanted help fast. Now that the punishments
were gone, people like Sergio were—tentatively—starting to listen. The
face of authority was changing. Where once there were police with batons
to beat you, there are now psychologists offering help.

It was a street team that persuaded Sergio to try a treatment center for
rehab, so he could become abstinent. He went. He tried. But it didn't
work: he couldn't stay off heroin.

When that shoe didn't fit, the street team didn't write him off as a failure. They tried another shoe to see if it fit better. They got him into a
longer-term program, called a therapeutic community, where he lived for
one and a half years, regularly saw a psychologist, and was given the
substitute drug methadone every day.

Sergio got a job. He got into a relationship. His girlfriend got pregnant.
And as his bonds with the world around him grew stronger, his bonds
with his drug began to weaken and wither. So he decided to stop the
methadone. Now he uses only cannabis or cocaine very occasionally, at
parties.

"My life has changed completely," he said when I met him in a chichi
café in Oporto with a piano player tinkling in the corner and a sycophantic
waiter bowing at our every request. He looked no different from the other
customers. He paid taxes, and he beamed when he talked about his excite-
ment at how he was about to become a dad. As we sat together, I couldn't
help thinking that in the countries where the drug war was still being
waged, he would be regarded even now as a criminal, and a failure.

We walked out onto the cobbled streets where once he had slept,
broken and filthy, and Sergio waved good-bye as he walked back to a life
made possible by the end of the drug war.

～

Yes, I kept thinking—things are better for addicts. I expected that. But
what about for kids? I am very close to my nephews and my niece—this
book is dedicated to them—and for all the horrors of the drug war, my
biggest worry about ending it has always been that more kids might end
up using drugs. This would damage them in all sorts of ways, but here's
just one: there is strong scientific evidence that persistent cannabis use

affects how adolescent and teenage brains develop, and can permanently lower their IQ. One of my best friends when I was a kid smoked a lot of weed, and he feels it harmed him for life. He may be right. Developing brains are more fragile than adult brains: they need to be protected.

In a classroom full of Portuguese sixteen-year-olds at the Romeu Correia High School, we are watching as a girl named Sabrina is offered her first taste of cocaine. She is tall and lean and gorgeous and she wants to be a supermodel. The man offering the white powder is in his twenties, handsome and seductive. The class is discussing what she should do. Should she go with him? Should she snort it?

These are the children of the drug revolution. They were five years old when all drugs were decriminalized, so they have never known the drug war.

For many people of my generation growing up in the 1980s, drug education consisted mainly of being told that if you tried drugs, your life would be ruined, and that was that. As soon as you smoked your first spliff and survived, you dismissed your teachers as liars on the issue of drugs, and you stopped listening—even to the parts you needed to hear. As Portugal changed its drug laws, it was also in the process of abandoning Just Say No prevention programs and replacing them with something radically different.

The teacher, Luz Baiao, explains to these kids that they can discuss their thoughts about what Sabrina should do candidly. Since what they are talking about hasn't been a criminal offense any time they can remember, they seem to take that for granted. They are staring at the whiteboard, where this scenario has been projected for them to talk about.

It would be very risky to use this drug, one of the kids says, because it is more addictive than the marijuana he has tried a few times at parties with his friends. All of life is risk, another boy says, rebutting him. Yes, a girl replies, but that's no reason to take risks unnecessarily.

The class giggles a little at the subject matter, but they seem engaged. This is clearly a conversation that takes place between teenagers everywhere. I can remember how we would have it when I was that age—on buses, in the park, at parties—but we were alone, with only our own ignorance to reflect back at each other.

Luz mediates neutrally. She listens. She doesn't ever look judgmental, or shocked. So when she refers to the real risks involved in taking this drug, the kids seem to listen, precisely because she is not pretending it is the whole picture.

After a debate, the class reaches the conclusion that Sabrina would be foolish to use the cocaine, and they vote for her to say no. They reach this conclusion on their own. They are not, I think, trying to please their teacher. They are expressing their own thoughts. The social disapproval of hard drugs didn't die with the old drug laws. Indeed, it may be stronger now, since there's no rebellion in drug use anymore.

This approach brings teenage decisions into discussion with the adult world, instead of pretending they don't exist. In Portugal, the dilemmas of teenage life aren't playing out in a sealed-off cocoon of adolescence: they play out in conversation with parents and teachers and the guidance they can offer. After criminalization ends, a new, more candid conversation can begin.

It occurs to me as I watch the students that the philosophy expressed in these lessons runs through all the reforms in the country since 2001. Prohibition is based on externally preventing people from using drugs through fear and force; the Portuguese alternative is based on the belief that drugs aren't going away, so you need instead to give people the internal tools—the confidence, the knowledge, the support—to make the right decisions for themselves.

The school bell rings and the kids shuffle out of the classroom. They have, I realize, had honest conversations with adults, in place of the boo-and-hiss pantomime my generation was offered.

~

This is the kind of mature approach liberals have been advocating for years. But there is a strange anxiety in seeing your proposals put into practice. What if they fail? What if we end the drug war, and drug use explodes? What if punishing people really does keep large numbers of people sober? What if more people end up, like too many of the people I love, addicted? What if you saw other disasters start to emerge—ones I can't even predict now?

One man, more than any other, issued this warning before Portugal began its drug revolution. His name is João Figueira, and he is the chief of the Lisbon Drugs Squad, the closest equivalent in Portugal to the head of the DEA, or the chief inspector of Scotland Yard's Narcotics Division. He is a carefully spoken, mild-mannered man with an enormous mustache of a type unseen outside the pages of late Victorian fiction. He greets me in a dim police station corridor where the yellow fluorescent lighting makes the walls look sickly, and we squeeze into an arthritic elevator to reach his office.

His concerns at the time of decriminalization spoke for many people in Portugal. As we saw earlier, he warned that once the criminal penalties were lifted, "we could have an explosion of consumption . . . [where] lots of people start consuming, and then we lose control of the situation."

More than anyone else in the country, his men saw the changes on the streets, up close, and immediate. It was a fear that—if we are totally candid—some of us in the drug reform movement shared.

So João Figueira watched the results happen in real time, very closely, expecting vindication.

And he found something else.

"The things we were afraid of," he says, "didn't happen." Two highly respected and impartial bodies have studied the outcomes: the European Monitoring Centre for Drugs and Drug Addiction (EMCDDA), and the *British Journal of Criminology*. They have no horse in this race. Their role is solely to figure out what actually happened.

They discovered there has been a slight increase in overall drug use, from 3.4 to 3.7 percent of the population.

But Portugal started with a low rate of use, except for heroin, and it stayed low compared to other countries. The EMCDDA found Portugal is ninth lowest out of twenty-eight European countries when it comes to cannabis use, fifth lowest when it comes to amphetamines, and fifth lowest when it comes to ecstasy. Over a decade after full decriminalization, Portugal has, they found, "a level of drug use that is, on the whole, below the European average and much lower than its only European neighbor, Spain."

But what about the three forms of drug use that the prohibitionists understandably offer as the reason why we must continue fighting the drug war—addiction, deaths due to drug use, and teenage drug use? These figures were collected carefully.

The Portuguese Ministry of Health says that the number of problematic drug users has literally been halved, from a hundred thousand to fifty thousand. The *British Journal of Criminology* confirms it is down, but found a more modest decline, from 7.6 people per thousand to 6.8, while confirming that injecting drug use has indeed been almost halved, from 3.5 injectors per thousand people to 2. When they compared the situation to the nearby countries of Spain and Italy, which are still waging the drug war, they found that "Portugal is the only of these nations to have exhibited declines" in problematic drug use.

So there are fewer addicts after decriminalization. At the same time, the *British Journal of Criminology* found that overdose has been "reduced significantly," and the proportion of people contracting HIV who get it from drug use has fallen from 52 percent to 20 percent. This means that fewer young people like Vitor—the musician whom João sat in his clinic in the Algarve having long conversations with, at the birth of this transformation—are getting sick.

Figueira thinks he knows why all this has happened. It is, he tells me, because "we don't see a drug addict as a [criminal] anymore. He's someone that needs help. And everyone thinks it. Then they consider themselves sick people—they don't consider themselves [to be] against the society. It's a big change." It means that now, "they are not marginalized. They are just like a traffic accident. They are not on the other side of the line. They are regular citizens. They have a problem."

In the old days, he says, when somebody you knew became an alcoholic, "we treated those guys as friends—they need[ed] help," not abuse. He now realizes "drug consumers are on exactly the same level . . . In fact, it is exactly the same situation. It is a sickness that needs to be treated." Now, instead of being hounded to the gutter, they are helped to a hospital. In the years since heroin was decriminalized in Portugal, its use has been halved there—while in the United States, where the drug war continues, it has doubled.

~

But what, I found myself worrying, about teenagers? Are the kids in Luz's class more or less likely to use drugs than my nephews and niece? They are the most vulnerable group, because an increase in use there would affect their brain chemistry for the rest of their lives.

"Children aged 15–16 [in Portugal] also reported one of the lowest lifetime prevalence of cannabis use in Western Europe (13 percent)," the EMCDDA found, while their level of cocaine use is almost half the EU average. It is slightly down since decriminalization started: in 1999, 2.5 percent of sixteen-to-eighteen-year-olds used heroin. By 2005, after six years of this model of decriminalization, it was down to 1.8 percent. "I spent a lot of time on the streets walking and arresting consumers," João Figueira says, and he believed in it—so he describes what he sees on the streets now with a tone of mild amazement.

He stresses that the new drug policy has brought a transformation, too, in the lives of people who have never once touched a drug. It was "very common" before the end of the drug war that heroin addicts would rob people to get their next fix, he says, but the "crimes related to drug consumption are now finished. It doesn't happen. The crimes on street level related to drug consumption—there aren't [any] anymore." They are all either on methadone, in treatment, or recovering, so "they don't need to rob cars or assault people." He adds: "This is a complete change."

And this change has caused another transformation—in how people see the police. "I don't think [people in poor neighborhoods] see the police now as enemies. I think this is important. This is different." I think of Leigh Maddox back in Baltimore, and how she told me this would happen after the end of the drug war. This in turn, Figueira says, makes investigating all forms of crime easier: "We spare lots of resources, human resources, paperwork, money" to go after real criminals. In the past, he spent his time "arresting consumers without any result." Now, he says, "there are results."

He is careful to add one caveat: These results are not due to the change in the law alone. The heroin use in the 1980s and 1990s was so widespread and so damaging that it spurred a backlash among young people who looked at their older siblings and resolved never to follow those particular track marks to disaster. So some of these changes would have happened even without the transformation in the drug laws—but not, he is confident, all of it.

João Figueira describes himself as "very conservative." At first, he says, when the laws were changed, "the left wing said 'let's do this' and the right wing said 'no, no, no'—and in fact on the results we have, there is no kind of ideological [debate anymore] because it has nothing to do with ideology. What happened here worked," he explains. "What happened here was a good result and the statistics we have prove it. There is no ideology in this . . . Now everyone, conservatives or socialists, accepts the situation." Since the drug policy revolution, Portugal has had two governments of the left, and two governments of the right. All have kept the decriminalization in place. None of the political parties wants to go back.

I felt a sense of physical relief as he spoke, and as I reviewed these figures. It has turned out, it seems, that strengthening people's internal resistance to drugs works a lot better than trying to terrorize them away from drugs with force. The alternative works. And the best proof is that virtually nobody in Portugal is arguing for a return to the old ways.

"All the Portuguese society accepts it completely. It is a system that is settled," Figueira says. As I traveled around Portugal, I struck up conversations with people on trains and in cafés and on the streets, and it was startling to me to see how quickly decriminalization had become the common sense of the country. People described the idea of busting users and addicts with puzzlement, as if it were a strange medieval practice from the distant past. A few people argued that the benefits for addicts are too generous, but that is the only criticism I heard. Nobody sees this as a Hollywood ending. Everybody knows addiction continues, and it remains a tragedy. But there is a lot less of it.

João Figueira looks at me and, from behind his bushy mustache, he smiles. "I was not expecting," he says, "that this would work so well."

~

After I left my meeting with him, I walked the streets of Lisbon for hours lost in a head-rush of optimism, because I saw now, for the first time, how narrow the gap is between even the most passionate prohibitionists and people who want to radically change the laws.

Most of the people I have met on this journey who support the drug war are not like Harry Anslinger, driven by racism and hatred and personal inadequacy. They are like João Figueira: admirable people who have a series of understandable worries about the alternative. They support the drug war out of compassion for all the people they fear might become victims if we relaxed the laws. They are good people. They are acting out of decency.

It occurred to me as I walked up and down those Lisbon streets that we all—the vast majority of drug warriors, and the vast majority of legal-izers—have a set of shared values. We all want to protect children from drugs. We all want to keep people from dying as a result of drug use. We all want to reduce addiction. And now the evidence strongly suggests that when we move beyond the drug war, we will be able to achieve those shared goals with much greater success.

At the start of my journey, I set out to find an answer to a contradic-tion within myself, and within our culture—between the impulse to be compassionate to addicts, and the impulse to crush and destroy our addictive impulses. Now, at last, I see—and really feel—that it is not a contradiction at all. A compassionate approach *leads* to less addiction. The conflict within me—the one I found so disturbing—is not a conflict at all. It's not a question of one impulse winning over the other. They can both win—if we just do it right.

If this insight were more widely understood, I asked myself, how would it change our debate? I think we'd start to see this isn't a debate about values. It's a debate about how to achieve those values. In the United

States alone, legalizing drugs would save $41 billion a year currently spent on arresting, trying, and jailing users and sellers, according to a detailed study by the Cato Institute. If the drugs were then taxed at a similar rate to alcohol and tobacco, they would raise an additional $46.7 billion a year, according to calculations by Professor Jeffrey Miron of the Department of Economics at Harvard University. That's $87.8 billion next year, and every year. For that money, you could provide the Portuguese style of treatment and social reconnection for every drug addict in America.

I know there are people who say that the United States, or Britain, or other large countries can't learn from other countries—that Portugal is so small and so different it has nothing to teach a superpower. As João Figueira waved good-bye to me from his police station where no drug user will ever be busted again, I pictured Leigh Maddox, who told me back in Baltimore that this model could save her city too. I kept walking.

~

That afternoon, as I strolled through the squares of Lisbon, middle-aged men skulked up to me and flashed packets of drugs. "You want? You want?" they asked insistently.

It's important to understand the limits of the Portuguese experiment. They have decriminalized the personal possession but not the sale of drugs. This is a strange hybrid: everyone knows that to possess drugs, you have to buy them—so under this system, you mostly still have to go to these criminals and their gangs. This means the new Portuguese laws save Marcia Powell and the women in Tent City, but they do not stop Arnold Rothstein or Rosalio Reta or their local affiliates.

True, it has dented their business a little in some ways. When the methadone vans started going out across the country's streets, the drug dealers stoned the vans and smashed up the offices of the health workers, because—as João Goulão says—"it was the first time there was a decrease in the[ir] earnings" in their memories. But they still control the bulk of the trade. Decriminalization can't take it away from them; only legalization can.

The architects of the Portuguese drug revolution believe this will come, in time. I asked João Goulão if he was sympathetic to this argument. "Yes," he said, "and I believe this is the trend. But I also believe that this trend needs a vast consensus among nations, and I don't believe that the political environment even here in Europe is very in favor of such a movement. But it will happen—in the future."

~

Back in the yellow sands of the Algarve in 1996, before the laws were changed, before the treatment was expanded, before the drug war ended, another young addict—the last in this book—was staggering in to see a doctor.

Antonio Gago was a stringy and strung-out boy who, at the age of fourteen, had started coping with the fact he was being abused by his dad by smoking heroin. He was twenty-one, and he knew only that all the local addicts had Dr. João Goulão's personal phone number: he handed it out to anybody he thought might need it. At first, João got Antonio a daily supply of methadone—but, perhaps more important, he listened. He seemed to think Antonio's feelings and thoughts mattered. Even on his days off, he would sometimes meet Antonio, and sit with him. One Christmas Day, Antonio received a call from João, who was contacting all his addicted patients one by one. "You're going to get what you want—a new life," he said.

"You can have more honesty with a doctor like this," Antonio told me, years later. "I never felt any kind of condemnation, and that helped me to open up my life and my heart a little bit more." He started to talk about the real reasons why he used drugs: the things his father did. "I had to cover that up with the drugs," he says.

João helped him to get into rehab, and when Antonio came out and sank back into heroin, he wasn't judgmental. He was just there.

When João was put in charge of the country's drug policy, he started to fund long-term therapeutic communities where addicts can live and be helped to rebuild their lives over a period of years. This, at last, was the shoe that fit Antonio. Living at a center called Team Challenge in idyllic green fields on the outskirts of Lisbon, surrounded by the quiet whir of wind farms, he learned for the first time how to trust. He was amazed that the people he meets leave him alone with their wallets or their children. He never thought that would happen to him again. Step by step, he was gaining the confidence to leave his drug use behind. When I met him, he had been abstinent for years.

Now, every morning, Antonio goes out in a van to find the addicts on the streets who are still lost in their pain, to give them whatever they need—whether it's food, or clean needles, or the knowledge that there is a safe place they can come to, for free, for love, when they are ready. He believes in giving out lots of hugs. All across the country, there are armies of former addicts employed like this, to rescue the people they left behind on the streets.

And it was only when I met Antonio and saw his little white van that I thought I really began to understand what had happened in Portugal in the decade since the death of the drug war. Prohibition—this policy I have traced across continents and across a century—consists of endlessly spreading downward spirals. People get addicted so we humiliate and shame them until they become more addicted. They then have to feed their habit by persuading more people to buy the drugs from them and become addicted in turn. Then those people need to be humiliated and shamed. And so it goes, on and on.

But in Portugal after the drug war, the state helped people to get better, and then those people helped more people to get better, and then they helped still more people to get better—and so the downward spiral of the drug war has been replaced by a healing ripple that spreads slowly out across the society.

~

On my last day in Lisbon, I thought of João as a young man on the streets of Lisbon, watching the tyranny fall—and I thought I could now see why he believes this is the continuation of the spirit of 1974. The Portuguese people rose up then to say that every single one of them deserved a life and a voice, and that they would not be beaten down or shut up ever again. And now their drug policy says that every one of them—even the weakest and sickest of their siblings—deserves not to be beaten down or shut up but to be embraced, and offered hope, and love.

In a true democracy, nobody gets written off. Nobody gets abandoned. Nobody's life is declared to be not worth living. That was the spirit of the revolution. The revolution lives.

CHAPTER 17

The Man in the Well

When I started this book, no country had ever gone further than decriminalization: Portugal was the end of the line. But then, as I was writing, history began to shift beneath my feet.

One country—a tiny nation sandwiched between Argentina and Brazil—took a step nobody had taken since Harry Anslinger's war began in the 1930s. They fully legalized a drug. And, at the same time, a rebellion began at the very heart of the drug war, when two American states, in ballot initiatives, voted to do the same.

I was about to discover the answer to a question that had hung over me from the start. What happens when you legalize a drug? I booked my flights, and I discovered that the president who stands at the end of the drug war has a story far stranger than I could have imagined. I interviewed his wife, his closest friends, his biographer, his critics, his chief of staff, and finally him. This is what I learned from them.

~

José Mujica looked up at the light. It seemed that the roof of the long, damp well where he had been kept prisoner for two and a half years was covered with only a flimsy sheet of aluminum. If he could reach it, if he could stretch, he could—surely—push it aside, and he would be free. He would be back in the world at last.

He was as emaciated as a concentration camp prisoner by now, and he stank from drinking his own piss.

"It taught me to talk—talk to the person that we all have inside," he told me years later. "Since I couldn't talk to the world, I tried to stay alive by calling on the world I had inside myself." He would pick up one of the many bugs crawling all around him, hold it to his ear, and then—inside the tremendous silence—he would hear the insect shouting to him very loudly. He had also made friends with the frogs. When he was thrown water by the guards, he would try to share a little with them. "Those were the only nonaggressive live beings I had surrounding me in those days," he would explain to another interviewer later.

But Mujica did not let the insects and frogs shout their messages to him for long, because he was afraid for them. The government, he believed, had planted a secret listening device in his ear, to hear everything he could hear and to read his thoughts. He knew this was true, because he had a burning sensation in his ear, and because the people who would do this to him could—he was convinced—do anything.

Perhaps it was for the best that Mujica didn't know that the metal at the top of the well couldn't be pushed away, by him, or by anyone. It was part of a tank. The dictators who had seized power in Uruguay were not taking any chances. They wanted him sealed away from the world. "The only thing worse than solitude," he tells me softly, "is death."

As he and his friends were being sealed into separate wells, the guards told them: "You guys are being held as hostages. If anybody on the outside does anything crazy, we'll kill you. We'll kill you."

José Mujica had grown up not far from this prison in Montevideo. It was in one of those neighborhoods where the countryside bleeds into the city, and half-built slums form the scar tissue in between. As a boy, he had watched the farm fields just beyond the city wither and empty out one by one. The farmers who had worked those fields were streaming hungrily into the town to try to hustle a living. Mujica's father lost everything and died when the boy was just seven. His mother grew flowers, and the young Mujica was sent out to sell them. It was only because they all worked constantly that they did not starve.

By the time Mujica got to the university, the country's economy had gone into a deep depression. Kids with distended stomachs toddled around the slums, wasting away, and the political mood began to darken. Some of the worst of the Nazi war criminals—including Josef Mengele—were living in the country, with the tacit approval of the regime. Then one day, a senior general in the Uruguayan military revealed that the army was planning a military coup. Mujica and his friends believed they couldn't just sit back and watch, so they formed a group called the Tupamaros and started to hijack food trucks destined for wealthy areas, driving them to poor neighborhoods and giving all the contents away. They went to the sugarcane workers and gave them arms, so they could take over their fields themselves. They began to seize control of whole cities, and they quickly became known as the "Robin Hood guerrillas."

They chose to name a woman as their honorary leader—Miss Marple, the elderly spinster who solves crimes in Agatha Christie's novels. She represented for them the principle of justice, and that, they said, is what they were fighting for.

Like the French Resistance, the Tupamaros were organized into different "pillars," all operating separately—so that if one pillar was captured, the movement would live on. José and his wife Lucia belonged to pillar number 10. They lived underground and spent their time being bundled from one safe house to the next, planning operations—until one day, as Mujica was waiting to meet a contact in a bar, suddenly, something hit him in the chest.

The police shot him six times, but they didn't let him die. They needed him as a hostage, to discipline his comrades.

Mujica does not talk about the torture he endured while in prison, but some of the other survivors from that time told me about what happened to them. The guards were fond of "the submarine," where you hold a man's head underwater until he is about to drown, and then suddenly yank him out. They also applied electric shocks to men's cheeks, nipples, and testicles.

From his well, Mujica was only allowed to write to Lucia, his wife, once. She was being held in prison, too; she was also being tortured. If we ever get out of this, he told her, we are going to get a little plot of land somewhere—a farm—and make it ours.

There must have been days when it seemed that this would never end, that this would be his reality forever. In a well nearby, one of his comrades had died, although Mujica didn't know it yet, and wouldn't for years. And then, one day, alone, José Mujica heard a human voice. Then there were lots of voices. It was a chant. "Your struggle is our struggle!" the voices said. "Your struggle is our struggle! We are here! We believe in what you're doing! We are here! We believe in what you're doing!"

This time, it was not a hallucination. It was the beginning of the end of the dictatorship.

Mujica kept the promise to Lucia that he had scribbled in the silence of the well. They bought a tiny shack on the outskirts of the city with an iron roof and a little stretch of farmland, and there, they planted flowers, like the ones his mother had grown in his childhood, long ago.

~

One night in November 2009, José Mujica and his wife returned to this shack, to find it looking a little different. All their neighbors were there, cheering and singing, and there were barbecues all around them, where everyone was cooking their best meat and offering it around in jubilation. Mujica had just been elected president of Uruguay. He announced that he would not be moving into the Presidential Palace. He would be staying right here, in his shack, for his full five-year term. He would be giving 90 percent of his income to the poor and living on $775 a month. And as for the presidential limousine—no, thanks. He would take the bus.

In Uruguay, the president is sworn in on inauguration day by the most popularly elected senator. That senator was Lucia. He introduced a law providing a laptop for every child in Uruguay, and he legalized same-sex marriage and abortion. But there was another issue waiting for him.

His cabinet had been watching the news from northern Mexico as it was cannibalized by cartels. Uruguay similarly sits on the transit route for marijuana and cocaine being transported to Europe. The cartels already have a role in controlling Paraguay, the country next door. If the cartels chose to seize Uruguay, they realized, the country would be defenseless. Mujica would have liberated his nation for nothing.

So he began to look at the history of drug policy and realized, he told me, that "we have for over one hundred years been following the policy of repressing drugs—and after one hundred years we have realized that it has been a resounding failure . . . We have to try other ways."

But what is the alternative? It was explained to them that when you legalize drugs, you bankrupt most of the cartels. Government regulation can provide a product that is cheaper, higher quality, and not sold in dark alleyways. The drug dealers would go the way of alcohol-selling gangsters into the dustbin of history. Mujica decided he would start with marijuana, on the assumption that over time, other drugs would follow, until they were all regulated.

Previously, presidents across the world had held back from legalization because of two fears. The first was of the United States. The second was of their own people. But President Mujica, from his shack, was noticing a crucial shift. In the United States, several states were poised to vote to fully legalize marijuana—to allow it to be grown and sold to adults, as we'll see later. And he resolved to persuade his people to do likewise. In solitary confinement, he tells me, he had learned "that life is a fine thing—[so] above and beyond everything, we have to defend life . . . We shouldn't sacrifice a generation in the name of a dream."

To figure out how to make legalization work, he turned to two men from the land of his old honorary leader, Miss Marple: Britain.

~

Many people will begin to travel some way down the road leading away from the drug war, but then they smack into a concrete wall. Written on that wall is the word "legalization," and next to the *l* word, there is a mural of a man named Timothy Leary. He was the most famous face of 1960s drug legalization, a Harvard professor who dropped out to preach that everybody should take drugs and sail away on the trip that would finally bring Western civilization crashing down.

His eyes flashing, Leary evangelized on a cascade of TV shows that he was the founder of a new religion, with cannabis and LSD as its sacraments. These drugs should, he said, be given to twelve-year-olds so they can "fuck righteously and without guilt"—and to prove the point he gave them to his own young teenage children, even as they went slowly insane.

"Please wake up," Leary's daughter wrote to him in letters while he swallowed more tabs than Pac-Man. "You are destructive and evil." She later dissolved into insanity and committed suicide. Leary had already told his friends: "You know, I really am a psychopath."

At first, Leary had argued that drugs made you blissed-out and pacifist. Then he argued that his followers should shoot policemen because "total war is upon us." When he ended up on the run in Algeria, he told the Islamic fundamentalists there that they should like him "because he had screwed up the brains of so many American middle-class white people." By the end of his life, he was arguing we should all live in space, because "I've always been an enemy of gravity."

Leary was the most credentialed salesman of legalization the American people had seen since Henry Smith Williams. Today, many people still believe that legalization would be an expression of his values—that drug use is a good thing and should be encouraged; that it would make drugs available to children; that legalization would lead to much more widespread drug use; and that it would end with the destruction of our culture as we know it.

But the people Mujica sought out make the case for legalization for precisely the opposite reasons. They want to legalize drugs because they want to get them out of the hands of our kids, defend the basic values of law and order, and reduce anarchy and violence. They don't want a world where drug use becomes more exciting and revolutionary. They want a world where it becomes much more boring. They are a pair of English policy wonks called Danny Kushlick and Steve Rolles. Danny had been working for years with prisoners on probation, and he was sick of watching his clients die of overdoses. Steve was a scientist investigating the effects of ecstasy, who stood with a clipboard taking notes at raves and noticed that people on ecstasy were much more friendly and less violent than the alcohol drinkers he was used to. It was startling, he says, to see the police round them up and take them off to the cells.

Together, Danny and Steve formed a group called the Transform Drugs Policy Institute, to answer a question nobody else in the world was answering in any detail: In practice, on your street, what does legalization mean? If we end the drug war, how will drugs be distributed? Who will be allowed to use them? What would change?

I have been discussing these issues with Danny and Steve for nearly ten years now, and they have become my friends. As they began their investigations, Danny and Steve knew that most people believed legalizing drugs would mean there would be a crack-and-meth aisle in every branch of CVS, between the candy bars and the flavored water. Legalization, its opponents believe, means a free-for-all.

But as they looked at the evidence, Danny and Steve came to believe that it would mean the opposite. Today, the trade in drugs consists of unknown gangsters selling unknown chemicals to unknown users, in the dark. That is the definition of a free-for-all. The only way to regulate this trade, they believe, is to turn on the lights—and the first thing they discovered is that to legalize drugs, you don't have to invent anything new. The structures already exist, all around us.

At the moment, we have a licensed and regulated way to sell the two deadliest recreational drugs on earth—alcohol and tobacco.

This wasn't always the case. For a time, various governments experimented with suppressing them by force. In the seventeenth century, Czar Michael Fedorovitch of Russia decreed that "anyone caught with tobacco should be tortured until he gave up the name of the supplier." Around the same time, Sultan Murad IV of the Ottoman Empire introduced the death penalty for smoking. In both countries, people still smoked. So we set up a system where adults can buy this drug legally— but at the same time we make it clear, as a culture, that it makes you sick, you can't do it in most public places, and most of us find the habit unpleasant.

As a result of this policy where tobacco is legal but increasingly socially disapproved of, cigarette smoking has fallen dramatically. In 1960 in the United States, according to the General Household Survey, 59 percent of men and 43 percent of women were smokers. Today, it's 26 percent of men and 23 percent of women—a halving. There have been similar trends across the developed world. Just because something harmful is legal doesn't mean people rush to use it: more and more are turning away from it.

So Danny and Steve concluded that we need to divide drugs into at least two different tiers, depending on how powerful they are. In the first tier, you find the less potent drugs, like marijuana. For them, their solution is: treat it like tobacco and booze. That would mean—in Europe, at least—no advertising. No promotions. Sell them in plain packages, with no logos but lots of health warnings, through licensed vendors. Impose strict age restrictions. Sell them in dull designated stores. If anyone uses drugs in public, while driving, at work, or while performing any responsible task that requires concentration, severely punish them. If they sell them to kids, strip them of their licenses. In other words—expand the web of regulation covering booze and cigarettes to cover them.

At the next tier, you find the more potent drugs, such as heroin. Again, Danny and Steve say, we already have a form of regulation suitable for them. Across every country in the developed world, there is a network of doctors and pharmacists who prescribe powerful chemicals, on the basis of your doctor's assessment of whether you need them. As you read this, they are handing out opiates and amphetamines and everything in between, for medical purposes. This, too, can be expanded—just as they've done in Switzerland. Under this model, addicts would be prescribed their drug by their doctor, while being offered all sorts of programs to help them stop using.

Expanding these two tiers of regulation that already exist would, they argue, end most of the problems caused by the drug war today. It would mean people who go right now to armed gangsters on street corners will go either to licensed stores, or to doctors and pharmacists, for their drugs.

This isn't a vision in which we lose control of drugs, Danny and Steve argue—it's a vision in which we gain control, at last. Legalization is the only way of introducing regulation to the drug market. If this were done, the people selling drugs wouldn't be shooting each other, any more than your local neighborhood barkeeps send hit men to slaughter each other. The users would know what they were taking. And through taxation, we would have a huge new revenue stream to educate kids and invest in reducing the real causes of addiction.

We have run this historical experiment once before, they point out, and we know what one of the effects will be. When alcohol was legalized again in 1933, the involvement of gangsters and murderers and killing in the alcohol trade virtually ended. Peace was restored to the streets of Chicago. The murder rate fell dramatically, and it didn't rise so high again until drug prohibition was intensified in the 1970s and '80s.

At its heart, legalization is, Danny tells me, "a drama reduction program. Because all the excitement, the salaciousness, the sexiness of drugs is very much in their prohibition, not their regulation. Somebody once said to me—what you really need to do is get a movie made of what legalization would look like. And I said—Jesus, that would be the most boring film in the world. Because it would be. It's going to be watching somebody walk into a shop and say, 'Please can I have some MDMA?' and they will say, 'Yes, here's some. That'll be £4.50 please.' There's a real danger as we move toward the end [of the war] and the beginning of the new [system] that we continue to associate the horrors and the excite-ment of prohibition with a new regime that is [actually] incredibly boring." The culture of terror will turn—slowly, but ineluctably—into a culture of tedium.

~

But what happens next? I had seen clearly that prohibition doesn't work, and Portugal shows that decriminalization is a significant advance. But what about legalization? The difference is simple. When you decriminalize, you stop punishing drug users and drug addicts—but you continue to ban the manufacture and selling of the drugs. They are still supplied by criminal drug dealers. When you legalize, you set up a network of stores or pharmacies or prescription where users and addicts can buy their drugs.

One crucial question hangs over this vision—one that understandably stops many people from buying this whole argument. If we make drugs more easily available, won't more people use them? And a whole range of concerns follows from that. There are, for me, three in particular. If more people use them, won't more people become addicted? Won't more people overdose? And won't more kids get hold of drugs? If you are thinking of moving beyond decriminalization into legalization, these are the central questions that have to be answered.

To determine whether drug use would increase, I started to go through the evidence carefully—and I soon found that it is mixed. There are two important pieces of proof from the past—the quasi legalization of marijuana in the Netherlands, and the end of alcohol prohibition in the United States. They offer different lessons.

In 1976, the Dutch introduced a new drug policy. They announced if you had up to 30 grams of marijuana on you, the police wouldn't take it away. This is, in effect, decriminalization of personal use. All legal punishments for cannabis use among adults ended. What happened next? According to all the available evidence, over the next seven years, levels of drug use remained the same. Then the Netherlands took another step, which was to allow cannabis to be sold openly in licensed cafés. This was a move from the decriminalization of personal possession to—effectively—the legalization of selling the drug itself. They backed away from calling it legalization, because that would breach the UN treaties authored by Harry Anslinger. But it is, for all intents and purposes, a very modest form of legalization.

And the results, it turns out, were equally clear. There *was* an increase in the use of the drug. Among the group most likely to smoke weed, eighteen-to-twenty-year-olds, the proportion of people who had used cannabis in the previous month rose from 8.5 percent to 18.5 percent. For other age groups, there was a smaller but still real rise. This increase did not happen in other European cities at that time, so it is reasonable to assume it was a result of this policy. Some of this increase was probably due to the fact that people are more likely to openly admit to smoking cannabis when it is no longer a crime—but it is unlikely that this explains all of the rise.

This finding suggests that there is no significant increase in drug use if a country decriminalizes possession, but some increase when they legalize sale. The reason seems to be pretty obvious: it's about ease of access. We all, I think, know people who would not approach a street dealer for a drug in an alleyway, but who might buy it if it were sold in a store or pharmacy in the local shopping mall.

It's important to be candid about this rise, but also important not to exaggerate its scale. Cannabis use rose a little, but it is still low in the Netherlands. Some 5 percent of Dutch citizens reported smoking cannabis in the previous month, which is lower than the United States at 6.3 percent and the EU average of 7 percent. Cannabis consumption didn't spiral out of control, and it remains low compared to other countries.

But there's a significant complicating factor to this rise—one explained to me by Danny. Try, as you read this, to see "drug use" as an overall number—everyone in the world tonight who is taking a drug counts as one drug user. You'd include everyone buying a joint or taking an ecstasy pill. But should you include every pint of beer and every shot of whisky in that tally? If you don't count alcohol as drug use, then drug use would go up. But if you do count alcohol as drug use, then there is some evidence suggesting overall drug use will *not* go up after legalization. Why? What seems to happen when you legalize marijuana is that a significant number of people looking to chill out transfer from getting drunk to getting stoned. After California made it much easier to get marijuana from your doctor—anyone claiming a bad back was given a permit—traffic accidents fell by 8 percent, because lots of people made this shift, and driving when you're stoned (while a bad idea) is nowhere near as dangerous as driving drunk.

That's why Danny believes that talk about a rise in "drug use" is the wrong way of thinking about it. The more interesting question, he says, is how patterns of drug use will change. If we legalized ecstasy and lots of people transferred from getting drunk on a Saturday night to taking ecstasy on a Saturday night, that would count in the official statistics as an increase in "drug use." In fact, he says, it would be an improvement. Our streets would be less violent. Domestic violence would fall. Fewer people would get liver diseases. This is a more complex calculation, he says, than can be measured on a narrowly statistical balance sheet.

~

I understand Danny's point, and I respect it, and want it to be right—but I don't think it tells the whole picture.

Here's an inconvenient fact for those of us who favor reform. There is strong evidence that during alcohol prohibition, fewer people drank, and after it ended, more people drank. It's hard to tell precisely, because measuring an illegal activity is always tough, but you can look at rates of cirrhosis of the liver, which corresponds with heavy alcohol use, and get a fairly good sense. Drinking seems to have fallen by between 10 and 20 percent during Prohibition, and after it ceased, there was a very slow rise back over several decades. They weren't transferring to other intoxicants—there wasn't anything else. They were staying sober—in substantial numbers. It wasn't just a fall in drinking either. It was a fall in alcoholism.

Why? The best explanation is that there are significant numbers of people who want to obey the law because it is the law. If something is illegal, that has a deterrent effect all on its own. Then, on top of that, if you ban something, it does become somewhat harder for most people to get hold of. I have complained in this book that the people who support the drug war sometimes use propaganda to promote their cause, so it's important that I resist the temptation to produce propaganda of my own. Those of us who have come to believe we should end the drug war have to be candid. The evidence suggests there will probably be a modest but real increase in use. Some significant share of that will be people transferring from alcohol, but probably not all of it. It should be acknowledged: one of the successes of prohibition is that it probably does hold down drug use somewhat.

I have been trying for more than a year now to absorb what this fact means. When I discussed it with Danny one afternoon in the café at the British Library, he pointed out that most of us don't object to drug use in and of itself. We worry about the harms caused by drug use. If I told you that your neighbor smoked a spliff or snorted a line of coke last weekend, I doubt you would be deeply concerned. But you would—rightly—be worried if she was a teenager, or if she became an addict, or if she overdosed. It is not drug use that worries us, but the harms caused by drug use.

And the evidence about these harms is quite striking. Legalization slightly increases drug use—but it significantly reduces drug harms.

Let's start with teenagers. In the best available study, a large number of American teens in surveys explained that they found it easier to buy marijuana today than to buy beer or cigarettes. When I first read this, I found it puzzling. I only really understood why one afternoon on my travels when I was told about a road to Damascus that ran through a parking lot in New Jersey.

This story was told to me in the winter of 2012, when I went to Trenton, New Jersey—a concrete wilderness town that bears an uncanny resemblance to the Gaza Strip. In an office overlooking the wheezing city, Fred Martens told me a story about his past. One day in the early 1970s, he had been waiting in the lot outside a shopping mall, to buy marijuana, PCP, heroin, and meth, and then bust the dealer's ass. This was the era of Dirty Harry, and Fred was an undercover cop who could easily have been Clint Eastwood's character, packing a Magnum and a sneer. "I had no qualms," he told me, "about putting a gun in an informant's mouth and telling him, 'If you're fucking lying to me, I'll blow your fucking brains out. Do you get it?'"

But something was about to happen that would make Fred rethink his support for the drug war.

A kid approached him. He seemed to be about twelve years old.

"Mister, mister," he said, "do me a favor. Could you buy me a bottle of wine in the liquor store?"

Fred kicked him in the ass and snapped, "Get out of here." He went back to waiting for a drug dealer so he could make his buy and make his bust.

But "that's when the realization hit me," he told me. "I'm saying to myself—this kid needs me to get him a bottle of liquor, when he can go get any drug he wants in the parking lot without me. What was better regulated—the liquor, or the drugs in this parking lot? It was . . . an epiphany. What is this all about?" The insight stayed with him as a source of doubt for years, and it made him come out, in the end, for legalization.

Nobody in my nephews' schools, it occurred to me as Fred talked, is selling Budweiser or Jack Daniel's. But there are plenty of people selling weed and pills. Why? Because the people who sell alcohol in our culture have a really strong incentive not to sell to teenagers: if they do, they lose their license and their business. The people who sell other, prohibited drugs in our culture have a really strong incentive to sell to teenagers: they are customers like everybody else.

If we legalize, there will be a barrier standing between our kids and drugs that does not exist today. This isn't theoretical; the societies that have tried this have shown it to be the case. Some 21 percent of Dutch teenagers have tried marijuana; in the United States, it is 45 percent. I picture my nephews and my niece. If I decide to support legalization, it won't be despite them—it will be because of them.

~

Addiction seems more worrying. It is common sense that if more people use drugs, more people will become addicted to drugs. During alcohol prohibition, fewer people drank—and fewer died of alcoholism and the diseases it causes. This weighs really heavily on me. If more people ended up like the people I love, the people who set me on this journey—desperate and broken—that would be a major reason not to change the existing policy.

But then I contrast this evidence with the evidence from Portugal. More people used drugs, yet addiction fell substantially. Why? Because punishment—shaming a person, caging them, making them unemployable—traps them in addiction. Taking that money and spending it instead on helping them to get jobs and homes and decent lives makes it possible for many of them to stop.

At the end of alcohol prohibition, they didn't use the massive new tax revenues to invest in educating kids about alcohol, and turning the lives of alcoholics around. Portugal showed us there is another way.

~

But what about overdose? This, surely, is the hardest point to answer. If more people use drugs, more will end up accidentally taking fatal doses. It seems obvious.

But in fact—as I saw in Vancouver and Geneva—the places that have expanded legal access to hard drugs have seen an enormous fall in overdoses. Why? There are two big reasons. The first is that at the moment, if you buy a drug from a gangster, you have no idea what is in it. Imagine ordering generic "alcohol" from the bar, not knowing whether it is an alcopop or absinthe. You'd be far more likely to drink too much and collapse. In a regulated store, by contrast, you know what you are getting.

The second reason is the iron law of prohibition, which I explained earlier. When you ban a drug, it's very risky to transport it—so dealers will always choose the drug that packs the strongest possible kick into the smallest possible space. That means that under prohibition you can only get the most hard-core form of a drug. Beer disappeared during alcohol prohibition, and moonshine shone; as soon as alcohol prohibition ended, moonshine vanished.

After drug prohibition ends, it's reasonable to expect that the milder forms of drugs that were popular before prohibition will come back, just as beer did. So the rise in drug use will most likely consist not of an army of crack addicts, but of an increase in people drinking stronger tea and smoking weaker spliffs. Nobody has ever overdosed on coca tea.

~

I can feel, as I write this, that I am persuading myself that the full legal regulation of all drugs is a good idea—but then a set of prickly questions comes into my mind, and they won't go away.

What about the most powerfully intoxicating drugs? Would you let people buy meth? Would you let people buy crack?

When it comes to a drug like crack or meth, what does legalization even mean? Are we suggesting openly selling it? If not, would doctors even be willing to prescribe it?

I keep putting this question to legalizers across the world. Their first response is usually to sigh and point out that those drugs make up 5 percent or less of the market for illegal drugs. So let's start, they say, with the other 95 percent. Take the politically possible steps today. We'll get to this conversation years from now, when it is no longer totally hypothetical.

But this, it seems to me, is to dodge the question. So when you push further and ask the question again, you find that legalizers fall into three broad camps on these drugs.

Some would leave a few drugs banned, as tiny islands of prohibition in a sea of regulation. They are aware that this would mean that small networks of drug gangs would persist, but there would be far fewer of them, because now they'd be meeting only a really small niche market for the most hard-core users.

At the opposite end of the spectrum, you find some pure libertarians. They say: You have a right to damage your own body. It's your choice. If you are allowed to ski, or box, or race at 300 mph on a private track, you should be allowed to ingest whatever chemicals you want. The job of government is not to protect you from yourself. If people want to buy crack, let them buy crack. Sell it along with the other drugs, in regulated stores.

In between these two positions, there is a middle way: Build a third tier of regulation, beyond open sale or prescription. You'd establish safe designated rooms in our big cities, where people would be allowed to buy and use these more hard-core drugs, with doctors on hand, provided they didn't leave until the drugs had worn off. It'd be like the safe injection rooms I saw in Vancouver and Switzerland, but with a broader range of drugs on offer, and tighter rules. The argument for this is that the hard-core users are going to take their drugs anyway: at least this way they do it in a place where they can be kept away from everyone else, and where there are people to care for them, and patiently point the way toward getting help.

~

But I remained nervous, nonetheless, about expanding legal access to these drugs, for an obvious reason—one I had known since I was a child. Crack and meth contain such powerful chemical hooks that almost everyone who tries them will become addicted. I had learned this—without ever looking at the evidence. When I was shown the actual facts by real experts, I was startled.

As an experiment, I'd like to quickly test how well you know this. Can you stop for a moment and write in the margin of this book what proportion of crack users you think become addicts? Don't read on until you've written down your estimate.

In April 2012, the brilliant drug reformer Ethan Nadelmann appeared on the MSNBC discussion show *Hardball*. The host, Chris Matthews, was clearly initially persuaded by Ethan's case for change—but then he backed off. He explained his worry: "Ten people could have a glass of wine and maybe one in ten or one in a hundred would become quickly addicted to alcohol. But I'm told . . . if you try crack cocaine once, you're liable to be addicted." That is what I believed, too.

But then I interviewed Dr. Carl Hart, one of the world's leading experts on this question, at his offices in Columbia University, and what he showed me was so surprising I had to keep going back to see him repeatedly over the course of a year before I really accepted what he was saying. He talked me through the best scientific evidence, which he later expanded on in his book *High Price*. He showed me that the evidence is that, of the people who have tried crack, just 3 percent have used it in the past month, and at most 20 percent were ever addicted at any point in their lives.

Look again at the figure you wrote down. Is the real figure higher or lower than your guess? My initial estimate would have been 90 percent. I was wrong by 70 percent.

Now I know that instead of the vast majority of users becoming addicted, as I and Chris Matthews thought, the vast majority of users—even of these substances—do *not* become addicted. When Rob Ford, the mayor of Toronto, was revealed to have used crack, and a month later Paul Flowers, the head of a major bank in Britain, was caught buying meth and forced to resign, there was general bemusement. This wasn't our picture of a crack or meth user—people with responsible jobs, who appeared to have functioned for quite a long time. Clearly, we thought, they were freakish exceptions. But in fact, according to the best available data, they are actually more typical users of the drug than Marcia Powell or Chino's mom, Deborah.

This feels strange to say. It seems intuitively wrong to me. But it is what the facts show. Why is this so surprising to all of us, me included? It took me a while to puzzle it out, but I think this is the reason.

We still think—as I discussed earlier—of addiction as mainly caused by chemical hooks. There's something in the drug that, after a while, your body starts to crave and need. That's what we think addiction is. But chemical hooks are only a minor part of addiction. The other factors, like isolation and trauma, have been proven to be much bigger indicators. Yet the drug war *increases* the biggest drivers of addiction—isolation and trauma—in order to protect potential users from a more *minor* driver of addiction, the chemical hook. If we legalize, somewhat more people will be exposed to the chemical hook in drugs—but the even larger drivers of addiction, trauma and isolation, will be dramatically reduced.

As I try to understand this, I keep picturing the women back in Tent City on their chain gang. Imagine if, instead, you used that money Portugal-style to put them in a lovely clinic, teach them how to cope with pain, and help them get a job. Now imagine that kind of transformation spreading across a society, even one in which more people use drugs. Would addiction go up, or down?

~

How, in the end, can you decide whether you support drug legalization, and for which drugs? I can't decide that for you. It comes down to what you, personally, value more. What I did was draw up a balance sheet, and try to figure what I personally value more.

I urge you to draw up your own balance sheet. Here's mine.

In the column arguing against legalization, I wrote that drug use will probably go up. It won't be massive—we know that from both of the historical precedents—but it will be real. Some people today refuse to take drugs because it is a crime to do it, and because they fear either getting arrested or buying from criminals in alleyways. The day after legalization, this reason for reservation will no longer be there. That is a significant drawback.

I searched very hard for other arguments to put in this column. I couldn't find any, but you may have some: please e-mail them to me.

In the column next to it, arguing for legalization, I found myself writing out the following arguments:

Across the world, armed criminal gangs selling drugs will be financially crippled, from the Crips to the Zetas. The survivors will be pushed into much less profitable markets, where they will be able to do much less harm. As a result, the culture of terror that currently dominates whole neighborhoods and countries—from Brownsville, Brooklyn, to Ciudad Juárez—will gradually abate. (This happened after the end of alcohol prohibition.) The murder rate will significantly fall. (This also happened after the end of alcohol prohibition.) Enormous amounts of police time will be freed up to investigate other crimes. Trust in the police will begin to come back to poor communities. (This happened in Portugal.)

Teenagers will find it harder to get drugs. (This happened in the Netherlands.) Overdoses will significantly decline, and the rate of HIV transmission will fall dramatically. (Both happened in Switzerland, the Netherlands, and Vancouver.) The drugs people use will, in the main, be milder than today. (Remember the iron law and the end of alcohol prohibition.) There will be a lot more money to spend on treating addicts and dealing with the underlying causes of addiction. Many addicts who currently get worse behind bars will get better in hospitals and then in new jobs. This means addiction will fall. (This happened in Portugal.)

Millions of people who are currently imprisoned for nonviolent offenses, at great expense to the taxpayers and to their communities, will walk free. Huge numbers of African American and Latino men who are currently locked out of the workforce, student loans, and public housing will be allowed back in. Shaming addicts will be replaced by caring for addicts.

Once I had drawn up my list, I compared the pros and cons of each side. Your calculation of the benefits may well vary from drug to drug. Mine did. When it comes to marijuana and the party drugs like ecstasy, up to and including cocaine, I think the harm caused by a small increase in use is plainly outweighed by all these gains. That's why I would sell them in regulated stores, like alcohol. And with drugs like crack and meth? I am inclined to the middle option—allow safe regulated spaces where users can buy and take them, supervised by doctors.

I can't support a policy that sacrifices people like Chino Hardin and Marcia Powell and Marisela Escobedo in order to prevent people who want to use drugs from taking them. I don't want to live in that world

~

When Danny and Steve began to advise the government of Uruguay, they showed President Mujica how to begin to build this better path.

Their blueprint—along with the advice offered by other drug reform groups—showed Mujica how to set up a legal, regulated framework for selling marijuana. After all the controversy, the proposals were pretty straightforward. In 2014, a legal structure was set up to let pharmacies across Uruguay sell marijuana to people over the age of twenty-one who produce a valid ID. The crop will be grown legally across the country, and taxed. Each home is also allowed to grow a small number of marijuana plants for personal use.

Nobody will ever be imprisoned for using this naturally growing plant again. Adults will be free to choose marijuana or alcohol on a Saturday night without any risk of punishment. Maybe, Mujica tells me, this policy will fail—but what we are doing now under prohibition "is a failure every day." It is hard to see, he says, how the new policy could fail worse.

Seen in the long sweep of human history, Danny says, it's not this new wave of legalization of drugs that is radical. "The radical move," he tells me, "was prohibition"—the experiment that lasted a century and was based on the idea that it could eradicate entire plant species from the face of the earth and stop humans from getting high.

When Danny launched Transform in the mid-1990s, he named 2020 as the year he believed would mark the end of the global drug war. He always said presidents would be coming to his door, asking how to do it. People laughed. They're not laughing now.

~

On the sunlit winter's day when I visit the presidential shack, the first thing I noticed is President Mujica's underwear, flapping in the wind on a clothesline. His wife, Lucia, is standing by the door. There is not, she explains, much to see. It is, indeed, a shack, with a rather rickety-looking iron roof. There are three rooms: a tiny bedroom, a tiny kitchen, and a narrow living space that connects them, with some books, a small wood fire, and a painting that was given to them by Evo Morales, the Bolivian president. That's it. The tour of the Uruguyan equivalent to the White House takes all of ninety seconds. It occurs to me that my own prime minister, David Cameron, would not keep his shoes here.

Mujica "would be different if he weren't kept prisoner," Lucia tells me, "because he had so much time to think, it became clear to him what was important in life." He learned "to live with light baggage in jail. He learned that happiness doesn't come from what you have, but from what you are."

Later, when I speak to him on the telephone, Mujica tells me: "If I have too much luggage, too much property, too many material goods, that makes me worry I have to defend this stuff—then in that case I will not have time left to take care of the things I really love, and then I lose my freedom." He is in a philosophical mood. "I am seventy-eight years old," he says. "I had a dream of changing the history of man—the possibility of creating a humanity where men don't exploit each other. A utopia that we call socialism. We thought it was much closer in time . . . Many decades have gone by, and without renouncing our dreams, we learned that the impossible takes a bit longer."

Outside the entrance to their shack, staring back at Mujica every morning as he leaves to run the country, there is a well. It provides the water for the flowers that grow all around him. Mujica grows his flowers, and he allows others to grow theirs.

CHAPTER 18

High Noon

So I had learned how drug legalization could work practically, but now I wanted to know—how do you make it work politically? How do you go to the heart of the country that has been imposing the drug war on its citizens and on the world for a hundred years, and persuade people there is a better way? I kept thinking of the line from the old song: If you can make it there, you'll make it anywhere.

In Colorado and Washington State, two small bands of friends and allies decided to get the question of whether to legalize, tax, and regulate marijuana onto their states' ballots, so everyone could vote on it—and within seven years, they had won. I resolved to track down the people who achieved this and find out how they did it. And here's the surprising thing. The different campaigns, it turns out, have different explanations. The men who led the victory in Colorado disagree with the women who won in Washington.

By teasing out this difference, I found two different routes out of the drug war—ones we all need to think about now.

~

Standing on the street, staring intently, Mason Tvert issued a challenge to the mayor of his city—to fight a duel at high noon. Back when Colorado was the Old West, these threats of shootouts to the death were as common as cowboys, but the last recorded instance was in a quarry back in 1904.

Until now. In 2006, standing outside the Denver County Courthouse, Mason was reviving the tradition. It would be seen later by some people as the beginning of the duel that changed the course of the drug war.

The offer was simple. John Hickenlooper, the elected leader of Denver, was a rich man who made his fortune by setting up a brewpub and selling beer to the public—yet he insisted it would be crazy to sell marijuana in exactly the same tightly regulated way. Mason Tvert—a large twenty-four-year-old Jewish American guy with a rhythmic foghorn voice—believed the drug had been proven by scientists to be safer than alcohol. He wanted to prove it again. So he sat next to several large cases of beer, a fake joint in his hand and a real joint in his pocket. For every hit the mayor took of alcohol, Mason pledged, he would take a hit of marijuana—and we would see who died first.

Hickenlooper announced he would be out of town and so, alas, could not take part. He would continue to vehemently oppose legalization for years as he rose to become the governor of Colorado—until something unprecedented in the history of the United States took place.

~

Mason Tvert first became fired up about marijuana policy when he was subpoenaed before a multijurisdictional grand jury. He was a freshman at the University of Richmond, Virginia, studying political science, and it was the middle of his finals week when the police told him he needed to report to them. Mason knew that all he had done was smoke some marijuana—but he was interrogated like a suspect in a terror plot. It quickly became clear that another student had been busted and had started to give up names. The cops demanded to know: Where do you buy your marijuana? What suppliers do you know? How high up the chain does this go? Mason explained he got it in parking lots after rock concerts, and he knew nothing else of use to them—but he was terrified.

But as he reflected on his predicament, he remembered that the college would allow and even officially approve of parties where huge amounts of alcohol were openly consumed—so he began to ask himself a question. Why is alcohol sanctioned and smiled at, while the police crack down constantly on weed—when it seemed to him that the weed smokers cause a lot less trouble than the drinkers?

After he left college, Mason wanted to change a situation he regarded as crazy, and he began to look at the details. A friend of his, Steve Fox, had noticed a quirk in the opinion polling about the marijuana laws. If you believed that marijuana was more dangerous than alcohol, you were very likely to support banning it. If you believed that marijuana was less dangerous than alcohol, you were very likely to support legalizing it. But the facts showed, he was sure, that marijuana *is* safer than alcohol. This, Mason became convinced, was the key to unlocking legalization—so he moved to Denver and set up a group called Safer Alternative for Enjoyable Recreation (SAFER) Colorado. It was designed to explain the facts about marijuana. He raised a banner outside Mayor Hickenlooper's office. "What is the difference between the mayor and a marijuana dealer?" it asked. "Mayor Hickenlooper deals a more dangerous drug."

He was told it was a waste of time, a crazy quixotic quest. "We spent years getting doors slammed in our faces," one of his closest allies, Brian Vicente, tells me. "Politicians wouldn't meet with us. They wouldn't return our phone calls. The police would threaten us from time to time. Our parents and others said, 'Why are you working on this? It's a hopeless cause.' But we just believed in it." They were determined to be free to use their drug of choice.

~

Four thousand miles away, in Anchorage, Alaska, Tonia Winchester was sitting in her school's DARE program—the educational initiative cheerled into existence by Nancy Reagan to make kids pledge to "Just Say No." She took its message so deeply to heart that she rose to become the president of her school's chapter. She was convinced that "all people who use marijuana are bad and deserve to be in jail." She tells me: "I thought that if you used marijuana, the next thing you knew, you'd be addicted to heroin and shooting up every day. That was my upbringing. I avoided drugs." Tonia had never liked marijuana personally, and she never would—even as she led it to legalization in Washington State.

When she left school, she trained to become a lawyer and rose to become a prosecutor in Waunakee, a city in central Washington. One of her main jobs was to take on marijuana users and punish them. She had always believed in the cause.

But gradually, she began to notice a few things that were making her feel uncomfortable. Why were the people she was prosecuting overwhelmingly Latino and African American, when "the majority of people who use marijuana are white men"? she asked. Why is "a white man not going to get pulled over and arrested for marijuana possession"? She began to wonder if she was part of a racist system—and then, in dark moments, she started to question something about herself. Were some of her own decisions being driven by unconscious prejudices? If she saw that a defendant had a Hispanic last name, she noticed, she automatically assumed he or she wasn't a citizen and could be deported. She was starting to ask herself: How did you end up thinking like this? Is this what you want to spend your life doing?

And then she noticed something even worse. The people she was charging weren't just from ethnic minorities—they were often kids. One day, she was told to prosecute an eighteen-year-old boy who had been smoking a bowl of marijuana with his friends in a parked car in a parking lot. He had a scholarship to college. If he was convicted, he would lose his scholarship, and it would be hard for him to get a job for the rest of his life.

This wasn't an isolated case. "Have you ever seen large food production plants, where the cows are just coming in—and they come in, and come in, and come in?" she asks me. It was like that: "It's a conveyor belt of people coming in and out of the system . . . Case called. Sentence entered, paperwork filled out. You go to the bailiff. Next case . . . The drama is afterward, when they go to get a job and they can't because they have a conviction, when they can't pay their fines and end up having to spend more time in jail . . . It's a never-ending spiral of hopelessness."

Her doubts slowly built up, like polluted water behind a dam—until one day she was working through a pile of marijuana prosecutions and she noticed that there was a pile of domestic violence prosecutions waiting for her that she didn't have the time to get to. Busting weed was the priority for her bosses, and it carried a mandatory jail sentence—while domestic violence didn't. In that moment, she made a promise to herself.

I am going to get out of this system, she pledged, and I am going to get rid of this bad law. She hadn't changed her mind about marijuana. She would never like it. She had changed her mind about the marijuana laws. Not long after, she teamed up with another lawyer—a young mother named Alison Holcomb, who had been working on similar cases, and had resolved to make sure her son would grow up in an America where nobody was treated like this ever again. They were virtually alone in launching this fight at first—almost nobody else was working to get this onto the ballot, because they thought it was a hopeless cause.

∼

Both of these campaigns wanted to undo the work of Harry Anslinger—but in very different ways. Mason wanted to focus on undoing Harry's claims about the effects marijuana has on its users. Tonia wanted to focus on undoing Harry's claims about the benefits of prohibition. All the successful drug reform campaigns I had seen up to this point—like the one in Switzerland—had at their heart conservative messages about restoring order, bankrupting criminals, and protecting children. That, Tonia believed, was the right approach for Washington—but in Colorado, Mason was going to try a different way.

Mason believes the main reason marijuana should be legalized is that ever since Anslinger, people have profoundly misunderstood it. It is, in fact, safer than the beer they drink on a Saturday night. "Alcohol is a poison," he tells me. "It is a toxic substance that can result in overdose deaths. Its use alone—not including accidents and injuries—is responsible for [about] forty thousand deaths in the United States each year. No deaths are attributed to marijuana use. [Alcohol has] been found to be a more addictive substance. It is certainly far more problematic socially—in that alcohol has been found to be a major contributing factor in acts of violence and reckless behavior."

Now look, he says, at marijuana. "There's no significant evidence showing marijuana is problematic in that way. In fact the evidence suggests marijuana tends to reduce risk-taking behavior and makes people less likely to become violent. It's less harmful to the body and it's less harmful to society. So if someone makes the choice to use marijuana instead of drinking, they are making a safer choice."

This changes the debate, he believes—because if you legalize, some people will choose to transfer from getting drunk to getting stoned on a Saturday night. Legalization, then, wouldn't be "adding a vice"—it would be "providing adults with a less harmful recreational alternative." He even argued that, although he is against teenagers using marijuana, if they switch from drinking alcohol to smoking pot, "that's a net positive."

So above a liquor store, the campaign to legalize marijuana bought a billboard showing a smiling woman in a white cardigan. She was saying: "For many reasons, I prefer marijuana over alcohol. Does that make me a bad person?" A previous billboard showed a girl in a bikini—in a parody of a beer advertisement—saying: "Marijuana: No hangovers, no violence, no carbs!" More controversially, Mason had noticed academic research that shows men are eight times more likely to attack their partners after drinking, but no more likely to do it after smoking cannabis. That's why

SAFER paid to put up a billboard showing a woman who had been beaten up, and urging people to vote for marijuana legalization to reduce domestic violence.

At every stage, Mason wanted to underscore that the current laws "steer people toward using the more harmful substance." When the local cops arrested a ring of marijuana dealers, he stood outside the press conference arranged by the Drug Enforcement Agency with wanted posters of John Hickenlooper, the mayor of Denver, explaining that he had made his fortune selling a more harmful drug and so—logically—he should be busted too. Mason said he had conducted an investigation into all the "alcohol dealers" in town by looking up the licensed stores in the Yellow Pages, and he asked why they weren't being raided and paraded like the weed dealers.

His campaign called this tactic "marijuana jujitsu"—pushing the onus back onto the prohibitionists to justify their crazy system. Mason believes this is the only path to reform. "Until people understand marijuana's not as harmful as they've been led to believe, they're not going to support making it legal," he says.

In all the debates during the campaign—all over the rocky and snowy terrain of Colorado—he set himself a rule. He would never make an argument for ending the prohibition of marijuana in which you could simply replace the word "marijuana" with the word "methamphetamine." He would never solely say, for example, that marijuana prohibition is a waste of resources, or empowers criminal drug gangs, or that it burns through money that could be used for better causes—because if that's true for marijuana, why not meth? Once you talk yourself into that corner, he says, you have lost the argument with the public. "Marijuana is illegal because of the perception of harm surrounding it," he says. "Our message addresses that perception of harm head-on, whereas traditional messages have avoided that and simply focused on problems associated with prohibition."

~

Over in Washington, Tonia Winchester was standing in the snow outside a Cougar football game, trying to gather the three hundred thousand signatures necessary to trigger a statewide ballot initiative to legalize marijuana. Many of the people who passed would smile and thank her—and many of them would snap at her angrily. She heard endless variants on "It's a devil drug. You're doing the devil's work! You're corrupting our youth!"

When people stopped to talk, she offered a very different message from Mason's. "I'm not asking you to like marijuana or even think it's a good thing," she would explain. "In fact, I don't use marijuana myself, and I would prefer if people didn't use marijuana. We're not talking about liking marijuana or advocating its use. We're talking about a policy that has not benefited society, and has actually caused more harm than good."

She would talk about her life as a former prosecutor, how she had seen the marijuana laws wreck people's lives—and how she should have been spending her time prosecuting people who cause real harm. "In my mind always, no matter who I was talking to, the first fork in the road of discussing marijuana legalization was—Can I get them to the point where they realize we are not talking about liking marijuana?" she told me. "We're not talking about advocating for the use of marijuana. We're not talking about enjoying marijuana."

Only around 15 percent of the people of Colorado and Washington like marijuana enough to smoke it. That means 85 percent don't like or want it. Tonia thought that trying to mobilize those people in defense of marijuana itself would never work. She wanted to show, instead, how marijuana prohibition affects everyone—whether they smoke the drug or not. When you sound as if you are praising marijuana, she believes, you only trigger negative stereotypes in people's minds. "I saw people's attitudes toward me change when they saw me walk into the room and I wasn't wearing Rastafari clothes and dreadlocks," she says. "I have really successful friends who are smart and brilliant and intelligent, and when they admit to smoking pot, they see people's opinions of them change . . . *I* still have to combat my own stereotypes of what it means to be a pot smoker."

So the Washington campaign made a conscious decision not ever to argue that marijuana is safer than alcohol, because, as Tonia puts it, "it's a stupid argument and it doesn't persuade people . . . [They] have a visceral negative reaction to marijuana, and it's only by overcoming that that you can actually get them voting for legalization." If you try to tell people that marijuana isn't bad, most of them—even people who could be persuaded of legalization—will quickly come back at you with all their negative thoughts about marijuana. "And I'm not sure there is anywhere to move from that argument point to then get somebody back to supporting legalization," Tonia says. "You've backed yourself into a corner."

But it is not just that they doubted that Mason's argument would persuade people—they also doubted it was true. Professor Roger

Roffman, an expert on addictive disorders, was one of the leading figures in the campaign, and he had been campaigning for marijuana legalization since 1967, ever since he returned from Vietnam. But when he heard people during the campaign saying the drug is "safe," he felt obliged to explain: "This is perhaps what you'd like to believe, but the science doesn't support it. Dependence is a risk. Driving accidents are a risk. Teenagers using marijuana early and regularly and becoming derailed . . . is a risk, and to say marijuana is harmless is misinformed, and it's misinforming those people you're talking to."

The Washington campaign argued that drugs should be legalized not because they are safe, but because they are dangerous. It's precisely because they are risky that we need to take them back from the gangsters and cartels, and hand them to regulated stores—and use the tax money we gain to pay for prevention and treatment. They wouldn't have dreamed of telling parents their kids would be better off using marijuana rather than alcohol. Instead, they would explain: "Street dealers don't check ID." Legalization, they said, would restrict access to weed for teens. The Children's Alliance— the major children's charity in Washington State—came out for a yes vote on legalization.

This difference in philosophy didn't just produce different campaigns— it produced different models of legalization.

In Washington, the model was built on the conviction that marijuana causes harm and we need to counteract those harms. So they decided to earmark the tax revenue from selling marijuana for drug prevention programs in schools and drug treatment for addicts. In Colorado, they didn't—the money is going toward building new schools instead. In Washington, the legalization legislation introduces a strict new ban on driving while stoned. In Colorado, they resisted this proposal. In Washington, you are not allowed to grow it at home. In Colorado, you are.

Both campaigns argued that legalization would improve public health—but in contrasting ways. In Colorado, it seemed to me they primarily argued that it would make people healthier by getting them to transfer from alcohol to marijuana. In Washington, they argued it would make people healthier by making it possible to raise taxes to undo some of the harm caused by their marijuana use. It was a subtle—but crucial—difference.

~

One night, in Washington, the campaigners finally got confirmation that their initiative was going to be on the ballot, and they threw a big party at the home of a local travel writer. Alison Holcomb—the leader of the campaign alongside Tonia—was exhausted, and she wandered out and went to sit for a moment, alone. The sky was glowing pink and purple, and it was the first time in months that she had time to take off the blinders, and think about what they were really doing.

"That was when I finally realized that Washington State voters," she told me, "were going to have the chance to change the world. I remember when I was looking up at the clouds thinking—that is the same sky that is over Mexico, the same sky that is over Europe, the same sky that is all over the world—and there were so many people worldwide that were waiting to see what would happen. To see if we would do it. I had that little moment . . . when I realized how big it was."

~

As the war on marijuana was drawing to a close in both these states, I kept hearing strange echoes of the start of this war.

Marijuana was first banned by Harry Anslinger as part of a racist panic against Latinos: they are coming up into the United States, he warned, and bringing their "loco weed" with them. It was an argument that mobilized the public to back him. Now, all these years later, Tonia and Alison were explaining to the public that Latinos were still the focus of this crackdown. Yet this time—after decades of change—the public saw this not as a reason to support the war, but as a reason to oppose it. The country had become more compassionate.

Yet I could feel the habits of the early drug war coming back again and again, like acid reflux. At the start, Harry had used the full force of the law to intimidate and silence dissenters like Henry Smith Williams. It was still happening. One evening, one of Mason's closest allies—an attorney with Latino roots named Brian Vicente—drove out to a county on the eastern plains of Colorado, to give a presentation on their arguments.

Suddenly, the local sheriff burst in with his officers. "If I had my way," he yelled, "I would pull marijuana users out of their cars as they were driving by and shoot them"—and he mimed shooting them with his fingers.

Brian sped out of the county, terrified. But the intimidation didn't only come from law enforcement. Later, Brian went to one of Denver's leading Latino radio stations to make the case for legalization. He knew the state has many citizens who came from Mexico, some fleeing the drug war violence—so he wanted to explain to them that legalization would strip the cartels of a large part of their income and begin the process of bankrupting them.

The DJs looked at him, appalled, and said he could not say that on the air. "We don't want to say that on the radio," they explained, "because we're afraid we're going to get killed.'" They were convinced, Brian says, that if they advocated legalization, "there would be some sort of retribution in Colorado" from the Mexican cartels, who have representatives operating in the state, growing marijuana in the national parks, and smuggling hard drugs up into the country.

As he told me this, I remembered that right at the start of the drug war, gangsters supported prohibition, even bribing Harry Anslinger's agents to impose it more rapidly. Now, at the end of the drug war, they were violently intimidating people who wanted to end prohibition. What, I wondered to myself, does this reveal about who really benefits from this war?

~

As I talked to people from both Washington and Colorado, I kept asking myself: Which of these campaigns is right? Which approach should people across the world take as we try to end this war?

Instinctively, I agreed more with Tonia and Alison in Washington. If I were a prohibitionist, I'd want to be able to characterize legalizers as a group of angry stoners demanding their right to smoke and saying it's a good thing if others try it too. But I had a niggling sense that I was being too simplistic in viscerally rejecting Mason's arguments. Why, I asked myself, are people more receptive to the arguments for legalization and regulation of marijuana today than they were in, say, the 1930s, or the 1980s?

There are many reasons—but one is that they no longer believe the most extreme myths about marijuana. They haven't just changed their minds about prohibition—they have changed their minds about the drug. If you read out Harry Anslinger's warnings today that marijuana routinely turns people into slavering murderers, even conservative audiences laugh out loud. That must be a factor in why people chose to legalize—mustn't it?

Anslinger had to create hysteria about the drug in order to ban it; isn't an essential part of undoing the ban undoing the hysteria?

When I discussed this with Tonia and Alison, it turned out their view was more complex than I had first understood. They readily acknowledge there is some truth in this argument. Back when she left school, Tonia thought marijuana was evil because it reduced everyone to being a slothful slacker. "Once people started to realize they knew homosexuals who were in wonderful, loving relationships—once the humanization of it happened—people got to accept it a little more in their lives," she says. "That's how it was with me and drugs and drug use. I know a lot of incredibly smart, articulate, productive members of society that recreationally use marijuana . . . For me it was just realizing that my ideas of what I thought people were like who used drugs were totally incorrect—and allowing those beliefs to be shattered when facts presented themselves."

So they acknowledge—at least implicitly—that we need some aspects of Mason's message. He goes too far, they think, but the message that it is safer than we were told for a long time is an important part of softening public opinion. Perhaps, I wonder, we need Mason's argument as a long-term cultural undercurrent, and Tonia and Alison's arguments as the harder seal-the-deal campaign. When I put this to Mason, he argued that this was the plan all along—you communicate that marijuana is safer, and "then push the traditional arguments once they're primed and more receptive."

And yet, and yet—other parts of Mason's arguments strike me as wrong, both politically and in practice. I try to imagine telling skeptical parents that it's a good thing if their kid smokes weed rather than drinking beer. I can't think of anything that would make them run into the arms of the prohibitionists faster. Indeed, if that was really the proposal of the legalizers, I'd be tempted to vote against them: I would rather my nephews drank beer than smoked a drug that really can damage their IQ permanently.

But here's the strange thing. For all the differences between the campaigns, both of them won—by big margins. In Colorado, 55 percent voted for it and 45 percent voted against. In Washington, it was almost exactly the same. Both of the campaigns that had been ridiculed as unrealistic at the start won by a 10 percent margin.

Once people in Colorado saw marijuana being sold legally in stores, the support for legalization went up even more. After two months of sale, the gap between support for legalization and opposition to legalization grew from 10 percent to 22 percent, with only 35 percent of people still against it. The fears about legalization began to bleed away once people could see it in practice.

~

A question hangs on the difference between these two campaigns, and it is the question—perhaps more than any other—that will determine the future of the war on drugs: In time, can we apply this same message to other drugs? Mason has a blunt answer. He says: "Are we just going to see this broad legalization of any other drugs [where they are sold to any adult who can produce proof of age]? No. Absolutely not. It's not going to happen."

I can see where he is coming from. Who would want to challenge their mayor to an alcohol vs. cocaine duel? An alcohol vs. methamphetamine standoff?

"All drugs," Mason says, "should be treated based on their relative harms. These are different substances—they demand different treatment." So while marijuana should be legal and regulated for adult use because it is safer than alcohol, he believes many other drugs are more dangerous—and so the same logic can't apply. Mason is no conservative on this question, and he is strongly in favor of other kinds of drug policy reform—he wants to see drug use by individuals decriminalized across the board, for example, and he says that other drugs could and should be legally regulated in the future. "But in terms of it being regulated and produced and distributed? I don't think any other drug would be treated the same way as marijuana."

Tonia and Alison approach this question differently. Their case for legalizing marijuana was not that it is safe, but that the drug laws do more harm than the drug itself—and this, they believe, is an argument that can and will be expanded to many other chemicals. One by one, they believe, some drugs will be brought into a framework of legal regulation that will look something like marijuana regulation. It will take a generation or more, they say—but the time will come.

All sides of the marijuana debate agree that if this wave of marijuana legalization succeeds, it will break open a discussion about changing our approach to other drugs. Mason thinks we can move a long way—and Tonia thinks we can go further still, to full legalization. If the sky does not fall in Washington and Colorado, this whole debate will radically open up.

~

As I try to figure out how to advance the next stage of drug legalization, I keep coming back to one of the hardest questions I have come across in writing this book. Mason argued that marijuana is safer than we generally think it is—especially compared to alcohol. So: Are other drugs safer than we think they are, too? Are they, in fact, safer than alcohol? Should that be part of our argument?

When I first came across it, this seemed to me a stupid question—especially with my family's history. I have seen what these drugs can do. Yet Professor David Nutt, the former chief scientific adviser to the British government on drugs, published a study in *The Lancet*—Britain's leading medical journal—going through every recreational drug, and calculating how likely it was to harm you, and to cause you to harm other people. He found that one drug was quite far ahead of all the others. It had a harm score of 72. The next most harmful drug was heroin—and it had a harm score of 55, just ahead of crack at 54 and methamphetamine at 32. It wasn't even close. The most harmful drug was alcohol.

This is so radically counterintuitive that it was only after I talked it over with Professor Nutt in detail, and then Professor Carl Hart and others, that I understood it fully. Nutt points out that the other drugs can be very harmful, too—but it is simply a provable fact that they harm few people, and cause them to harm fewer people in turn. He explains that this doesn't tell you that these drugs are safe—merely that alcohol is considerably more dangerous than we realize.

So could it be that Mason's argument might hold for many other prohibited drugs after all—they really are safer than alcohol? This is a complex message, and it is not reducible to a neat sound bite. Try saying: "These drugs can be very harmful—but they are not as harmful as you have been told by your government for years, and they are not as harmful as alcohol." That's not a message that I can slip into a five-minute shout-fest on cable TV. It requires lots of unpacking and explanation and qualification. It is easily caricatured as an argument that drugs are in fact safe—which is not at all what this evidence shows.

Yet Professor Hart—a neuropharmacologist at Columbia University—told me it is essential to apply Mason's argument to other drugs, and he made a strong case. "You cannot vilify marijuana the way Harry Anslinger did" today, he tells me, "because we have this vast experience with marijuana, so if you tell people [that] if you smoke marijuana you're going to go out and kill your parents—nobody is going to believe that. But if you [said that] in Harry Anslinger's time, people did believe [it]." Today, if "you tell people [that] if they do methamphetamine they'll kill someone, people will believe that. Or if you tell people [that] if they smoke crack they'll go and kill someone, people will believe that—although it's just not possible." So until we debunk this "mythical view of drugs," he says, we will be stuck forever in Anslinger's war.

I feel divided about this. Part of me thinks Professor Hart is right: people will never choose to bring drugs into the legal realm of regulation so long as they believe they are demonic substances that hijack most of their users and destroy them. When they discover that these drugs are in fact less dangerous than alcohol, and addiction is caused mainly by trauma and isolation rather than the drug itself, they will be more receptive to new approaches. They will think about the drugs differently—and that, in turn, will make them change their minds about the cage we put drugs in.

But another voice within me says: This will seem crazy to many people. These drugs *are* harmful to lots of people. Nobody disputes that. Most of the banned drugs are closer to alcohol, with its massive harms, than they are to marijuana. Why would understanding the horrible damage caused by alcohol change how you think about the only-slightly-less-horrible harm that can be caused by crack or meth? You won't win an argument about the drugs. You can win an argument about the drug war. Why choose the harder argument, when you don't have to?

The division between Mason's approach and Tonia's is a division that runs through my own mind, and I can't resolve it. But I know there is one way it will be resolved, in time. Over the next few decades, there will be campaigns that test both of these messages. Some will try to change how we think about drugs, and some will only try to change how we think about the drug laws. Which will succeed? Soon we will know.

∼

Governor John Hickenlooper never did accept Mason's offer of a marijuana vs. alcohol duel—but six months after marijuana was legalized, the governor told Reuters, "It seems like the people that were smoking before are mainly the people that are smoking now. If that's the case, what that means is that we're not going to have more drugged driving, or driving while high. We're not going to have some of those problems. But we are going to have a system where we're actually regulating and taxing something, and keeping that money in the state of Colorado . . . and we're not supporting a corrupt system of gangsters." He began to refer to legalization as "common sense," and added later, "Let's face it, the war on drugs was a disaster."

I think that means Mason did get to fight his duel at high noon in the end—and it is clear who won.

∼

After the people of Colorado had spoken, it was the job of the bureaucrats across the state to figure out how to do something that had not been done for more than seven decades—how to sell marijuana legally. In the fall of 2013, I sat in a café with Barbara Brohl, the head of the Department of Revenue in Colorado, to find out how they plotted their course through this unexpected task.

"It's a new world," she tells me, her eyes widening a little. Barbara would not tell me how she voted on the legalization measure, because it is her job to impartially carry out the will of the people of Colorado, whatever that might be. The people told her to figure it out—so here she was, figuring it out. The end vision endorsed by the Coloradan people was pretty simple. Any citizen over the age of twenty-one can buy up to one ounce of marijuana on any given day from one of the 136 licensed stores, and they can consume it at home. They are also allowed to grow a small amount at home for personal use.

For over an hour, Barbara talked me through the questions her department has had to answer in order to get there. Some of them are: Who should be licensed to grow the marijuana? Who should be licensed to sell the marijuana? What should the level of excise taxes be? What should the level of sales taxes be? If you tax the weed based on weight, does that create an incentive to make more potent marijuana to beat the taxes? If your tax is based on THC levels—the chemical component that makes users high and giggly—how do you test that? How do you stop the marijuana from being taken out of state? What kind of edible marijuana products should be permitted? Under federal law there is a strictly limited number of chemicals that can legally be injected into beef—so does a beef jerky with marijuana violate that?

We talked through the dense thickets of bureaucratic bargaining, drinking caffeine to keep ourselves alert. A typical sentence Barbara utters is this: "We needed to address how the state regulatory agencies and the local regulatory agencies were going to work together." Another one is: "In the medical field, we have early vertical integration, which meant there was common ownership between the cultivation facility and the medical marijuana center where sales occur—and what that meant was we would have to license and approve both facilities before either license could be approved."

And slowly, while the intricate logistics of marijuana licensing were explained to me, I felt a strange sensation washing over me. I couldn't quite figure out what it was—and then it hit me. I was bored. For the first time in the entire process of writing this book, my eyes were glazing over. It's not Barbara, who is delightful. It's the sudden pressure drop. With legalization, the fevered poetry of the drug war has turned into the flat prose of the drug peace. Drugs have been turned into a topic as banal as selling fish, or tires, or lightbulbs.

As Barbara speaks, all the killing—from Arnold Rothstein to Chino's gang to the Zetas—is being replaced by contracts. All the guns are being replaced by subordinate clauses. All the grief is being replaced by regulators and taxes and bureaucrats with clipboards.

This, it occurs to me, is what the end of the drug war looks like. It is not a mound of corpses. It is not a descent into a drug-fueled frenzy. It is a Colorado soccer mom talking about excise taxes in a gray conference room long into the night. Brian Vicente, an attorney who played a key role in the Colorado campaign, told an interviewer: "For years, the only discussion was: 'How long should we be locking people up for possessing marijuana?' Now we're discussing what the font should be on the label of a marijuana brownie."

I am bored at last, and I realize a tear of relief is running down my cheek.

If You Are Alone

I would pick up the phone and dial their numbers—but then I would hang up before they answered.

Throughout my travels into the drug war, I kept returning to London, and I knew that I should go to see the people whose addictions had propelled me there in the first place, my relative and my ex-boyfriend. But something kept stopping me. I was not ready—despite all I had seen—to finally resolve the conflict within myself between the prohibitionist and the legalizer. I busied myself with other things.

~

I kept picturing all the people I came across on this journey who lost somebody they loved in this war—and an image occurred to me.

Two global wars began in 1914. The First World War lasted four years. It came to be remembered as a byword for futility—miles of men killing and dying to seize a few more meters of mud. The drug war has lasted, as I write, for almost one hundred years and counting.

I am trying now to imagine its victims laid out like the dead of that more famous war, concentrated in one vast graveyard.

Who is here, beneath a sea of anonymous white crosses?

Billie Holiday, and all the songs she never got to sing.

The patients from Edward Williams's shuttered clinic, who Anslinger's agents said should be drowned because "that's all any of them are good for."

Arnold Rothstein, with his fake white teeth and his pledge that if he died, his men would get revenge.

Chino's mother, Deborah Hardin.

Ed Toatley, the undercover agent shot in the head by a drug dealer, whose death stirred Leigh Maddox to begin her fight against this war.

Tiffany Smith, shot on her front porch before she even knew what a drug was.

Marcia Powell, shut into a cage and cooked.

All the people whose bodies Juan Manuel Olguín stands over, his angel wings fluttering in the Juárez breeze.

All the people Rosalio Reta tortured and killed for the Zetas.

In time, probably, Rosalio Reta himself.

Marisela Escobedo, who walked through the desert and the dust storms to find her daughter's killer, only to find there was no law left.

Bud Osborn's friends, overdosing behind dumpsters on the Downtown Eastside, before his uprising began.

Julia Scott, the young mother in Liverpool who said she would die if her heroin prescription was cut off, and was proved right.

João Goulão's patients back in the Algarve, killed before he could lead Portugal to decriminalize.

And for each of these people, there are many tens of thousands more like them whom I will never know, and whose names will never be recorded.

~

I forced myself to ring. I knew the people I loved weren't in that grave-yard yet—I would have been told—but I didn't know if they were still heading toward it.

My relative sat on her sofa and smiled. She had been clean for over a year. She was, she explained a little manically, working for an addiction help line, ten hours a day, every day. She was still finding it hard to be present at times, I could tell. But she was alive, and she was progressing.

A short while later, one afternoon, I met up with my ex in the café at the British Library. He was obviously clean: there was color in his face, and it was rounder and fleshier. He explained he was going to Narcotics Anonymous every day, and he hadn't used in almost a year, either. Before, he only ever talked about his drug use defensively—it works for me, so fuck off—or in a slump of self-loathing: I am an idiot, I have ruined my life. Now he expressed himself more reflectively. He could talk a little about how he had been using the drugs to deal with the pain from his childhood, which had been unbearable.

So I began to draft a happy ending to this story. Then, a few months later, he texted me, and explained that he had relapsed; he needed drugs, as he put it, that move faster than the speed of his pain. He was in a crack house in East London.

I had been taught by our culture what you are supposed to do in situations like this. I had learned it from endless films, and from TV shows like *Intervention*. You confront the addict, shame him into seeing how he has gone wrong, and threaten to cut him out of your life if he won't get help and stop using. It is the logic of the drug war, applied to your private life. I had tried that way before. It always failed.

Now I could see why. He coped with his childhood by cutting himself off. He obsessively connected with his chemicals because he couldn't connect with another human being for long. So when I threatened to cut him off—when I threatened to end one of the few connections that worked, for him and me—I was threatening to deepen his addiction.

The desire to judge him—and my relative, and myself—seemed to have bled away. The old noisy voices of judgment and repression were only whispers now. I told him to call me anytime. I told him I'd go to Narcotics Anonymous meetings with him. I told him that if he was tempted to relapse I'd sit with him, however long it took, until his urge to use passed. I didn't threaten to sever the connection: I promised to deepen it.

As I write this, he is passed out on my spare bed. He has been bingeing on heroin and crack every other day for the past few weeks: he's worried he might lose his job, so he wants to break this pattern. He asked yesterday if he could stay here for a little while, to get through at least that first forty-eight hours without relapsing. After that, he says, it gets easier. Maybe it will. I looked at him just now, lying there, his face pallid again, and as I stroked his hair, I think I understood something for the first time. The opposite of addiction isn't sobriety. It's connection. It's all I can offer. It's all that will help him in the end. If you are alone, you cannot escape addiction. If you are loved, you have a chance. For a hundred years we have been singing war songs about addicts. All along, we should have been singing love songs to them.

One thing has the potential—more than any other—to kill this attempt at healing. It is the drug war. If these people I love are picked up by the police during a relapse, and given a criminal record, and rendered unemployable, then it will be even harder for them to build connections with the world. This is not Arizona, or Russia, or Thailand: the chances of middle-class white British people being busted are slim. But it still takes place—some twenty-four thousand people in Britain are cautioned or charged every year for cannabis possession alone, never mind other drugs.

And if that happens? Then they will be lost, like so many of the people I met on the road.

I am trying to learn to apply this lesson to myself. In the past, when I felt inclined to swallow pills and soar off into mania, I reacted with shame and tried to suppress these feelings. It only made my binges deeper. I still have days when I feel the urge to nuke my feelings with a well-aimed exocet of chemicals. When this comes, I try to remember what I learned from Bruce Alexander and Bud Osborn. You don't need a chemical; you need a connection. So I go to the people I love and sit with them. I listen to them. I try—as hard as I can—to be present in that moment, not someplace in the past or future. And I have found—so far—that the impulse passes, in time.

I have stopped fighting a drug war in my own head. I am conscious—now more than ever—that this is a privilege I get because I am white, and middle class, and I live in a corner of Western Europe where the worst of the drug war is not fired into the faces of people like me. I keep thinking of all the people I have met who didn't get this privilege, because of the color of their skin, or because they were born in the wrong place. It isn't right. It shouldn't be this way—and it doesn't have to be.

~

In the 1930s, Harry Anslinger recanted his support for alcohol prohibition. He wrote: "The law must fit the facts. Prohibition will never succeed through the promulgation of a mere law if the American people regard it as obnoxious. Temperance by choice is far better than the present condition of temperance by force." If this logic had been extended to a few more substances, the drug war graveyard would still be a rolling green field.

The day after Christmas in 2013, Billie Holiday's godson, Bevan Dufty—whom she had suckled, telling his mother with a laugh, "This is my baby, bitch!"—was sitting in a San Francisco clinic. He was in charge of helping the homeless in the city, and he was there to help a heroin addict who was in withdrawal and had just been thrown off his methadone program. The addict turned to Bevan and said he wanted to rip the skin off his body, because he couldn't bear to be without the drug for one more minute.

When he was a four-year-old, Bevan had seen the cops refusing to let his parents in to see Billie Holiday on her deathbed. Soon after they withdrew her methadone, she died.

Bevan looked around the clinic, at all the people surrounding him in a similar state. "It's sixty-five years in this drug war, and here I am—looking at all these people whose lives are just shells," he told me. As he looked from face to face, he said, "all I could do was think—where have we come, in all these years?"

~

There are days when the fight to end the drug war seems too steep a cliff to scale. But when I feel like despairing, I remember a few things. In his second inauguration speech as president, Barack Obama named the Stonewall riots as one of the great moments in American history. As he spoke, I found myself imagining standing with that small group of drag queens and gay men that night in June 1969 outside the Stonewall Inn in Greenwich Village as they were tear-gassed and beaten by the police—as they had been beaten by the police so many times before, and as people like them had been beaten for two thousand years.

They were representatives of one of the most despised minorities in the world. Hatred of them was encoded into every major religious text, and in the laws of every nation on earth. Even in liberal New York City, they were pariahs, and people who saw the rioters were disgusted by them. Their fight-back was a cry of desperation—a howl in the dark.

"Listen," I imagine saying to them that night. "You won't believe me now, but forty-five years from now, a black president is going to say in his inauguration speech that what you are doing now is one of the greatest moments in the history of America. It will get the biggest cheer of the day. There will be a million people—mostly straight—lining the Mall cheering—just for you. You are going to win. It will happen slowly, in tiny increments, day after day, year after year, and there will be long stretches when it seems that you are losing. But person by person, you will win this argument. You will get there. You will win."

It would have seemed like science fiction, but many of the men and women who took part in the Stonewall riots that night lived to see it happen. It happened in a single human lifetime, and it happened because they started somewhere, and they fought.

If they had stood apart, as isolated individuals, despairing, nothing would have changed. If they had waited for politicians in Washington to see sense, they would have waited forever. Instead they came together—finding each other, nervously, when it meant risking their freedom and their reputations—and then they went out and persuaded people, street by street, in the face of scowls and hatred, until slowly they transformed the culture and the world.

When we talk about ending the drug war, we are a little like the gay activists of 1969—the final end to the war is so distant we can't see it yet, but we can see the first steps on the road, and they are real, and they can be reached.

So when I feel depressed, I say to myself: It seems tough today? It seemed a whole lot tougher for the first generation of openly gay men and women. The cost for their taking a stand was a potential prison sentence. They didn't give up; they got up.

And then I think of the people I met on this journey, who have already begun the fight against the drug war. Chino was a convicted drug dealer who nobody wanted to hear a word from. He didn't give up; he got up and demanded the closure of the child jail he was tossed into—and he won. Bud Osborn was a homeless junkie nobody wanted to even look at. He didn't give up; he got up—and as a result of his decision, people survive, on average, for ten years more of life in his neighborhood, and they sealed off the streets to celebrate his life when he died.

What I learned from Chino and Bud is—whoever you are, if you are a human being with a voice, you can start to persuade people, and if your arguments are good enough and you never stop, you will make converts, and they will join you, and you will win. And even when you appear to be losing, you might be starting a process that will win further down the line. Edward Williams was defeated—his clinic was closed and he was driven out of public life. But seventy years later, I found his story, and it inspired me to finish this book. Billie Holiday was defeated—they put her in jail and helped cause her death. But seventy years later, all over the world, every day, people listen to Billie Holiday's songs, and it makes them feel strong. In the last years of her life, Billie Holiday was convinced she would be forgotten. If you are brave, if you refuse to be defeated, there will be a ripple effect from your actions that you may never see—but it will be there, transforming lives.

Any individual can start the fight, and any country in the world can break the chain and start the process of legalization. If Uruguay—a tiny nation of three million, led by an anarchist dissident—is brave enough, why isn't Britain, or Australia, or any other nation? They will be—if we make them.

Not long before she died, Billie Holiday said: "One day, America is going to smarten up . . . It may not happen in my lifetime. Whether or not it does is no skin off mine, because I can't be hurt any more than I have been." Not long before she was murdered, Marisela Escobedo appealed to us all to join her. "If you are alone," she said, "you're not going to achieve anything. If we are together," she said, we can win.

If you are alone, you are vulnerable to addiction, and if you are alone, you are vulnerable to the drug war. But if you take the first step and find others who agree with you—if you make a connection—you lose your vulnerability, and you start to win. You can put down this book and make that connection now.

~

Before we part, there are two last things you should know about Harry Anslinger. That he became a drug user—and that he became a drug dealer.

In the 1950s, Harry became aware that an extremely important member of Congress was a heroin addict. "He headed one of the powerful committees of Congress," he wrote. "His decisions and statements helped to shape and direct the destiny of the United States and the free world."

Harry went to this man in the corridors of Washington, D.C., and told him sternly he must stop using the drug. "I wouldn't try to do anything about it, Commissioner," replied the legislator. "It will be the worse for you." He would go to the gangsters to get it whatever Harry did, "and if it winds up in a public scandal and that should hurt this country, I wouldn't care . . . The choice is yours."

All over America, Anslinger had cut off legal avenues to drugs and forced addicts to go to gangsters for a filthy supply. But he had always pictured it being done to the "unstable, emotional, hysterical, degenerate, mentally deficient and vicious classes."

Now, before Harry, there was a man he respected, and he was an addict. So he assured the legislator that there would be a safe, legal supply for him at a Washington, D.C., pharmacy so he would never have to go to the gangsters or go without. The bureau even picked up the tab until the day the congressman died. A journalist uncovered the story and was about to break it. Harry told him that if he published a word, Harry would have him sent to prison for two years. He smothered the story.

Years later, when everybody involved was dead, Will Oursler—who wrote Anslinger's books with him—told the *Ladies' Home Journal* who this member of Congress was: Senator Joe McCarthy. Anslinger had admitted it to him and then looked away. McCarthy—the red-faced red-baiter—was a junkie, and Anslinger was his dealer. Nobody ever believes the drug war should be waged against somebody they love. Even Harry Anslinger turned into Henry Smith Williams when confronted with an addict he cared about.

Years later, after Harry retired, he developed angina, and he began to use the very drug he had been railing against: he took daily doses of morphine. Anslinger died with his veins laced with the chemicals he had fought to deny to the world.

I try now to picture Harry as the first dose of opiates washes through his system and it makes him still and calm. What does he think in that moment? Does he think of Henry Smith Williams and Billie Holiday and his order to his agents to "shoot first" when they saw drugs? Does he think of the scream he heard all those years before as a little boy in a farmhouse in Altoona, and of all the people he had made scream since in an attempt to scrub this sensation from the human condition—or does he, for a moment, with the drugs in his hand, hear, at last, the dying of the scream?

If you would like to know what you can do to stop the war on drugs, go to www.chasingthescream.com/getinvolved

If you would like to be kept informed of actions you can take and developments in this subject, sign up to the mailing list at www.chasingthescream.com/mailinglist

Other ways to be kept informed on this issue are to like this book's Facebook page, at www.facebook.com/chasingthescream, and to follow me on Twitter at www.twitter.com/johannhari101.

A Note on Narrative Techniques

Around the start of each chapter, as you might have noticed, I explain to the reader how I know the information I am about to present.

In the case of the historical chapters, I learned it from a mixture of primary and secondary sources, which are laid out in the endnotes, along with a small number of interviews with historians and with the few remaining people who were present during the events I narrate.

In the case of the chapters about people who have lived more recently, I have drawn primarily on extensive interviews with the subjects, and with people who know them. For the quotes that were spoken directly to me, you can hear the audio on the book's website, at www.chasingthe scream.com.

In many sections, I describe what a person was thinking and feeling. These are based on the accounts they gave in their interviews with me, or in additional accounts—such as court records, or interviews given to other writers, or in their own writing. All of these sources are laid out in the endnotes.

After my chapters were written, I read or showed the relevant chapters to the people whose lives I was chronicling at any length, to ensure that all my statements were faithful to their recollections; all these fact-checking conversations are recorded. In many cases, they offered clarifications and further information, and these were then incorporated into the text.

I went through this process with Chino Hardin, Leigh Maddox, Gabor Maté, Liz Evans, Bruce Alexander, Bud Osborn, John Marks, Ruth Dreifuss, João Goulão, Sergio Rodrigues, Danny Kushlick, Steve Rolles, Mason Tvert, Brian Vicente, Tonia Winchester, and Alison Holcomb. The only living subjects of the book who are described at length and have not been read or shown all the material about them in this way are Rosalio

Reta, for reasons explained in the endnotes for that chapter, and José Mujica, who had a country to run so couldn't spare the time.

I did my best to independently verify all accounts I was told with the documentary record and other witnesses wherever possible. I did not pay or otherwise compensate any of my sources, beyond occasionally buying them lunch.

As indicated in the text, there are three places where I changed the names of people to protect their identities: Chino's sexually-assaulted ex-girlfriend, whom I refer to as Dee, one of the addicts in Vancouver, referred to as Hannah, and one of the addicts in the clinic in Switzerland, referred to as Jean. In the first case, I did this to protect the identity of a sexual assault survivor who would have been identifiable to other people who knew her at that time. In the second case, it was because Liz Evans wanted to maintain the privacy of her former client, who has now died but might have been recognizable from this description to her family. In the third case, I did this because "Jean" was confessing to criminal acts and could have faced investigation or prosecution if this had been put into the public domain. The audio of both was provided to the publishers of this book. No other details have been in any way altered anywhere in this text.

Acknowledgments

I was dependent on a large number of people to write this book. I thank most of all everyone who agreed to be interviewed by me, especially the subjects of the book, who often shared very painful memories. They were remarkably open, because they believe it is important that people know the cost of this war, and I am grateful to them.

There are six people in particular I discussed this book with for years, and it was shaped and reshaped by their many questions and insights: Alex Higgins (not the snooker player), Rob Blackhurst, Stephen Grosz, Matt Hill, Alex Ferreira, and Alison MacDonald. I am very much in their debt.

Anton Mueller at Bloomsbury was a remarkably sensitive and clever editor and made this a radically better book. I'm also grateful at Bloomsbury to George Gibson, Bill Swainson, and Imogen Corke.

I am indebted to my wonderful agents—Peter Robinson in London and Richard Pine in New York.

In London, Danny Kushlick and Steve Rolles have been my guides through this subject for a decade now. They consistently produce the best research in the world on drug prohibition. In Ciudad Juárez and northern Mexico, my guide, translator, and friend was Julian Cardona, a remarkable journalist and a remarkable person. I am also grateful to Sandra Rodriguez of *El Diario* in Juárez. In El Paso, Sandra, Carlos, and Alejandra Spektor were invaluable in connecting me with the victims of the Mexican drug war as part of the brilliant organization they have cofounded, Mexicanos en Exilio. I am also grateful for translation there to Josie Font.

In Phoenix, Arizona, I couldn't have gotten by without the extraordinary Peggy Plews, who fights a daily heroic struggle in defense of the rights of prisoners in Arizona and is constantly exposing atrocities against them, along with Donna Leone Hamm, Stephen Lemons, and Mike Mann. Their work exposing the war on drug addicts in their state goes on. In Baltimore, Donny Andrews was my guide, while in Las Vegas, Dr. Rob Hunter explained gambling addiction to me and kindly let me sit in on a meeting of his Gamblers Anonymous group. In New York City, Rachel Schubert, Christopher Rogers, Antonia Cedrone, Carlos Saavedra, and Gentian Mullaj helped me a great deal. Everyone at the brilliant Drug Policy Alliance was really helpful, especially Tony Newman and Ethan Nadelmann.

In Vancouver, I am grateful to everyone at the Portland Hotel Society, and especially Liz Evans. In Washington, D.C., Jasmine and Billie Tyler were invaluable guides and are wonderful people, and my great friend Jake Hess kept me sane, as he has in so many places before, not least the West Bank. In Uruguay, Alex Ferreira was my brilliant guide. I was also helped by Hannah Hetzer, Geoffrey Ramsey, and Will Carless. Dario Moreno translated my interview with the president. In Stanford, Charlie Keeden did some digging in the George White archives for me.

I also thank many other people who read this book and commented on it in ways that made it better, or helped me in some other way: Patrick Strudwick, Jessica Smerin, Josepha Jacobson, Adam Thirlwell, Russell Brand, Lizzie Davidson, Noam Chomsky, Sarah Punshon, Daniel Bye, Tom Angell, Evgeny Lebedev, Ammie al-Whatey, Rachel Seifert, Glenn Greenwald, Arianna Huffington, Eugene Jarecki, Sarah Morrison, Jeremy Heimans, Alnoor Lahda, Ali Weiner, Jack Bootle, Alex Romain, Ronan McCrea, Matthew Bloch, Greg Sanderson, Josh Cullimore, Anna Powell-Smith, David Pearson, Dorothy Byrne, Rupert Everett, Peter Marshall, Chris Wilkinson, Owen Jones, Damon Barrett, Matthew Todd, Stephen Fry, Matt Getz, Deborah Orr, Sally-Ann Larson, Zoe Ross, Crispin Sommerville, Jamie Byng, Joss Garman, Ben Stewart, Anna Moschovakis, Dennis Hardman, Simon Wills, my parents, Violet and Eduard Hari, my brother and sister, Steven and Elisa, and my sister-in-law, Nicola.

Harm Reduction International covered the costs of my trip to the World Federation Against Drugs convention in Stockholm, Sweden, in return for a short report on what I saw: thank you, Mike Trace, for facilitating this. *Le Monde Diplomatique* sent me on assignment to Uruguay, and I drew on some of the same material in my report for them and my article about President Mujica: thank you, Renaud Lambert and Serge Halimi, for making this possible. Airbnb and Greyhound buses made it possible for me to afford to stay in so many different places. Amanda Fielding and the Beckley Foundation shared much of their cutting-edge scientific research with me.

The two best biographers of Billie Holiday, Julia Blackburn and Donald Henderson Clarke, were very generous in sharing their insights and lessons, and Julia's archive was invaluable. Billie Holiday's godson, Bevan Dufty, was extremely kind with his help and sharing his mother's notes and insights. My classicist friends Caroline Higgins and Natalie Haynes went over the section about the Eleusinian Mysteries and corrected some errors.

Many scientists and doctors with specialties in this field made the time to talk to me and explain several key facts. I am grateful in particular to David Nutt, Sophie Macken, Carl Hart, Raquel Peyraube, Paul Enck, Sunil Aggarwal, Scott Kellogg, Daniele Piomelli, Lance Dodes, Ambros Uchtenhagen, Barbara Broers, Richard DeGrandpre, Dylan Evans, Howard Becker, and Fabrizio Benedetti. Several people did excellent work on the text: Joe Daniels as fact checker, Emily DeHuff as copy editor, Laura Phillips on production, Alan J. Kaufman and Kirsty Howarth as lawyers, and Stuart Rodger in transcribing many of the interviews.

Frank Wynne did a fantastic job designing and maintaining the website, and was really patient with my technological illiteracy.

The following people pointed out errors or omissions in the text for the hardcover that have been corrected in this edition: Jonas van Hoffmann, Erin Flanigan, John Fitzgerald, Andres Seidler, Brent Stone, María José Viejo, Nancy Carroll, Alison Wrbik, Mark Whitfield, Ron Dodd, Seth Mnookin, Clare Barlett and Charles Cairns, Erin Klassen, Ben Richards, Patrick Riesterer, Mansfield Frazier, and John Harris. I am grateful to all of them. For a list of those corrections in full, go to http://chasingthescream.com/questions/.

All errors are mine alone. If you spot any, please e-mail me at chasingthescream@gmail.com and I will post them on the website and have them corrected in any future editions. On the first of each month, for a year after this book is published, I will post questions from readers and go through them, and I will go through any requests for corrections and lay out my thinking on whether they are correct.

To save the best for last—I am especially indebted to Elton John, David Furnish, and Andrew Sullivan, the fairy godfathers of gays everywhere; Jemima Khan, Naomi Klein, and Eve Ensler, the fairy godmothers of lefties everywhere; and Barbara Bateman, my own personal fairy godmother. I couldn't have done this without you.

Notes

Any quote not listed here was said directly to the author and can be heard on the book's website: www.chasingthescream.com/audio

Introduction

1 Almost one hundred years This has been independently verified by the publisher of this book through contact with my ex-boyfriend and through the public writings of my relative.

1 I had been swallowing fistfuls of fat white narcolepsy pills for years This account of my own drug use has been independently verified by the publisher of this book with the doctor who treated me all through this period and after.

1 I realized one morning Shortly before this, I was involved in a journalistic controversy. I want to stress that this controversy—and things I did that were wrong—had nothing to do with this drug use. I did these things wrong both before and during the period I used these drugs; so there is no relationship between the two.

2 I arrived in New York City This was one of several reasons I went to New York that summer; it is the only one relevant to this book.

3 This journey would end up taking me across nine countries They were: the United States, Canada, Britain, Mexico, Portugal, Switzerland, Sweden, Uruguay, and Vietnam.

Chapter 1: The Black Hand

7 The pledge to wage "relentless warfare" Anslinger archives, box 1, file 10, "Address by Commissioner of Narcotics before the National Conference on Crime."

7 Only then did I begin to see who he really was This view of Anslinger as a "moral entrepreneur" who pioneers the drug war as a way to keep his department and bureaucracy alive was first articulated by the sociologist Howard Becker in his classic book *Outsiders: Studies in the Sociology of Deviance*. I subsequently interviewed Becker. My reading of the Anslinger archives confirmed to me that Becker was right, and remarkably prescient.

8 In 1904, a twelve-year-old boy was visiting Harry Anslinger, *The Murderers: The Shocking Story of the Narcotics Gang*, 17–18; Jill Jonnes, *Hep-Cats, Narcs, and Pipe-Dreams: A History of America's Romance With Illegal Drugs*, 91

8 Why would a grown woman howl like an animal? Anslinger, *The Murderers*.

8 "I never forgot those screams" Ibid.

8 "emotional, hysterical, degenerate, mentally deficient and vicious" Larry Sloman, *Reefer Madness*, 258.

8 His three-year-old son was standing over his sleeping older brother David Pietrusza, *Rothstein: The Life, Times, and Murder of the Criminal Genius Who Fixed the 1919 World Series*, 17.

8 He would later declare Nick Tosches, *King of the Jews*, 32. Leo Katcher, *The Big Bankroll: The Life and Times of Arnold Rothstein*, 18–19.

9 Her mother was convinced John White, *Billie Holiday*, 18–19.

9 It gave her a feeling Billie Holiday interview with Mike Wallace, November 8, 1956—as found in *Julia Blackburn archives*, Box 18, Linda Kuehl notes VIII.

9 The most popular cough mixtures http://www.bbc.co.uk/blogs/thereporters/markeaston/2010/12/can_we_imagine_a_britain_where.html, accessed December 9, 2012. See also Marek Kohn, *Dope Girls*, 33.

10 When Billie Holiday stood on stage This description is based on the images of her that appear in episode 5 of Ken Burns's series *Jazz*.

10 It was on one of these nights, in 1939 Julia Blackburn, *With Billie*, 112.

10 "Southern trees bear a strange fruit" The history of this song is beautifully described in David Margolick, *Strange Fruit: Billie Holiday, Café Society, and an Early Cry for Civil Rights*.

10 Before, black women had—with very few exceptions John White, *Billie Holiday*, 24–25.

10 fury at the mass murder of her brothers John Chilton, *Billie's Blues*, 69.

10 But Billie did it because the song Billie Holiday, *Lady Sings the Blues*, 84.

10 "the beginning of the civil rights movement" Margolick, *Strange Fruit*, 19.

10 Her harassment by Harry's Federal Bureau of Narcotics Blackburn, *With Billie*, 111.

10 He had just been appointed Anslinger, *The Murderers*, 16–24. Douglas Valentine, *The Strength of the Wolf: The Secret History of America's War on Drugs*, 21. Jonathon Erlen and Joseph F. Spillane, eds., *Federal Drug Control: The Evolution of Policy and Practice*, 66.

10 As he looked out over his new staff Harry Anslinger, *The Protectors: Our Battle Against the Crime Gangs*, 24.

11 These men were notoriously corrupt Anslinger, *The Murderers*, 42.

11 Many drugs, including marijuana, were still legal Arthur Benavie, *Drugs: America's Holy War*, 25; Rufus King, *The Drug Hang-Up*, 45; Erlen and Spillane, *Federal Drug Control*, 39.

11 And then—almost before he had settled into Richard Davenport-Hines, *The Pursuit of Oblivion: A History of Narcotics*, 275.

11 would make all of Harry's hair fall out Valentine, *Strength of the Wolf*, 298.

11 like a wrestler printed in primary colors Sloman, *Reefer Madness*, 196. Valentine, *Strength of the Wolf*, 32.

11 Harry believed that the response King, *Drug Hang-Up*, 69–71; Erlen and Spillane, *Federal Drug Control*, 61.

11 His dad was a Swiss hairdresser John McWilliams, *The Protectors: Harry J. Anslinger and the Federal Bureau of Narcotics*, 1930–62, 25.

11 He was forced to go out to work on the railroad Ibid.

11 He was a determined boy Ibid., 26.

11 It was his task to supervise Anslinger, *The Murderers*, 18.

11 something called a "Black Hand" Ibid., 18–20

12 What could this Black Hand be? McWilliams, *Protectors*, 27.

12 But one morning, Harry found one of his work crew Ibid.

12 you gave the Mafia money or else Anslinger, *Murderers*, 19.

12 "If Giovanni dies, I'm going to see to it that you hang" McWilliams, *Protectors*, 28; Anslinger, *Murderers*, 19.

12 no more real than the Loch Ness Monster McWilliams, *Protectors*, 28. Anslinger, *Murderers*, 17, 81. Arthur Schlesinger, *Robert Kennedy and His Times*, vol. 1, 268.

12 the idea that anyone could believe something so silly Anslinger, *Protectors*, 82.

12 An "invisible world-wide government" secretly controlling events Anslinger, *Murderers*, 79.

13 one day, he thought, he would use this information His archives contain many such clippings.

13 From there, he traveled on to Hamburg Erlen and Spillane, *Federal Drug Control*, 64.

13 and the Hague King, *Drug Hang-Up*, 70.

13 Harry stared into their skeletal faces Ibid., 64; Anslinger, *Murderers*, 25.

13 **"revolution, strikes and chaos"** Anslinger, *Murderers*, 20–24.

13 **Frightened, assuming he was one of the Kaiser's men** Ibid., 20–21.

13 **The decision had been made** Ibid., 22–23.

13 **"a decent peace might have been written"** Ibid., 23–24.

13 **"The sight of a large city in ruins"** Anslinger archives, Box 1, File 1.

13 **"All bridges down"** Ibid.

14 **Harry was standing in a hotel lobby in Berlin** Anslinger, *Murderers*, 23.

14 **After this, and for the rest of his life** *Playboy*, February 1970, "The Drug Revolution," 74. In this conversation, Anslinger links, as he did throughout his career, drug use to the idea of civilizational collapse.

14 **In 1926, he was redeployed** King, *Drug Hang-Up*, 70; Anslinger, *Murderers*, 11.

14 **This was the height of alcohol prohibition** Anslinger, *Protectors*, 10–15.

14 **He believed they were filled with "loathsome and contagious diseases"** Sloman, *Reefer Madness*, 36.

14 **"Just give me a high-powered rifle"** Anslinger, *Protectors*, 42.

14 **until they were all locked up** McWilliams, *Protectors*, 33.

15 MEXICAN FAMILY GO INSANE Sloman, *Reefer Madness*, 20.

15 **Harry had long dismissed cannabis as a nuisance** Erlen and Spillane, *Federal Drug Control*, 68–69; McWilliams, *Protectors*, 14.

15 **He insisted it was not addictive** Erlen and Spillane, *Federal Drug Control*, 76.

15 **He believed the two most-feared groups** Richard Bonnie and Charles Whitehead, *The Marijuana Conviction: A History of Marijuana Prohibition in the United States*, 32–40.

15 **"Result: pregnancy"** McWilliams, *Protectors*, 53.

15 **Twenty-nine of them wrote back** Sloman, *Reefer Madness*, 39.

15 **Finally, you will reach the inevitable end point: "Insanity."** Erlen and Spillane, *Federal Drug Control*, 75.

15 **"You could easily get stoned and go out and kill a person"** http://www.redhousebooks.com/galleries/assassin.htm, accessed March 20, 2013.

15 **Marijuana "turns man into a wild beast"** William O. Walker, *Drug Control in the Americas*, 111.

15 **"if the hideous monster Frankenstein"** Bonnie and Whitebread, *Marijuana Conviction*, 117.

16 "The marihuana evil can no longer be temporized with" McWilliams, *Protectors*, 61.

16 He would fund no independent science King, *Drug Hang-Up*, 82.

16 they were "treading on dangerous ground" Walker, *Drug Control in the Americas*, 113.

16 Instead, he wrote to police officers Erlen and Spillane, *Federal Drug Control*, 73.

16 "a sane, rather quiet young man" Sloman, *Reefer Madness*, 63.

16 He then entered a "marihuana dream" Ibid., 61.

16 "The press, at Harry's prompting" http://hightimes.com/lounge/ht_ admin/8215, accessed April 1, 2013.

16 Anslinger was not the originator of these arguments See Isaac Campos, *Home Grown: Marijuana and the Origins of Mexico's War on Drugs*.

16 People began to clamor for the Bureau Erich Goode et al., *Moral Panics: The Social Construction of Deviance*, 196–202.

16 Many years later, the law professor John Kaplan Extract from "Marijuana—The New Prohibition" by John Kaplan. See http://www.drugtext .org/Marijuana-The-New-Prohibition/iv-marijuana-and-aggression.html, accessed April 7, 2013.

17 The psychiatrists who examined him said Sloman, *Reefer Madness*, 62.

17 The examining psychiatrists thought his cannabis use Ibid.

17 "Parents beware!" Steve Fox, Paul Armentano, and Mason Tvert, *Marijuana Is Safer: So Why Are We Driving People to Drink?*, 51.

17 He was building up a scrapbook Anslinger, *Murderers*, 82, 86.

17 His raids were proving him right Anslinger, *Protectors*, 203–4.

17 Some were corrupt Anslinger, *Murderers*, 83.

17 some simply didn't want to disturb Anslinger, *Protectors*, 214–15.

17 When the police chief of New Orleans Anslinger, *Murderers*, 87.

17 It made them forget the appropriate racial barriers Carolyn Gallaher, *On the Fault Line: Race, Class, and the American Patriot Movement*, 140.

17 Later, when one of his very few black agents Valentine, *Strength of the Wolf*, 63.

18 When the American Medical Association Sloman, *Reefer Madness*, 207.

18 Harry instructed his men to falsely Valentine, *Strength of the Wolf*, 64.

18 he was associated with a "criminal organization" David Patrick Keys and John F. Galliher, *Confronting the Drug Control Establishment: Alfred Lindesmith as a Public Intellectual*, 13, 137.

18 had him wiretapped See also John F. Galliher, David P. Keys, and Michael Elsner, *"Lindesmith v. Anslinger:* An Early Government Victory in the Failed War on Drugs," *Journal of Criminal Law and Criminology* 88:2, Winter 1998, 661–82.

18 and sent a team to tell him to shut up Richard Lawrence Miller, *The Case for Legalizing Drugs,* 77.

18 Harry couldn't control the flow of drugs Keys and Galliher, *Confronting the Drug Control Establishment,* 160; King, *Drug Hang-Up,* 62–63.

18 So I tracked down everyone I spoke with Yolande Bavan, Annie Ross, Eugene Callendar, Bevan Dufty, and Lorraine Feather.

18 "like the jungles in the dead of night" Anslinger archives, box 9, file 54, "Musicians."

18 "unbelievably ancient indecent rites of the East Indies are resurrected" Ibid. Anslinger was far from alone in these beliefs: see Harry Shapiro, *Waiting for the Man: The Story of Drugs and Popular Music,* 56–61.

18 "reek of filth" Shapiro, *Waiting for the Man,* 72.

18 His agents reported back to him Anslinger archives, box 9, file 54, "Musicians." This appears to be an internal FBN report but is not marked as such.

18 The Bureau believed that marijuana slowed down your perception of time Sebastian Marincolo, *High: Insights on Marijuana,* 106.

19 "Music hath charms," Anslinger archives, box 9, file 54, "Musicians."

19 For example, the song "That Funny Reefer Man" Ibid.

19 men like Charlie Parker Anslinger brags about his men busting Parker in *The Protectors,* 157–60.

19 Louis Armstrong Terry Teachout, *Pops: The Wonderful World of Louis Armstrong,* 156–58, discusses Armstrong's history of marijuana use and how Anslinger's legal charges affected him. See also Shapiro, *Waiting for the Man,* 60.

19 Thelonious Monk Shapiro, *Waiting for the Man,* 74, 89–90.

19 he longed to see them all behind bars Shane Blackman, *Chilling Out: The Cultural Politics of Substance Consumption, Youth and Drug Policy,* 83. Sloman, *Reefer Madness,* 149. Shapiro, like Sloman, calls it a "pogrom": *Waiting for the Man,* 67.

19 "Please prepare all cases in your jurisdiction" http://druglibrary.org/schaffer/History/whiteb1.htm, accessed October 1, 2012. Bonnie and Whitebread, *Marijuana Conviction,* 183.

19 "Shoot first" "'Shoot First' is nation-wide slogan for raids on dope peddlers," *Pathfinder* magazine, January 23, 1952, 24.

19 not "the good musicians, but the jazz type" Shapiro, *Waiting for the Man*, 73. Bonnie and Whitebread, *Marijuana Conviction*, 185.

19 Anslinger's men could find almost no one among them who was willing to snitch Jonnes, *Hep-Cats, Narcs, and Pipe Dreams*, 129.

19 whenever one of them was busted Bonnie and Whitebread, *Marijuana Conviction*, 185. Shapiro, *Waiting for the Man*, 71.

19 In the end, the Treasury Department told Anslinger Anslinger, *Protectors*, 150–64.

19 Billie Holiday was born a few months after the Harrison Act Holiday, *Lady Sings the Blues*, 5.

19 it would become her lifelong twin Her birth name was Eleanora; for the sake of clarity I've called her Billie all the way through, even though she only adopted the name when she was a child.

Also—throughout this chapter I have treated as a broadly reliable source *Lady Sings the Blues*, which was co-written with William Dufty. There is a debate about how reliable this memoir is, but her 1995 biographer Stuart Nicholson went through it and found that, for example, on one of the most famously contested passages, her description of her rape as a child, it was an accurate account. See Nicholson, *Billie Holiday*, 6. Billie herself claimed at one point that Dufty had written her entire memoir—"Shit, man, I ain't never read that book"—but the publisher had in fact made her sign every page of the manuscript to verify it matched her recollections. See Margolick, *Strange Fruit*, 33–34.

19 Sadie, became a prostitute Holiday, *Lady Sings the Blues*, 5.

19 He later died of pneumonia Robert O'Meally, *Lady Day: The Many Faces of Billie Holiday*, 67. White, *Billie Holiday*, 51; Holiday, *Lady Sings the Blues*, 68–69; BBC "Reputations" documentary *Billie Holiday: Sensational Lady*; Shapiro, *Waiting for the Man*, 99.

19 It was the last city without a sewer system in the United States Holiday, *Lady Sings the Blues*, 6.

19 clouds of stinking smoke White, *Billie Holiday*, 14.

19 Every day, little Billie would wash and clean her great-grandmother Ibid., 17; Holiday, *Lady Sings the Blues*, 8; O'Meally, *Lady Day*, 171.

20 One store that sold hot dogs Holiday, *Lady Sings the Blues*, 13.

20 "I just plain decided one day I wasn't going to do anything" Ibid., 86.

20 a man in his forties named Wilbert Rich Ken Vail, *Lady Day's Diary: The Life of Billie Holiday, 1937–1959*, 4. In her autobiography, *Lady Sings the Blues*, Billie refers to him as "Mr. Dick."

20 She screamed and clawed at the man Holiday, *Lady Sings the Blues*, 15–16, 103.

20 Billie was punished with a year in a reform school Donald Clarke, *Billie Holiday: Wishing on the Moon*, 34. There is a dispute over how long Mr. Dick was in jail—Clarke says three months, Billie's memoir says five years: see Holiday, *Lady Sings the Blues*, 17.

20 they decided they needed to "teach her a lesson" BBC "Reputations" documentary *Billie Holiday: Sensational Lady*.

20 Billie hammered on the doors White, *Billie Holiday*, 18. Other people confined in that institution later confirmed to interviewers that it was a very brutal place: see O'Meally, *Lady Day*, 79–81. See also Julia Blackburn archives, box 18, Linda Kuehl notes, vol. VIII, interview with Peter O'Brien and Michelle Wallace.

20 she was determined to find her mother Holiday, *Lady Sings the Blues*, 20. In her memoir, Billie says her mother sent for her, but most other accounts say she ran away to find her.

20 When she arrived on the bus Julia Blackburn archives, box 18, Linda Kuehl notes, vol. VIII.

20 A madam offered her a 50 percent cut Maely Dufty files provided by her son, Bevan Dufty—document headed "Introduction."

21 Billie's mother was telling her to marry Louis *Ebony* magazine, July 1949, 32.

21 Billie was caught prostituting Holiday, *Lady Sings the Blues*, 23. Some people think she had in fact been pimped in Baltimore at an even younger age: see O'Meally, *Lady Day*, 84–87.

21 they punished her BBC "Reputations" documentary *Billie Holiday: Sensational Lady*.

21 At first her favorite was White Lightning Blackburn, *With Billie*, 43. Clarke, *Billie Holiday: Wishing on the Moon*, 35. Mike Gray, *Drug Crazy*, 107.

21 One night, a white boy called Speck from Dallas Julia Blackburn archives, box 18, Linda Kuehl notes, vol. VIII, interview with Willard. His last name isn't given.

21 You just heat up the heroin in a spoon As described in *The Long Night of Lady Day*, BBC documentary, 1984.

21 When Billie wasn't drunk or high Chilton, *Billie's Blues*, 127.

21 so shy she could barely speak Ibid., 22.

21 She would still wake in the night screaming Holiday, *Lady Sings the Blues*, 103–4.

21 "I got a habit, and I know it's no good" Eugene Callender interview.

21 He pointed her toward an old piano man in the corner Holiday, *Lady Sings the Blues*, 34.

21 By the time she finished her next song White, *Billie Holiday*, 29.

21 She stabbed a bottle into his face Clarke, *Billie Holiday: Wishing on the Moon*, 230.

21 Another time in another bar Ibid. See also Julia Blackburn archives, box 18, Linda Kuehl notes, vol. VIII, Sylvia Simms interview.

21 Yet when it came to the men in her life Nicholson, *Billie Holiday*, 198.

21–22 After her greatest performance at Carnegie Hall BBC "Reputations" documentary *Billie Holiday: Sensational Lady*.

22 Harry had heard whispers Blackburn, *With Billie*, 209. I wanted to check the original sources for this material about Jimmy Fletcher. The only primary source about him is Linda Kuehl's interview with him. I contacted Toby Byron, who owns the archive. He told me—dismayingly—that the transcript of the interview with Fletcher has been lost. That means we will have to rely on secondary sources from now on. Both Julia Blackburn and Donald Clarke—who read the original transcript—describe it in detail, and also talked with me on the phone about it.

22 if he sent white guys into Harlem Douglas Valentine interview.

22 He was and would remain an "archive man" Blackburn, *With Billie*, 207.

22 Many agents in this position would shoot heroin with their clients Douglas Valentine interview.

22 "I never knew a victim," Clarke, *Billie Holiday: Wishing on the Moon*, 254.

22 He first saw Billie in her brother-in-law's apartment Blackburn, *With Billie*, 207.

22 Billie's greatest talent, after singing, was swearing BBC "Reputations" documentary *Billie Holiday: Sensational Lady*.

22 if she called you a "motherfucker," Blackburn, *With Billie*, 94.

22 "So why don't you do that?" Ibid., 212.

23 When Billie sang "Loverman, where can you be?" Maely Dufty files, document marked "Introduction."

23 she begged them to stop Yolande Bavan interview. See also Julia Blackburn archives, box 18, Linda Kuehl notes, vol. VIII, interview with Peter O'Brien and Michelle Wallace.

23 "No Guts Holiday" William Dufty, "The True Story of Billie Holiday," article 3, *New York Post* series, Julia Blackburn archive, box 18, file VII.

23 "It's tough enough coming off" Holiday, *Lady Sings the Blues*, 118.

23 "I don't want you to lose your job" Blackburn, *With Billie*, 213.

23 Not long after, he ran into her in a bar Ibid. The dog's name is given in Julia Blackburn archives, box 18, Linda Kuehl 1, interview with Memry Midgett.

23 "she was the loving type" Blackburn, *With Billie*, 214.

23 The man Anslinger sent to track Ibid., 216. Ibid., 11.

23 they had to tape up her ribs John Levy interview, Linda Kuehl notes, vol. VII, box 18.

24 "I don't want no cunt" Louis MacKay interview, Linda Kuehl notes, vol. VIII, Julia Blackburn archives, box 18.

24 He traveled to D.C. to see Harry Blackburn, *With Billie*, 211.

24 she was put on trial Ibid., 11.

24 "The United States of America versus Billie Holiday" Holiday, *Lady Sings the Blues*, 127.

24 She refused to weep on the stand Chilton, *Billie's Blues*, 116.

24 "I want the cure" Holiday, *Lady Sings the Blues*, 129–30.

24 a year in a West Virginia prison http://www.nybooks.com/articles /archives/2005/jul/14/street-diva/?pagination=false, accessed March 12, 2014.

24 a pigsty Vail, *Lady Day's Diary*, 103.

24 she did not sing a note BBC "Reputations" documentary *Billie Holiday: Sensational Lady*. White, *Billie Holiday*, 93.

24 Billie tracked Jimmy Fletcher down Clarke, *Billie Holiday: Wishing on the Moon*, 252.

24 "Most federal agents are nice people" Holiday, *Lady Sings the Blues*, 125–26.

24 "Billie 'paid her debt' to society" Maely Dufty files, "Introduction."

24 This meant she wasn't allowed to sing anywhere White, *Billie Holiday*, 94.

25 "You're damn right you will!" Blackburn, *With Billie*, 162.

25 "Do you think I can do it?" Ibid., 255.

25 She dreamed of getting a big farm Ibid., 304. Holiday, *Lady Sings the Blues*, 169–70. She was turned down as a foster parent because of her drug conviction. See Shapiro, *Waiting for the Man*, 97.

25 One day, she went out with a teenage friend to Central Park Julia Blackburn archive, box 18, Notes from Linda Kuehl 1, section marked "Billie H. Goes to Cuba."

25 Everywhere she went, there were agents asking about her Julia Blackburn archives, box 18, Linda Kuehl notes, article from *Ebony*: "I'm Cured Now" [no date].

25 She began to push away even her few remaining friends Julia Blackburn archives, box 18, Linda Kuehl notes, vol. VIII, interview with Peter O'Brien and Michelle Wallace.

26 They had a friendly chat Ray Tucker, "News Behind the News," Anslinger archives, box 5, file 9.

26 he wrote to her studio McWilliams, *Protectors*, 101. It is likely that Judy Garland is the unnamed woman from among "our loveliest film stars" who Anslinger describes having "conducted a running battle for months . . . to save" in *Murderers*, 184–86.

26 a Washington society hostess he knew Anslinger, *Murderers*, 166.

26 The main reason given for banning drugs The best account of how this fits into the long history of racism in the United States is Michelle Alexander's important book *The New Jim Crow*. There is also an excellent account of this in Timothy A. Hickman, *The Secret Leprosy of Modern Days*, 60–92. I first learned of the key role of this prejudice against the Chinese in early drug prohibition from Richard Lawrence Miller, who discusses it in Eugene Jarecki's documentary *The House I Live In*. It is also discussed in his books *Drug Warriors and Their Prey*, 26, and *The Case for Legalizing Drugs*, 88–91.

26 it was part of the point Shapiro, *Waiting for the Man*, 87.

26 "the increase [in drug addiction] is practically 100 percent among Negro people," Anslinger archives, box 1, file 12, "Modern Medical Interviews."

26 "60 percent of the addicts" Anslinger archives, box 1, file 10, "New York Forum: Saturday, April 28, 1962, Program Transcript." In fact, before criminalization, the official registers of addicts showed they were overwhelmingly white. It was only after criminalization that they started recording addicts as overwhelmingly black—suggesting these figures were the result of racist enforcement rather than a real reflection of how addiction was distributed throughout the American population. See King, *Drug Hang-Up*, 108–9.

26 NEGRO COCAINE "FIENDS" NEW SOUTHERN MENACE Ioan Grillo, *El Narco: Inside Mexico's Criminal Insurgency*, 28.

27 INCREASED THE CALIBER OF THEIR GUNS Hickman, *Secret Leprosy*, 77–78.

27 "The cocaine nigger" Ibid. See also the comments of Hamilton Wright before Congress in same book, 116. Even the idea that African Americans disproportionately used cocaine, or that it was a factor among psychotic African Americans, seems to be a myth: at the height of the "cocaine nigger" scare, of 2,100 African Americans admitted to an asylum in Georgia, only two were confirmed cocaine users. See Walker, *Drug Control in the Americas*, 14.

27 But there was another racial group King, *Drug Hang-Up*, 27–28; Erlen and Spillane, *Federal Drug Control*, 12–13.

27 In the mid-nineteenth century Benson Tong, *The Chinese Americans*, 2; there's a good account of the reasons for the migration on pp. 21–22. David Musto, *The American Disease*, 6. Craig Reinarman and Harry Levine, eds., *Crack in America: Demon Drugs and Social Justice*, 6. John Gibler, *To Die in Mexico: Dispatches from Inside the Drug War*, 44–45; Kohn, *Dope Girls*, 2–3. One of the books that best helped me to understand the history of this prejudice against the Chinese in America is Yunte Huang's terrific *Charlie Chan: the Untold Story of the Honorable Detective and His Rendezvous with American History*.

27 their "own special Oriental ruthlessness," Anslinger, *Murderers*, 29-36.

27 the "panties" they revealed Anslinger, *Murderers*, 37. In general, he talks a lot about things being smuggled inside women's vaginas (see Anslinger, *Protectors*, 4) or "ample bosoms" (49). He seems to have deliberately injected sex into his accounts.

27 "the yellow race would rule the world" Bruce Alexander, *Peaceful Measures*, 32; Emily Murphy, *The Black Candle*, 188–89.

27 "and when the time was ripe would command the world" Murphy, *Black Candle*, 5.

27 In Los Angeles, twenty-one Chinese people were shot Huang, *Charlie Chan*, 124.

27 until the courts ruled the policy was unconstitutional Tong, *Chinese Americans*, 81.

28 "The choking smoke spread its heavy mantle" Jefferson M. Fish, ed., *How To Legalize Drugs*, 244.

28 a vastly obese white slab of a man Anslinger, *Protectors*, 79.

28 "I have a lot of friends who are murderers" Albarelli, *Terrible Mistake*, 392.

28 he kept a photo of the man he had throttled Clarke, *Billie Holiday: Wishing on the Moon*, 296. Holiday, *Lady Sings the Blues*, 160–61. Anslinger, Protectors, 80. Some of the details of this account are disputed in Albarelli, *Terrible Mistake*, 402–3. He says the victim was Chinese, not Japanese, and that he was shot, not strangled.

28 "a very attractive customer," Blackburn, *With Billie*, 219.

28 "at a loose end . . . to kick her over" Ibid., 220.

28 he was a sadist Valentine interview.

28 he would go swimming in the filthy waters Albarelli, *Terrible Mistake*, 394.

29 "She was the big lady wherever she went" Julia Blackburn archive, Box 18, Linda Kuehl notes 1.

29 Billie was sitting in white silk pajamas Julia Blackburn archive, Box 18, Linda Kuehl notes 1, George White section.

29 they charged her with possession Maely (Dufty) Lewis, *Killer Jazz*, 3, as provided by Bevan Dufty. See also George White archives, box 1, folder 12; Vail, *Lady Day's Diary*, 118; Nicholson, *Billie Holiday*, 173.

29 "appeared a little defensive" George White archives, box 1, folder 12; Maely (Dufty) Lewis, *Killer Jazz*, 3.

29 "They'll remember me" Yolande Bavan interview.

29 "I did not think much of Ms Holiday's performance" George White archives, box 1, folder 12.

29 she would experience no withdrawal symptoms Holiday, *Lady Sings the Blues*, 159–63.

29 She checked herself in at a cost of one thousand dollars Vail, *Lady Day's Diary*, 119. Maely Dufty disagreed with this—she recalled that Billie was using at this time, and said she had found heroin on her, and she did go into withdrawal that night. *Killer Jazz*, 4.

29 He was fond of pretending to be an artist Martin A. Lee and Bruce Shlain, *Acid Dreams: The CIA, LSD, and the Sixties Rebellion*, 32–33.

29 he would spike their drinks with LSD This was often (but not always) at the behest of the CIA, as part of their MK-ULTRA program to discover a "truth drug" that could be used on their enemies. This is one of the oddest little stories I came across, and worth reading about. If it wasn't so well documented I would assume it was a paranoid Cold War fantasy. See Douglas Valentine, *The Strength of the Pack*, 16–18, 346–50. See also Albarelli, *Terrible Mistake*, 216–22, 435, 237–41, 279, 379–81. White's behavior aroused suspicion within the CIA itself: see 279–81, 289–90, 412. He continued spiking women for years: see 427. The CIA compiled a list of his known victims in the late 1970s when MK-ULTRA became a scandal; see Albarelli, *Terrible Mistake*, 578–79.

29 One of his victims was a young actress Albarelli, *Terrible Mistake*, 279.

29 he drugged her Ibid., 290.

29 "lie, kill, cheat, steal, rape and pillage" McWilliams, *Protectors*, 168. Lee and Shlain, *Acid Dreams*, 35.

29 "The hounding and the pressure" Nicholson, *Billie Holiday*, 174.

29 "enough anxieties to kill a horse" Maely (Dufty) Lewis, *Killer Jazz*, 4.

30 "found her not guilty" There's an important account of this trial in "He's My Man! Lyrics of Innocence and Betrayal in the People vs Billie Holiday" by

Sarah Ramshaw of Queen's University, Belfast, published in *Canadian Journal of Women and the Law* 87, 2004, accessed at http://papers.ssrn.com/sol3/papers.cfm?abstract_id=2041361 on March 14, 2013.

30 "Her voice was cracking" Anslinger, *Protectors*, 157.

30 she suddenly collapsed Clarke, *Billie Holiday: Wishing on the Moon*, 433; White, *Billie Holiday*, 110–11. Vail, *Lady Day's Diary*, 204. Chilton, *Billie's Blues*, 193.

30 they said she was a drug addict and turned her away Maely Dufty files, "Introduction"; Nicholson, *Billie Holiday*, 223.

30 One of the ambulance drivers recognized her Maely Dufty files, "Introduction."

30 As soon as they took her off oxygen Clarke, *Billie Holiday: Wishing on the Moon*, 434.

30 "Some damnbody is always trying to embalm me" Vail, *Lady Day's Diary*, 205.

30 had several leg ulcers White, *Billie Holiday*, 109–10. See also Julia Blackburn archives, box 18, Linda Kuehl notes, vol. VIII, interview with Dr. Kurt Altman for the Arena documentary; see also William Dufty, "The True Story of Billie Holiday," article 3, *New York Post* series, Julia Blackburn archive, box 18, file VII.

30 unlikely to survive for long Blackburn, *With Billie*, 297.

30 "You watch, baby" Maely Dufty files, "Introduction."

30 said they had found less than one-eighth of an ounce of heroin Chilton, *Billie's Blues*, 194.

30 They claimed it was hanging on a nail on the wall Maely Dufty files, "Introduction."

30 They summoned a grand jury Clarke, *Billie Holiday: Wishing on the Moon*, 440.

30 telling her that unless she disclosed her dealer Blackburn, *With Billie*, 296.

30 They confiscated Davenport-Hines, *Pursuit of Oblivion*, 275, 282.

30 handcuffed her to the bed Eugene Callender interview.

31 They had orders to forbid any visitors Blackburn, *With Billie*, 296.

31 her friends were told there was no way to see her Annie Ross interview.

31 Her friend Maely Dufty screamed at them Maely Dufty, "Introduction."

31 then the methadone was suddenly stopped Clarke, *Billie Holiday: Wishing on the Moon*, 442. Some of her earlier biographers disputed the claim she was using heroin in the last period of her life. See Chilton, *Billie's Blues*, 193.

31 "I had very high hopes that she would be able to come out of it alive" BBC documentary *The Long Night of Lady Day*.

31 "I've always been a religious bitch" BBC "Reputations" documentary *Billie Holiday: Sensational Lady*.

31 Callender had built a clinic for heroin addicts in his church Eugene Callender interview.

31 They took a mug shot of her on her hospital bed Blackburn, *With Billie*, 298.

31 They grilled her on her hospital bed Clarke, *Billie Holiday: Wishing on the Moon*, 438.

31 she blamed the drug war itself Holiday, *Lady Sings the Blues*, 126.

31 "Imagine if the government chased sick people . . ." Ibid., 132.

32 she was terrified that she would burn in hell Blackburn, *With Billie*, 253; Julia Blackburn archives, box 18, Linda Kuehl file 1, Memry Midgett interview.

32 "as if she had been torn from life violently" BBC "Reputations" documentary *Billie Holiday: Sensational Lady*.

32 She was intending to give it to the nurses Dufty piece for *New York Post*, Julia Blackburn archives, box 18.

32 At Billie's funeral, there were swarms of police cars Eugene Callender interview.

32 "there would be no more 'Good Morning Heartache'" Anslinger, *Protectors*, 157.

32 "The last addict's died" Anslinger archive, box 1, file 14, poem titled "L'Envoie."

Chapter 2: Sunshine and Weaklings

33 a story that, as far I can tell, has been almost entirely forgotten Henry Smith Williams is mentioned in passing in *Reefer Madness*, so we know Larry Sloman read him; and there are a few academic articles about the Smith Williams brothers.

33 He wore small wire-framed glasses This description of HSW is based on the images of him that appear on Google Images, e.g. http://www.google.co.uk /imgres?q=henry+smith+williams&um=1&hl=en&sa=N&biw=1175& bih=618&tbm=isch&tbnid=VuZQj3kCGqlkwM:&imgrefurl=http://www .librarything.com/author/williamshenrysmith&docid=3-CWd

RI5IGZ6yM&imgurl=http://pics.librarything.com/picsizes/a1/0b/a10b615c5
a2c06d63706645415143314f6744.jpg&w=162&h=242&ei=GhqIUPP
HJ-y10QW7yYG4BQ&zoom=1&iact=rc&dur=366&si g=109334892739419
133305&page=1&tbnh=140&tbn w=93&start=0&ndsp=24& ved=1t:429,r:3,
s:0,i:78&tx=47&ty=67, accessed October 25, 2012.

33 addicts were "weaklings" Henry Smith Williams, Drugs Against Men, ix.

33–34 "the idea that every human life has genuine value . . ." Ibid., 74.

34 drugs led only to destruction Henry Smith Williams, *Survival of the Fittest*, 35; Henry Smith Williams, *Adding Years to Your Life*, 111–13.

34 It was the scam of the century This is the central premise of all of Henry Smith Williams, *Drug Addicts Are Human Beings*.

34 Edward was the one of the most distinguished experts E. H. Williams, *Opiate Addiction: Its Handling and Treatment*; see also http://www.bhrm.org/papers/1920-1941.pdf, accessed May 23, 2013.

34 "The man is a wreck . . . physical and mental comfort" Williams, *Drug Addicts*, 149.

34 He will be able to function again See chapters 3 and 22 of Williams, *Drug Addicts*.

35 the Supreme Court ruled in 1925 http://www.ncbi.nlm.nih.gov/pmc/articles/PMC1655029/pdf/calwestmed00219-0042.pdf, accessed May 4, 2014.

35 He was said to know more about the chemistry and biology . . . ten thousand patients Williams, *Drug Addicts*, iii.

35 his brother's arrest William L. White, *Slaying the Dragon: The History of Addiction Treatment and Recovery in America*, 120.

35 "Mrs. Winslow's Soothing Syrup" Musto, *American Disease*, 94.

35 65 milligrams of pure morphine http://www.cracked.com/article_15669_the-10-most-insane-medical-practices-in-history.html, accessed May 4, 2014.

35 used them without a problem Robert J. MacCoun and Peter Reuter, eds., *Drug War Heresies*, 197.

36 "had they seen cigarette stains on the fingers of a daughter" Williams, *Drug Addicts*, 17, 49.

36 "props for the unstable nervous system" Williams, *Drugs Against Men*, xii.

36 An official government study Williams, *Drug Addicts*, 15. Miller, *Case for Legalizing Drugs*, 6.

36 Some 22 percent of addicts were wealthy Richard DeGrandpre, *The Cult* *of Pharmacology: How America Became the World's Most Troubled Drug Culture*, 126. Ibid., 104.

36 they were rarely out of control or criminal King, *Drug Hang-Up*, 18–19.

36 "Here were tens of thousands of people . . ." Williams, *Drug Addicts*, 9.

36 the criminal gangs charged a dollar Ibid., 11; King, *Drug Hang-Up*, 65.

37 "the greatest and most potent maker of criminals in any recent century" Williams, *Drug Addicts*, 12.

37 a very clear and deliberately designed loophole Ibid., xviii; Hickman, *Secret Leprosy*, 121–24; King, *Drug Hang-Up*, 33–34, 40; Wright, *Case for Legalizing Drugs*, 93.

37 Patients who had come in as unemployed physical wrecks Williams, *Drug Addicts*, 24.

37 The mayor of Los Angeles Caroline Jean Acker and Sarah W. Tracey, eds., *Altering American Consciousness*, 231.

37 the Federal Bureau of Narcotics was furious Anslinger, *Protectors*, 48–49.

38 "department stores for kleptomaniacs" Erlen and Spillane, *Federal Drug Control*, 127.

38 savaged the clinics as dens of sin Acker and Tracey, *Altering American Consciousness*, 230; Bonnie and Whitebread, *Marijuana Conviction*, 100–101.

38 "They'll make fair fish food . . ." Williams, *Drug Addicts*, 37.

38 almost all the addicts lost their jobs Musto, *American Disease*, 178.

38 dozens of them died Williams, *Drug Addicts*, 70.

38 defying the clear ruling of the Supreme Court Ibid., 170; King, *Drug Hang-Up*, 44–46. John Martin Murtagh and Sara Harris, *Who Live in Shadow*, 114–16.

38 "the Supreme Court has no army to enforce its decisions," "The Czar Nobody Knows," *New York Post*, Anslinger archives, box 5, file 10.

38 95 percent were convicted Williams, *Drug Addicts*, 22.

38 but some faced five years in prison Ibid., 91. A good account of the wider persecution can be found in King, *Drug Hang-Up*, 47–58.

38 horrified juries Anslinger archives, box 1, file 9.

38 "The moral effect of his conviction" Acker and Tracey, *Altering American Consciousness*, 238.

38 "Anybody that came out with any academic work . . ." Sloman, *Reefer Madness*, 199. See also King, *Drug Hang-Up*, 71.

39 the sooner they died off Henry Smith Williams, *Luther Burbank*, 316.

39 He went to meet Harry Anslinger Anslinger archives, box 8, file 8, memo marked "California."

39 "why such a man had been attacked" Anslinger archives, box 3, file 6, HSW letter to Beck.

39 "hysteria" Anslinger archives, box 3, file 6, letter titled "Memorandum for Mr. Gaston" by Anslinger.

39 every single one of the seventeen doctors Acker and Tracey, *Altering American Consciousness*, 238.

39 found guilty King, *Drug Hang-Up*, 61.

39 a year Acker and Tracey, *Altering American Consciousness*, 238.

39 never again In 1955, Dr. Hubert Howe testified before a Senate subcommittee explaining that he and his colleagues would like to prescribe opiates "but doctors have been scared away by the Federal Bureau." See King, *Drug Hang-Up*, 125–26. See also 139–40.

39 "Doctors," Harry boasted Anslinger, *Protectors*, 219.

39 William G. Walker, said Acker and Tracey, *Altering American Consciousness*, 242.

39 "made a sieve out of him" Anslinger, *Murderers*, 221–22.

40 "absolutely worthless" Ryan Grim, *This Is Your Country on Drugs: The Secret History of Getting High in America*, 44.

40 the story of Chris Hanson Alfred Lindesmith, writing in *The Washington Post*, as reproduced at http://www.onlinepot.org/addictandthelaw /AddictandtheLaw/chapter01.htm. *Liberty* magazine, February 26, 1938, 43. Anslinger, *Protectors*, 53–54. Anslinger doesn't name Hansen in this passage about a crooked agent, but it seems clear from the context that he is discussing him. We know this because the "Lady in Red" whom he discusses was a key part of Hansen's case: see the *Liberty* magazine report cited above.

40 Woo Sing National Archives, San Francisco, court cases Nevada, files 9580 and 9581. Williams, *Drug Addicts*, 100–101.

40 *by the drug dealers themselves* There are three possible interpretations of Hanson's criminality. The first is Henry Smith Williams's interpretation: that he was working for them all along, closing the clinics because they wanted him to. The second is that he was working for them all along, but his bribery consisted only of the kind of thing drug dealers pay the police for today: to turn a blind eye. And the third is that he started taking their bribes only after he left California and was posted to Nevada. I favor Henry's interpretation: Hanson's own colleagues at the FBN wondered out loud if he had been working for them during his time heading the L.A. bureau. See *Official Detective Stories*, August 1, 1939, 43.

41 no alternative Acker and Tracey, *Altering American Consciousness*, 255.

41 crushing the weak Henry Smith Williams, *Survival of the Fittest*, 309–10. This isn't a simple change. Sometimes Williams voices his old prejudices, although with less vigor than before—they are eroding. See Williams, *Drugs Against Men*, ix.

41 "in trouble with Uncle Sam" King, *Drug Hang-Up*, 61.

41 The exact year Sloman, *Reefer Madness*, 83.

41 "the kindliest fashion" "The Tsar Nobody Knows," *New York Post*, Anslinger archives, box 5, file 10.

Chapter 3: The Barrel of Harry's Gun

42 took his war global The historian David Bewley-Taylor has done brilliant work on this, and it was only possible to fully retrace what Anslinger had done in the international sphere through his brilliant work.

42 Baltimore Anslinger archives, box 2, file 20.

43 flooding America McWilliams, *Protectors*, 150; Erlen and Spillane, *Federal Drug Control*, 194.

43 "cold, calculated" Davenport-Hines, *Pursuit of Oblivion*, 275, 284.

43 "a fifth column" *This Week* magazine, March 7, 1948, 22. See also Anslinger, *Murderers*, 207–11.

43 none of these claims Valentine, *Strength of the Wolf*, 68.

43 "no evidence" McWilliams, *Protectors*, 153. Valentine, *Strength of the Wolf*, 211.

43 all over the world For the full story, see chapters 2 and 4 of David Bewley-Taylor, *The U.S. and International Drug Control 1909–1997*. See also chapter 21 of King, *Drug Hang-Up*.

43 Thailand, for example Anslinger, *Protectors*, 19.

43 Charles Siragusa King, *Drug Hang-Up*, 225.

44 "made up my mind" Bewley-Taylor, *U.S. and International Drug Control*, 105.

44 "belongs to the strong" Ibid., 48.

44 "quarantined" Anslinger archives, box 5, file 8, article headlined "Gains in War on Dope Told by Anslinger"—no byline or reference to which newspaper.

44 disappeared Jonnes, *Hep-Cats, Narcs, and Pipe Dreams*, 104; John Rainford, *Consuming Pleasures*, 150; Blackburn, *With Billie*, 53.

44 hospitalized Jonnes, *Hep-Cats, Narcs, and Pipe Dreams*, 104.

45 "major source" McWilliams, *Protectors*, 184.

Chapter 4: The Bullet at the Birth

49 baby-faced Donald Henderson Clarke, *In the Reign of Rothstein*, 19.

49 feminine hands Ibid., 9.

49 never fidgeted or drank Leo Katcher, *The Big Bankroll: The Life and Times of Arnold Rothstein*, 227. Carolyn Rothstein, *Now I'll Tell*, 31.

49 chew gum David Pietrusza, *Rothstein: The Life, Times, and Murder of the Criminal Genius Who Fixed the 1919 World Series*, 10.

49 suits Rothstein, *Now I'll Tell*, 19.

49 "Often on my way home" Pietrusza, *Rothstein*, 3.

49 Lindy's Pietrusza, *Rothstein*, 3.

49 network of fraud "Rothstein: Puzzle in Life, Still Enigma in Death," *Pittsburgh Press*, Nov 13, 1928, p. 1.

50 "water hole" Rothstein, *Now I'll Tell*, 232.

50 *Guys and Dolls* *Guys and Dolls* was based on Damon Runyon's short stories, which were inspired by Arnold and Carolyn. See http://www.new republic.com/article/109050/american-shylock-arnold-rothstein-1882 –1928#, accessed February 24, 2012.

50 "the laughter . . ." Rothstein, *Now I'll Tell*, 50.

50 replace the cash Rothstein, *Now I'll Tell*, 19.

50 ran away Katcher, *Big Bankroll*, 30.

50 "two million fools" Nick Tosches, *King of the Jews*, 34.

51 obsessively counted Rothstein, *Now I'll Tell*, 40. Pietrusza, *Rothstein*, 2.

51 only their statistics Rothstein, *Now I'll Tell*, 78

51 he first met Ibid., 42.

51 "all he shot was craps" Pietrusza, *Rothstein*, 43; Rothstein, *Now I'll Tell*, 20.

51 her engagement ring Rothstein, *Now I'll Tell*, 30.

51 and hung up Ibid., 142–43.

51 "I knew my limitations" Clarke, *Reign of Rothstein*, 305.

51 **he would pay jockeys** Rothstein, *Now I'll Tell*, 97.

52 **"Prohibition is going . . ."** Pietrusza, *Rothstein*, 198.

52 **mass alcohol poisoning** Daniel Okrent, *The Rise and Fall of Prohibition*, 221.

52 **fake company names** Jonnes, *Hep-Cats, Narcs, and Pipe Dreams*, 77.

52 **small-time hoodlums** Katcher, *Big Bankroll*, 238.

52–53 **controlled the entire trade** Valentine, *Strength of the Wolf*, 7.

53 **threw him out** Rothstein, *Now I'll Tell*, 172.

53 **The *World* newspaper** Tosches, *King of the Jews*, 209.

53 **"as gracious to him"** Clarke, *Reign of Rothstein*, 5.

53 *plato o plomo* Ed Vuiliamy, *Amexica*, 4.

53 **two detectives** "Indict Arnold Rothstein: Charged With Shooting Two Detectives," *New York Times*, June 7, 1919.

53 **The judge dismissed** Tosches, *King of the Jews*, 288. Clarke, *Reign of Rothstein*, 6–7, 40–48.

53 **"a little pistol practice"** Ibid., 52.

54 **He paid a dentist** Rothstein, *Now I'll Tell*, 130.

54 **with his own cash** Pietrusza, *Rothstein*, 321.

54 ***New York Times* reported** Ibid., 323.

55 **"a culture of terror"** Reinarman and Levine, *Crack in America*, 68. Steven Pinker hints at this in his excellent book *The Better Angels of Our Nature*, in which he points out that "as drug trafficking has increased" in Jamaica, Mexico, and Colombia, "their rates of homicide have soared." See page 89. Miller, *Case for Legalizing Drugs*, 67–68.

55 **"the fear with which . . ."** Clarke, *Reign of Rothstein*, 50.

55 **the stickpin** Rothstein, *Now I'll Tell*, 120.

55 **police were constantly watching** Ibid., 34.

55 **"lose all dignity"** Ibid., 52.

56 **raking in the chips** Ibid., 34.

56 **Not like hers** Ibid., 16.

56 **around five or six** Ibid., 31-3.

56 **never be enough** Katcher, *Big Bankroll*, 214.

56 **"It's too late"** Clarke, *Reign of Rothstein*, 32.

56 **"think that over"** Ibid., 304.

56 **he seemed afraid** Rothstein, *Now I'll Tell*, 116.

56 **"the wrong man"** Ibid., 238.

56 **"bound and gagged"** Ibid., 240.

57 **West Seventy-Second Street** Ibid., 241.

57 **a divorce** Ibid., 237.

57 **November 5, 1928** Katcher, *Big Bankroll*, 1.

57 **a bullet to the gut** Sherwin D. Smith, "35 Years Ago: Arnold Rothstein was mysteriously murdered," *New York Times Magazine*, October 27, 1963.

57 **"Get me a taxi"** Rothstein, *Now I'll Tell*, 246.

57 **"If I live"** Jonnes, *Hep-Cats, Narcs, and Pipe Dreams*, 72.

57 **a day to die** Stanley Walker, *The Night Club Era*, 11. David Wallace, *The Capital of the World: A Portrait of New York City in the Roaring Twenties*, 260.

57 **a new will** Clarke, *Reign of Rothstein*, 289.

57 **got nothing** "Rothstein Estate Is Held Insolvent," *New York Times*, October 6, 1935.

57 **never made** Rothstein, *Now I'll Tell*, 252.

57 **Rothstein's corpse** "Section of Polite Society Is on Trial with McManus," *Miami News*, November 24, 1929, p. 7.

57 **"It was as if no one"** Tosches, *King of the Jews*, 317.

57 **acquitted by the jury** "McManus, Gambler, Dies in New Jersey," *New York Times*, August 30, 1940, p. 38.

58 **war for drugs** Charles Bowden, *Murder City*, 18.

58 **"over the corpses of another"** Anslinger, *Murderers*, 17.

58 **Darwinian evolution** John Marks—the subject of a later chapter—in "The Paradox of Prohibition," undated but clearly written during this period, mailed to me by John Marks, uses the image of "the natural selection of gangsters" and calls it "the Darwinian effect of prohibition." I had used this image myself before reading this: it seems to be a common image in drug reform literature.

Chapter 5: Souls of Mischief

61 **A friend of mine** Tony Newman of the Drug Policy Alliance.

62 **Almost seventy years . . .** Chino's birth name was Pemanicka; he was known as Pam and then Jason for a while, settling on the name Chino around the age of fifteen. For the sake of clarity, I have called him Chino all the way through this text.

63 **electrical storm with skin** I have used this phrase before, in a column for the *Independent*, describing Bette Davis.

64 **"you're amazed at the quiet"** Pritchett, *Brownsville, Brooklyn: Blacks, Jews, and the Changing Face of the Ghetto*, 261.

65 "He never failed to fashion" Rothstein, *Now I'll Tell*, 96.

66 "And more than three quarters" I first learned about this study in *The Fix* by Michael Massing 39. I then read the original report, P. Goldstein & H. Brownstein (1992), "Drug Related Homicide in New York: 1984 and 1988," *Crime and Delinquency* 38, 459–76.

66 Just as the war on alcohol Reinarman and Levine, *Crack in America*, 118.

66 The National Youth Gang Center James Gray, *Why Our Drug Laws Have Failed and What We Can Do About It*, 77.

70 fewer than 2 percent Elizabeth Pisani, *The Wisdom of Whores*, 231.

70 by 75 percent Pisani, *Wisdom of Whores*, 232.

70 threatened with arrest Interviews with Allan Clear and Judith Rivera.

73 a 22 percent chance See MacCoun and Reuter, *Drug War Heresies*, 26–27.

77 abuse by prison guards http://www.villagevoice.com/2008-04-08/news/rikers-fight-club/, accessed February 5, 2013; http://www.nytimes.com/2009/02/04/nyregion/04rikers.html?_r=1, accessed February 5, 2013; http://www.nytimes.com/2014/08/05/nyregion/us-attorneys-office-reveals-civil-rights-investigation-at-rikers-island.html, accessed October 2, 2014.

78 Chino was standing on a New York street corner There were times when I was listening to Chino's story that I found it hard to believe. Could all this really be true? So I met with his best friend from when he was a teenager, his colleagues, and his cousin. They all told a similar story about him. Chino's arrest records—because his criminal offenses are from before the age of eighteen—are sealed under New York law. However, by phone and e-mail on January 16, 2014, I was able to confirm with the New York Courts system that a person with Chino's name and birth date did indeed commit multiple criminal offenses in Brownsville, Brooklyn, during the period Chino had described to me, though they could not tell me the nature of the offenses. There were significant parts of the story I couldn't verify with anyone else—as with Arnold Rothstein, drug dealers don't keep documentation. But all the parts I could check matched what Chino was telling me.

79 white people are slightly more likely Alexander, *New Jim Crow*, 97.

80 kill the head of Coors Glenn Greenwald was one of the first people to make this point to me, I think. I had made a variant of this point in previous articles. This is a very common analogy used by drug reformers, and I suspect it was thought of by many of us simultaneously. The earliest example of its use that I can find is on page 68 of James Gray's *Why Our Drug Laws Have Failed and What We Can Do About It*.

81 Professor Jeffrey Miron Jeffrey Miron, *Drug War Crimes*, 47.

81 in order to control an illegal trade Miron, *Drug War Crimes*, 48.

81 between 25 and 75 percent Ibid., 51. The RAND Corporation has interesting research on this, too. See http://www.rand.org/content/dam/rand/pubs/occasional_papers/2010/RAND_OP325.pdf, accessed January 14, 2014.

Chapter 6: Hard to Be Harry

85 I interviewed sixteen They were: Joe Arpaio in Arizona; Leigh Maddox in Maryland; Stephen Dowling in New York City; Fred Martens in New Jersey; Howard Wooldridge in Washington, D.C.; João Figueira in Lisbon; Joe Toft in Reno, Nevada; Michael Levine in upstate New York; Neil Franklin in Baltimore; Peter Moskos in New York City; Olivier Gueniat in Neuchâtel, Switzerland; Terry Nelson in Fort Worth, Texas; Marisol Valles García in the United States. (I have been asked not to name the city, to protect her safety, since she had to flee Mexican cartels); Richard Newton in El Paso, Texas; and Charlie Mandigo from Washington State.

89 talking to her colleague Ed Toatley This passage describing Ed Toatley is also informed by my conversation with his colleague Neill Franklin.

90 "clean up that damned corner" Timothy Noah, ed., *After Prohibition*, 94-7.

91 studied the murder statistics Miron, *Drug War Crimes*, 50.

91 confirmed in many other studies The Global Commission on Drug Policy, led by former U.S. secretaries of state and other governmental leaders, looked at the evidence and concluded: "Virtually all studies on the subject have concluded that increased levels of enforcement activity have been associated with increased drug market violence." See *The War on Drugs and HIV/AIDS: How the Criminalization of Drug Use Fuels the Global Pandemic*, 14. See also http://www.rand.org/content/dam/rand/pubs/occasional_papers/2010/RAND_OP325.pdf, accessed January 14, 2014.

91–92 "than an Academy Award winner" Anslinger, *Protectors*, ix. Anslinger, *Murderers*, 15.

92 "I didn't give it a second thought," Del Quentin Wilbur, "Drug Dealer Gets Life for Killing State Trooper," *Baltimore Sun*, December 15, 2001, "Telegraph," 1A.

93 "my Damascus moment" Leigh said this in her speech to the Cato Institute in the fall of 2011. I was in the audience. The audio can be heard at http://www.cato.org/events/ending-global-war-drugs, accessed February 5, 2013.

93 Ed's five year old son Daniel Stephen Manning, "Slain Trooper Remembered as Model Policeman," Associated Press, November 3, 2000, accessed via LexisNexis April 1, 2013. Wilbur, "Drug Dealer Gets Life."

93 The 1993 National Household Survey MacCoun and Reuter, *Drug War Heresies*, 114.

93 Indeed, at any given time DeGrandpre, *Cult of Pharmacology*, 174.

94 "Fogg, you know you're right" https://christiansagainstprohibition.org/node/383, accessed January 8, 2014.

96 once you have been busted Alexander, *New Jim Crow*, 153.

96 Justice Thurgood Marshall Benavie, *Drugs: America's Holy War*, 14.

97 "Your white flag" Leigh's speech to the Cato Institute, fall of 2011.

Chapter 7: Mushrooms

98 playing on the sidewalk http://articles.baltimoresun.com/1992-01-20/news/1992020097_1_tiffany-gunmen-baltimore, accessed October 2, 2012.

98 It had been a fun day http://articles.baltimoresun.com/1991-07-11/news/1991192151_1_tiffany-smith-rosedale-turf-war, accessed October 2, 2012.

99 They renamed the block http://articles.baltimoresun.com/2008-12-11/news/0812100212_1_tiffany-devone-leave-baltimore, accessed October 2, 2012.

Chapter 8: State of Shame

104 The female chain gang I had my audio recorder on almost the whole time I was in Tent City and when I went out with the chain gang, so I have full audio of everything recounted in this chapter.

104 I WAS A DRUG ADDICT On this particular day, women with domestic violence charges and child support violations were also on this particular chain gang.

104 One girl is free I have chosen not to give their full names because I don't want to deepen their humiliation.

105 Michelle starts vomiting After a while they took her to medical; the other women told me that that only ever happens when journalists are there. Arpaio claims that the chain gang is voluntary: see Arpaio, *Joe's Law*, 126. But the guard overseeing the chain gang says: "They don't ask to be on there. We put them." The women confirmed this. They are put in the Hole and the only way out is often the chain gang. One woman told me she chose it because it was better to get out than to feel trapped inside; but most did not choose it.

105 "you got a good guy here!" This chapter is informed in particular by interviews with Donna Leone Hamm, Steve Lemmons, and Peggy Plews.

105 "**concentration camp**" http://www.nytimes.com/2012/07/22/opinion /sunday/in-arpaios-arizona-they-fought-back.html?_r=0, accessed November 10, 2012.

106 built a leper colony Anslinger achives, box 1, file 10. Arpaio, *Joe's Law*, 94.

107 fifteen cents Ibid., 213.

107 "**unspecified meat**" http://abcnews.go.com/ABC_Univision/Politics /problem-sheriff-joe-arpaios-tent-city-analysis/story?id=19804368 and http:// www.theguardian.com/commentisfree/2012/jun/27/joe-arpaio-maricopa-county -king-cruel , both accessed October 2, 2014.

107 "**no-one see this note**" I have this note, as well as the name of the prisoner and her ID number, and the documentary filmmaker Rachel Siefert filmed the note the day it was handed to me.

108 they consider themselves lucky The only exception is that some have a cellmate; they are trapped together in a tiny space where they even have to shit in front of each other.

109 pay for his medical care I initially learned about this case from Peggy Plews in my interview with her. She wrote about the case first at http:// arizonaprisonwatch.blogspot.co.uk/2011/06/new-az-juvenile-corrections-director_14.html. It was documented in the Amnesty International report "Cruel Isolation: Amnesty International's Concerns About Conditions in Arizona Maximum Security Prisons," 22n30.

109 turned into an animal shelter http://www.google.co.uk/#hl=en& sclient=psy-ab&q=joe+arpaio+animal+shelter&oq=joe+arpaio+animal+ shelter&gs_l=hp.3..0j0i5j0i5i30l2.61655.63380.1.63561.14.11.0.3.3.0.201.1081 .4j5j1.10.0.les%3B..0.0...1c.1.lUd2A56VcoA&pbx=1&bav=on.2,or.r_gc.r_pw .r_qf.&fp=686a68ff5cd60d08&bpcl=37643589&biw=1175&bih=618, accessed November 10, 2012.

109 imprisons more people MacCoun and Reuter, *Drug War Heresies*, 24.

109 if all US prisoners Graham Boyd, "The Drug War Is the New Jim Crow," *NACLA Report on the Americas*, vol. XXXV, no. 1, (July/August 2001): 18.

110 More men have been raped http://nplusonemag.com/raise-the-crime -rate, accessed December 12, 2012.

110 She was here because a year ago Presentence investigation in case CR9611017, *The State of Arizona vs. Marcia Joanne Powell*.

111 She was taken to see See Arizona Department of Corrections investigation, summary.

111 appointed a guardian Letter from James Hass, Office of the Public Defender, Maricopa County, to the Adult Probation Department, laying out his recommendations for sentencing of Marcia Powell, July 11, 2008. See also e-mail from Gary Strickland to Karyn Klaussner on May 29, 2009, showing

the prison was aware she had an appointed guardian, as published in the official inquiry. See also the finding of the Superior Court of Maricopa County
July 7, 2008, defining her as an "incapacitated adult."

111 **But the doctor concluded** Arizona Department of Corrections Inspector
General's Report into the death of Marcia Powell.

111 **"coffee and cigarettes"** Arizona Department of Corrections Inspector
General's Office Administrative Investigations memorandum, September 6,
2009, interview with Correctional Officer Evan Hazelton.

111 **Shat herself** Testimony of Correctional Officer Electra Allen to the
Inspector General for the official investigation, September 2, 2009. See also
letter from Donna Leone Hamm of Middle Ground Prison Reform to Richard
Romley, Acting Country Attorney of Maricopa County, May 14, 2010. Also
letter by the same to Kathleen Ingley of the Arizona Republic, September 24,
2009.

111 **"something about Jay-Z"** Arizona Department of Corrections, memorandum to Division Director John Hallahan, September 6, 2009.

111 **"it is too hot!"** Arizona Department of Corrections Inspector General's
Office Administrative Investigations memorandum, September 1, 2009.

111 **"the funniest thing"** This is a quote from the witness statements that
accompany the publication of the official investigation. The names of the prisoners who were witnesses are all redacted, but their original written statements
were published. The witnesses repeatedly stress that they are frightened to
give a statement but they believe it is morally the right thing to do.

111 **only go to 108 degrees** Letter from Arizona Department of Corrections
Inspector General Frigo, June 1, 2009, to Warden T. Schroeder. See also
http://blogs.phoenixnewtimes.com/bastard/2010/09/marcia_powells_death
_unavenged.php, accessed April 2, 2013.

111 **as if in an oven** http://www.phoenixnewtimes.com/2009-10-01/news
/arizona-s-shameless-about-the-human-cage-death-of-marcia-powell-and
-you-might-not-want-to-worship-pot-like-the-church-of-cognizance-but
-why-the-heck-can-t-you-just-smoke-it/, accessed April 2, 2013.

112 **Legally required** http://blogs.phoenixnewtimes.com/bastard/2009/05
/marcia_powell_update_the_guard.php, accessed April 2, 2013.

112 **"dry as parchment"** http://blogs.phoenixnewtimes.com/bastard/2010
/09/marcia_powells_death_unavenged.php, accessed April 2, 2013.

112 **Three prison officers were fired** http://blogs.phoenixnewtimes.com
/bastard/2010/09/marcia_powells_death_unavenged.php, accessed April 2, 2013.
http://dmcantor.com/blog/2010/09/07/arizona-prison-guards-not-charged
-in-marcia-powell-death, accessed April 2, 2013. http://www.phoenix
newtimes.com/2009-10-01/news/arizona-s-shameless-about-the-human

-cage-death-of-marcia-powell-and-you-might-not-want-to-worship-pot
-like-the-church-of-cognizance-but-why-the-heck-can-t-you-just-smoke-it/,
accessed April 2, 2013.

112 Abu   Ghraib   scandal   http://www.democracynow.org/2004/6/2/it
_happened_here_first_exporting_americas, accessed April 2, 2013.

112 three years in foster care *The State of Arizona vs. Marcia Joanne Powell*,
case no. CR9611017—Presentence Investigation.

114 newspaper reports of the deaths See "Teenager Suspected in Missouri
Triple Slaying," Associated Press, March 28, 2004, accessed via LexisNexis
February 29, 2013.

115 "a nationwide emergency" *The State of Arizona vs. Marcia Joanne
Powell*, case no. CR9611017—Presentence Investigation.

Chapter 9: Bart Simpson and the Angel of Juárez

116 more   than   sixty   thousand   http://www.bbc.co.uk/news/world-latin
-america-10681249, accessed December 6, 2013.

116 TIME IS SHORT I was also accompanied on this part of my trip by the
filmmaker Rachel Siefert.

116 I met him some time after He had last stood over a corpse in this way a
few months before, he told me.

116 90 percent of the cocaine http://www.cnn.com/2013/09/02/world
/americas/mexico-drug-war-fast-facts/, accessed December 6, 2013.

116–117 Between $19 and $29 billion http://www.ice.gov/doclib/cornerstone
/pdf/cps-study.pdf, accessed December 6, 2013, via CNN report named above.

117 Billie Holiday came Nicholson, *Billie Holiday*, 208.

118 "we want a better society" Juan does not support legalization; he
believes the drug war will be ended by the Christianization of society and
moral warnings. "I am sure in my heart some of the hit men will see my
message."

119 and then she left Guards came in and out throughout the interview—
about two hours in, a female guard sat down and listened for most of the rest
of the time.

120 In 2009, Rosalio Reta was at summer camp In this book, wherever I've
written about living persons and summarized facts about their internal lives,
if they form a big part of the book, I've read or sent the material I have written
to them to make sure I'd gotten everything right. Rosalio is one of only two
exceptions to this. (The other is President Jose Mujica, who had a country to
run so didn't have time to read my work).

About the raw facts of his life with the Zetas, with a few exceptions that are explained in the text, Rosalio has always told a fairly consistent story about his life. But, as you will see, when it comes to how he explains why he did what he did, his story has changed radically over time. He initially said he chose to be a Zeta; later he said he was forced to become one.

It became clear in our long conversation that he wants every journalist who talks to him to present this second narrative—that he was kidnapped and forced to be a hit man—as the truth, and to dismiss the earlier narrative as false. As I spoke to him, I found that Rosalio is very angry with every journalist who has ever written about him, because they haven't done this. For example, he said of the journalist Rusty Fleming, who interviewed him and later wrote about it: "The majority of what he said is bullshit." When I asked Rosalio for specifics about what Fleming got wrong, he said he had Fleming's article in his cell and said: "None of that is true." But then he conceded: "It is similar to what happened, but in his own words . . . Yeah, that was true."

It soon became clear to me that the root of Rosalio's anger with journalists is that they will not vindicate his new narrative, which he wants them to present exclusively in his words and without any skepticism. He told me all journalists have distorted him because "they always tend to switch things around and instead of looking like a victim, I look like the villain. It's not fair. That's the only thing I ask of you. Don't put me in a position like that. You don't know what I went through." He said later: "It's not right of him, trying to say a story in his own way. It's not right." He said later that journalists "use the same theory but put it in their own words." He said to me: "I don't want you to turn this into your own words and do like everyone else."

I asked him if he thinks the whole interview should consist only of his own words and nothing else, and he said: "Yeah." I did not agree to this condition, and I told him explicitly that, "I can't just use your words."

So it became clear to me later that my normal fact-checking process—the one I went through with, for example, Chino Hardin and Leigh Maddox, where I asked them to go through it and say sentence by sentence if what I had written was totally accurate—wouldn't make sense with Rosalio. The only write-up of his story that he would agree was accurate would be one that entirely exculpated him, and I do not think it would be factual or reasonable to present the story he is offering now as the full truth. (Indeed, his story slipped and changed during our interview, as is clear in the text.)

The claim that he never enjoyed the violence he carried out is flatly contradicted, for example, by the wiretap evidence gathered by the police, which is quoted in this chapter.

This left me with a dilemma: Is his story reliable enough to include in the book, and if it is, how should I tell it? There is no doubt he did indeed serve with the Zetas—he is in prison for it, and the wiretaps provide explicit evidence. And crucially, as you will see, when it comes to the actual actions he carried out, he has been broadly consistent. It is his account of his motives and rationale that have changed—not, with the exception of how he got started, his account of the facts themselves. I am also inclined to believe he is telling the truth about the facts because the part of the story he has told consistently is the most unflattering part of the story: the raw facts of it show him to have been a serial killer, and he confirms those facts. I came to the conclusion that if a person is consistently over years describing a story in which he committed massive crimes, and there is a large body of legal evidence to show they occurred, then I believe it is legitimate to relay his story.

However, this interview is written up in a different way from the other interviews, to reflect the higher degree of ambiguity about some points. First, I did not send this account to Rosalio. I am sure he would react the same way he reacted to Rusty Fleming's: he will say it is wrong because it doesn't present him purely as a victim, but—as with Fleming—he will not be able to name any specific errors, since I have only relayed what he told me in our recorded four-hour conversation, and the evidence from other reliable sources. Second, where he has told different stories at different times about some events, I have explained this in the text, to allow the reader to reach her or his own conclusion. I included this endnote to be as transparent as possible about how I came to the conclusions in this book.

120 He remembered the techniques An account of the Zeta training camps that matches with Rosalio's descriptions can be found in George W. Grayson, *The Executioner's Men*, 46–48.

120 "If I retreat" Grillo, *El Narco*, 105.

120 He committed industrial killings Grayson, *Executioner's Men*, 181.

120 brought them to Fort Bragg http://www.aljazeera.com/indepth/features /2010/10/20101019212440609775.html, accessed October 5, 2012.

121 "Not even death" Grillo, *El Narco*, 96.

121 defected, en masse Sergio Rodriguez, *The Femicide Machine*, 62.

121 These breakaways Gibler, *To Die in Mexico*, 59; Grayson, *Executioner's Men*, 46–47.

121 He grew up "Mexican cartels lure American teens as killers," *New York Times*, June 23, 2009, http://www.nytimes.com/2009/06/23/us/23killers.html ?pagewanted=all, accessed October 5, 2012.

121 "if you're not a cop" http://www.foxnews.com/on-air/war-stories /2009/08/20/day-i-met-cartel-assassin, accessed October 5, 2012.

122 "I thought I was Superman" http://articles.cnn.com/2009-03-12 /justice/cartel.teens_1_drug-cartels-los-zetas-mexican-gulf-cartel? _s=PM:CRIME, accessed October 5, 2012.

123 **"Others sleep as peacefully"** "Mexican cartels lure American teens as killers."

123 **made him a Zeta** Grayson, *Executioner's Men*, 179.

123 **For three years, he was working** Ibid., 180–81.

123 **the Expendables** "Mexican drug cartels recruit US teenagers as 'expendables,'" *Digital Journal*, October 18, 2011. See also Grayson, *Executioner's Men*, 36.

124 **Each body is a billboard** Howard Campbell, *Drug War Zone*, 29.

125 **always awake, always watching** http://articles.cnn.com/2009-03-12 /justice/cartel.teens_1_drug-cartels-los-zetas-mexican-gulf-cartel?_s =PM:CRIME.

125 **But in the midst of the terror** Grayson, *Executioner's Men*, 91–92.

125 **paid $500** Grillo, *El Narco*, 254.

125 **paid $375,000** http://www.foxnews.com/on-air/war-stories/2009/08/20 /day-i-met-cartel-assassin, accessed October 5, 2012.

125 **a fancy safe house** "Mexican cartels lure American teens as killers."

126 **"They just died and shit"** Luke Dittrich, "Four Days on Mexico Border Control," *Esquire*, June 8, 2009.

126 **The local cops disposed** Grayson, *Executioner's Men*, 183.

126 **"I've killed men while they were"** Ibid., 36, 181.

126 **including their pregnant women** http://www.aljazeera.com/indepth /features/2010/10/20101019212440609775.html, accessed October 5, 2012.

126 **display them in public** Ibid.

126 **sew it onto a soccer ball** http://www.telegraph.co.uk/news/worldnews /centralamericaandthecaribbean/mexico/6962500/Murder-victim-has-face -stitched-on-football.html, accessed October 8, 2012. Grillo, *El Narco*, 6.

126 **Carolyn Rothstein said** Rothstein, *Now I'll Tell*, 119.

127 **"There's no police now"** This is corroborated by most accounts. See for example chapter 4 of Grayson, *Executioner's Men*, 67–82, where he refers to the Zetas as having "dual sovereignty" and forming a "shadow government."

127 **60 to 70 percent** Bowden, *Murder City*, 45.

128 **within forty-eight hours** This is explained most clearly in "Young Guns."

130 **But it was the war for drugs** As referenced before, this is a concept coined by Charles Bowden: see Bowden, *Murder City*, 18.

130 **become number one** http://www.guardian.co.uk/world/2012/oct/09 /zetas-boss-heriberto-lazcano-death-confirmed, accessed October 6, 2012.

130 captured by the Mexican police http://www.theguardian.com/world /2013/jul/16/mexico-drugs-trade, accessed November 20, 2013.

Chapter 10: Marisela's Long March

131 tracking down the people I was introduced to Juan Fraire Escobedo by the extraordinary group Mexicanos en Exilio, who campaign for the right of Mexicans fleeing drug war violence to be granted asylum in the United States.

135 "I don't have words" http://mariselaescobedo.com/media.html, accessed April 24, 2014.

136 just 2 percent Bowden, *Murder City*, 238.

136 "It is only a few" http://mariselaescobedo.com/vid_protests.html, accessed February 26, 2013, and translated for me by Francis Whatlington.

137 The heat on these roads This description is based on my own experience of being driven on these roads, when I went to Creel to interview a woman whose husband and sons had all disappeared. I later wrote about their story in *Le Monde Diplomatique.*

138 "Then let him kill me" Ken Ellingwood, "Mexico Under Siege," *Los Angeles Times*, December 18, 2010.

138 he shot her This was captured on video. Part of it can be seen at http://www.youtube.com/watch?v=i9P1gNCAZNw or http://www.youtube.com /watch?v=jfH5U3JnCDs, accessed April 2, 2013, and in the documentary *8 Murders a Day.*

139 the cartels' control You can hear Juan giving an account of his experiences at http://www.texasobserver.org/justice-in-exile/, accessed April 2, 2013.

139 Anslinger himself wrote Anslinger, *Protectors*, 10–11.

139 Not what the family http://hispanicnewsnetwork.blogspot.co.uk/2012 /11/barraza-bocanegra-killed-in-zacatecas.html, accessed November 23, 2013.

140 leading expert on drugs Gretchen Kristine Pierce, "Sobering the Revolution: Mexico's Anti-Alcohol Campaigns," Ph.D. diss., University of Arizona, 2008. Accessed at http://books.google.co.uk/books?id=xNS1YGSi9t kC&printsec=frontcover&dq=sobering+the+revolution&hl=en&sa=X&ei =KZyuU5rgH5TG7AbmooCQCw&ved=0CCEQ6AEwAA#v=onepage&q =sobering%20the%20revolution&f=false.

140 appointed him chief Bewley-Taylor, *U.S. and International Drug Control*, 42.

140 the same discoveries He explicitly condemned Harry's approach: see Walker, *Drug Control in the Americas*, 125.

140 does not cause psychosis Ibid., 68.

140 **"myth of marijuana"** Campos, *Home Grown*, 226.

140 **"It is impossible"** Walker, *Drug Control in the Americas*, 67.

140 **prevent criminals** UNESCO report "Globalisation, Drugs and Criminalisation: Final Research Report on Brazil, China, India and Mexico," 2002, 60, at http://www.unesco.org/most/globalisation/drugs_vol1.pdf, accessed October 21, 2012.

141 **"criminals first"** Walker, *Drug Control in the Americas*, 126.

141 **forced from office** Ibid., 67, 133.

141 **writhed in agony** Ibid., 127–32.

141 **"victory for Harry"** Ibid., 132.

141 **"a sign of success"** http://www.bbc.co.uk/news/world-latin-america -12992664, accessed October 21, 2013.

Chapter 11: The Grieving Mongoose

145 **"a drug-free world"** http://www.guardian.co.uk/commentisfree/2009 /mar/05/war-on-drugs-prohibition, accessed July 1, 2012.

145 **"no such thing"** "Warning Campaign Launched Against Club Drugs," Associated Press, December 3, 1999, accessed via LexisNexis July 1, 2012.

145 **adviser to two U.S. presidents** Ronald Siegel, *Intoxication: Life in Pursuit of Artificial Paradise*, 14.

145 **out of its mind** Ibid., 72.

146 **"after sampling"** Ibid., 11.

146 **"In every country"** Ibid., 13.

147 **They got so drunk** Ibid., 105; see also Siegel interview.

147 **"they can barely crawl"** Siegel, *Intoxication*, 198.

147 **Only 10 percent** http://www.unodc.org/documents/commissions/CND -Session51/CND-UNGASS-CRPs/ECN72008CRP17.pdf, 3–4 as accessed July 12, 2012. I am grateful to Steve Rolles of Transform and Dr. Carl Hart for highlighting this fact for me. This fact is also discussed in https://news.vice .com/article/cryptomarkets-are-gentrifying-the-drug-trade-and-thats -probably-a-good-thing as accessed September 24, 2014. For studies finding a similar ratio, see DeGrandpre, *Cult of Pharmacology*, 231.

147 **Even William Bennett** See Miller, *Drug Warriors*, 5.

147 **lying in a gutter** Jacob Sullum, *Saying Yes*, 10.

148 **the World Health Organization** http://transform-drugs.blogspot.co.uk /2009/06/report-they-didnt-want-you-to-see.html, accessed December 2, 2013.

148 "the norm not the exception" Sullum, *Saying Yes*, 9.

149 the pleasure of getting wasted Siegel, *Intoxication*, 14. See also Siegel interview.

149 to get a head rush Stuart Walton, *Out of It*, 10.

149 High in the Andes Mike Jay, *High Society*, 14.

149 Shakespeare's house http://www.telegraph.co.uk/science/science-news/4760882/Did-Shakespeare-seek-inspiration-in-cocaine.html, accessed June 24, 2014.

149 George Washington Okrent, *Last Call*, 8.

149 "The ubiquity" Walton, *Out of It*, 2; Arnold Trebach, *The Heroin Solution*, xi.

149 "the fourth drive" Walton, *Out of It*, 208.

149 "new, astonishing" R. Gordon Wasson, Albert Hofmann, and Carl A. P. Ruck, *The Road to Eleusis: Unveiling the Secret of the Mysteries*, 17.

150 Sophocles, Aristotle Walton, *Out of It*, 38–39.

150 The annual ritual Ibid., 38; Wasson, Hofmann, and Ruck, *Road to Eleusis*, 51–53.

150 for two thousand years Wasson, Hofmann, and Ruck, *Road to Eleusis*, 9. See also Herodotus, *Histories* 8.65, and Isocrates, *Panegyricus* 4.157.

150 "nothing less than" McWilliams, *Protectors*, 186.

150 and other writers Wasson, Hofmann, and Ruck, *Road to Eleusis*.

150 as it was being suppressed Ibid., 55.

150 passed around the crowd Walton, *Out of It*, 38; Wasson, Hofmann, and Ruck, *Road to Eleusis*, 76–85; Carl Kerényi, *Eleusis: Archetypal Image of Mother and Daughter*, 177–80.

150 caused hallucinations D.C.A. Hillman, *The Chemical Muse: Drug Use and the Roots of Western Civilisation*, 209. See also Wasson, Hofmann, and Ruck, *Road to Eleusis*, 25–34, 47–48. There is no consensus among classicists around these conclusions. Some agree with them and some do not. They are not, however, the views of cranks, but of distinguished scholars in the field. George Luck, professor emeritus of classics at Johns Hopkins University, says it has been "establish[ed] beyond the shadow of a doubt, I think, that the drink served during the initiation rites at the Eleusinian mysteries contained ergot," the hallucinogenic fungus, and that "this . . . fully accounts for the marvelous visions of another world that made this religious experience so unique." See Carl A. P. Ruck, *Sacred Mushrooms of the Goddess: Secrets of Eleusis*, 161.

150 arranged by public officials Hillman, *Chemical Muse*, 209.

150 "Caught in possession" Walton, *Out of It*, 44.

150 **"were drug users"** See Hillman, *Chemical Muse*, 3, 6.

151 **only in tiny sips** Walton, *Out of It*, 27.

151 **This "forcible repression"** Walton, *Out of It*, 38.

152 **"We are discovering"** Ibid., 11.

152 **where it can breathe** Ibid., xvii.

152 **"intoxicology"** Ibid., xxv.

152 **"Intoxication plays"** Ibid., ix.

Chapter 12: Terminal City

153 **By then, the only milk** This is based on Gabor's account of Judith's memories: she died before I could meet her. See Gabor Maté interview. She both described these events to Gabor and kept a diary at the time, which Gabor had read. Gabor also describes these experiences in *Scattered Minds*, 87–93.

154 **on a train platform in Budapest** Ibid., 91.

154 **"I'll come"** Gabor Maté, *In the Realm of Hungry Ghosts*, 241.

154 **the only clothing** Maté, *Scattered Minds*, 92.

155 **It will kill itself** Reinarman and Levine, *Crack in America*, 148.

155 **his former colleagues and patients** These included Bud Osborn, Dean Wilson, and Liz Evans.

156 **this neighborhood is** There's a good discussion of the neighborhood in Douglas Coupland's *City of Glass*, 87; he talks about this being the end of the line on page 111.

156 **an echoing concrete husk** It was later developed into housing and apartments.

157 **straight in the jugular** As shown in the documentary *The Fix*.

157 **"People in Vancouver"** Charles Demers, *Vancouver Special*, 85.

157 **Liz was put in charge** Maté, *Hungry Ghosts*, 11.

158 **A Fellini film** Ibid., 9.

158 **A thirty-six-year-old man named Carl** Ibid., 37.

158 **"a warm, soft hug"** Ibid., 165.

159 **"no significant risk"** Ibid., 141.

159 **snort a roulette wheel** Maté, *Hungry Ghosts*, 140.

160 **"of an order of magnitude"** Ibid., 201–2.

160 **as obesity is to cause heart disease** http://providence.net/bariatrics /internal.php?page=obesity-facts, accessed February 27, 2013, says: "Nearly 70 percent of diagnosed cases of cardiovascular disease are related to obesity."

160 published in *American Psychologist* I originally learned about the report from Sullum, *Saying Yes*, 15. I then read the original study: see *American Psychologist*, May 1990, 612–30.

160 "a symptom, not a cause" Sullum, *Saying Yes*, 15. If that seems odd, remember the strong evidence showing that childhood trauma can actually physically stunt a child's growth—and putting them into a loving home can make it start again. See Daniel E. Moerman, *Meaning, Medicine and the Placebo Effect*, 133.

160 "The basic cause" Maté, *Hungry Ghosts*, 189.

161 "I don't know much" *Ebony*, July 1949, 32.

161 "grow up in homes" Anslinger, *Murderers*, 174.

162 "The reason for her being an addict" Julia Blackburn archives, box 18, Linda Kuehl notes 1, Memry Midgett interview.

162 "People think sometimes" Julia Blackburn archives, box 18, Linda Kuehl notes, vol. VIII, interview with Peter O'Brien and Michelle Wallace.

163 flung into their faces As explained to me by Liz Evans.

163 his grandfather had it coming Maté, *Hungry Ghosts*, 75.

163 passages of Goethe's poetry Ibid., 82–83.

163 "Heil Hitler" Ibid., 84.

164 binge on CD buying Ibid., 120.

164 "behind my eyes" Ibid., 118.

164 Now, as an adult, Maté, *Hungry Ghosts*, 21.

165 "before the use of" Ibid., 30.

Chapter 13: Batman's Bad Call

168 I read about an experiment I think I first read about it in Lauren Slater's brilliant book *Opening Skinner's Box*.

170 This wasn't some freak DeGrandpre, *Cult of Pharmacology*, 124, 203; Miller, *Drug Warriors*, 17.

170 You can get rid of the drug There is a similar, and much more common-place, example of this: 90 percent of addicts who are detoxified in clinics—who, in other words, are looked after until their entire bodies are free of the drug, and all withdrawal symptoms have stopped—go back to using. See Miller, *Case for Legalizing Drugs*, 30.

170 symptoms were often minor Miller, *Case for Legalizing Drugs*, 5–6.

171 "Well, he says they're not very serious" This exchange is as recalled by Bruce.

171 a little bit sniffly Billie Holiday's withdrawal, as discussed earlier, was so threatening to her life not because withdrawal is inherently life-threatening, but because she was so weak. A person whose immune system is weak can be killed by an ordinary flu.

171 The medical researchers John Henry Merryman, ed., *Stanford Legal Essays*, 284. http://www.spectator.co.uk/features/3212846/withdrawal-from -heroin-is-a-trivial-matter/, accessed March 3, 2013; http://ps.psychiatry online.org/article.aspx?articleID=62279, accessed January 8, 2014.

171 a series of experiments on rats DeGrandpre, *Cult of Pharmacology*, 29. See also "The Effect of Housing and Gender on Morphine Self-Administration in Rats," *Psychopharmacology* 58, 175–79.

171 "Only one drug is so addictive" http://www.youtube.com/watch?v =7kS72J5Nlm8&list=PL6301BC630AE6F23E&index=106&feature=plpp _video, viewed November 1, 2012.

172 What, he wondered, if This discussion of the experiment is informed heavily by the two original studies of Rat Park by Alexander and colleagues: "The Effect of Housing and Gender on Morphine Self-Administration in Rats," *Psychopharmacology* 58, 175–79, and "Effect of Early and Later Colony Housing on Oral Ingestion of Morphine by Rats," *Pharmacology, Biochemistry and Behaviour*, vol. 15, 571–76.

172 Within its plywood walls Slater, *Opening Skinner's Box*, 165.

172 He called it Rat Park See "The View from Rat Park" by Bruce K. Alexander, http://globalizationofaddiction.ca/articles-speeches/177-addiction -the-view-from-rat-park.html, accessed November 1, 2012.

172 He took a set of rats Slater, *Opening Skinner's Box*, 168.

173 "nothing that we tried" Bruce K. Alexander, *Globalizing Addiction: A Study in Poverty of the Spirit*, 195. Although in other interviews and in his writing Bruce has talked about the idea of rats being addicted as a shorthand for their heavily using drugs, he stressed to me that we perhaps need to be more careful with these terms: "What would that look like in a rat? I think the question is moot, really, we just don't know what addiction would look like in a rat . . . How could you possibly know if a rat was addicted?" Since rats cannot tell us about their psychological state we cannot know about their cravings and longings. We can talk about heavy and compulsive use, which can be measured; but Bruce believes "addiction" also implies a mental state, which we can't measure in rats. To be clear, "addiction," when I use it in this chapter about rats, is shorthand for very heavy use when they are in unhappy situations.

173 Out in Southeast Asia Dan Baum, *Smoke and Mirrors*, 49.

173 This wasn't just journalistic hyperbole Reinarman and Levine, *Crack in America*, 10; Maté, *Hungry Ghosts*, 142.

173 This meant there were more As reported in the documentary *The Most Secret Place on Earth: The CIA's Covert War on Laos*.

173 The American military had cracked down Baum, *Smoke and Mirrors*, 50.

173 Senator Robert Steele Ibid., 48. There's a useful discussion of drug use by U.S. troops in Vietnam in Valentine, *Strength of the Pack*, 117–32.

173 Senator Harold Hughes Reinarman and Levine, *Crack in America*, 10; Sally Satel and Scott O. Lilienfeld, *Brainwashed: The Seductive Appeal of Mindless Neuroscience*, 49–50.

173 The *Archives of General Psychiatry* Maté, *Hungry Ghosts*, 142. DeGrandpre, *Cult of Pharmacology*, 117.

173 They turned out to have Maté, *Hungry Ghosts*, 146.

174 "Take a man out" Baum, *Smoke and Mirrors*, 62. Miller, *Case for Legalizing Drugs*, 54–55.

174 one idea above all See Bruce K. Alexander, "The Rise and Fall of the Official View of Addiction," http://globalizationofaddiction.ca/articles-speeches/240-rise-and-fall-of-the-official-view-of-addictionnew.html, accessed March 12, 2013.

175 The Gin Craze See Jessica Warner, *Craze: Gin and Debauchery in an Age of Reason*.

175 A meth binge See Nick Reding, *Methland: The Death and Life of an American Small Town*.

175 "today's flood of addiction" Bruce K. Alexander, "The View From Rat Park," http://globalizationofaddiction.ca/articles-speeches/177-addiction-the-view-from-rat-park.html, accessed March 12, 2013.

175 a new word: "bonding" http://www.cedro-uva.org/lib/cohen.addiction.html, accessed February 5, 2012. See Peter Cohen, "Is the Addiction Doctor the Voodoo Priest of Western Man?" at http://www.cedro-uva.org/lib/cohen.addiction.html, also published in *Addiction Research*, special issue, vol. 8, no. 6: 589–98.

177 better than being alone More recent evidence reinforces this. When there have been heroin shortages in Europe in the twenty-first century, far from getting clean, users have in fact turned to even deadlier intoxicants. See https://reportingproject.net/occrp/index.php/en/ccwatch/cc-watch-indepth/1901-heroin-shortages-drive-users-to-deadly-alternatives, accessed March 30, 2013.

177 summing up a conference Robert DuPont is the founder of the National Institute for Drug Abuse (NIDA), the body which has done more than any other to popularize the notions of addiction as "brain-hijacking" and "chemical slavery." I wanted to put the points raised by Bruce Alexander, Gabor Mate, and others—suggesting that addiction has radically different causes that render these metaphors inaccurate—to the current head of NIDA, Nora Volkow, but she declined my interview requests. (She was one of only a handful of people who did so, through the whole process of writing the book.)

I believed it was nonetheless important to give a full response to these points in the book from a distinguished scientist who is broadly aligned with NIDA and the NIDA worldview. Given that I could not get the key NIDA scientist to talk on the record and respond to these claims, I weighed carefully who would be the next best person to put these points to. Robert DuPont personally does not use the specific metaphors of hijacking and slavery, and does not like them, because he believes they undermine the idea that addicts are personally responsible for their recovery. I concluded he was nonetheless the best person I could get on the record to respond to these points from a NIDA-aligned perspective, for three reasons.

One: he is the founder of NIDA. Two: he was the key speaker at a conference and a movement which uses this way of thinking about addiction as a reason to prohibit drugs, and he understands that milieu better than anyone else I can think of.

Three, most crucially: The core point I wanted to test was whether NIDA scientists had engaged with the radically different theories about addiction that Alexander and Mate have been laying out. It was very clear from speaking to DuPont that this is not the case; this was further confirmed by the fact that I could find no evidence of NIDA engaging with them anywhere, which suggested to me that he is representative of NIDA in this respect. In addition Bruce Alexander and all the dissident scientists I interviewed demonstrated to me that these ideas are systematically ignored. If Nora Volkow would like to reconsider and to offer me an interview, I would be very happy to include the response of the current head of NIDA to these theories, alongside those of the previous head that are described here. I am keen to offer the fullest possible response, and to explore all sides of this really important debate about what causes addiction.

I am grateful to John Harris, writing in the Guardian, for suggesting more explanation was needed of this point in his review for the newspaper: he was right.

180 in a lecture in London http://www.thersa.org/events/audio-and-past -events/2011/addiction-what-to-do-when-everything-else-has-failed, accessed December 15, 2012.

180 Countless studies prove Matthew E. Brashears, "Small Networks and High Isolation? A Reexamination of American Discussion Networks," *Social Networks* 33 (2011): 331–41.

183 Also the deadliest Benavie, *Drugs: America's Holy War*, 12.

183 kills 650 Ibid., 11.

183 while cocaine kills 4 DeGrandpre, *Cult of Pharmacology*, 85.

Chapter 14: The Drug Addicts' Uprising

187 This is his story This account of the origins of VANDU is based on my interviews with Bud and others who were there at the time and later—Ann Livingstone, Dean Wilson, Donald MacPherson, Liz Evans, Philip Owen, Gabor Maté, Bruce Alexander, Clare Hacksell, Coco Cuthbertson, Laura Shaver—and writings and documentaries as referenced in the endnotes.

188 He was a homeless http://www.cosmik.com/aa-december99/bud_osborn.html, accessed April 1, 2013.

189 and he never stopped John Armstrong, "Poet had a choice of gutters," *Vancouver Sun*, April 6, 1996.

189 "the consequences of flaunting" Bud Osborn, *Hundred Block Rock*, 13.

190 Later, he wrote Ibid., 26.

194 "saw a pitch-black hole" Osborn, *Hundred Block Rock*, 33.

194 "I spent considerable time" Ibid., 111.

195 "People overdose because" Benavie, *Drugs: America's Holy War*, 43.

195 European countries that provide Pisani, *Wisdom of Whores*, 232.

197 lock them away Maté, *Hungry Ghosts*, 101.

197 "I'm totally and violently opposed" Susan Boyd, Donald MacPherson, and Bud Osborn, eds., *Raise Shit! Social Action Saving Lives*, 92.

197 "vampires" and "werewolves" Ibid., 84.

197 "wouldn't piss on them" http://www.scribd.com/doc/103641727/Independent-Counsel-Report-to-Commissioner-of-Inquiry-August-16-2012, accessed October 25, 2012.

197 "Why don't they just" Boyd, MacPherson, and Osborn, *Raise Shit!* 189.

197 a killer whale Ibid., 35.

197 a dramatic gesture A good discussion of this process can be found in "The Establishment of North America's First State-Sanctioned Injection Facility: A Case Study in Cultural Change," *International Journal of Drug Policy* vol. 17 (2006): 73–82, available online at http://www.communityinsite.ca/pdf/culture-change-case-study.pdf, accessed April 1, 2013.

197 Each cross represented http://news.streetroots.org/2012/03/14/vancouver-bc-s-drug-revolution, accessed April 1, 2013.

197 Their names were written As seen in the documentary *The Fix*.

197 "killing fields" Boyd, MacPherson, and Osborn, *Raise Shit!*, 19.

197 handed out leaflets Greg Joyce, "Downtrodden March in Vancouver," *Edmonton Journal*, July 12, 2000, accessed via LexisNexis November 5, 2012.

198 "a thousand crosses in oppenheimer park" Bud Osborn, *Sign of the Times*, 26–30.

198 WHO WILL BE THE NEXT Boyd, MacPherson, and Osborn, *Raise Shit!* 50.

198 DRUG USERS ARE PEOPLE TOO Ibid., 59.

199 getting Bud to sit on the board Ian Mulgrew, "Health Board's Rabble-rousing Social Conscience," *Vancouver Sun*, July 24, 1999, accessed via LexisNexis November 5, 2012.

200 a pink blouse in a heap Osborn, *Hundred Block Rock*, 79.

200 He wrote "the war on drugs" Boyd, MacPherson, and Osborn, *Raise Shit!*, 89.

201 VANDU cofounder Dean Wilson . . . I know about this moment because it was featured in the excellent documentary *The Fix*.

203 The local business owner Price Vassage Ibid. This quote comes from the documentary.

203 The average life expectancy http://www.theprovince.com/news/Life +expectancy+Downtown+Eastside/7202585/story.html, accessed November 5, 2012.

203 One newspaper headline http://www2.canada.com/theprovince/news /story.html?id=6ee496bd-5a4c-4bca-8323-42d3f4d91df1, accessed February 27, 2013.

203 The *Globe and Mail* newspaper reported Robert Matas, "BC Drug Deaths Hit a Low Not Seen in Years," *Globe and Mail*, December 9, 2008, accessed via LexisNexis November 2, 2012.

204 He was found dead in his apartment http://www.vancouversun.com /news/Osborn+true+hero+Downtown+Eastside/9816842/story.html, accessed May 14, 2014.

204 For his memorial service I could not make it there, alas. This was described to me by Liz Evans, who was there.

Chapter 15: Snowfall and Strengthening

205 It was time, I realized I had been back and forth to Britain all through the researching of this book, but this was the point when I decided to return for good and focus my energies on researching the effects of the drug war outside North America.

205 to find everyone I could Namely John Marks, Russell Newcombe, Pat O'Hare, Cindy Fazey, Allan Parry, and Andrew Bennett.

206 "trying to make water flow uphill" http://www.bbc.co.uk/news/uk -england-merseyside-16355281, accessed April 24, 2013.

207 a little less than the United States The best explanation of British drug policy today is in Alex Stevens's excellent book *Drugs, Crime and Public Health: The Political Economy of Drug Policy.*

207 black men are ten time more http://www.guardian.co.uk/society/2010 /oct/31/race-bias-drug-arrests-claim, accessed April 24, 2013.

207 On the twenty-seventh of November 1918 Kohn, *Dope Girls*, 84–85.

207 "the sickening crowd" Ibid., 129.

207 "the nigger 'musicians'" Ibid., 120.

207 EVIL NEGRO CAUGHT Ibid., 158.

207 Sir Humphrey Rolleston Trebach, *Heroin Solution*, 90.

207 "Relapse," he found Ibid., 93.

207 So he insisted King, *Drug Hang-Up*, 190–207; G. Bammer, "Drug Abuse: The Heroin Prescribing Debate; Integrating Science and Politics," *Science* 5418 (1999): 1277–78.

207 As Mike Gray explains Gray, *Drug Crazy*, 155.

208 "stabilized addict" Trebach, *Heroin Solution*, 104.

208 When Billie Holiday came Holiday, *Lady Sings the Blues*, 182–83.

208 in Hong Kong Anslinger archives, box 1, file 10, "New York Forum: Saturday April 28th 1962, Program Transcript."

208 Anslinger couldn't crush them King, *Drug Hang-Up*, 212–14; Ambros Uchtenhagen, "Heroin Maintenance Treatment: From Idea to Research to Practice," *Drug and Alcohol Review* 30 (March 2013): 130–37.

208 it had gone up Elizabeth Young, "The Needle and the Damage Done," *Guardian*, August 20, 1994.

208 He told them to stop Linnet Myers, "Europe Finds U.S. Drug War Lacking in Results," *Chicago Tribune*, November 2, 1995.

209 He assumed Newcombe would Gray, *Drug Crazy*, 158. John Marks, "To Prescribe or Not to Prescribe," *Mersey Drugs Journal* (September/October 1987): 5.

209 All doctors agree I first learned this from an excellent series of articles and a documentary *The Truth About Heroin*, by the British journalist Nick Davies, in 2001.

209 He explained to journalists Ed Bradley, "Success of Britain's Addict Treatment Program," *60 Minutes* segment, December 27, 1992, CBS News transcript.

210 By 1942, he was boasting Anslinger archives, box 1, file 8.

210 cigarettes soaked in heroin Will Self, *Junk Mail*, 92.

210 He also prescribed cocaine Sally Woods, "Heroin and Methadone Substitution Treatments," unpublished Ph.D. thesis, Liverpool John Moores University, 2005.

210 "If you were an alcoholic" Young, "Needle and the Damage Done."

210 Inspector Michael Lofts studied Myers, "Europe Finds U.S. Drug War Lacking."

211 a 93 percent drop Edward Pilkington, "The Smack Doctor," *Guardian*, October 26, 1995.

211 Lofts told a newspaper Ibid.

211 "boring boring, boring" Self, *Junk Mail*, 91.

211 "I went back once" Bradley, "Success of Britain's Addict Treatment Program."

211 "I need heroin" Ibid.

211 John overstated it See Self, *Junk Mail*, 94.

211 "Since the clinics opened" Gabriele Bammer and Grayson Gerrard, eds., "Heroin Treatment: New Alternatives. Proceedings of a Seminar held on 1st November 1991, Ian Wark Theatre, Canberra," National Center for Epidemiology and Population Health.

212 "Heroin use was concentrated" Davenport-Hines, *Pursuit of Oblivion: A History of Narcotics*, 275, 282.

212 "maturing out," or "natural recovery" A good discussion of this subject is found in Harald Klingemann, "Natural Recovery from Alcohol Problems," chapter 10 of *The Essential Handbook of Treatment and Prevention of Alcohol Problems*, edited by Nick Heather. See also Satel and Lilienfeld, *Brainwashed*, 54–56.

212 Most addicts will simply stop Self, *Junk Mail*, 93.

212 after around ten years of use Miller, *Case for Legalizing Drugs*, 53.

212 "If they're drug takers determined" Bradley, "Success of Britain's Addict Treatment Program."

212 "drug addicts would multiply" *Bulletin on Narcotics*, January–April 1954, 6.

212 thought the rate of use would hold steady Marks, "Paradox of Prohibition."

213 a twelvefold decrease John Marks, "The North Wind and the Sun," *Proceedings of the Royal College of Physicians of Edinburgh*, vol. 21, no. 3 (July 1991). Heroin prescription has a considerably better success rate than methadone prescription. In the only randomized heroin and methadone prescription trial, 71 percent of patients given methadone dropped out, compared to just

26 percent of heroin patients. The methadone patients were also far more likely to have committed crimes and to be using their drug heavily. See Woods, "Heroin and Methadone Substitution Treatments," and Uchtenhagen, "Heroin Maintenance Treatment."

213 discovered what he believes is the explanation He explains this both in his interview with me (see Russell Newcombe audio) and in Nick Davies's brilliant documentary *The Truth About Heroin*.

213 £100 a day Marks, "Paradox of Prohibition."

213 a pyramid-selling scheme Marks, *Paradox of Prohibition*, 7. This phenomenon had in fact been noticed before, by another doctor. In the late 1950s in the United States, Dr. Walter Treadway wrote: "It is known that addicted individuals, having acquired a supply, are very apt to dispose of part of it for a consideration, thus assuring their own future purchases. It is also known that these addicted peddlers, or addicted pushers as they are often called, may assiduously endeavor to recruit new addicts, often for the same reason." See King, *Drug Hang-Up*, 178.

214 The department store Marks and Spencer Marks, "North Wind and the Sun."

214 "As police officers ..." Pat O'Hare, "Merseyside, the First Harm Reduction Conferences, and the Early History of Harm Reduction," *International Journal of Drug Policy* 18 (2007), 141–44.

214 on a CNN phone-in show http://fair.org/press-release/media-downplay -bigotry-of-jesse-helms/, accessed April 26, 2013.

215 "We've got a lot of heat" Marks also discusses this here: http://www .runcornandwidnesweeklynews.co.uk/runcorn-widnes-news/runcorn -widnes-local-news/2010/08/19/dr-john-marks-talks-about-the-controversial -harm-reduction-drug-treatment-programme-in-widnes-55368-27086372/, accessed November 28, 2012.

215 John was powerless Woods, "Heroin and Methadone Substitution Treatments," 45–46.

215 from 1982 to 1995 Marks, "Paradox of Prohibition."

215 Of the 450 patients Peter Carty, "Drug Abuse: The End of the Line," *Guardian*, December 10, 1997.

215 10 to 20 percent John Marks, "Preventing Drug Misuse," *Psychiatry Online*, vol. 1, issue 7, paper 2.

216 Ruth thought of Wall Street The history of these street scenes is summarized well in Ambros Uchtenhagen, "Heroin-Assisted Treatment in Switzerland: A Case Study in Policy Change," *Addiction*, doi: 10.111/j.1360 -0443.2009.02741.x.

216 everything the Swiss thought Joelle Kuntz, *Switzerland: How an Alpine Pass Became a Country*, 7.

217 flush your toilet http://www.guardian.co.uk/travel/blog/2007/aug/02/itsillegaltowhatofficer, accessed January 22, 2012.

217 "A wonderful couple" See Holiday, *Lady Sings the Blues*, 137.

218 the worst HIV epidemic Joanne Csete, *From the Mountaintops*, 17; Uchtenhagen, "Heroin-Assisted Treatment in Switzerland: A Case Study in Policy Change."

218 told her that they had been Interview with Dr. Ambros Uchtenhagen. He also describes his mission there in "Heroin-Assisted Treatment in Switzerland: A Case Study in Policy Change." See also O'Hare, "Merseyside," 141–44.

218 a really large experiment Csete, *From the Mountaintops*, 18; Uchtenhagen, "Heroin-Assisted Treatment in Switzerland: A Case Study in Policy Change"; Ambros Uchtenhagen, "The Medical Prescription of Heroin to Heroin Addicts," *Drug and Alcohol Review* 16 (1997), 297–98.

219 I will call him Jean When I was introduced to Jean by Dr. Rita Manghi and her colleagues at the clinic in Geneva, he agreed to speak on the condition that I do not use his real name or post the audio of the interview online. The reason he gave for this is that his story involved him admitting to criminal acts from before the law was changed—such as drug-smuggling—for which the statute of limitations has not passed. For that reason, this is the only instance where I am not posting the audio for these quotes on the website. The conversations were recorded and the audio has been provided to Bloomsbury. Dr. Manghi also confirmed to the publishers in writing that she introduced me to several patients in her clinic, and they included "Jean."

220 "The addict is never satisfied" "Narcotic Addiction," *Spectrum* magazine, March 1, 1957, 139.

220 "A person in the condition of" *The Narcotics Officer's Handbook*, 79–80. Anslinger also makes this point in *The Murderers*, 219.

220 to stabilize their doses Csete, *From the Mountaintops*, 19.

221 a path to it Over a three-year period, of the 353 patients leaving the heroin program studied in *Prescription of Narcotics for Heroin Addicts: Main Results of the Swiss National Cohort Study* (Uchtenhagen et al., 6), 83 left to choose an abstinence-based therapy. See Uchtenhagen et al., *Prescription of Narcotics*, 7.

221 an empty glass inside them There was a slight language barrier between us, but this is my best understanding of the metaphor.

221 only 15 percent http://www.time.com/time/health/article/0,8599,1926160,00.html, accessed January 22, 2013.

221 55 percent ... 80 percent Denis Ribeaud, "Long-term Impacts of the Swiss Heroin Prescription Trials on Crime of Treated Heroin Users," *Journal of Drug Issues* 34:163 (2004), 173, doi: 10.1177/002204260403400108, http://jod.sagepub.com/content/34/1/163.

221 "almost immediate" Ibid., 188.

221 68 percent ... 5 percent http://hivlawandpolicy.org/resources/view
/753, accessed January 22, 2013.

222 fell dramatically Jurgen Rehm and colleagues, "Mortality in heroin-
assisted treatment in Switzerland 1994-2000," *Drug and Alcohol Dependence*
79 (2005), 137–43.

222 had a home Uchtenhagen et al., *Prescription of Narcotics*, 6.

222 A third of all Ibid.

222 94.7 percent Ribeaud, "Long-term Impacts," 173.

222 thirty-five Swiss francs Uchtenhagen et al., "Prescription of Narcotics
for Heroin Addicts," 89.

222 forty-four francs a day Ibid., 94. Woods, "Heroin and Methadone
Substitution Treatments," 33.

222 fifty thousand signatures Csete, *From the Mountaintops*, 16.

223 In 1997 ... 68 percent Ibid., 27-8. Uchtenhagen et al., "Prescription of
Narcotics," 96.

223 These campaigns showed At the same time, she tried to champion the
legalization of cannabis, but this effort was rejected by the Swiss people.

223 could end prohibition around the world It was Joanne Csete's brilliant
pamphlet that made me realize this.

223 "Six months ago" This wording is from Ruth's memory.

224 "Anyone who plays" Peter Reuter and Robert MacCoun, "Heroin
Maintenance: Is a US Experiment Needed?" *One Hundred Years of Heroin*, ed
by D. Musto.

224 "There will be no" Privately, she says, he was "really, really" interested in
the country's methadone program.

226 twenty-five years in jail http://www.mapinc.org/newscsdp/v07/n531/
a05.html, accessed February 20, 2014.

226 hold up a pharmacy http://www.nytimes.com/2011/02/07/us/07
pharmacies.html?ref=prescriptiondrugabuse, accessed February 20, 2014.

228 three times more powerful The strength of opiates is compared in
standard medical textbooks using something called an "equianalgesic chart."
See for example http://globalrph.com/narcoticonv.htm and http://clincalc.com
/Opioids/ http://www.medscape.com/viewarticle/542574_3. There are several
that enable you to compare different opiates and figure out how much more or
less of one opiate is equivalent to another. They show the medical consensus
that diamorphine (the form of heroin given to patients in hospitals) is considerably stronger than Oxycontin. (All accessed May 14, 2014.) See also the
NHS Scotland report "The Management of Pain in Patients with Cancer,"

November 2009, 21, published on the NHS website: http://www.palliativecare guidelines.scot.nhs.uk/documents/PAINCANCERREV_BPS_NOV09.pdf, accessed June 20, 2014.

228 almost never turns people Maté, *Hungry Ghosts*, 141.

228 since the Great Depression The work of the Nobel Prize–winning economists Joseph Stiglitz and Paul Krugman provides the best documentation of this trend that I know.

229 go to any college football game This discussion of the phenomenon is based both on Gray, *Drug Crazy*, and on my interview with Gray. See also http://www.cato.org/pubs/pas/pa157.pdf, accessed November 20, 2012.

230 "iron law of prohibition" http://www.cato.org/pubs/pas/pa-157.html, accessed March 3, 2013.

230 The day before alcohol prohibition Gray, *Drug Crazy*, 68. http://www .cato.org/pubs/pas/pa157.pdf, accessed November 20, 2012.

230 a zone of alcohol prohibition Gray, *Drug Crazy*, 68.

230 Mrs. Winslow's Soothing Syrup Musto, *American Disease*, 94.

230 Vin Mariani Terence McKenna, *Food of the Gods*, 212.

231 teas and soft drinks Steve Rolles, *After the War on Drugs: Blueprint for Regulation*, 125.

Chapter 16: The Spirit of '74

235 In the early hours of the morning A good account of the Portuguese revolution is given in chapter 7 of Malcolm Jack's book *Lisbon: City of the Sea*, and it helped to inform this section.

235 The authorities ordered people Phil Mailer, *Portugal: The Impossible Revolution?* 38-9.

235 tossed a single red carnation Hugo Gil Ferreira and Michael W. Marshall, *Portugal's Revolution: Ten Years On*, 5.

235 People climbed onto the tanks Martin Kayman, *Revolution and Counter-Revolution in Portugal*, 74.

236–237 The 1960s were canceled here Artur Domoslawski, *Drug Policy in Portugal: The Benefits of Decriminalizing Drug Use*, 13.

237 the use of heroin Ibid., 15. Kellen Russoniello, "The Devil (and Drugs) in the Details: Portugal's Focus on Public Health as a Model for Decriminalization of Drugs in Mexico," *Yale Journal of Health Policy, Law and Ethics* 12 (2012), 382.

237 By the early 1990s Michael Specter, "Getting a Fix," *New Yorker*, October 17, 2011.

237 "We were out of options," ibid.

238 "drug users should be treated" Russoniello, "The Devil (and Drugs) in the Details," 385.

238 had a brother addicted to heroin João told me the name of both the politician and his brother, who subsequently died of an unrelated cause, but he asked me not to make their names public to respect the privacy of the family. Several other people raised this story with me: it appears to be common knowledge in Portugal.

238 recreational drug users "should, above all" *European Monitoring Center for Drugs and Drug Addiction report* "Drug Policy profiles: Portugal" on Portugal 2012, p12.

239 would trigger a catastrophe Otto Pohl, "Portugal shifts aim in drug war," *Christian Science Monitor*, October 11, 2001.

239 In Portugal, the ratio Specter, "Getting a Fix," *New Yorker*, Oct 17, 2011.

239 spends one million dollars Tara Herivel and Paul Wright, eds., *Prison Profiteers*, 27–35.

239 He believed that if you This account of the thinking behind the changes in Portuguese drug laws was also informed by Mirjam van het Loo et al., "Decriminalization of Drug Use in Portugal: the Development of a Policy," *Annals of the American Academy of Political and Social Science* 582, July 2002, 49–63.

240 The job of the Dissuasion Commission Russoniello, "The Devil (and Drugs) in the Details," 386–88.

241 any addict who wants to stop You will be asked to pay 20 percent of the costs if you are judged to be able to afford it.

242 So this institution is here João agrees with Bruce Alexander and Gabor Maté that even if the currently banned drugs could be somehow be made to disappear, addicts would simply shift to other addictions. "I believe most of them would develop other kinds of addictions—legal substances or other kinds," he says: "What really matters is the relation the individual has with the substance, and not the substance itself."

244 Would they come forward Artur Domoslawski, *Drug Policy in Portugal*, 18.

245 At first, these teams This account of how street teams work is also informed by the street team I spent an afternoon with in Lisbon.

246 Where once there were police He attributes the fact that the police no longer beat addicts at anything like the same rate not primarily to the decriminalization, but to the fact that one addict died in a beating.

247 permanently lower their IQ http://www.pnas.org/content/early/2012/08/22/1206820109.abstract via http://www.bbc.co.uk/news/health-19396351 both accessed November 21, 2012.

247 In a classroom full of Portuguese They were speaking in English—the lesson was integrated into an English lesson—but some of them spoke it a little awkwardly (although a lot better than in any foreign language class I've ever seen in Britain). This is my best understanding of what they were saying. It was all recorded.

249 from 3.4 to 3.7 percent http://www.boston.com/news/world/europe /articles/2011/01/16/drug_experiment/, accessed January 9, 2014. See also http://www.npr.org/2011/01/20/133086356/Mixed-Results-For-Portugals -Great-Drug-Experiment, accessed same date.

249 The EMCDDA found Portugal *European Monitoring Centre for Drugs and Drug Addiction (EMCDDA) Statistical Bulletin 2010.*

249 The *British Journal of Criminology* BJC article http://www.scribd.com /doc/46235617/What-Can-We-Learn-From-The-Portuguese-Decriminal ization-of-Illicit-Drugs, page 1006.

250 from 52 percent to 20 percent Ibid., 1015. Domoslawski, *Drug Policy in Portugal*, 40.

250 it has doubled http://www.latimes.com/nation/shareitnow/la-sh -heroin-comeback-20140203,0,5569498.story, accessed February 20, 2014; http://www.bostonglobe.com/magazine/2014/02/23/philip-seymour-hoffman -and-danger-romanticizing-heroin/dJhAQgBSmvtzNpPK4HYTRP/story .html, accessed February 23, 2014.

250 "Children aged 15–16" *European Monitoring Center for Drugs and Drug Addiction report* "Drug Policy profiles: Portugal" on Portugal 2012, 20.

250 Down to 1.8 percent Domoslawski, *Drug Policy in Portugal*, 19.

253 a detailed study by the Cato Institute http://www.cato.org/sites/cato.org /files/pubs/pdf/DrugProhibitionWP.pdf, accessed February 5, 2013.

253 an additional $46.7 billion http://www.ibtimes.com/pros-cons-drug -legalization-us-246712, accessed December 7, 2012.

Chapter 17: The Man in the Well

256 I interviewed My interviewees were President Mujica, Lucia Topolansky (his wife), Mauricio Rosencof (also a dissident kept in the well and one of Mujica's oldest friends), Miguel Angel Campodonico (Mujica's biographer), Rolando Sasso (editor of Mujica's speeches, also a political prisoner under the dictatorship), Representative Julio Bango, Representative Sebastian Sabini, drug czar Julio Calzada, the writer Eduardo Galeano (his old friend), his chief of staff Diego Carnepa, Dr. Raquel Parquet (an expert on drug treatment who has advised the government), Federico Grana, Geoffrey Ramsay, Guillermo Garat, Juan Tubino, Juan Vaz, and his opponents Representatives Geraldo Amarilla and Veronica Alonzo.

257 he had a burning sensation *Mujica en Búsqueda*, 21.

257 It was only because they all worked *Mujica en Búsqueda*, and this account of his childhood is also informed by interviews with Topolansky, Campodonico, and Sasso.

258 to hijack food trucks http://nationalinterest.org/commentary/josé -mujica-uruguays-robin-hood-guerrillas-9066?page=1, accessed October 8, 2013.

258 "Robin Hood guerillas" Ibid.

258 Miss Marple http://www.dailytimes.com.pk/default.asp?page=story_24 -9-2005_pg9_1, accessed December 23, 2012; http://inside.org.au/reading -agatha-christie/, accessed same date. See also M.E.L. Mallowan, "Mallowan's Memoirs: Agatha and the Archaeologist," http://www.thetimes.co.uk/tto/arts /books/article2450603.ece, 223–24, accessed same date.

258 shot him six times Sasson interview.

258 "Your struggle is our struggle!" *Memorias del Calabozo* by Rosencof et al, 371.

259 They bought a tiny shack http://upsidedownworld.org/main/uruguay -archives-48/2385-celebrating-compromises-in-uruguay-mujica-inaugurated -as-president, accessed October 8, 2013.

259 One night in November 2005 Topolansky interview.

259 giving 90 percent http://www.bbc.co.uk/news/magazine-20243493, accessed December 15, 2012.

260 bring Western civilization crashing Robert Greenfield, *Timothy Leary: A Biography*, 333.

260 His eyes flashing, Leary Ibid., 273.

260 "fuck righteously" Ibid., 355.

260 to his own young teenage Ibid., 168.

260 they went slowly insane Many other passionate advocates of LSD were horrified by his belief that it should be given to juveniles. See ibid., 427.

260 "Please wake up" Ibid., 308.

260 dissolved into insanity Ibid., 380, 557.

260 "You know, I really . . ." Ibid., 108.

260 "total war is upon us" Ibid., 392.

260 "because he had screwed up" Ibid., 397.

260 "an enemy of gravity" Ibid., 532.

262 "anyone caught with tobacco" Szasz, *Ceremonial Chemistry*, 198.

262 according to the General Household Survey Medical Research

Council website: http://www.mrc.ac.uk/Achievementsimpact/Storiesofimpact/Smoking/index.htm, accessed February 10, 2013.

263 The murder rate fell dramatically Miron, *Drug War Crimes*, 47.

264 In 1976, the Dutch introduced MacCoun and Reuter, *Drug War Heresies*, 240.

264 According to all the available evidence Ibid., 256. This was also broadly true of U.S. states that decriminalized marijuana possession in the 1970s. See Mary O'Leary, "Data shows pot use probably won't grow," *New Haven Register*, June 12, 2011.

264 from 8.5 percent to MacCoun and Reuter, *Drug War Heresies*, 257.

264 This increase did not Ibid., 258.

265 Some 5 percent of Dutch citizens http://ca.reuters.com/article/top News/idCATRE7992IX20111010, accessed December 1, 2012.

265 lower than the United States http://stash.norml.org/bigbook/monthly-adult-use-by-state.html, accessed March 3, 2013.

265 transfer from getting drunk http://dmarkanderson.com/Point_Counterpoint_07_31_13_v5.pdf, accessed November 27, 2013. http://www.guardian.co.uk/science/2012/jun/19/david-nutt-alcohol-cannabis-cafes, accessed November 20, 2012.

265 fell by 8 percent http://articles.chicagotribune.com/2013-10-31/news/ct-oped-1031-chapman-20131031_1_medical-marijuana-marijuana-use-drug-use, accessed December 2, 2013.

266 between 10 and 20 percent Miron, *Drug War Crimes*, 26. Miron notes that it has been falling before national prohibition was introduced; but this may be because most states had introduced their own prohibitions during this period.

266 a very slow rise back MacCoun and Reuter, *Drug War Heresies*, 28.

266 easier to buy marijuana Tom Feiling, *The Candy Machine: How Cocaine Took Over the World*, 270.

267 and it made him come out There were some caveats to his support for legalization; these emerged in our conversation.

267 Some 21 percent of Dutch teenagers http://norml.org/news/1999/01/07/dutch-marijuana-use-half-that-of-america-study-reveals, accessed December 2, 2013; see also "Addiction" doi:10.1111/j.1360-0443.2011.03572.x; Robert J. MacCoun, "What Can We Learn from the Dutch Coffee Shop System?" Working Paper for Rand Corporation. As accessed http://www.rand.org/content/dam/rand/pubs/working_papers/2010/RAND_WR768.pdf on June 24, 2014.

270 the MSNBC discussion show *Hardball* See http://www.msnbc

.msn.com/id/47064492/ns/msnbc_tv-hardball_with_chris_matthews/t/hardball-chris-matthews-monday-april/#.T9-Ds82TSqk, accessed May 1, 2012.

270 just 3 percent have used For good references, read Jacob Sullum's account of Hart's theories, at http://www.forbes.com/sites/jacobsullum/2013/11/04/everything-youve-heard-about-crack-and-meth-is-wrong/, accessed November 10, 2013. Miron, *Drug War Crimes*, 48. See also page 40 of the RAND Report at http://www.rand.org/content/dam/rand/pubs/occasional_papers/2010/RAND_OP325.pdf, accessed January 14, 2014.

Chapter 18: High Noon

275 the people who achieved this From the Colorado campaign I talked on the record to Mason Tvert, Steve Fox, Art Way, Joe Megyesy, Brian Vicente, Christian Sederberg, Tom Tancredo, Barbara Brohl, and Betty Aldworth. From the Washington campaign I talked to Alison Holcomb, Tonia Winchester, Pete Holmes, Roger Rofmann, Maru Mora Villapando, and Charlie Mandigo.

275 The men who led There was also a woman in the leading team in Colorado, Betty Aldworth. Her analysis, however, was closer to the Washington team's. There were also some male spokespeople for the Washington team, but they were not its leaders.

275 a duel at high noon http://archive.saferchoice.org/safercolorado06/pressroomcf1a.html?id=1159426802, accessed January 2, 2014.

275 a quarry back in 1904 http://cdnc.ucr.edu/cgi-bin/cdnc?a=d&d=SFC19040726.2.31, accessed January 2, 2014.

276 the course of the drug war While this initial duel received little press, the wider duel between Mason Tvert and John Hickenlooper—which began, in some ways, here—played a huge role in the drug war.

276 by setting up a brewpub http://www.theatlantic.com/politics/archive/2012/09/colorados-beer-brewing-governor-critiques-the-white-house-beer/262018/, accessed January 2, 2014.

276 see who died first At the same time, he issued the same challenge to Pete Coors—the owner of the Coors beer empire—who was a prominent Republican in the state. The challenge was bipartisan.

276 could not take part http://www.youtube.com/watch?v=yaN5ERdnHrw, accessed January 2, 2014.

276 he was terrified Mason was later told he did not have to testify.

276 parties where huge amounts http://thecollegianur.com/2012/10/10

/richmond-alumnus-is-leading-advocate-to-legalize-marijuana/29323/, accessed January 2, 2014.

277 "deals a more dangerous drug" Fox, Armentano, and Tvert, *Marijuana Is Safer*, 139.

279 No deaths are attributed The Safer Colorado website provides sources for these claims. See http://archive.saferchoice.org/content/view/24/53/, accessed January 6, 2014. See also http://jop.sagepub.com/content/early/2011/09/03/0269881111414751, accessed same date.

279 "making a safer choice" Mason interview. See also Fox, Armentano, and Tvert, *Marijuana Is Safer*, xviii–xix and chapter 3 of the book, where he backs up these statements.

279 "adding a vice" Fox, Armentano, and Tvert, *Marijuana Is Safer*, xx.

279 "make me a bad person" http://archive.saferchoice.org/content/view/1335/10/, accessed January 2, 2014.

279 "Marijuana: No hangovers" http://www.cannabisculture.com/articles/4837.html, accessed January 2, 2014.

279 eight times more likely http://archive.saferchoice.org/content/view/24/53/, accessed January 2, 2014; see also http://www.ncbi.nlm.nih.gov/pubmed/14656545, accessed January 6, 2014.

280 reduce domestic violence http://archive.saferchoice.org/content/view/387/38/, accessed January 2, 2014.

280 "marijuana jujitsu" Steve Fox interview; see also Fox, Armentano, and Tvert, *Marijuana Is Safer*, 125.

280 "Our message addresses that perception" Later, via e-mail, Mason clarified that this was only one stage in their work. After reading an earlier draft of this chapter, he wrote to me: "We focused on the marijuana-is-safer-than-alcohol message up until the 2012 campaign, at which time we began making the traditional anti-prohibition arguments while still making the SAFER argument, and then for the final few months made only the traditional anti-prohibition arguments. This is really a critical part of the whole thing. The goal was to make sure people understood marijuana is less harmful than alcohol, then push the traditional arguments once they're primed and more receptive. You make it sound like we completely rejected all standard anti-prohibition arguments."

281 She wanted to show, instead http://www.youtube.com/watch?v=qAou98YFqo4, accessed February 6, 2014.

285 "then push the traditional arguments" Mason said this to me via e-mail during my fact-checking process, February 14, 2014.

285 can damage their IQ Mason argues that the scientific study indicated that this link is false.

286 The fears about legalization http://www.huffingtonpost.com/2014/03/19/marijuana-legalization-colorado_n_4989191.html, accessed May 6, 2014.

286 the same logic can't apply Initially, I had taken from our conversation that Mason believed all other prohibited drugs were more dangerous than alcohol. In an e-mail as part of my fact-checking process, he clarified that this is not the case, writing: "I am 100% sure that many illegal substances—particularly psilocybin, MDMA, LSD—are not remotely as dangerous as alcohol."

286 "I don't think any other drug" As part of my fact-checking, I showed this chapter to Mason, as I did with all the major living figures I have written about (except as noted above). I then had an e-mail discussion with him intermittently for quite a long time clarifying his position. I want to lay out the contours of that conversation here, to make it as clear as possible how I reached my conclusions about Mason's policy positions, and—just as importantly—because I think our conversation reveals something useful about the debate that will happen as the drug war ends.

In my initial interview with Mason, he said other drugs "should" be treated differently from marijuana, because they cause different (and by implication greater) harms. I asked: "Do you think over time the model of regulation that you've achieved for marijuana, or other models of regulation, can be applied to other drugs that are currently banned?" He replied: "I don't think they will be, no." When I said: "That's a division within the drug reform movement as well, isn't it?" he replied: "Well, it's only a division between reasonable, realistic people, and non."

I therefore, in my initial draft, presented Mason as opposed to legalization of any drug other than marijuana or alcohol because that was how I'd understood his position, which I described as different to Alison and Tonia's, since they both said to me that they believe legalization of other drugs can and should happen in time.

When he read this initial text, Mason felt it was incorrect to describe him as having a different position to Tonia and Alison—who believe in more extensive legalization covering other drugs—and reiterated that he believes in reforms like the decriminalization of personal drug use. This disagreement, I soon realized, came in part from a difference between us about what these individual words mean. He wrote to me that "words like 'legalize' (and even 'decriminalize') are ambiguous to the point of worthlessness." I didn't agree: I believe the words "legalize" and "decriminalize" do have quite distinct and clear meanings, and I tried to clarify them.

I was using "decriminalization" to mean the decriminalization of personal drug use by individuals—so you wouldn't be arrested or jailed for having, say, a bag of coke or some LSD for personal use. And for me, "legalization" means that the sale of the drug would be reclaimed from criminal gangs, and transferred to stores and pharmacies (or some other legitimate route).

So based on my initial interview with him and using these as my working definitions, I couldn't see how Mason's position was not opposed to legalization beyond marijuana and alcohol, so I kept asking questions. In response to these requests for clarification, Mason suggested I clarify my description of his position by stating only that he thinks legalization of other drugs is "unlikely." I asked him to explain his position further. I had taken from our initial conversation that he thought most other drugs *should* not be legalized—but now it seemed he was saying only that they probably *would* not be legalized.

He continued to argue that the term "legalization" is meaningless, and suggested that legalizing a drug is different to regulating a drug. To me, legalization and regulation are synonymous—they mean the same thing. Legalization is a process of setting up a regulatory framework in which a drug can be sold and consumed.

But to Mason they are not. In the end we agreed a form of words that we both believe is accurate to describe his position, and that's what I use in this chapter—that he thinks other drugs could and should be legalized, but not in the same way as marijuana.

I wanted to lay out all this information here so the reader can reach their own conclusions, but also because I thought it might be useful to explain to readers that even someone as informed and committed and smart on this issue as Mason doesn't agree with some of the terms I am using here to describe the solutions. One part of the fight to end the drug war, it occurred to me from this email conversation with him, will be getting agreement on how to describe the alternatives. Even people who essentially agree—like Mason and I—can end up having apparent disagreements because we haven't reached a consensus on what these words mean.

287 A study in the *Lancet* http://www.economist.com/blogs/dailychart/2010/11/drugs_cause_most_harm, accessed January 6, 2014; http://www.thelancet.com/journals/lancet/article/PIIS0140-6736(10)61462-6/, accessed March 30, 2014.

288 "It seems like the people that" http://www.vox.com/2014/7/3/5868249/colorado-governor-who-opposed-legalizing-pot-now-says-its-going-fine, accessed July 3, 2014.

289 "common sense" http://www.huffingtonpost.com/2013/05/28/hickenlooper-signs-colora_n_3346798.html, accessed January 2, 2014.

289 "Let's face it, the war" https://news.yahoo.com/colorado-governor-marijuana-legalization-221049661.html, accessed July 4, 2014.

290 "a marijuana brownie" http://online.wsj.com/news/articles/SB20001424052748703559504575630760766227660, accessed January 14, 2014.

Conclusion: If You Are Alone

291 in one vast graveyard I first thought of this image of an alternative drug war graveyard when reading Adam Hochschild's amazing history of the resistance to the First World War, *To End All Wars*, in which he imagines a graveyard for all the resisters.

294 twenty-four thousand people http://www.release.org.uk/blog/drugs-its-time-better-laws, accessed January 14, 2014.

294 "The law must fit the facts" Sloman, *Reefer Madness*, 34.

296 They didn't give up I think I picked up this formulation—don't give up, get up—from the Australian campaign group Get Up, which was cofounded by my friend Jeremy Heimans.

296 it makes them feel strong I think it was Julia Blackburn, Billie Holiday's biographer, who first talked to me about how Billie Holiday's songs make people strong—it's a formulation I love and that really stayed with me.

296 she would be forgotten Yolande Bavan interview.

297 "One day, America is" Julia Blackburn archives, "The Story of Billie," article V, by William Dufty, box 18, file VII.

297 "If you are alone" Interview with Juan Fraire Escobedo, recalling his mother's words.

297 "He headed one of the powerful" Anslinger, *Murderers*, 172–73.

297 "The choice is yours" http://druglibrary.org/schaffer/library/joe_mccarthy.htm, accessed February 24, 2013.

297 "unstable, emotional, hysterical" Sloman, *Reefer Madness* 258.

298 He smothered the story Anslinger, *Murderers*, 173.

298 Anslinger had admitted it http://druglibrary.org/schaffer/history/e1970/drugswashdc.htm.

298 he took daily doses of morphine McWilliams, *Protectors*, 187. Even Anslinger's highly sympathetic biographer, John McWilliams, calls this "an incredible irony for the man who devoted his adult life to the enforcement and control of such narcotics." See ibid.

Bibliography

Acker, Caroline Jean and Sarah W. Tracy, eds. *Altering American Consciousness.* Amherst, MA: University of Massachusetts Press, 2004.

Acker, Caroline Jean. *Creating the American Junkie: Addiction Research in the Classic Era of Narcotic Control.* Baltimore, MD: Johns Hopkins University Press, 2006.

Albarelli, H. P., Jr. *A Terrible Mistake: The Murder of Frank Olson and the CIA's Secret Cold War Experiments.* Walterville, OR: Trine Day, 2009.

Alexander, Bruce K. *The Globalization of Addiction: A Study in Poverty of the Spirit.* Oxford: Oxford University Press, 2008.

———. *Peaceful Measures: Canada's Way Out of the "War on Drugs."* Toronto: University of Toronto Press, 1990.

———. "Rise and Fall of the Official View of Addiction." Published on the Globalization of Addiction website: http://globalizationofaddiction.ca/

Alexander, Michael. *Jazz Age Jews.* Princeton, NJ: Princeton University Press, 2001.

Alexander, Michelle. *The New Jim Crow.* New York: New Press, 2010.

Andreas, Peter, ed. *Policing the Globe: Criminalization and Crime Control in International Relations.* Oxford: Oxford University Press, 2006.

Anslinger, Harry. *The Murderers: The Shocking Story of the Narcotics Gang.* New York: Garden City Press, 1962.

———. *The Protectors: Our Battle Against the Crime Gangs.* New York: Farrar, Straus and Co., 1966.

———, and William F. Tompkins. *The Traffic in Narcotics.* New York: Funk and Wagnalls, 1953.

Arpaio, Joe, and Len Sherman. *Joe's Law: America's Toughest Sheriff Takes On Illegal Immigration, Drugs, and Everything Else That Threatens America.* New York: Amacom Books, 2008.

Attwood, Shawn. *Hard Time: Life with Sheriff Joe Arpaio in America's Toughest Jail.* New York: Skyhorse Publishing, 2011.

Balko, Radley. *Overkill: The Rise of Paramilitary Police Raids in America.* Washington, D.C.: Cato Institute, 2006.

———. *Rise of the Warrior Cop.* New York: PublicAffairs, 2013.

Barrett, Damon, ed. *Children of the Drug War: Perspectives on the Impact of Drug Policies on Young People.* London: International Debate Education Association, 2011.

Baum, Dan. *Smoke and Mirrors.* New York: Little, Brown, 1996.

Becker, Howard. *Outsiders: Studies in the Sociology of Deviance.* New York: Free Press, 1966.

Beith, Malcolm. *The Last Narco: Hunting El Chapo, the World's Most Wanted Drug Lord.* New York: Penguin, 2010.

Benavie, Arthur. *Drugs: America's Holy War.* New York: Routledge, 2009.

Bennett, William J., John R. DiIulio, and John P. Walters. *Body Count: Moral Poverty . . . and How to Win America's War Against Crime and Drugs.* New York: Simon and Schuster, 1996.

Bergmann, Luke. *Getting Ghost: Two Young Lives and the Struggle for the Soul of an American City.* New York: New Press, 2008.

Bewley-Taylor, David. *The United States and International Drug Control, 1909–1997.* New York: Continuum, 1999.

———. *International Drug Control: Consensus Fractured.* Cambridge, UK: Cambridge University Press, 2012.

Blackburn, Julia. *With Billie: A New Look at the Unforgettable Lady Day.* New York: Vintage, 2005.

Blackman, Shane. *Chilling Out: The Cultural Politics of Substance Consumption, Youth and Drug Policy.* New York: Open University Press, 2004.

Bonnie, Richard J., and Charles H. Whitebread. *The Marijuana Conviction: A History of Marijuana Prohibition in the United States.* New York: Lindesmith Center, 1999.

Bowden, Charles. *Down by the River: Drugs, Money, Murder and Family.* New York: Simon and Schuster, 2004.

———. *Murder City: Ciudad Juárez and the Global Economy's New Killing Fields.* New York: Nation Books, 2010.

———. *A Shadow in the City.* New York: Harcourt, 2005.

Bowden, Mark. *Killing Pablo.* New York: Penguin, 2001.

Boyd, Susan, Donald MacPherson, and Bud Osborn, eds. *Raise Shit! Social Action Saving Lives.* Vancouver: Fernwood Publishing, 2009.

Brand, Russell. *My Booky Wook*. London: Hodder, 2007.

——. *Booky Wook 2: This Time It's Personal*. London: HarperCollins, 2010.

Burroughs, William. *Junky*. New York: Penguin, 2003.

Butler, Paul. *Let's Get Free: A Hip-Hop Theory of Justice*. New York: New Press, 2009.

Callender, the Reverend Eugene. *Nobody's a Nobody: The Story of a Harlem Ministry Hard at Work to Change America*. New York: CreateSpace Independent Publishing Platform, 2012.

Campbell, Howard. *Drug War Zone: Frontline Dispatches from the Streets of El Paso and Juárez*. Austin, TX: University of Texas Press, 2009.

Campbell, Larry, Neil Boyd, and Lori Culbert. *A Thousand Dreams: Vancouver's Downtown Eastside and the Fight for Its Future*. Vancouver: D&M Publishers Incorporated, 2009.

Campbell, Nancy, J. P. Olsen, and Luke Walden. *The Narcotic Farm: The Rise and Fall of America's First Prison for Drug Addicts*. New York: Abrams, 2008.

Campos, Isaac. *Home Grown: Marijuana and the Origins of Mexico's War on Drugs*. Chapel Hill, NC: University of North Carolina Press, 2012.

Carpenter, Ted Galen. *Bad Neighbor Policy: Washington's Futile War on Drugs in Latin America*. New York: Palgrave Macmillan, 2003.

Carroll, Jim. *The Basketball Diaries*. New York: Penguin, 1995.

Chadwick, Charlie, and Howard Parker. "Wirral's Enduring Heroin Problem: The Prevalence, Incidence and the Characteristics of Drug Use in Wirral, 1984–87." The Misuse of Drugs Research Project, presented to the Wirral Drug Advisory Committee, Department of Social Work Studies, University of Liverpool, 1988.

Chilton, John. *Billie's Blues*. New York: Quartet Books, 1975.

Clarke, Donald. *Billie Holiday: Wishing on the Moon*. Cambridge, MA: Da Capo Press, 2000.

Clarke, Donald Henderson. *In the Reign of Rothstein*. Ann Arbor, MI: University of Michigan Press, 2006.

Clegg, Bill. *Portrait of an Addict as a Young Man: A Memoir*. New York: Jonathan Cape, 2010.

Cordano, Jose Alberto. *Mujica en Búsqueda*. Montevideo, Uruguay: Búsqueda: Editorial Fin de Siglo, 2009.

Courtright, David, Don Des Jarlais, and Herman Joseph: *Addicts Who Survived: An Oral History of Narcotic Use in America, 1923–1965*. Knoxville, TN: University of Tennessee Press, 1989.

Coupland, Douglas. *City of Glass*, rev. ed. Vancouver: Douglas and McIntyre, 2009.

Csete, Joanne. *From the Mountaintops*. London: Open Society Foundation, 2011.

Davenport-Hines, Richard. *The Pursuit of Oblivion*. New York: W. W. Norton, 2003.

DeGrandpre, Richard. *The Cult of Pharmacology: How America Became the World's Most Troubled Drug Culture*. Durham, NC: Duke University Press, 2006.

Demers, Charles. *Vancouver Special*. Vancouver: Arsenal Pulp Press, 2009.

Dhywood, Jeffrey. *World War D: The Case Against Prohibitionism: A Roadmap to Controlled Re-legalization*. Columbia Communications, Inc., 2011.

Domoslawski, Artur. *Drug Policy in Portugal: The Benefits of Decriminalizing Drug Use*. New York: Open Society Foundations, 2011.

Edwards, Griffith, ed. *Addiction: Evolution of a Specialist Field*. London: Blackwell, 2002.

Elsner, Alan. *The Gates of Injustice: The Crisis in America's Prisons*. New York: FT Press, 2004.

Elton, Ben. *High Society*. London: Black Swan, 2003.

Eppinga, Jane. *Arizona Sheriffs: Badges and Bad Men*. Phoenix, AZ: Rio Nuevo, 2006.

Epstein, Edward Jay. *Agency of Fear: Opiates and Political Power in America*. New York: Verso Books, 1990.

Erlen, Jonathon, and Joseph F. Spillane, eds. *Federal Drug Control: The Evolution of Policy and Practice*. Binghamton, NY: Haworth Press, 2004.

Escohotado, Antonio. *A Brief History of Drugs: From the Stone Age to the Stoned Age*. South Paris, ME: Park Street Press, 1999.

Evans, Dylan. *Placebo: The Belief Effect*. London: HarperCollins, 2003.

Feiling, Tom. *The Candy Machine: How Cocaine Took Over the World*. New York: Penguin Books, 2009.

Ferentzy, Peter. *Dealing with Addiction: Why the Twentieth Century Was Wrong*. Raleigh, NC: Lulu Enterprises Incorporated, 2010.

Ferreira, Hugo Gil, and Michael W. Marshall. *Portugal's Revolution: Ten Years On*. Cambridge: Cambridge University Press, 1986.

Fine, Doug. *Too High to Fail: Cannabis and the New Green Economic Revolution*. New York: Gotham Books, 2012.

Fish, Jefferson M., ed. *How to Legalize Drugs*. Northvale, NJ: Jason Aaronson, 1998.

Fox, Steve, Paul Armentano, and Mason Tvert. *Marijuana Is Safer: So Why*

Are We Driving People to Drink? White River Junction, VT: Chelsea Green, 2009.

García, Alfredo. *Pepe Coloquios.* Montevideo, Uruguay: Fin de Siglo, 2009.

García Márquez, Gabriel. *News of a Kidnapping.* New York: Vintage, 2008.

Gerber, Rudolph Joseph. *Legalizing Marijuana: Drug Policy Reform and Prohibition Politics.* Westport, CT: Greenwood Publishing, 2004.

Gerhardt, Sue. *Why Love Matters.* London: Routledge, 2004.

Gibler, John. *To Die In Mexico: Dispatches from Inside the Drug War.* San Francisco: City Lights, 2011.

Glenny, Misha. *McMafia.* London: Bodley Head, 2008.

Goblet d'Alviella, Eugène. *The Mysteries of Eleusis: The Secret Rites and Rituals of the Classical Greek Mystery Tradition.* Wellingborough: Aquarian Press, 1981.

Gonzalez Rodriguez, Sergio. *The Femicide Machine.* Los Angeles: Semiotext(e), 2012.

Graham-Mulhall, Sara. *Opium: The Demon Flower.* Montrose: Montrose Publishing Company, distributed by World Foundation for Public Enlightenment on Traffic in Opium, 1928.

Gray, Judge James P. *Why Our Drug Laws Failed and What We Can Do About It: A Judicial Indictment of the War on Drugs.* Philadelphia, PA: Temple University Press, 2001.

Gray, Mike. *Drug Crazy.* New York: Random House, 1998.

Grayson, George W., and Samuel Logan. *The Executioner's Men: Los Zetas, Rogue Soldiers, Criminal Entrepreneurs, and the Shadow State They Created.* New Brunswick, NJ: Transaction, 2012.

Greenfield, Robert. *Timothy Leary: A Biography.* New York: Harcourt, 2006.

Greenwald, Glenn. *With Liberty and Justice for Some.* New York: Metropolitan Books, 2011.

Grillo, Ioan. *El Narco: Inside Mexico's Criminal Insurgency.* New York: Bloomsbury Press, 2011.

Grim, Ryan. *This Is Your Country on Drugs: the Secret History of Getting High in America.* Hoboken: John Wiley and Sons, 2009.

Harney, Malachi, and John Cross. *The Narcotic Officer's Notebook.* Springfield, IL: Charles C. Thomas, 1973.

Heather, Nick, ed. *The Essential Handbook of Treatment and Prevention of Alcohol Problems.* Hoboken: John Wiley and Sons, 2004.

Hentoff, Nat. *At the Jazz Band Ball.* Berkeley, CA: University of California Press, 2010.

———. *The Jazz Life*. Cambridge, MA: Da Capo Press, 1961.

Herivel, Tara, and Paul Wright, eds. *Prison Profiteers: Who Makes Money from Mass Incarceration*. New York: New Press, 2007.

Hickman, Timothy A. *The Secret Leprosy of Modern Days: Narcotic Addiction and Cultural Crisis in the United States, 1870–1920*. Amherst, MA: University of Massachusetts Press, 2007.

Hillman, D.C.A. *The Chemical Muse: Drug Use and the Roots of Western Civilization*. New York: St. Martin's Press, 2008.

Holiday, Billie, with William Dufty. *Lady Sings the Blues*. London: Penguin UK, 1984.

Huang, Yunte. *Charlie Chan: The Untold Story of the Honorable Detective and His Rendezvous with American History*. New York: W. W. Norton, 2010.

Huidobro, Eleuterio. *Le Fuga de Punta Carretas*. Montevideo, Uruguay: Banda Oriental, 2012.

———, and Mauricio Rosencof. *Memorias del Calabozo*. Montevideo, Uruguay: Banda Oriental, 1988.

Huxley, Aldous. *The Doors of Perception*. New York: Vintage, 2004.

Inkster, Nigel, and Virginia Comolli. *Drugs, Insecurity and Failed States: The Problems of Prohibition*. London: Routledge, 2012.

Jack, Malcolm. *Lisbon: City of the Sea; A History*. London: I. B. Tauris, 2007.

Jarvis, Brian. *Cruel and Unusual: Punishment and U.S. Culture*. Sterling, VA: Pluto Press, 2004.

Jay, Mike. *Emperors of Dreams: Drugs in the Nineteenth Century*. Sawtry, Cambridgeshire: Dedalus, 2000.

———. *High Society: Mind-Altering Drugs in History and Culture*. London: Thames and Hudson, 2010.

Jonnes, Jill. *Hep-Cats, Narcs, and Pipe Dreams*. New York: Scribner, 1996.

Kaiser, David. *How the Hippies Saved Physics: Science, Counterculture, and the Quantum Revival*. New York: W. W. Norton, 2011.

Katcher, Leo. *The Big Bankroll: The Life and Times of Arnold Rothstein*. Cambridge, MA: Da Capo Press, 1994.

Kayman, Martin. *Revolution and Counter-Revolution in Portugal*. Wolfeboro, NH: Merlin Press, 1987.

Kerényi, Carl. *Eleusis: Archetypal Image of Mother and Daughter*. Princeton: Princeton University Press, 1967.

Keys, Daniel Patrick, and John F. Galliher. *Confronting the Drug Control Establishment: Alfred Lindesmith as a Public Intellectual*. New York: SUNY Press, 2000.

King, Alexander. *May This House Be Safe from Tigers*. London: Heinemann, 1960.

King, Rufus. *The Drug Hang-Up: America's Fifty-Year Folly*. New York: W. W. Norton, 1972.

Kobler, John. *Capone: The Life and World of Al Capone*. Cambridge, MA: Da Capo Press, 1992.

Kuntz, Joelle. *Switzerland: How an Alpine Pass Became a Country*. Historiator Editions, 2008.

Lasch, Christopher. *The Culture of Narcissism: American Life in an Age of Diminishing Expectations*. New York: W. W. Norton, 1991.

Lee, Martin A., and Bruce Shlain. *Acid Dreams: The CIA, LSD, and the Sixties Rebellion*. Grove Press, 1985.

Levine, Michael. *Deep Cover: The Inside Story of How DEA Infighting, Incompetence and Subterfuge Lost Us the Biggest Battle of the Drug War*. Backprint, Lincoln, NE: Authors Guild, 2000.

Liddy, G. Gordon. *Will*. New York: St. Martin's Press, 1998.

Lindesmith, Alfred. *The Addict and the Law*, online ed. http://www.druglibrary.eu/library/books/adlaw/.

Longmire, Sylvia. *Cartel: The Coming Invasion of Mexico's Drug Wars*. New York: Palgrave, 2011.

Lowes, Peter. *The Genesis of International Narcotics Control*. Geneva, Switzerland: Librarie Droze, 1966.

Lynch, Mona. *Sunbelt Justice: Arizona and the Transformation of American Punishment*. Redwod City, CA: Stanford University Press, 2010.

Lynch, Timothy, ed. *After Prohibition: An Adult Approach to Drug Policies in the 21st Century*. Washington D.C.: Cato Institute, 2000.

MacCoun, Robert J., and Peter Reuter, eds. *Drug War Heresies: Learning from Other Vices, Times, and Places*. Cambridge, UK: Cambridge University Press, 2006.

Mailer, Phil. *Portugal: The Impossible Revolution?* London: Solidarity London, 1977.

Malinowska-Sempruch, Kasia, and Sarah Gallagher, eds. *War on Drugs, HIV/AIDS and Human Rights*. New York: International Debate Education Association, 2004.

Marez, Curtis. *Drug Wars: The Political Economy of Narcotics*. Minneapolis, MN: University of Minnesota Press, 2004.

Margolick, David. *Strange Fruit: Billie Holiday, Café Society, and an Early Cry for Civil Rights*. Edinburgh: Canongate Books, 2001.

Marincolo, Sebastian. *High: Insights on Marijuana*. Indianapolis, IN: Dog Ear Publishing, 2010.

Martinez, Oscar J. *Border Boom Town: Ciudad Juárez Since 1848*. Austin, TX: University of Texas Press, 1978.

Massing, Michael. *The Fix*. Berkeley, CA: University of California Press, 2000.

Maté, Gabor. *In the Realm of Hungry Ghosts: Close Encounters with Addiction*. Berkeley, CA: North Atlantic Books, 2010.

———. *Scattered Minds: The Origins and Healing of Attention Deficit Disorder*. Toronto, ON: Knopf Canada, 1999.

———. *When the Body Says No: Exploring the Stress-Disease Connection*. Hoboken, NJ: John Wiley and Sons, 2011.

McKenna, Terence. *Food of the Gods: A Radical History of Plants, Drugs and Human Evolution*. New York: Random House, 1992.

McKibben, Bill. *Deep Economy: The Wealth of Communities and the Durable Future*. New York: Holt Paperbacks, 2007.

McWilliams, John C. *The Protectors: Harry J. Anslinger and the Federal Bureau of Narcotics, 1930–62*. Newark, DE: University of Delaware Press, 1991.

Merryman, John Henry. *Stanford Legal Essays*. Stanford, CA: University of California Press, 1975.

Miller, Richard Lawrence. *The Case for Legalizing Drugs*. Santa Barbara, CA: Praeger, 1991.

———. *Drug Warriors and Their Prey: From Police Power to Police State*. Santa Barbara, CA: Praeger, 1996.

Miron, Jeffrey. *Drug War Crimes: The Consequences of Prohibition*. Chicago: Independent Institute, 2004.

Molloy, Molly, and Charles Bowden, eds. *Confessions of a Cartel Hit Man*. London: Arrow Books, 2012.

Moskos, Peter. *Cop in the Hood: My Year Policing Baltimore's Eastern District*. Princeton, NJ: Princeton University Press, 2008.

Murphy, Emily. *The Black Candle*. Toronto, ON: Thomas Allen, 1922.

Murtagh, John Martin, and Sara Harris. *Who Live in Shadow*. London: New English Library, 1960.

Musto, David. *The American Disease: Origins of Narcotic Control*. Oxford, UK: Oxford University Press, 1987.

Musto, David, ed. *One Hundred Years of Heroin*. Westport, CT: Greenwood, 2002.

Nawa, Fariba. *Opium Nation: Child Brides, Drug Lords, and One Woman's Journey Through Afghanistan*. New York: Harper Perennial, 2011.

Newark, Tim. *Boardwalk Gangster: The Real Lucky Luciano*. New York: St. Martin's Press, 2010.

Nicholson, Stuart. *Billie Holiday*. London: Victor Gollancz, 1995.

Nutt, David. *Drugs Without the Hot Air: Minimising the Harms of Legal and Illegal Drugs.* Cambridge, UK: UIT Cambridge, 2012.

Okrent, Daniel. *Last Call: The Rise and Fall of Prohibition.* New York: Simon & Schuster, 2012.

O'Meally, Robert. *Lady Day: The Many Faces of Billie Holiday.* New York: Arcade Publishing, 1993.

O'Rourke, Beto, and Susie Byrd. *Dealing Death and Drugs: The Big Business of Dope in the U.S. and Mexico.* El Paso, TX: Cinco Puntos Press, 2011.

Osborn, Bud. *Hundred Block Rock.* Vancouver: Arsenal Pulp Press, 1999.

——. *Signs of the Times.* London: Anvil Press, 2005.

Parenti, Christian. *Lockdown America: Police and Prisons in the Age of Crisis.* New York: Verso, 1999.

Pietrusza, David. *Rothstein: The Life, Times, and Murder of the Criminal Genius Who Fixed the 1919 World Series.* New York: Basic Books, 2003.

Pinchbeck, Daniel. *Breaking Open the Head: A Psychedelic Journey into the Heart of Contemporary Shamanism.* New York: HarperCollins, 2003.

Pisani, Elizabeth. *The Wisdom of Whores: Bureaucrats, Brothels, and the Business of AIDS.* London: Granta, 2009.

Pritchett, Wendell E. *Brownsville, Brooklyn: Blacks, Jews, and the Changing Face of the Ghetto.* Chicago: University of Chicago Press, 2002.

Putnam, Robert D. *Bowling Alone: The Collapse and Revival of American Community.* New York: Simon & Schuster, 2000.

Quinones, Sam. *True Tales from Another Mexico.* Albuquerque, NM: University of New Mexico Press, 2001.

Rastello, Luca. *I Am the Market: How to Smuggle Cocaine by the Ton and Live Happily.* London: Granta, 2010.

Reding, Nick. *Methland: The Death and Life of an American Small Town.* New York: Bloomsbury, 2009.

Reed, Jeremy. *Saint Billie.* London: Enitharmon Press, 2001.

Reinarman, Craig, and Harry Levine, eds. *Crack in America: Demon Drugs and Social Justice.* Berkeley, CA: University of California Press, 1997.

Rempel, William C. *At the Devil's Table: The Untold Story of the Insider Who Brought Down the Cali Cartel.* New York: Random House, 2011.

Rolles, Steve. *After the War on Drugs: Blueprint for Regulation.* Bristol, UK: Transform, 2009.

Rosencoff, Mauricio and Eleutorio Huidobro. *Memorias del Calobozo.* Montevideo, Uruguay: Bandas Orientale, 2004.

Rothstein, Carolyn. *Now I'll Tell.* New York: Vanguard Press, 1934.

Ruck, Carl A. P. *Sacred Mushrooms of the Goddess: Secrets of Eleusis.* Berkeley, CA: Ronin Publishing, 2006.

Rudgley, Richard. *The Alchemy of Culture: Intoxicants in Society.* London: British Museum Press, 1993.

Sasso, Rolando W., ed. *Pepe en la Radio, Pensando el Pais.* Montevideo, Uruguay: Ediciones Participando, 2010.

Satel, Sally, and Scott O. Lilienfeld. *Brainwashed: The Seductive Appeal of Mindless Neuroscience.* New York: Basic Books, 2013.

Schlesinger, Arthur. *Robert Kennedy and His Times.* Vol. 1. London: Deutsch, 1978.

Schlosser, Eric. *Reefer Madness: Sex, Drugs, and Cheap Labor in the American Black Market.* London: Penguin, 2003.

Self, Will. *Junk Mail.* London: Bloomsbury, 1995.

Shapiro, Harry. *Shooting Stars: Drugs, Hollywood and the Movies.* London: Serpent's Tail, 2003.

———. *Waiting for the Man: The Story of Drugs and Popular Music.* London: Helter Skelter, 2003.

Shapiro, Nat, and Nat Hentoff. *Hear Me Talkin' to Ya: The Story of Jazz as Told by the Men Who Made It.* New York: Penguin, 1962.

Siegel, Ronald K. *Intoxication: Life in Pursuit of Artificial Paradise.* New York: Simon & Schuster, 1989.

Simon, David, and Ed Burns. *The Corner: A Year in the Life of an Inner-City Neighborhood.* London: Canongate, 2009.

Slater, Lauren. *Opening Skinner's Box: Great Psychological Experiments of the Twentieth Century.* New York: W. W. Norton, 2004.

Sloman, Larry. *Reefer Madness: A History of Marijuana.* New York: St. Martin's Griffin, 1998.

Sondern, Frederic. *Brotherhood of Evil: The Mafia.* London: Hamilton and Co, 1961.

Stevens, Alex. *Drugs, Crime and Public Health: The Political Economy of Drug Policy.* London: Routledge, 2011.

Strickland, Joy. *In the Mourning: A Mother's Journey from Tragedy to Triumph.* Dallas, TX: Strickland, 2010.

Sullum, Jacob. *Saying Yes: In Defense of Drug Use.* New York: Penguin, 2003.

Szasz, Thomas. *Ceremonial Chemistry: The Ritual Persecution of Drugs, Addicts, and Pushers.* London: Routledge and Segan Paul, 1975.

———. *Our Right to Drugs: The Case for Free Markets.* New York: Praeger, 1992.

Teachout, Terry. *Pops: The Wonderful World of Louis Armstrong*. London: JR Books, 2009.

Thompson, Hunter S. *Hell's Angels: A Strange and Terrible Saga*. London: Michael Joseph, 2009.

Thornton, Mark. *The Economics of Prohibition*. Salt Lake City, UT: University of Utah Press, 1991.

Tong, Benson. *The Chinese Americans*. Boulder, CO: University Press of Colorado, 2003.

Tosches, Nick. *King of the Jews: The Greatest Mob Story Never Told*. New York: Hamish Hamilton, 2005.

Trebach, Arnold S. *The Heroin Solution*. New Haven, CT: Yale University Press, 1982.

Uchtenhagen, Ambros, et al. *Prescription of Narcotics for Heroin Addicts: Main Results of the Swiss National Cohort Study*. Basel; London: Karger, 2000.

Vail, Ken. *Lady Day's Diary: The Life of Billie Holiday, 1937–1959*. London: Castle Communications, 1996.

Valentine, Douglas. *The Strength of the Pack: The Personalities, Politics and Espionage Intrigues That Shaped the DEA*. Walterville, OR: TrineDay, 2009.

———. *The Strength of the Wolf: The Secret History of America's War on Drugs*. New York: Verso Books, 2004.

Vulliamy, Ed. *Amexica: War Along the Borderline*. London: Bodley Head, 2010.

Wallace, David. *Capital of the World: A Portrait of New York City in the Roaring Twenties*. Guildford, CT: Lyons Press, 2011.

Walker, Stanley. *The Night Club Era*. Baltimore, MD: Johns Hopkins University Press, 1999.

Walker, William O. *Drug Control in the Americas*. Albuquerque, NM: University of New Mexico Press, 1981.

Walton, Stuart. *Out of It: A Cultural History of Intoxication*. London: Penguin, 2001.

Warner, Jessica. *Craze: Gin and Debauchery in an Age of Reason*. London: Profile, 2003.

Wasson, R. Gordon, Albert Hofmann, and Carl A. P. Ruck. *The Road to Eleusis: Unveiling the Secret of the Mysteries*. New York: Harcourt, 1978.

Watt, Peter, and Roberto Zepeda. *Drug War Mexico: Politics, Neoliberalism and Violence in the New Narcoeconomy*. London, Zed Books, 2012.

Weston, Paul, ed. *Narcotics USA*. New York: Greenberg, 1952.

Whipple, Sidney. *Noble Experiment: A Portrait of America Under Prohibition*. London: Methuen, 1934.

White, John. *Billie Holiday: Her Life and Times*. Universe Books, 1987.

White, William M. *Slaying the Dragon: The History of Addiction Treatment and Recovery in America*. Bloomington, IL: Chestnut Health Systems, 1998.

Williams, E. H. *Opiate Addiction: Its Handling and Treatment*. New York: The Macmillan Co., 1922.

Williams, Henry Smith. *Adding Years to Your Life*. New York: Hearst's International Library Co., 1914.

———. *Drug Addicts Are Human Beings*. Washington, D.C.: Shaw Publishing Company, 1938.

———. *Drugs Against Men*. Reprint. New York: Arno Press, 1981.

———, ed. *The Historians' History of the World*. Vol 3. Encyclopedia Britannica Company, 1926.

———. *Luther Burbank*. New York, Hearst's International Library Co., 1915.

———. *The Science of Happiness*. New York; London: Harper & Brothers Publishers, 1909.

———. *The Survival of the Fittest*. New York: R.M. McBride & Co., 1932.

Woods, Sally C. "Heroin and Methadone Substitution Treatments." Unpublished thesis, Liverpool John Moores University, 2005.

Yardley, Tom. *Why We Take Drugs: Seeking Excess and Communion in the Modern World*. London, New York: Routledge, 2012.

Documentaries

8 Murders a Day, produced by Charlie Minn (2011).

Bastards of the Party, produced by Alex Alonso and Lisa Caruso (2005).

Billie Holiday: Sensational Lady (BBC "Reputations" series), produced by David F. Turnbull (2001).

Cocaine Unwrapped, produced by Rachel Siefert (2011).

Dateline NBC: Inside Mexico's Drug War, produced by Solly Granatstein and Rayner Ramirez (2011).

Endgame: AIDS in Black America, produced by Raney Aaronson (2012).

The Fix, produced by Nettie Wild and Betsy Carson (2012).

Gladiator Days, produced by Marc Levin (2002).

The House I Live In, produced by Eugene Jarecki (2013).

Jazz, directed by Ken Burns, produced by Wynton Marsalis (2000).

Nothing Personal, "Young Guns," episode 5, produced by Steve Schirripa (2011).

Our Drug War, produced by Angus MacQueen (2011).

Pablo's Hippos, produced by Lawrence Elman and Antonio Von Hildebrand (2010).

Return Engagement, directed by Alan Rudolf (1983).

Sins of My Father, directed by Nicolas Entel (2009).

Archives and Libraries

Harry Anslinger archives at Penn State University, Pennsylvania

George White archives at Stanford University, California

National Archives at San Francisco, California

Wellcome Trust Library, London

Federal Bureau of Narcotics archives, Virginia

New York Public Library, New York

Library of Congress, Washington, D.C.

British Library, London

Julia Blackburn Archives at Brotherton Library, University of Leeds

Public records office, Phoenix, Arizona

Index

A NOTE ON THE AUTHOR

Johann Hari is a British journalist who has written for the *New York Times*, *Le Monde*, the *Los Angeles Times*, the *Independent*, the *Guardian*, *Slate*, the *New Republic*, and the *Nation*. He has reported from many countries, from the Congo to Venezuela. He was twice named Newspaper Journalist of the Year by Amnesty International UK, awarded the Martha Gellhorn Prize for turning political writing into an art, and later named Journalist of the Year by Stonewall. He can be followed on Twitter: @johannhari101.